THE NEW CREATIVE COOKBOOK

Edited by Charlotte Turgeon

Blitz Editions

Created and manufactured by arrangement with
Ottenheimer Publishers, Inc.
© MCMLXXXVI, MCMLXCI by Ottenheimer Publishers, Inc.

This British edition edited by Carole Fahy,
Anton Wills-Eve and Pamela Wills-Eve
All Rights Reserved

Printed in Hong Kong

ISBN 1 85605 023 8

Contents

Appetisers

Pineapple, Cucumbers and Melon with Spicy Peanut Dressing

4 servings

dressing
1 tablespoon peanut oil
Dash chilli sauce
2 oz/60 grams peanut butter, smooth or crunchy
2 tablespoons hot water
2 tablespoons soy sauce
2 tablespoons red wine vinegar
1 tablespoon sesame oil

salad
1 small, fresh pineapple
2 medium cucumbers
1 medium cantaloupe melon
1 large ripe banana
4 oz/115 grams fresh spinach
1 small bunch spring onions, thinly sliced

In a small pan heat the peanut oil and chilli sauce over a high heat for a few seconds. Pour into a small bowl and whisk in the peanut butter and hot water. Add soy sauce, vinegar and the sesame oil and whisk again.

Keep all the salad ingredients in separate bowls. Peel and core the pineapple, slice and cut into wedges. Remove a few narrow strips of green peel from the cucumbers, using a vegetable peeler. Halve the cucumbers lengthways, de-seed and cut in half lengthways again. Cut into ½-inch/1-cm slices. Peel melon. Halve lengthways and de-seed. Cut into ½-inch/1-cm slices. These ingredients can be prepared in advance and arranged on the plate just before serving.

To serve, cover a round, chilled serving dish with the spinach leaves and arrange the fruit in circles around the edge starting with the pineapple, then a circle of cucumber inside it, then a ring of melon inside that. Peel the banana, quarter it lengthways and cut into ½-inch/1-cm slices. Place in the centre of the dish and sprinkle spring onions over all the ingredients and moisten them with the dressing. This salad looks better if you do not toss it in the dressing, but serve a little of each ingredient onto cold salad plates at the table.

Peanut Butter Dip

2 oz/60 grams peanut butter
2 oz/60 grams finely shredded carrot
2½ fl oz/75 ml orange juice

In a small bowl, stir together the peanut butter, carrot and orange juice until well mixed. Serve as a dip for fresh fruits and vegetables.

Apple, Nut and Horseradish Dip

2 apples, peeled and cored
1 tablespoon lemon juice
4 tablespoons yoghurt
1 tablespoon horseradish
2 tablespoons ground walnuts

Grate the apples and add the lemon juice immediately to prevent discolouring. Blend in the remaining ingredients.

Serve this dip immediately with crisps, savoury biscuits or raw, fresh vegetables for dipping.

Clam or Mussel Pie

Sweet Potato Fingers

10 servings

4 to 6 cooked sweet potatoes
1 oz/30 grams flour
Fat for deep frying
3 oz/85 grams brown sugar
1 teaspoon salt
½ teaspoon nutmeg

Cut the sweet potatoes into strips or fingers. Score lightly with a fork. Coat each finger well with flour.

Heat the fat in a frying pan and fry the potato fingers until golden brown. Drain on kitchen towel and sprinkle with a mixture of brown sugar, salt and nutmeg. This should make about 40 fingers.

Roasted Pecan Nuts

24 servings

6 lb/3 kilos pecan nuts
4 oz/115 grams butter
Salt

Place the nuts in a rectangular baking tin and roast for 30 minutes at 250°F/120°C/gas mark ¼. Dice the butter and sprinkle over the nuts. Stir once or twice until the nuts and butter are well mixed.

Season well with salt and roast the nuts for a further hour, stirring and adding salt several times. The nuts are ready when crisp and the butter completely absorbed.

Fish Pâté

4 to 6 servings

8 oz/225 grams pike or other firm white fish
1 egg
½ pint/¼ l cream
Salt
Pepper
2 oz/60 grams pistachio nuts, chopped
8 thin slices fresh salmon
8 fillets of sole

Mince the pike in a food processor until it becomes a smooth mousse. Carefully mix in the egg and the cream. Stir well with a wooden spoon. Season with salt and pepper and fold in the nuts. Leave to cool in a refrigerator.

Grease a round cake tin or a ring mould. Salt and pepper the salmon and sole lightly and place them, overlapping, in the tin leaving the end of each slice hanging over the edge of the tin. Fill with the fish mousse. Fold the ends of the fish back over the mousse. Smooth the surface. Cover with foil. Pre-heat the oven to 350°F/180°C/gas mark 4. Place the dish

of pâté in a baking tin of water and cook for 35 to 40 minutes. Leave to cool before turning out, upside down. Serve with dill, Hollandaise sauce and rice.

Chicken Liver Pâté

6 to 8 servings

12 oz/345 grams streaky bacon slices, unsmoked
11 oz/315 grams chicken liver
2 eggs
½ pint/¼ l double cream
½ oz/15 grams butter
1 oz/30 grams flour
½ teaspoon salt
¼ teaspoon ground black pepper
½ bunch chives
2 large leaves sage, or ¼ teaspoon dried sage
1 sprig thyme
2–3 leaves marjoram, or ¼ teaspoon dried marjoram
2 oz/60 grams hazelnuts

Line a 2 pint/1¼ litre pâté dish with the bacon slices so that most of the inside edges of the dish are covered. Place several of the bacon slices across the dish and leave several of the shorter pieces just overhanging the edge.

Mix the rest of the ingredients together in an electric mixer or food processor until everything is finely blended. Pour the mixture into the pâté dish. Place in a baking tin of water in a pre-heated oven at 400°F/200°C/gas mark 6 for about 60 minutes. Cool before turning out of the dish.

Colourful Relish Dip

4 servings

¼ pint/140 ml soured cream
2½ fl oz/75 ml salad dressing
1 teaspoon sugar
½ teaspoon salt
2 tablespoons finely chopped spring onions
2 tablespoons finely chopped radishes
2 tablespoons finely chopped cucumber
2 tablespoons finely chopped green pepper
½ clove garlic, finely chopped
Crudités

Mix together the soured cream, salad dressing, sugar, salt, spring onions, radishes, cucumber, green pepper and garlic. Leave to cool in a refrigerator.

Serve in a small bowl surrounded by crudités such as cauliflower, carrot, celery and cucumber.

Fish Pâté

Lamb Pâté

14 to 16 servings

1 lb/450 grams lean minced lamb
11 oz/315 grams minced fat pork
1½ teaspoons salt
½ teaspoon pepper
½ teaspoon thyme
1 to 2 cloves garlic, crushed
3 eggs
1 oz/30 grams flour
½ pint/¼ l cream

Mix together the meats and spices. Add the eggs one at a time. Stir in the flour and cream. Fry a small amount to test for taste and adjust seasonings and spices as required.

Pour the mixture into a greased 3 pint/1½ litre loaf tin or oblong pâté dish. Cover with foil and place the dish in a baking tin of water. Cook in a pre-heated oven at 375°F/190°C/gas mark 5 for about one hour or until the surrounding fat and juices are clear. Leave to cool in the dish.

Serve with a currant sauce.

Blackcurrant Sauce

About 6 servings

12 oz/345 grams blackcurrant jelly
2½ fl oz/75 ml lemon juice
¼ teaspoon coarsely ground black pepper

Melt the jelly over a low heat. Add lemon juice and pepper. Leave the sauce to cool. Serve with lamb pâté.

Fried Cheese

4 to 6 servings

8 oz/225 grams Camembert cheese cut in 1-inch/
    2½-cm cubes
3 egg whites, lightly beaten
4 oz/115 grams crumbled cornflakes
2 pints/1¼ l corn oil

Dip the cheese cubes into the egg whites and then into the crumbs. Leave to dry for a few minutes then repeat the coating.

Fill to one third a heavy saucepan or fondue pot with the corn oil. Heat over a medium heat.

Fry the cheese, a few pieces at a time, for one minute or until golden brown. Drain on kitchen paper. Serve with jam if desired. Makes about 24.

Cheddar Cheese Puffs

8 servings

1 lb/450 grams cheddar cheese, grated
4 oz/115 grams butter or margarine, softened
4 oz/115 grams flour, sifted
½ teaspoon salt
½ teaspoon paprika
48 stuffed green olives

Blend together the cheese and butter. Add the flour, salt and paprika. Mix well. Encase each olive in 1 teaspoon of the mixture. At this point, you can keep the puffs in the refrigerator for up to 10 days.

Bake the puffs at 400°F/200°C/gas mark 6 for 15 minutes. Serve hot.

Cheese Straws

6 servings

2½ oz/75 grams butter
8 oz/225 grams flour, sifted
½ teaspoon cayenne pepper
1 teaspoon salt
1 lb/450 grams Cheddar cheese, grated

Cream the butter well. Sift the dry ingredients together and add to the butter. Add the cheese.

Roll the dough out thinly on a floured surface and cut into strips. Bake in a pre-heated oven at 400°F/200°C/gas mark 6 for 10 minutes. Makes 36 cheese straws.

Stuffed Bread Dip

About 12 servings

14 fl oz/400 ml sour cream
14 fl oz/400 ml mayonnaise
2 tablespoons chopped parsley
2 tablespoons chopped onion
2 tablespoons salt
6 small dried olives
½ teaspoon crushed garlic
2 oz/60 grams Parmesan cheese
2 oz/60 grams grated Cheddar cheese
1 round granary loaf

Apart from the loaf, mix all the ingredients together well. Leave the mixture to stand overnight or for several hours before serving. Slice a piece of bread off the top of the loaf to act as a lid. Scoop the rest of the bread out of the centre of the loaf and break into pieces.

Put a bowl into the hole in the bread and fill this with dip just before serving. Place the broken bits of bread around the bowl.

Cheddar Walnut Spread

about 12 servings

1 lb/450 grams mature Cheddar cheese, grated
8 oz/225 grams walnuts, finely chopped
3 oz/85 grams spring onions (white part only),
    chopped
2 tablespoons dry white wine
1 teaspoon caraway seeds
4 oz/115 grams butter or margarine, softened

Mix together the cheese, nuts, onions, wine and caraway seeds. Stir in the butter to give a smooth mixture. Chill, covered, and bring to room temperature before serving.

Cheese Mousse

about 10 servings

½ pint/¼ l milk
2 medium eggs, separated
5 oz/140 grams Parmesan cheese, finely grated
3 oz/85 grams cottage cheese
Grated rind and juice of 1 medium lemon
¼ pint/140 ml whipping cream, stiffly beaten
1 sheet gelatine
3 fl oz/85 ml water
¼ teaspoon salt
Large pinch white pepper
Large pinch nutmeg
Dash paprika
2 drops Tabasco

Heat the milk until lukewarm. Lightly whisk the egg yolks in a mixing bowl. Gradually add the milk, whisking continuously. Stir in the Parmesan and cottage cheeses and mix well. Stir in the lemon juice and rind.

Fold the whipped cream into the mixture. Soften the gelatine in water and dissolve over a low heat. Pour slowly into the mixture, stirring continuously. Beat the egg whites until stiff and fold them into the mixture. Add the seasonings. Turn into a greased, 2 pint/1¼ litre, ring mould. Chill until set. Turn out onto a serving dish.

Serve with savoury biscuits or pretzels.

Potted Herb Cheese

About 12 servings

1½ lb/675 grams Cheddar cheese, grated
1 tablespoon whipping cream
2 tablespoons sherry
3 oz/85 grams butter
1 teaspoon chopped chives
1 teaspoon tarragon leaves
1 teaspoon sage
1 teaspoon thyme
1 teaspoon chopped parsley
Clarified butter

Place all the ingredients, except the clarified butter, in the top of a double saucepan over hot water. Stir, over a medium heat, until the cheese and butter melt and the ingredients are thoroughly mixed. Pour into a storage jar and chill until cold.

Cover with a ¼-inch/½-cm deep layer of clarified butter. Cover and store in a refrigerator. Before serving bring back to room temperature and then serve with fingers of hot buttered toast or tiny hot biscuits.

Anchovy Eggs

4 servings

6 soft boiled eggs
1½ oz/45 grams butter
½ teaspoon mustard
2 tablespoons tomato ketchup
1 tablespoon mushroom ketchup
1 tablespoon Worcester sauce
Salt and pepper
4 rounds buttered toast, spread with anchovy paste

Mix together the butter, mustard, ketchups and Worcester sauce in a chafing dish. Simmer.

While simmering add the eggs and seasonings, having broken the eggs well with a fork and mixed them in well to the sauces. As the mixture begins to stiffen turn it out, still hot, onto the toast and serve immediately.

Chicken Liver Pâté

Party Cheese Ball

8 servings

3 oz/85 grams cream cheese
1 tablespoon finely chopped onion
4 oz/115 grams soft smoked cheese
1 teaspoon Worcester sauce
1 teaspoon stuffed green olives, chopped
2 oz/60 grams blue cheese, crumbled
Chopped nuts

Soften the cheese. Mix it together with all the ingredients except the nuts. Cool in a refrigerator until firm. Form the mixture into a ball and roll it in the chopped nuts.

Cheese Yule Log

About 16 servings

6 oz/170 grams cream cheese, softened
8 oz/225 grams blue cheese, crumbled
3 tablespoons chilli sauce
2 tablespoons grated onion
1 tablespoon Dijon mustard
1 teaspoon Worcester sauce
1½ lb/700 grams mature Cheddar cheese, grated
2 oz/60 grams green pepper, chopped

Coarsely crushed pretzels
Garnish, if desired
Assorted savoury biscuits

Beat the first six ingredients together, in a large mixing bowl, until smooth. Stir in the Cheddar cheese and green pepper. Shape the mixture into a log. Wrap in foil and chill for a few hours. Just before serving roll the log in the crushed pretzels. Garnish and serve with the savoury biscuits.

Cheese Snacks

6 servings

4 oz/115 grams Cheddar cheese, grated
2½ oz/75 grams margarine
2½ oz/75 grams flour
½ teaspoon celery salt

Beat the cheese and margarine together until smooth. Gradually add the flour and celery salt. Form into balls and place on an ungreased baking sheet. Flatten each one with a fork. Leave to cool in the refrigerator overnight or for at least 6 hours. Bake in a pre-heated oven at 425°F/220°C/gas mark 7 for 10 minutes. Makes 24 balls.

Marinated Mussels

8 to 10 servings

2 lb/900 grams shelled mussels
2 onions, finely chopped
2 cloves garlic, crushed
4 fl oz/110 ml olive oil
3 oz/85 grams parsley, chopped
2 tablespoons lemon juice
½ teaspoon salt
1 teaspoon pepper

garnish
2 to 3 hard-boiled eggs
1 small lettuce
2 to 3 tomatoes
Sprigs of dill

Drain the mussels well and place in a bowl. Mix together the onion, garlic, oil, parsley, lemon juice, salt and pepper and pour over the mussels. Cool in the refrigerator for 2 to 3 hours.

Rinse the lettuce. Tear the larger leaves in half and place on a large plate. Place the marinated mussels with most of the marinade on the lettuce. Place wedges of egg and tomatoes around the mussels. Garnish with sprigs of dill.

Lamb Pâté

Mussel Balls

6 to 8 servings

1 lb/450 gram jar mussels, chopped
3 sticks celery, chopped
1 onion, finely chopped
Salt and freshly ground pepper to taste
6 hard-boiled eggs, diced
8 oz/225 grams moist breadcrumbs

Drain the mussels and keep the juice. Add sufficient water to the juice to make up to 1 pint/½ litre of liquid. Mix together the celery, onion and 15 fl oz/425 ml of the mussel juice in a saucepan. Simmer until the vegetables are tender.

Add the mussels, salt and pepper to the pan and simmer for about 10 minutes. Add the eggs, the rest of the juice and the breadcrumbs. Mix well. Shape the mixture into small balls and chill thoroughly. Fry in deep fat at 350°F/180°C until browned. Serve immediately with cocktail sticks.

Mussel Puffs

4 to 6 servings

8 oz/225 gram jar mussels, drained and chopped
2 oz/60 grams Gruyère cheese, grated
1 clove garlic, crushed
1 tablespoon mayonnaise
Salt
White pepper
Cayenne pepper

Mix together all the ingredients, adding just enough mayonnaise to bind the mixture and salt and pepper to taste. This may be prepared in advance.

Pre-heat the grill. Spread the mixture, forming a crown, on toasted rounds of white bread. Grill for 3 to 4 minutes, being careful not to burn. Remove when golden and serve hot. Makes 16 to 18 puffs.

Fried Crab Canapés

10 to 15 servings

8 oz/225 grams crabmeat
4 water chestnuts, finely chopped
1 oz/30 grams cornflour
1 egg, lightly beaten
2 teaspoons Worcester sauce
½ teaspoon salt
Dash Tabasco
8 slices firm white bread
Oil for frying

Mix together all the ingredients except the oil and bread. Trim the crusts from the bread. Cut and slice into 4 triangles. Spread them with the crabmeat mixture.

Pre-heat deep fat to 375°F/190°C. Fry the triangles, crab-side down, for 1 minute. Turn over and fry for a further minute. Drain on kitchen towel and serve immediately. Makes 32 canapés.

Spinach and Crab Supreme

12 servings

1 bunch spring onions, chopped
1 clove garlic, crushed
4 oz/115 grams butter
1 tablespoon Parmesan cheese, grated
Salt, pepper and Tabasco to taste
1 lb/450 grams crabmeat, flaked
1 lb/450 grams chopped spinach, cooked as
   directed and drained

Sauté the onions and garlic in the butter in a small frying pan. Add this and the remaining ingredients to the cooked spinach, mixing well. Add extra seasonings if needed. Put this mixture into a chafing dish to keep warm.

Hot Crabmeat Appetiser

15 servings

1 lb/450 grams crabmeat
1 lb/450 grams soft whipped cream cheese
½ pint/¼ l milk
2 tablespoons chopped onion

Mix together the cream cheese, milk and onion. Fold in the crabmeat. Place the mixture in a greased casserole. Cover and heat for 30 minutes at 350°F/180°C/gas mark 4. Serve hot on savoury biscuits or pitta bread.

Party Crabmeat

50 servings

8 oz/225 grams butter
6 oz/170 grams flour
4 pints/2¼ l milk
3 lb/1¼ kilos crabmeat
1 lb/450 grams mushrooms, sliced and sautéed
½ pint/¼ l dry sherry
1 teaspoon lemon juice
1 teaspoon Worcester sauce
Pinch nutmeg
Parsley

In a large pan melt the butter, stir in the flour and add the milk. Stir constantly until the white sauce is thick.

Add the remaining ingredients and heat until the mixture is hot, taking care it does not burn. Serve from a chafing dish with toast or savoury biscuits.

Crab and Cheese Appetiser

4 servings

1 lb/450 grams cream cheese
12 oz/345 grams crabmeat
4 tablespoons mayonnaise
4 tablespoons milk
4 tablespoons onion, chopped
1 teaspoon horseradish
½ teaspoon salt
Paprika

Combine all ingredients and blend well. Spoon into an ovenproof dish and sprinkle with paprika. Bake at 375°F/190°C/gas mark 5 for 18 minutes. Serve with rye bread, crackers or savoury biscuits. Makes 8 to 12 appetisers.

Clam or Mussel Pie

6 servings

2 tablespoons shallots, finely chopped
2 oz/60 grams butter
4 oz/115 grams tinned clams or mussels
Salt
Pepper
2 tablespoons Madeira or dry white vermouth
3 eggs
4 fl oz/110 ml cream
2 tablespoons tomato paste

pastry dough

5 oz/140 grams flour, sifted
½ teaspoon salt
4½ oz/130 grams butter
4 tablespoons water
2 oz/60 grams grated cheese

Sauté the shallot in the butter for a few minutes over a low heat so that it becomes soft without becoming brown. Add the clams or mussels and stir carefully for 2 minutes. Season with salt and pepper. Pour in the wine, increase the heat and allow to boil for a few seconds. Leave to cool.

Beat the eggs together with the cream, tomato paste and salt and pepper. Add the clams or mussels a few at a time and adjust the seasoning.

Make the dough and refrigerate it for at least an hour. Roll out the dough and place it in a ring-form pie dish that has a detachable edge. Bake the pie crust in the oven at 400°F/200°C/gas mark 6 for about 10 minutes.

Pour the mixture into the pie crust and sprinkle cheese over it. Bake for 25 to 30 minutes at 400°F/200°C/gas mark 6 until the pie has risen and become golden brown.

Mushroom Oysters on the Shell

4 servings

30 oysters on the half shell
15 fl oz/425 ml thick white sauce, seasoned
2 tablespoons mayonnaise
1 oz/60 grams grated cheese
2 tablespoons melted butter
2 oz/60 grams ham, chopped
6 oz/170 grams mushrooms, chopped
2 tablespoons parsley, chopped
salt and pepper
Tabasco
Extra grated cheese to garnish

Poach the oysters in their own juice for five minutes in a hot oven. Set to one side.

Heat the white sauce over a low heat and add the mayonnaise and cheese.

Heat the butter until foaming and add the shallots, ham and mushrooms. Cook, stirring frequently, for 5 minutes. Add the parsley and the seasonings to taste. Simmer for 5 more minutes.

Lift the oysters from the half shells and discard the juice. Then spoon 1 or 2 teaspoons of the mushroom mixture into the shells. Place an oyster on top and spoon the cheese-flavoured sauce over each. Sprinkle a little extra grated cheese over the sauce.

Arrange on a shallow baking dish and bake in a moderate oven, 375°F/190°C/gas mark 5, until the sauce is bubbling and lightly browned. Serve immediately while hot.

Marinated Mussels

Kipper Mousse

4 servings

1 envelope gelatine
3 medium kippers
1 egg
2 oz/60 grams onion, finely chopped
1 oz/30 grams dill, snipped
Pinch thyme
¼ teaspoon salt
1 teaspoon lemon juice
8 fl oz/220 ml soured cream
Lettuce, shredded
Lemon and dill to garnish

Place the gelatine in a little cold water.

Clean the fish and finely mash up the meat, or put it through a food processor using the metal knife attachment. Blend in the egg. Add the onion and dill to the fish together with the thyme, salt and lemon juice.

Dissolve the gelatine over a low heat and add the fish mixture. Finally fold in the soured cream.

Pour into a mould or bowl and refrigerate so that the mousse becomes firm—about 2 hours. Spoon the mousse out onto lettuce leaves and garnish with lemon and dill.

Spiced Herrings

Spiced Herrings

8 servings

20 medium sized fresh herrings (about 4½ lbs/2 kilos)
1 fl oz/30 ml white vinegar
2 pints/1¼ l water
1 lb/450 grams sugar
2 oz/60 grams coarse salt
2 oz/60 grams table salt
2 tablespoons allspice, coarsely ground
2 tablespoons black pepper, coarsely ground
3 tablespoons oregano
3 bay leaves, crushed

Clean the herrings, removing the heads but keeping the spines. Quickly rinse the fish and leave to drain.

Mix the vinegar and water. Place the herrings in a bowl and pour the liquid over them. This marinade should completely cover the fish. If it does not, make some more to ensure that the fish is covered. Place the bowl in the refrigerator for 24 hours.

After 24 hours the flesh of the fish should be completely white, right through to the bone. Make a cut in the back to check. If the flesh is not white let the fish stand in the marinade for a further 6 hours, again making sure it is completely covered by the liquid.

Combine the sugar, 2 kinds of salt, allspice, black pepper, oregano and bay leaves. Remove the herrings from the marinade and let them drain before layering them in an earthenware pot with the spice mixture. Place something heavy over the herrings so that they sink down into the juices. Leave them for a further 4 to 7 days before eating.

Angels on Horseback

4 servings

12 oysters, shelled
4 to 6 rashers bacon

Cut the bacon into lengths just long enough to wrap once around each oyster. Secure with a wooden toothpick.

Bake in a pre-heated oven at 450°F/230°C/gas mark 8 for about 10 minutes on each side or until the bacon is brown and crisp. Watch carefully. Drain and serve hot. Makes 12.

Oysters Botany Bay

6 servings

48 fresh oysters, opened and left in the shell
4 tablespoons dry sherry
3 oz/85 grams butter
1 large clove garlic, crushed
5 oz/140 grams fresh white breadcrumbs
1½ tablespoons fresh parsley, chopped
2 teaspoons lemon rind, grated
Salt and freshly ground black pepper

Arrange the oysters on plates and drizzle the sherry over them. In a heavy frying pan, heat the butter and sauté the garlic in it. Stir in all the remaining ingredients and cook, stirring continuously, until the breadcrumbs are golden. Spoon the mixture over the oysters and place in an oven at 425°F/220°C/gas mark 7 for 5 minutes or until heated through. Serve immediately garnished with a lemon half.

Oysters Colette

12 servings

2 oz/60 grams anchovies
3 oz/85 grams pimiento
3 oz/85 grams Parmesan cheese, grated
2 fl oz/60 ml white wine
2 tablespoons parsley, chopped
1 lb/450 grams butter, creamed
96 oysters in the shell
6 oz/170 grams Gruyère cheese, grated

Blend together the anchovies, pimiento, Parmesan and wine. Mix them with creamed butter in a bowl. Add the chopped parsley, folding it into the mixture gently. Be careful not to blend it too vigorously as this may give the mixture a green colour.

Clean and open the oysters, leaving them on the half shell. Place them on baking sheets with ½ teaspoon butter on each oyster. Sprinkle gruyère on top of the butter.

Bake in an oven at 350°F/175°C/gas mark 4 until the butter is melted. Be careful not to overcook the oysters as they can become rubbery.

Kipper Mousse

Salmon Ball

About 8 servings

8 oz/225 grams cream cheese
1 large tin pink salmon
1 small onion, chopped
1 teaspoon parsley
1 tablespoon lemon juice
1 teaspoon horseradish

Soften the cream cheese and set aside. Drain the salmon. Then mix the salmon, chopped onion, parsley, lemon juice and horseradish together. Add the cream cheese to the salmon mixture. Form a ball and roll it in chopped nuts. (Delicious with celery and crackers).

Prawn Dip

About 12 servings

8 oz/225 grams cream cheese, softened
3 tablespoons milk
2 tablespoons fresh onion, grated
½ teaspoon Worcester sauce
8 oz/225 grams boiled prawns, finely chopped

Combine the cream cheese and milk in a small bowl and beat with an electric whisk until smooth. Add the onion and Worcester sauce and beat until fluffy. Stir in the prawns. Serve with savoury biscuits for dipping.

New Orleans Style Prawns

6 servings

2 pints/1¼ l water
4 spring onions, finely chopped
1 small clove garlic, crushed
Salt and freshly ground pepper to taste
1 small bay leaf
4 celery heart stalks, finely chopped
1 lb/450 grams medium-sized, shelled, deveined
    prawns
2 tablespoons olive oil
2½ fl oz/75 ml lemon or lime juice
2½ fl oz/75 ml chilli sauce
2½ fl oz/75 ml ketchup
1 tablespoon freshly grated horseradish
1 tablespoon German mustard
1 teaspoon paprika
Dash cayenne pepper

Pour the water into a medium-sized saucepan and bring to the boil. Add half of the spring onions, the garlic, salt, pepper, bay leaf and celery and cover. Simmer 5 minutes longer. Drain the mixture and remove the bay leaf.

Place the prawn mixture in a medium-sized bowl and cool. Place the remaining spring onions, olive oil, lemon juice, chilli sauce, ketchup, salt, horseradish, mustard, paprika and cayenne pepper in a small bowl and mix well. Pour over the prawn mixture and mix until well blended. Cover and place in the refrigerator to marinate in the sauce over night.

Serve the prawns and sauce in a glass bowl placed in a bowl of cracked ice. Serve with cocktail sticks.

Shrimp Ball

8 to 10 servings

8 oz/225 grams shrimps
2 tablespoons onion, finely chopped
¼ teaspoon salt
8 oz/225 grams cream cheese
1 tablespoon lemon juice
1 tablespoon horseradish

Mix together all the ingredients. Form into 2 balls. Roll them in either nuts or parsley. Serve on crackers or savoury biscuits. This dish freezes well.

Prawn Mould

12 to 16 servings

2½ fl oz/75 ml water
1 envelope gelatine
12 oz/345 gram tin tomato soup
8 oz/225 grams cream cheese
2 oz/60 grams onions, chopped
4 oz/115 grams celery, chopped
½ pint/¼ l mayonnaise
1 lb/450 grams cooked prawns, chopped

Soften gelatine in water. Warm soup and add gelatine and cream cheese. Mix well. Add the remaining ingredients.

Pour into an oiled 3 pint/1½ litre mould. Refrigerate until firm. Turn out to serve. Serve with triangles of brown bread and butter.

Fried Prawn Balls

10 servings

1 medium onion, grated
1 medium raw potato, grated
1½ lb/700 grams raw prawns, shelled, deveined,
    grated, chopped
1 egg
Salt and pepper to taste
Fat for deep frying

Mix the onion, potato and prawns in a large bowl. Stir in egg, salt and pepper. Potato will thicken the batter.

Heat the fat to 375°F/190°C and drop in the batter by spoonfuls. Fry until golden brown; remove with a slotted spoon. Drain on kitchen towel. Serve hot. Makes 36 to 48 balls.

Luxury Toast

4 servings

4 slices white bread
9 oz/255 gram tin asparagus
Butter
About 1 lb/450 grams prawns
2 egg whites
2 tablespoons chilli sauce
4 tablespoons mayonnaise
Lettuce leaves
Sprigs of dill

Fry the slices of white bread in lightly browned butter until they are crisp and golden brown on both sides. Allow them to cool. Pour off the asparagus juice, making sure the asparagus is well drained. Divide up the asparagus between the slices of bread, placing 2 rows of double asparagus on each side. Shell the prawns and divide them between the bread slices so that they seem to "ride" on top of the asparagus.

Beat the egg whites into very stiff peaks. Blend the chilli sauce with the mayonnaise before carefully folding this mixture into the egg whites. Spread the egg mixture over the prawns and asparagus so that they are totally covered. Cook immediately in the oven at 400°F/200°C/gas mark 6 until the mayonnaise soufflé has risen and become golden brown.

Serve immediately, garnished with lettuce and sprigs of dill.

Marinated Beef Appetiser

10 to 12 servings

2½ lb/1150 grams rump steak, trimmed and
   cubed
¼ pint/140 ml soy sauce
3½ oz/100 grams brown sugar
½ teaspoon cinnamon
1 tin pineapple chunks (medium)
4 oz/115 grams mushrooms

Mix together all the ingredients except the pineapple and mushrooms. Marinate for three hours minimum or 24 hours maximum. Remove meat from the marinade and grill until medium done.

Meanwhile, add the pineapple and mushrooms to the marinade and heat until bubbly. Return the cooked meat to the liquid and serve in a chafing dish.

Hot Tamales

15 to 20 servings

1½ lb/700 grams stewing steak
2½ lb/1150 grams chicken pieces, boned
Water
Salt

1 clove garlic, crushed
1 small onion, sliced
2½ fl oz/75 ml vinegar
½ pint/¼ l ketchup
1 teaspoon sugar
2 tablespoons chilli seasoning mix
6 tablespoons chilli powder
12 oz/345 grams cornmeal
Greaseproof paper

Place the steak and the chicken in separate saucepans and cover each with water and season to taste with salt. Add crushed garlic clove to the steak and then add sliced onion to the chicken. Bring to the boil, cover and cook until tender.

Drain the steak and chicken, reserving the stocks. Shred the chicken. Chop the steak. Place the steak in a saucepan with vinegar, ketchup, sugar, 1 teaspoon salt, chilli seasoning mix and 4½ tablespoons of chilli powder. Add enough stock to moisten slightly.

Measure 3 pints/1½ litres of combined chicken and beef stocks and strain before placing in a large saucepan. Add salt to taste and the remaining chilli powder. Bring to the boil and stir in the cornmeal. Cook slowly for 15 minutes, until very thick, then remove from heat.

For each tamale place 2–3 tablespoons corn mixture in the centre of a 7 × 5-inch/10x7½-cm greaseproof paper sheet. Press until thin. Add a heaped tablespoon of steak mixture and another of chicken mixture in the centre. Fold the paper and tie. Steam over boiling water for 1 hour. When thoroughly cooked store in the refrigerator. Re-heat by steaming or put in the top of a double boiler. Makes about 40 small tamales.

Meatball Appetisers

4 servings

1 lb/450 grams minced beef
1 oz/30 grams dry breadcrumbs
1 egg
4 fl oz/110 ml plus 2 tablespoons teryaki sauce
2 tablespoons oil
2 tablespoons light brown sugar
1 oz/30 grams butter

Combine beef, breadcrumbs, egg and 2 tablespoons sauce. Mix and shape into 1-inch/2½-cm meatballs. Brown in oil in a frying pan. Drain off the fat.

Add 4 fl oz/110 ml sauce, brown sugar and butter to the meatballs in the pan and simmer, covered, for 15 minutes or until done. Makes 24 meatballs.

Meatballs in Brandy Sauce

6 to 8 servings

meatballs
2 lb/900 grams minced beef
½ pint/¼ l milk
2 oz/60 grams breadcrumbs
1 tablespoon Worcester sauce

sauce
1 jar peach jam
6 oz/170 grams light brown sugar
¼ pint/140 ml brandy
¼ teaspoon nutmeg

Combine all meatball ingredients and roll into a ball; set to one side.

Combine the sauce ingredients. Add a small amount of meat drippings and simmer for 10 minutes. Add the meatballs to the sauce and coat thoroughly. Cover and simmer for 45 minutes to 1 hour. Makes 40 small meatballs.

Chafing Dish Meatballs

10 to 12 servings

2 lb/900 grams
1 egg, lightly beaten
1 large onion, grated
Salt to taste
12 oz/345 grams chilli sauce
10 oz/285 grams redcurrant jelly
Juice of 1 lemon

Mix together the meat, egg, onion and salt. Shape into small balls. Mix together the chilli sauce, redcurrant jelly and lemon juice. Drop the meatballs into the sauce and simmer until brown. Refrigerate or freeze.

To serve; bring to room temperature. Re-heat in chafing dish and serve with cocktail sticks. Makes 50 to 60 meatballs.

Party Croissant

8 servings

1 oz/30 grams yeast
2½ oz/75 grams butter or margarine
4 fl oz/110 ml lukewarm water
Salt
½ teaspoon sugar
2 eggs
1 tablespoon sesame seeds, without skins, plus extra to sprinkle over croissant
8 oz/225 grams flour

filling
5 oz/140 grams garlic cheese
4 oz/115 grams smoked ham, in thin slices
18–20 olives, stuffed

Crumble the yeast into a large bowl. Melt the butter in a pan and add the water. Pour a little of the liquid over the yeast and stir. Pour in the rest of the liquid. Add salt, sugar, 1 egg and the sesame seeds. Add nearly all of the flour and work until the dough is smooth and shiny. Leave to rise under a cloth for about 30 minutes.

Place the dough on a lightly floured surface and knead until it stops sticking to the surface. Roll out into a triangle. Spread the filling in an even strip across the widest part of the triangle. Roll up towards the point. Form into a croissant.

Place the croissant on a prepared baking sheet and leave to rise for approximately 20 minutes. Brush with the second egg and sprinkle with some sesame seeds. Bake at 400°F/200°C/gas mark 6 on the lowest shelf in the oven for about 20 minutes. Test with a baking needle.

Luxury Toast

Sausage Pies

10 to 12 servings

1 lb/450 grams shortcrust pastry, frozen
12 oz/345 grams sausage meat
20–24 cherry tomatoes, halved

De-frost and roll out the dough. Put to one side.

Break up sausage meat in a heavy frying pan. Cook until all the pink has disappeared, about 10 minutes. Drain on kitchen towel. Cool completely.

Roll out dough and cut into 4-inch/10-cm squares. Moisten the corner of each square with a little cold water. Place the squares on a lightly greased baking sheet. Spoon the drained sausage meat, about 1 spoonful per square, into the centre of each square. Pinch the corners to seal, but do not close completely. Bake at 450°F/230°C/gas mark 8 for 12 to 15 minutes. Place a half cherry tomato, skin side up, on top of the sausage—this is why the pastry was not sealed. Bake 10 minutes more or until the pastry is golden brown. Serve immediately. Makes 20–24 little pies.

Sausage Biscuits

12 servings

8 oz/225 grams mature Cheddar cheese, grated
1 lb/450 grams spicy pork sausage
1 lb/450 grams biscuit dough

Mix everything together in a bowl, working the sausage and cheese in well. Drop spoonfuls of the mixture onto an ungreased baking sheet and shape lightly with the fingers into individual biscuits. Bake at 400°F/200°C/gas mark 6 for about 15 minutes or until browned.

Serve the biscuits piping hot. Makes about 36 biscuits.

Sausage and Apple Snack

6 servings

1 lb/450 grams sausage meat
2 tablespoons parsley, chopped
½ teaspoon curry powder
½ teaspoon mixed herbs
1 oz/30 grams flour
Butter
2 eating apples
6 thin rashers bacon
A few sprigs parsley
Toast

Mix together the sausage meat, parsley, curry powder, herbs and seasoning and shape into 6 patties. Coat lightly with flour and fry in butter for about 5 minutes each side. Remove from the pan and keep hot.

Core, but do not peel the apples. Slice each apple into three and fry for about 2 minutes on each side.

Roll up the bacon. Put it on a skewer and fry or grill.

Put the sausage patties on a serving dish with an apple ring on top. Arrange the bacon rolls in the centre and garnish with parsley. Serve with hot, thin toast.

Savoury Appetiser Franks

About 10 servings

½ pint/¼ l ketchup
2½ fl oz/75 ml Teryaki sauce
2 oz/60 grams brown sugar, tightly packed
2 tablespoons vinegar
1 lb/450 grams Frankfurters, cut in 1-inch/2½-cm pieces.

In a medium saucepan, mix together all the ingredients except the sausages. Simmer for 10 minutes. Add the sausages and simmer for a further 15 minutes. To serve: keep warm in chafing dish or fondue pot. Makes about 50 appetisers.

Sweet and Sour Hot Dogs

10 to 20 servings

6 oz/170 grams mild mustard
2 oz/60 grams redcurrant jelly
2 lb/900 grams Frankfurters

Heat the mustard and jelly in top of a double saucepan. Slice the sausages diagonally ½-inch/1-cm thick. Add to the sauce and cook for 5 minutes. Refrigerate or freeze.

When ready to serve, place in chafing dish and heat. Serve with cocktail sticks. Makes 60 to 80.

Pigs in Bacon

4 to 6 servings

12 Frankfurters
2 teaspoons mustard or ketchup
4 oz/115 grams cheese
12 rashers bacon

Cut a slit lengthways in each Frankfurter, but do not slice through completely. Spread with mustard (or ketchup) and fill the slits with thin strips of cheese.

Roll a slice of bacon in a spiral around each Frankfurter and fasten with cocktail sticks. Cook until bacon is crisp, turning frequently. Makes 12.

Ham and Melon Balls

6 to 8 servings

6 to 8 oz/170 to 225 grams ham, very thinly sliced.
Honeydew or cantaloupe melon

Slice ham into pieces 1-inch/2½-cm wide by 4-inch/10-cm long. These will wrap comfortably around the melon balls.

Cut the melon into balls: place on kitchen towel to drain excess water. Wrap each melon ball with ham: secure with a cocktail stick. Refrigerate until ready to serve. Makes 24 to 36 balls.

Avocado Cream with Sherry

8 servings

1 tin consommé
1 pint/½ l cold water
5 ripe avocados
2 oz/60 grams finely chopped leek
Juice from ½ lemon
1 teaspoon garlic salt
4 fl oz/110 ml double cream
2 tablespoons sherry
Caviar or prawns to garnish

Mix the consommé with the cold water and chill.

Divide the avocados in half, remove the stones and peel off the skins. Mash the fruit in a blender together with the leek, lemon and the spices to give a smooth purée. Dilute with consommé and mix in the cream and the sherry.

Place on individual dishes. Garnish with caviar or prawns and a little dill and lemon. Refrigerate.

Devilled Ham Twists

About 12 servings

14 oz/400 grams devilled ham.
3 tablespoons walnuts, chopped
3 tablespoons onion, finely chopped
2 oz/60 grams pimiento-stuffed olives, finely chopped
½ teaspoon ground red pepper
6 fl oz/170 ml milk
12 oz/345 grams packet biscuit mix
Paprika

Stir ham, walnuts, onion, olives and red pepper together until well blended.

Make a soft dough by combining the milk and biscuit mix. Beat until stiff. Divide dough in half and roll into 2 12-inch/30-cm squares. Spread the ham mixture equally on half of each square. Fold the uncovered half over the ham mixture to form a 12 x 6-inch/30 x 15-cm rectangle. With a sharp knife, cut pastry into 36 rectangles. Twist each gently to form a bow and dust with paprika. Place on a greased baking sheet and bake for 15 minutes at 400°F/200°C/gas mark 6 or until lightly browned.

Avocado Cream with Sherry

Warm Avocado

Vegetable Antipasto

6 servings

1 small cauliflower head, sliced
2 medium carrots, cut into 2-inch/5-cm strips
2 celery sticks, cut into 1-inch/2½-cm pieces
1 green pepper, cut into 2-inch/5-cm strips
2 whole pimientos, drained and cut into strips
2½ oz/70 grams stoned green olives, drained
¼ pint/140 ml salad oil
¼ pint/140 ml water
3 tablespoons Worcester sauce
3 tablespoons white vinegar
1 oz/ 30 grams sugar
1 teaspoon salt
2 dashes Tabasco

In a large saucepan, combine all the ingredients. Bring to the boil, cover, reduce the heat and simmer for 10 minutes, stirring occasionally. Cool; refrigerate for at least 24 hours. Drain well.

Warm Avocado

4 servings

4 small eggs
2 pints/1¼ l water
2 teaspoons salt
1 teaspoon vinegar
1 egg yolk
1 teaspoon lemon juice
1 tablespoon cream
2 oz/60 grams butter
Pinch salt
Tarragon, finely chopped
Snipped parsley
2 large, ripe avocados
Juice of ½ lemon

Start by poaching the eggs. Break each egg into its own cup. Mix together the water, salt and vinegar and bring to the boil. Remove from the heat and slide 1 egg out of its cup into the water. Fold the egg white that spreads out in the water back to the egg with a spoon. Cook the egg carefully for about 4 to 5 minutes, so that the white becomes firm. Cook only one egg at a time. Remove the egg from the water, using a large draining spoon. Trim the egg with a pair of scissors so that it has an even edge and looks attractive. It should not be larger than the hole from the stone in the avocado half. Keep the eggs warm by placing over water at 100°F/38°C.

Mix together the egg yolk, lemon juice and cream in a small saucepan (it should not be an aluminium pan). Gently warm over a low heat, stirring continuously. Lift the pan every now and then from the heat so that it does not become too warm. As soon as the mixture starts to foam or thicken add the butter in small knobs while continuing to beat constantly. Beat until the sauce is thick and light and all the butter has been added. Remove from the heat and season with salt, tarragon and parsley. Keep warm by placing it in water at 100°F/38°C.

Halve the avocados, remove the stones and dig out a slightly larger hole using a spoon. Place the avocado halves in a frying pan. Pour in warm water until it just covers the avocados and add the lemon juice. Bring slowly to the boil without covering the pan. Remove the avocados with a draining spoon and place each of the 4 halves on a warm plate.

Pour a little of the sauce into each hole. Place a poached egg in each hole and cover with the rest of the sauce.

Toasted Asparagus Rolls

12 servings

24 thin slices white bread
8 oz/225 grams Cheddar cheese, grated
24 cooked, whole asparagus
2 oz/60 grams margarine or butter, melted

Trim crusts from the bread and arrange slices between two damp tea towels. Gently roll the bread thin. Sprinkle each slice with grated cheese. Place asparagus at one corner and roll up like a Swiss roll. Fasten with toothpicks.

Arrange the rolls on a greased baking sheet and brush each with melted butter or margarine. Bake at 400°F/200°C/gas mark 6 for 10 minutes or until lightly browned. Serve hot. Makes 24 rolls.

Leeks with Mustard and Cress

4 servings

1 lb/450 grams small leeks
Water
Salt
Mustard and Cress

dressing
1 tablespoon vinegar
½ teaspoon salt
½ teaspoon tarragon
1 tablespoon water
1 teaspoon mustard
3 to 4 tablespoons oil

Wash the leeks well, trimming the root ends and most of the green. In a wide, shallow pan bring the water to the boil, adding 2 teaspoons of salt per 2 pints/1¼ litres of water. Divide the leeks into 2 or three pieces, if they are very long. Cook for about 2 minutes, depending on thickness. Do not over cook.

Blend the ingredients for the dressing and beat for a few minutes to allow the salt to dissolve. Drain the leeks and place in a dish. Pour the dressing over them while they are still hot. Leave them to get cold and marinate for a couple of hours. Cut some mustard and cress onto the leeks when serving.

Melon Balls with Chutney and Ham

6 servings

dressing
3 tablespoons white wine vinegar
¼ pint/140 ml light olive oil
¼ pint/140 ml mango chutney
½ teaspoon salt
Pinch cayenne pepper
½ teaspoon curry powder

salad
1 lb/450 grams melon balls such as canteloupe, honeydew or watermelon, cut with the Small end of a melon ball scoop.
Half head romaine lettuce, shredded
4 oz/115 grams toasted pecan nuts
4 oz/115 grams prosciutto ham, very thinly sliced

Beat together the wine vinegar, olive oil, chutney, salt, cayenne pepper and curry powder. Put to one side, at room temperature, for 1 to 2 hours to develop the flavour. Just before serving place melon balls in a bowl, pour on the dressing and toss gently.

Line a shallow serving bowl with romaine lettuce. Toss the melon balls again and arrange them on the lettuce, making a mound in the centre. Sprinkle with the pecan nuts. Loosely roll up the slices of prosciutto and arrange them in a border around the melon.

Yoghurt Stuffed Mushrooms

6 to 8 servings

24 medium sized whole, fresh mushrooms
1 lb/450 grams ham, finely chopped
¼ pint/140 ml plain yoghurt mixed with 1 oz/30 grams flour
3 oz/85 grams walnuts, chopped
1 tablespoon fresh parsley leaves, chopped

Remove the stems from the mushrooms. Mix together the ham, yoghurt, walnuts and parsley. Place a heaped tablespoon of this mixture in the centre of each mushroom cap. Place on a lightly greased baking sheet. Bake at 400°F/200°C/gas mark 6 for about 12 minutes. Serve hot.

Toasted Mushroom Rolls

15 to 20 servings

8 oz/225 grams mushrooms
2 oz/60 grams butter
1½ oz/45 grams flour
½ teaspoon salt
¼ pint/140 ml single cream
2 teaspoons chives, finely chopped
1 teaspoon lemon juice
1 thin sliced loaf fresh white bread.

Clean and finely chop the mushrooms. Sauté for 5 minutes in butter. Blend in flour and salt. Stir in cream. Cook until thick. Add chives and lemon juice and leave to cool. Remove the crusts from the white bread and spread with the mixture. Roll up. Pack and freeze if desired.

When ready to serve: defrost, cut each roll in half and toast all over in a pre-heated oven at 400°F/200°C/gas mark 6. Makes 42.

Spinach Tarts

12 servings

8 oz/225 grams frozen spinach, chopped, well
  drained
2 eggs, beaten
4 oz/115 grams feta cheese or cottage cheese
½ teaspoon salt
1 lb/450 grams chilled shortcrust dough, cut into
  24 tart rounds

Mix together the first 4 ingredients. Put to one side.
Place the tart rounds on a greased baking sheet. Place
one teaspoon of filling on each one. Pinch the edges
together so that the spinach is almost covered. Bake
at 350°F/180°C/gas mark 4 for 10 minutes or until
pastry is cooked.

Note: left over filling can be baked in a casserole
dish. Makes 24 tarts.

Stuffed Pepper Slices

4 to 6 servings

1 red pepper
1 green pepper
8 oz/225 grams cottage cheese
2 tablespoons milk
1 tablespoon pimiento, chopped
1 tablespoon parsley, chopped
1 tablespoon watercress, chopped
1 tablespoon chives, chopped
¼ teaspoon salt
Large pinch white pepper
1 teaspoon lemon juice
1 envelope plain gelatine
4 fl oz/110 ml cold water
Lettuce leaves

Cut tops off the peppers, de-seed and wash.

Cream the cottage cheese in a blender (thin with
milk if necessary). Remove from blender and mix
with pimiento, parsley, watercress, chives, salt, pepper and lemon juice.

Soak gelatine in cold water. Dissolve completely
over simmering water. Add to the cheese mixture.
Fill the peppers with the mixture and chill in the
refrigerator for at least 2 hours.

Cut each pepper into 4 thick slices. Serve on lettuce.

Marinated Mushrooms

8 servings

1 lb/450 grams fresh mushrooms, sliced
2 spring onions, sliced
4 fl oz/110 ml corn oil
4 fl oz/110 ml wine vinegar
2 tablespoons parsley, chopped
½ teaspoon salt
½ teaspoon dry mustard
½ teaspoon dried basil leaves
Dash pepper

Mix together all the ingredients. Chill for several
hours.

Fried Mushrooms

3 to 4 servings

1 lb/450 grams mushrooms
1 oz/30 grams flour
1 teaspoon salt
Pinch black pepper
2 eggs, beaten
3 oz/85 grams fine breadcrumbs

Rinse, dry and trim the mushrooms. Mix together
the flour, salt and pepper. Dredge the mushrooms
in flour, dip in egg and roll in the breadcrumbs.

Pre-heat fat to 375°F/190°C. Fry mushrooms for 3
minutes.

Mushroom Toast with Garlic

6 servings

24 fine, white mushrooms
1 lemon
3½ oz/100 grams butter, at room temperature
3 cloves garlic, crushed
1 tablespoon shallot, finely chopped
2 tablespoons parsley, chopped
Salt
Pepper
6 slices white bread, crusts removed

Clean the mushrooms and drip small amount of
lemon juice over them so that they remain white.

Mix together the butter, garlic, shallot, parsley and
juice from a half lemon. Add salt and pepper to taste.

Fry the bread until golden brown on one side. Cut
the mushrooms into thin slices and place them on
the unfried side of the bread. Cover with the butter
mixture and place under the grill. Serve when the
butter has started to turn brown on top.

Stuffed Mushrooms

4 servings

8 large mushrooms
1 oz/30 grams butter or margarine
2 tablespoons onion, chopped
1 clove garlic, finely chopped
1 teaspoon dried parsley
2 oz/60 grams salt
1 oz/30 grams dry breadcrumbs
½ teaspoon oregano
½ teaspoon salt
2 tablespoons Parmesan cheese, grated

Remove stems from mushrooms. Melt butter. Brush the caps with melted butter. Chop the stems finely. Sauté onion, garlic, and chopped stems in melted butter for about 5 minutes. Add remaining ingredients; more butter may be needed if mixture is too dry.

Fill the caps with the mixture. Bake at 375°F/190°C/gas mark 5 for 20 minutes.

Potato Skins

8 servings

8 medium sized potatoes (4 to 5 lb/about 2 kilos)
1 oz/30 grams flour
Cooking oil
Seasoned salt

Scrub the potatoes and pierce with a fork. Rub lightly with oil and bake in a pre-heated oven at 400°F/200°C/gas mark 6 for about 50 to 60 minutes, or until tender. Leave to cool.

Cut the potatoes in half lengthways and scoop out most of the cooked flesh, leaving about ¼-inch/½-cm shell. Cut these shells in half lengthways, then in half crossways, to give eight pieces from each potato. Dip in flour, shake off excess, then deep fry in oil pre-heated to 375°F/190°C for about 2 minutes or until lightly browned.

Drain on kitchen towel. Sprinkle with seasoned salt and serve. Makes about 64 potato skins.

These can be made in advance and re-heated by placing on a baking sheet in a pre-heated oven at 375°F/190°C/gas mark 5 for about 10 minutes.

Leeks with Mustard and Cress

Soups

Cold Buttermilk Soup

6 to 8 servings

3 egg yolks
4 oz/115 grams sugar
1 teaspoon lemon juice
½ teaspoon lemon rind, grated
1 teaspoon vanilla
2 pints/1¼ l buttermilk

Beat egg yolks lightly in a large bowl, gradually adding sugar.

Add lemon juice, lemon rind and vanilla. Slowly add the buttermilk, continuing to beat (either with an electric beater on slow or with a wire whisk) until soup is smooth.

Serve soup in chilled soup bowls.

Beer and Bread Soup

6 to 8 servings

1 small loaf dark rye bread
1½ pints/850 ml water
1½ pints/850 ml brown ale
4 oz/115 grams sugar
1 whole lemon (both juice and grated rind)
Whipped cream

Break bread in small pieces into a mixing bowl. Mix water and beer and pour this over the bread. Allow it to stand for several hours.

When ready to serve, cook the mixture over a low heat, stirring occasionally, just long enough for it to thicken. (If the mixture is too thick, strain it through a coarse sieve.) Bring to the boil, add sugar, lemon juice and lemon rind.

Serve the soup with a spoonful of whipped cream on top.

Apple Soup

8 servings

1½ lb/700 grams cooking apples
5 pints/2½ l water
½ lemon, thinly sliced
1 stick cinnamon
2 oz/60 grams cornflour
2½ fl oz/75 ml water
Sugar to taste
2½ fl oz/dry white wine (optional)

Wash, quarter and core the apples; do not peel. Cook until soft in 2 pints/1 litre of water with lemon and cinnamon. Put the apples through a coarse sieve. Place them in a pot with the rest of the water and bring to the boil.

Mix the cornflour with the 2½ fl oz/75 ml of water and add to the pot, stirring constantly. Add sugar and the wine and serve hot.

Apple Yoghurt Soup

4 servings

1 hard boiled egg, chopped
4 oz/115 grams raisins
3 pints/1½ l plain yoghurt
1 cucumber, peeled and chopped
2 oz/60 grams spring onions
1 teaspoon salt
¼ teaspoon pepper
3 tablespoons curry powder (or to taste)
5 green, unpeeled cooking apples, cored and chopped
Milk
1 tablespoon fresh parsley, finely chopped (optional)

Combine all the ingredients except the milk and parsley. Thin with milk to the desired consistency. Chill. Sprinkle with parsley before serving.

Cream of Marrow and Apple Soup

8 servings

1 marrow (about 2 lb/1 kilo) peeled, seeded and
  coarsely chopped
2 Granny Smith apples, cored, pared and coarsely
  chopped
1 medium onion, chopped
2½ pints/1½ l chicken broth
4 oz/115 grams Cheddar cheese, grated
2 egg yolks
3 tablespoons Marsala wine
Salt and pepper

Combine marrow, apples, onion and chicken
broth in a large saucepan. Bring to the boil, cover
and simmer over a medium heat for 20 minutes or
until marrow is soft. Purée in portions in a blender
or processor.

In a large bowl mix the egg yolks and cheese together. Slowly stir them into the hot soup as it is
puréed until all the soup is mixed in. Re-blend or
process to a smooth mixture and return to the pot.
Add the wine, salt and pepper to taste. Re-heat; do
not boil.

Creamy Blackberry Soup

4 to 6 servings

1 lb/450 grams blackberries, washed and picked
  over
1 pint/½ l water
½ pint/¼ l maple syrup
½ teaspoon cinnamon
½ pint/¼ l soured cream

Place fruit in a saucepan with water, maple syrup,
cinnamon and cardamom. Cook over a low heat for
10 minutes. Remove from heat and leave to cool.

Stir in soured cream and chill well before serving.

Celery and Walnut Soup

4 servings

1 lb/450 grams fresh celery, cut in slices
1 medium onion, chopped
2 oz/60 grams butter
2 pints/1¼ l chicken broth
4 fl oz/110 ml double cream
3 oz/85 ml shelled walnuts
1 oz/30 ml butter
Celery salt
Freshly ground pepper
A small amount of sherry

Combine the sliced celery and onion. Place the
mixture in a frying pan with butter and allow to bubble slowly over a low heat. Stir occasionally. Simmer
for about 10 minutes, or until the celery feels soft.

Stir in three quarters of the chicken broth. Bring to
the boil and simmer for about 30 minutes.

Strain or mix in a food processor and pour the
soup back into the pot. Beat in the cream. Chop the
walnuts and fry them in butter for a few minutes;
then blend them into the soup. Add the celery salt,
pepper and sherry. Dilute with the rest of the chicken
broth if the soup feels too thick. Serve in a heated
tureen or in individual, warmed soup bowls. Decorate with a few small leaves from the celery. These
should swim on top of the soup.

Cherry Soup

4 to 6 servings

1½ lb/700 grams sweet red cherries
2 pints/1 l water
½ stick cinnamon (or ¼ teaspoon ground
  cinnamon)
3 or 4 slivers orange or lemon rind and juice of
  ½ lemon or orange.
½ pint/¼ l red wine
½ oz/15 grams cornflour
sugar to taste

Stone the cherries and put about three quarters of
them into a saucepan. Cover with water. Add the cinnamon, rind and orange juice. Cover and simmer
gently until the cherries are tender. Put through an
electric blender or food processor until smooth. Add
the wine.

Add the cornflour to cold water and mix until
smooth. Add a little hot soup to this mixture and pour
back into the soup. Stir in well, bring to the boil and
cook for 4 to 5 minutes. Add the reserved cherries
for the last few minutes and make sure they heat
through. Add sugar to taste and serve hot with cracker
biscuits, which can be crumbled into the soup if preferred.

Cranberry Soup

4 servings

12 oz/345 grams sugar
1½ pints/850 ml water
2 sticks cinnamon
¼ teaspoon ground cloves
1½ lb/700 grams cranberries, fresh or frozen
2 tablespoons lemon juice
1 tablespoon grated orange rind
Soured cream

Combine sugar, water, cinnamon sticks and cloves
in an 8 pint/4½ litre heavy saucepan. Cook over high
heat until the mixture comes to the boil, about 10
minutes. Add the cranberries and cook until the mixture returns to the boil and continue for another 2
minutes.

Reduce the heat to medium and cook for another 5 minutes or until the cranberries begin to burst. Remove from the heat and stir in the lemon juice and orange rind. Cool to room temperature.

Chill in a refrigerator for at least 4 hours or until ready to serve. Serve with a spoonful of soured cream.

Cranberry and Orange Soup

4 to 6 servings

1 lb/450 grams fresh cranberries
1 pint/½ l thin chicken stock or water
15 fl oz/425 ml white wine
2 or 3 pieces lemon rind
Pared rind of ripe orange
½ stick cinnamon
2–4 oz/60–115 grams sugar to taste
Juice of 2 oranges
Juice of ½ lemon

Wash cranberries; put into a pan with the stock and wine. Add the lemon and orange rind and stick of cinnamon and then simmer for about 10 minutes until the berries have softened. Remove the cinnamon and put the fruit through a tammy sieve. Sweeten to taste. Add the orange and lemon juices.

Serve chilled with thin orange slice as a garnish.

Orange Soup

6 servings

½ oz/15 grams cornflour
2 pints/1¼ l water
15 fl oz/425 ml orange juice
2 oz/60 grams sugar
Whipped cream
Thin slice orange

Mix the cornflour in 2½ fl oz/75 ml of cold water. Bring the rest of the water to the boil and add the cornflour mixture to the boiling water to thicken slightly. Add the orange juice and sugar.

Serve either hot or cold, garnished with a spoonful of whipped cream and a thin slice of orange.

Cream of Pumpkin Soup

3 to 4 servings

4 oz/115 grams onion, diced
1 oz/30 grams butter
1 pint/½ l chicken stock
1 lb/450 grams cooked pumpkin
1 teaspoon cinnamon
1 tablespoon sugar
¼ pint/140 ml double cream or soured cream

Sauté the onion and butter in a medium-sized heavy saucepan until the onion is transparent. Add ½ pint/¼ litre of stock and simmer until the onion is tender. Stir in the pumpkin, blending until smooth. Add the remaining stock, cinnamon and sugar and stir until all the flavours have blended. Finally, add the double cream and serve hot.

If you prefer soured cream garnish, omit the double cream and top each soup bowl with a generous spoonful of soured cream.

Strawberry Soup

6 servings

1½ lb/700 grams fresh strawberries, washed, hulled and sliced.
4 tablespoons sugar, sprinkled on berries
1½ pints/850 ml plain yoghurt
½ pint/¼ l fresh cream
Fresh mint leaf

Place half of the strawberries in a blender with the yoghurt and cream. Blend until smooth. Reserve a few berries to be used as a garnish. Fold the remaining strawberries into the mixture. Garnish with the reserved fruit and a fresh mint leaf. Serve cold.

Celery and Walnut Soup

Cod Soup with Orange

4 servings

11 oz/315 grams cod fillet (frozen or fresh)
2 pints/1¼ l fish stock
5 to 6 potatoes, cut into cubes
1 whole fennel, cut into cubes
1 leek, shredded
1 tin tomatoes
2 cloves garlic
salt
pepper
Juice from ½ orange
2 tablespoons snipped parsley

Allow the fish to partially thaw, if frozen, and cut it into 1 to 1½-inch/2½ to 3-cm wide cubes.

Bring the stock to the boil in a pot. Add the vegetables and the garlic. Season with salt and pepper and let the soup simmer for 10 to 12 minutes until the vegetables feel soft. Add the orange juice and simmer the soup for another 3 to 4 minutes. Serve the soup piping hot with snipped parsley sprinkled on top.

Old-Fashioned Beef-Vegetable Soup

6 servings

3 lb/1¼ kilos shin of beef on the bone
6 pints/3¼ l water
2 tablespoons salt
2 teaspoons Worcester sauce
¼ teaspoon pepper
1 medium onion, chopped
3 oz/84 grams barley
8 oz/225 grams celery, chopped
8 oz/225 grams carrot, sliced
8 oz/225 grams potato, sliced
8 oz/225 grams cabbage shredded
8 oz/225 grams peas
1 turnip, peeled and cubed
1½ lb/700 grams tomatoes
3 teaspoons dried parsley

Place the beef, water, salt, Worcester sauce and pepper in a large pot. Cover and simmer for 2½ to 3 hours. Remove the bone, cut off the meat in small pieces and return the meat to the pot.

Add the remaining ingredients and simmer for about 45 minutes.

Cod Soup with Orange

Pumpkin Soup

4 servings

1 oz/30 grams butter
2 tablespoons onion, chopped
½ teaspoon ginger
1 oz/30 grams flour
1½ lb/700 grams pumpkin
1 pint/½ l chicken stock
1 pint/½ l milk
Salt

Sauté butter, onion and ginger. Stir in flour. Add pumpkin; cook 5 minutes. Gradually add stock and milk; simmer 5 minutes. Season with salt.

Cheese Soup

4 servings

1 onion, finely chopped
1 oz/30 grams margarine
1½ oz/45 grams flour
2 pints/1¼ l broth
10 oz/285 grams grated cheese
1 egg yolk
4 fl oz/110 ml soured cream
Finely chopped celery
Chopped parsley

Sauté the onion in the margarine. Stir in the flour when the onion has become transparent. Cover with the broth, stirring constantly and simmer for 5 to 6 minutes.

Stir in the cheese and let it melt. It should not, however, be allowed to boil. Remove the pot from the heat; stir in the egg yolk and the soured cream. Serve immediately garnished with celery and parsley.

Cheddar Cheese Soup

6 servings

4 oz/115 grams carrots, finely diced
4 oz/115 grams celery, finely diced
4 oz/115 grams onion, finely diced
4 oz/115 grams green pepper, finely diced
1½ lb/700 grams cheddar cheese, grated
2 oz/60 grams butter
1 oz/30 grams flour
2 pints/1¼ l evaporated milk
¼ teaspoon salt
Pepper to taste
sherry or beer (optional)

Sauté vegetables in butter for 5 minutes only, so they remain crunchy. Stir in flour till a paste forms. Add broth and simmer 5 minutes. Add cheese very slowly. Add evaporated milk. Season to taste with salt and pepper and sherry or beer, if desired.

Parmesan Cheese Soup

5 to 6 servings

2 rashers bacon, chopped
1 large or 2 small onions, chopped
2 to 3 stalks celery, chopped
1½ oz/45 grams butter
4 oz/115 grams fresh white breadcrumbs
2–2½ pints/1¼-1½ l stock or consommé
Salt and pepper
Pinch cayenne pepper
1 bay leaf, 3 to 4 sprigs of parsley, tied together
4 to 6 oz/115 to 170 grams Parmesan or other strong hard cheese
Pinch dry mustard

optional garnish
2 egg yolks
¼ pint/140 ml cream
Paprika
Croutons

Cook bacon, onions and celery gently in melted butter, stirring frequently, until onions are golden brown. Add fresh breadcrumbs; mix well before adding stock or consommé. Add salt and pepper, cayenne pepper, bay leaf and parsley sprigs. Bring mixture to the boil, stirring constantly. Cover, simmer about 20 minutes. Remove bay leaf and parsley.

Add cheese; mix well. A little dry mustard can also be added. This soup can be made richer by adding a mixture of egg yolks and cream. Sprinkle with paprika; serve hot with croutons.

Californian Minestrone

6 servings

4 oz/115 grams belly of pork, cut into ½-inch/ 1¼-cm cubes
8 oz/225 grams onion, finely chopped
2 cloves garlic, minced
2½ lb/1¼ kilos white kidney beans, drained
3 pints/1½ l beef broth or stock
2 carrots, peeled and diced
2 sticks celery, sliced
1½ lb/700 grams tinned tomatoes
4½ teaspoons lemon juice
1 bay leaf
1 teaspoon salt
1 teaspoon chilli sauce
½ teaspoon basil
½ teaspoon oregano

In large pan, brown belly of pork lightly. Add onion and garlic; cook until tender. Add remaining ingredients and simmer 30 minutes.

Main Course Vegetable Soup

6 servings

4 oz/115 grams dried lima beans
4 oz/115 grams dried peas
2 oz/60 grams barley
2 oz/60 grams rice
2 oz/60 grams kidney beans
4 pints/2¼ l cold water
4 oz/115 grams celery, cut in pieces
2 potatoes, sliced
2 onions, sliced
1 white turnip, diced
8 oz/225 grams stewed or tinned tomatoes
1 teaspoon salt
¼ teaspoon pepper
1 ham bone (optional)

Wash beans, peas, barley, rice and kidney beans and soak overnight in cold water. Bring to boiling point. Add celery, potatoes, onions, turnip, tomatoes, salt and pepper. Simmer slowly 2 hours. Add water as it cooks away.

About half an hour before serving, add ham bone if desired and more seasoning if necessary. Remove bone before serving. This soup should be quite thick and is a meal in itself.

Spring Soup

4 to 6 servings

4 young carrots
2 to 3 young leeks, depending on size
1½ oz/45 grams butter
1 oz/25 grams flour
2 pints/1¼ l chicken stock
4 oz/115 grams cauliflower florets
3 oz/85 grams peas
3 oz/85 grams young green beans, sliced
Pinch sugar
2 tablespoons mixed parsley, chervil, mint and
  thyme
Salt and pepper
¼ pint/140 ml cream
2 egg yolks

Peel and dice carrots. Wash leeks thoroughly; cut white part into slices. Melt butter; cook these vegetables gently in a covered pan 5 to 6 minutes without allowing to brown. Sprinkle in flour, mix thoroughly, then add stock. Blend well until smooth; bring to the boil, stirring constantly. Cook a few minutes before adding cauliflower florets, peas, sliced beans and sugar. Simmer 15 minutes. Add herbs; cook a few more minutes, to draw out flavour of herbs. Season to taste.

Mix cream with egg yolks. Take a few spoonfuls of hot soup; mix well with cream and egg-yolk mixture before straining it back into soup, stirring constantly. Reheat, being very careful not to allow soup to boil, as this causes egg to curdle and spoils texture of soup.

Bean/Vegetable Soup

5 to 6 servings

4 pints/2¼ l water
1 lb/ 450 grams dried haricot beans
3 tablespoons oil
1 small onion, chopped
2 large cloves garlic, crushed
3 oz/85 grams parsley, snipped
1 teaspoon oregano
½ teaspoon basil
12 oz/345 grams chopped carrots
12 oz/345 grams courgette
1 lb/450 grams tinned tomato sauce (or the
  equivalent in fresh tomatoes)
2 tablespoons red wine vinegar
Salt and Tabasco sauce to taste

Bring water to the boil in a soup pot. Add beans and reduce heat to simmer. Cover and cook for an hour or until tender.

Meanwhile, heat the oil in a frying pan and sauté the onion, garlic, parsley, oregano and basil until the onions are tender. Add this to the cooked beans along with the vegetables and tomato sauce. Cover and simmer at least 30 minutes, then add the vinegar, salt and Tabasco sauce.

Gazpacho

6 to 8 servings

Soup
2 medium-sized cucumbers, peeled and coarsely
  chopped
5 medium-sized tomatoes, peeled and coarsely
  chopped
1 large onion, coarsely chopped
1 medium-sized green pepper, trimmed, seeded
  and coarsely chopped
2 cloves garlic, finely chopped
1–1½ lb/450–700 grams French bread, trimmed
  of crusts and coarsely crumbled
2 pints/1¼ l cold water
2½ fl oz/75 ml red wine vinegar
4 teaspoons salt
4 teaspoons olive oil
1 tablespoon tomato paste

Garnish

4 oz/115 grams croutons
4 oz/115 grams onions, finely chopped
4 oz/115 grams cucumbers, peeled and finely
  chopped
4 oz/115 grams green peppers, finely chopped

In a deep bowl, combine the cucumbers, tomatoes, onion, green pepper, garlic and crumbled bread; mix together thoroughly. Then stir in the water, vinegar and salt. Ladle the mixture, about 1 pint/½ litre at a time, into a blender or food processor and blend at high speed for 1 minute, or until reduced to a smooth purée. Pour the purée into a bowl and, with a whisk, beat in the olive oil and tomato paste.

Cover the bowl tightly with foil or cling film and refrigerate at least 2 hours, or until the soup is thoroughly chilled. Just before serving, stir soup lightly, then ladle it into a large, chilled tureen or individual soup plates.

Place croutons, onions, cucumbers and green peppers in separate serving bowls and let each diner add whatever garnish he desires.

Zorn Soup

8 servings

6 oz/170 grams dried green peas
6 pints/3½ l water
3 tablespoons salt
3 onions, peeled and cut into wedges
10 black peppercorns
2 bay leaves
About 3 lb/1¼-1½ kilos topside of beef
8 potatoes
4 carrots
1 wedge cabbage, about 8 oz/225 grams
Snipped parsley

Soak the peas in 2 pints/1¼ litres of the water and 1 tablespoon of the salt for 8 to 10 hours. Pour away the water. Place the peas in a pot with the remaining 4 pints/2¼ litres of water. Cook the peas together with the onions and spices for about 45 minutes. Skim away all the pea skins.

Rinse the meat under running water. Stick a meat thermometer into the beef so that the point of the thermometer comes to the middle of the thickest part of the meat. The entire stick of the thermometer should be in the meat. Place the meat in the pot. Boil over low heat for 1¼ to 1½ hours, until the thermometer shows 185 to 195°F/85–90°C.

Peel the potatoes and the carrots about 30 minutes before the meat is done. Cut the vegetables into chunks and cook them in the soup. Add the shredded cabbage about 10 minutes before the meat is done. Season to taste.

Cheese Soup

When the meat is done, remove the pot from the stove. Let it stand, covered, for about 20 minutes. Remove the meat from the soup, cut it into slices, and serve it on a plate with the soup, or cut pieces of the meat into the soup. Garnish with parsley and serve.

Avocado Soup

4 servings

2 ripe, soft avocados, stoned and peeled
1 teaspoon lemon juice
½ pint/¼ l cold chicken broth
½ pint/¼ l single cream
¼ pint/140 ml plain yoghurt
¼ pint/140 ml dry white wine
Salt to taste

Set aside a few thin slices of avocado brushed with lemon juice to use as a garnish. Place remaining avocado in a food processor or blender; blend until smooth. Add remaining ingredients; blend until smooth.

Serve soup very cold, garnished with reserved avocado slices.

Minestrone with Sausage and Greens

4 servings

8 oz/225 grams well-flavoured Italian sausage
(small, individual salamis)
1 medium onion, finely chopped
½ pint/¼ l brown stock
1 lb/450 grams tinned plum tomatoes and liquid
1¼ lb/570 grams tinned white kidney beans,
undrained
8 oz/225 grams lettuce, Swiss chard or spinach
Salt and pepper
Grated Parmesan cheese

Sauté whole sausages in 6 or 8 pint/3¼ or 4½ litre saucepan over moderate heat. When they begin to take on colour (about 5 minutes), add chopped onion and sauté until onion is soft, about 10 minutes. Add broth, tomatoes and beans and simmer for 10 minutes.

Wash lettuce, chard or spinach and shred coarsely. Add to the soup, bring to the boil and simmer for 15 more minutes (adding extra water if needed).

Remove sausages and slice. Return to soup and add salt and pepper to taste. Sprinkle cheese on top and serve very hot.

Sherry Bisque

8 to 12 servings

1 small ham hock
6 oz/170 grams split green peas
1 bay leaf
3 pints/1½ l beef broth
6 rashers bacon, diced
6 oz/170 grams onion, chopped
1 stalk celery, diced
1½ oz/45 grams flour
8 oz/225 grams tinned tomato purée
½ pint/¼ l chicken broth
4 fl oz/110 ml sherry
2 oz/60 grams butter
Freshly ground pepper to taste

Place ham hock, split peas, bay leaf and 2 pints/ 1¼ litres beef broth into 8-pint/4½-litre saucepan. Bring to the boil, reduce heat to simmer.

Sauté bacon until fat is rendered. Add onion and celery; cook until tender. Stir in flour; mix to blend. Add remaining 1 pint/½ litre beef broth; cook until slightly thickened. Add onion mixture to split-pea mixture; continue to cook until split peas are soft, about 1½ hours.

When done, remove ham hock. Purée mixture in blender or food mill. Add tomato purée, chicken broth and sherry. Add butter and pepper; stir until melted. Strain soup, if desired, before serving.

Cauliflower Soup

6 servings

1 medium-sized head cauliflower, cut in small
florets
2 oz/60 grams butter
6 oz/170 grams onion, chopped
1 oz/30 grams flour
1 pint/½ l chicken broth
1 pint/½ l single cream
½ teaspoon Worcester sauce
Pinch salt
8 oz/ 225 grams Cheddar cheese, grated
Chopped chives

Place cauliflower in boiling salted water and cook until tender; drain, reserving liquid. Cook onion until soft in melted butter. Blend in flour and broth and stir until mixture comes to the boil. Stir in ½ pint/¼ litre liquid drained from the cauliflower (use water if needed to make ½ pint/¼ litre), cream, Worcester sauce, salt and cauliflower. Heat to boiling. Add cheese and stir until it melts. Garnish with chopped chives.

Zorn Soup

Barley Soup

6 to 8 servings

About 8 pints/4½ l water
1 lb/450 grams brisket and/or 2 soup bones
1 onion, whole
2 stalks celery, sliced
2–3 carrots, whole
4 oz/115 grams barley

Bring all ingredients to the boil. Cover and simmer over low heat 2 to 3 hours. Remove onion. Mash carrots and place back in soup.

Cream of Barley Soup

4 servings

8 oz/225 grams barley
1 onion, sliced
1 carrot, sliced
2 stalks celery, sliced
1 bay leaf
3 or 4 sprigs parsley (or 1 tablespoon chopped parsley)
2–2½ pints/1¼-1½ l chicken stock
Chicken carcass or ham bone
¼ pint/140 ml cream
1 to 2 tablespoons chopped parsley, for garnish
Croutons

Wash barley; soak overnight if possible. Otherwise, cover with boiling water and soak 2 hours. Put vegetables into pan with drained barley, herbs, stock and chicken carcass or ham bone. Cover; cook gently until barley is tender, about 1½ to 2 hours. Discard bones and herbs. Set aside barley.

Strain soup through sieve, or blend soup and barley in electric blender or food processor. Reheat soup; adjust seasoning. Add cream just before serving. Sprinkle with parsley; serve with croutons.

Black Bean Soup

4 to 6 servings

8–12 oz/225–345 grams dried black beans
1 ham bone or some ham meat minus fat
2½-3 pints/1¼-1½ l water
2 medium onions, sliced
4 to 5 stalks celery, sliced
2 to 3 carrots, sliced
1 bay leaf, 5 or 6 sprigs parsley and 1 sprig thyme, tied together
2 cloves
½ teaspoon dry mustard
Pinch cayenne pepper
Stock or milk
2 hard-boiled eggs
4 to 6 slices lemon
Croutons

Wash beans in several changes of cold water; cover with cold water. Soak overnight; drain. Put beans into large thick pan; add water and ham bone. Cover pan; cook 2 hours.

Add onions, celery, carrots, herbs, cloves, mustard and cayenne; cover pan. Cook another 1 to 1½ hours, until beans are tender.

Remove bone and herbs. Put soup through fine sieve or blend in electric blender or processor. Reheat soup; if too thick, add enough stock or milk to make good texture. Adjust seasonings. Serve hot; garnish with eggs, lemon and croutons.

Iced Green Bean Soup

6 to 8 servings

1 lb/450 grams fresh green beans
3 pint/1½ l chicken stock
½ teaspoon thyme
¼ teaspoon savory
1 clove garlic, crushed
¼ pint/140 ml whipping cream
Salt and freshly ground pepper to taste

Snap the ends from the green beans and cut the beans into large pieces. Combine the beans and stock in a large saucepan, then add the thyme, savory and garlic. Bring to the boil, then reduce heat and cover. Simmer until the beans are tender. Drain and reserve the liquid.

Pour the reserved liquid back into the saucepan and boil until reduced to 2 pints/1¼ litres. Place the beans in a blender or processor and process until puréed. Stir into the liquid in the saucepan and mix well. Bring to the boil, then stir in the cream and just bring to the boil. Remove from heat and season with salt and pepper. Cool, then chill until cold.

Haricot Bean Soup

8 servings

2 lb/900 grams haricot beans
1½ lb/700 grams smoked ham hock
1 medium onion, diced
1 oz/30 grams butter
Salt and pepper to taste

Wash beans and run through hot water until they are white again. Put in pot with 8 pints/4½ litres of hot water. Add ham and boil slowly for approximately 3 hours, covered.

Sauté onion in butter and, when light brown, add to bean soup. Season to taste with salt and pepper, then serve. Do not add salt until ready to serve, as this toughens the beans.

Pinto Bean Soup

6 to 8 servings

14 oz/400 grams dried pinto beans
Water
2 cloves garlic
1 wedge onion
Salt
2 medium tomatoes, peeled
1 medium onion, quartered
1½ oz/45 grams butter or margarine
½ teaspoon chilli powder
4 oz/115 grams Munster cheese, cut in small
  cubes
Crisp fried tortilla strips or garlic-flavoured
  croutons

Soak beans overnight in hot water to cover generously. The next day, drain beans, place in a large saucepan and add fresh hot water, 1 clove garlic and onion wedge. Bring to the boil, reduce heat and simmer gently, covered, for 2 hours. Add salt to taste and simmer for a further 2 hours, or until tender.

Drain beans, reserving 1½ pints/850 ml bean liquid. Measure 2 lb/900 grams beans and save any extra for another use. Grind beans and reserved liquid in a blender or food processor and set aside.

Combine tomatoes, remaining clove garlic and quartered onion and blend until smooth. Melt butter in a large, heavy saucepan. Add the tomato mixture and cook over a high heat for about 15 minutes. Add puréed bean mixture and chilli powder. Season to taste with salt and simmer for 15 to 20 minutes.

To serve; place a few cheese cubes in each soup bowl. Pour hot soup over cheese and garnish with tortilla strips or croutons.

Brown Bean Soup

4 servings

11 oz/315 grams brown beans/red kidney beans,
  dried
3 pints/1½ l water
1 tablespoon salt
1 large leek
1 green pepper
1 tin tomatoes, strained
1 clove garlic, crushed (optional)
¼ teaspoon chilli powder
2 pints/1¼ l vegetable broth (use the cooking
  water)
11 oz/315 grams lean salt pork/corned beef
½ oz/15 grams butter or margarine
3 oz/85 grams watercress, snipped

Place the beans in a generous amount of water. Let stand overnight. Then pour off the water.

Place the beans in 3 pints/1½ litres water, add salt and boil for 1½ hours. Pour off the water, but save it for the broth.

While the beans are boiling, prepare and rinse the vegetables. Peel and finely chop them. Stir all the ingredients, except the pork, butter and watercress into the bean stew. Boil the soup over low heat for about 20 minutes. Stir the soup vigorously so that the beans break up. If you use a blender the bean pieces will become too small.

Cut the pork into strips and brown them in the butter. Serve the soup hot, garnished with the pork and the watercress.

Cabbage Soup

4 to 6 servings

1 small green cabbage, sliced
2 rashers streaky bacon
1 large onion, chopped
2 small leeks, white part only, sliced
2 carrots, sliced
1 potato, sliced
½ oz/15 grams flour
2 pints/1¼ l beef stock
2 tablespoons parsley, chopped
1 bay leaf
Salt and pepper
Pinch nutmeg
2 teaspoons of chopped dill or 1 teaspoon dill
  seeds
3–4 frankfurters

Slice and wash the cabbage, put into a pan of boiling salted water and cook for 5 minutes. Then drain and rinse under cold water. Meanwhile, chop the bacon and heat over gentle heat until the fat runs. Then add the onion, leeks, carrots and potato and stir over heat for a few minutes. Sprinkle in flour and blend well before adding stock. Add parsley, bay leaf, salt and pepper. Bring to the boil. Then reduce heat and simmer for 10 minutes before adding cabbage. Cook for 20 minutes more, or until the vegetables are tender but not mushy.

Adjust seasoning and add nutmeg and chopped dill, or a few dill seeds. Remove bay leaf. For garnish, fry frankfurters and cut in slices, putting a few slices into each serving.

Cream of Carrot Soup

4 to 6 servings

2 oz/60 grams butter
12 oz/345 grams young carrots, sliced
1 large onion, finely sliced
½ clove garlic, crushed
2 oz/60 grams rice

3 or 4 sprigs parsley (or ½ oz/15 grams dried parsley)
Thinly peeled rind from ½ orange
2 pints/1¼ l chicken stock
¼ teaspoon sugar
Salt and pepper
Juice of ½ orange
2½ fl oz/75 ml cream
2 egg yolks
Finely grated rind of ½ orange
2 teaspoons chopped parsley

Melt butter. Add vegetables, garlic and rice; mix well over gentle heat 5 minutes without browning. Add parsley, peeled orange rind, stock, sugar and seasonings; bring to the boil. Lower heat; simmer 30 to 40 minutes, until vegetables are tender.

Put into electric blender or food processor and blend until smooth. Return to pot; reheat, adding orange juice. If not thick enough, add cream and egg yolks. Mix egg yolks and cream well; add few spoons hot soup. Strain back into soup; stir constantly. Reheat soup without allowing to boil. Serve in soup cups; sprinkle with grated orange rind and parsley.

Cucumber Soup

10 to 12 servings

4 pints/2¼ l chicken broth
1 oz/30 grams butter
4 cucumbers
1 onion
1 oz/30 grams flour
Water
2 pints/1¼ l single cream or top of milk
Dill, fresh or dried
Salt to taste

Peel cucumbers and onion. Chop and sauté in butter over medium heat for a few minutes. Purée in food processor. Add purée to heated chicken broth and cook over a medium heat for 15 minutes.

Make a paste of flour and water and slowly stir into slightly heated cream. Gradually stir cream mixture into broth. Simmer until thickened. Season to taste. Transfer to a heated tureen and garnish with finely chopped dill or chill thoroughly in the freezer (do not freeze) and transfer to a chilled tureen and garnish.

Brown Bean Soup

Corn Soup

4 servings

6 ears corn
1 pint/½ l water
1 pint/½ l milk
Butter
½ teaspoon salt
Generous pinch pepper

Cut the corn from the cob. Boil it in the water for a few minutes until tender. Add the milk and bring it to the boil; then simmer for 10 minutes. Add a large lump of butter and salt and pepper.

Corn Chowder

4 to 6 servings

3 rashers bacon, chopped
3 tablespoons onion, chopped
10 oz/285 grams potatoes, peeled and diced
½ pint/¼ l water
1 pint/½ l cream-style corn
1½ pint/850 ml milk
½ teaspoon salt

Fry bacon until crisp. Remove from pan; save for later use.

Lightly brown onion in bacon fat. Add potatoes and water; boil gently 10 minutes. Add corn; cook 10 minutes longer. Stir in milk, salt and bacon. Heat until just hot. Serve at once.

Portuguese Cucumber Soup

6 servings

3 large cucumbers
4 tomatoes, skinned
1 small red sweet pepper
1 small green sweet pepper
1 clove garlic, crushed
2 tablespoons onion, finely chopped
2½ pints/1½ l chicken stock, clarified
½ teaspoon salt
1 tablespoon fresh lemon juice
¼ pint/140 ml dry white wine

Peel the cucumbers and remove the seeds, then grate the pulp coarsely. Place in a large glass bowl. Chop the tomatoes and add to the bowl. Remove the seeds and membranes from the peppers and chop coarsely. Add to the bowl. Add the remaining ingredients and mix. Chill before serving.

Creamy Marrow and Corn Soup

4 to 6 servings

1 lb/450 grams yellow marrow, peeled and grated
1 lb/450 grams fresh corn
1 pint/½ l boiling water
1 cup onion, chopped
½ cup green pepper, chopped
3 oz/85 grams butter or margarine
2½ pint/1¼ l milk
1 tablespoon salt
¼ teaspoon pepper

Place marrow and corn in boiling water. Simmer, covered, until tender. Meanwhile, cook onion and green pepper in butter until tender. Stir in flour and milk and stir until thickened. Add marrow mixture along with seasonings. Heat thoroughly.

Carrot Soup with Peanut Butter

4 servings

1½ pints/850 ml chicken stock
1 small onion, chopped
4 carrots, peeled and sliced
Pinch nutmeg
1 oz/30 grams peanut butter
1 tablespoon Worcester sauce

Soup with Red and Green Lentils

1 clove garlic, crushed
Dash Tabasco sauce

Simmer all ingredients together until tender, about 15 minutes. Remove half the carrots. Purée rest of ingredients. Add reserved carrots; reheat before serving. Garnish with chopped peanuts, apples and spring onions.

Hominy Soup

8 to 10 servings

3 pigs' trotters or 2 large, fresh pork hocks
1 boiling fowl (about 4 lbs/2 kilos), cut up
1 lb/450 grams lean pork, cut up
2 medium onions, finely chopped
2 cloves garlic, chopped
6 pints/3¼ l water
1 tablespoon salt
4 red chilli pods
3 tins hominy or equivalent cooked maize meal,
    drained
8 oz/225 grams radishes, sliced
4 oz/115 grams lettuce, shredded
4 oz/115 grams spring onions, sliced
4 oz/115 grams cheese, coarsely grated

In a large saucepan combine the trotters, chicken, pork, onions, garlic, water, salt and chilli pods. Bring to the boil. Reduce heat to low and cook for 2 hours. Add hominy or maize meal and cook until the meat starts to fall off the bone (3 to 3½ hours total cooking time).

Remove meat from broth. Cool meat and broth in refrigerator for several hours or overnight. Discard the chilli pods and remove meat from bones. Skim fat from surface of broth.

When ready to serve add meat to broth and heat. Serve hot in soup bowls with hot tortillas. Serve garnishes in separate bowls, so that each diner can garnish their plate to their own taste.

Cream of Lettuce Soup

8 servings

8 large outer iceberg lettuce leaves
10 ozs/285 grams frozen peas
1 teaspoon dried mint flakes
4 spring onions, chopped
14 fl oz/400 ml chicken broth, tinned
½ teaspoon salt
1 teaspoon sugar
½ pint/¼ l top of milk

Arrange lettuce leaves in bottom of a soup pot. Add peas, mint, onions, chicken broth, salt and sugar. Bring to the boil, cover and simmer over medium heat for 15 minutes. Purée in blender or processor; cool and refrigerate at least 6 hours or overnight. Add cream, mix well and serve cold.

Lentil Soup with Frankfurters

4 servings

8 oz/225 grams dried, quick-cooking lentils
3 pints/2 l water
2 rashers lean bacon, diced
1 leek, finely chopped
1 large carrot, finely chopped
1 celery stalk, chopped
1 onion, finely chopped
1 tablespoon vegetable oil
1 oz/30 grams flour
1 tablespoon ketchup
1 teaspoon salt
¼ teaspoon black pepper

Wash the lentils thoroughly. In a large saucepan, bring 3 pints/2 litres water to the boil. Add the lentils, bacon, leek, carrot and celery. Simmer, partially covered, for 30 to 40 minutes.

Meanwhile, in a frying pan, sauté chopped onion in vegetable oil until soft. Sprinkle flour over onion and stir. Lower heat, stir constantly and cook until the flour turns light brown. Do not burn flour. Stir ¼ pint/140 ml hot lentil soup into the browned flour; beat with a wire whisk until well blended. Beat in vinegar.

Add contents of frying pan to lentil pan and stir together. Cover and simmer for 30 minutes or until lentils are soft. Add the frankfurters and ketchup. Cook to heat frankfurters through. Season with salt and pepper and serve hot.

Soup with Red and Green Lentils

4 servings

1 large onion
2 to 3 cloves garlic
½ oz/15 grams butter
4 oz/115 grams red lentils
4 oz/115 grams green lentils or the same amount
    of white beans
1½ pints/850 ml meat broth
Soured cream

Chop the onion into large pieces and crush the garlic cloves. Melt the butter in a large pot and brown the onion and garlic.

Stir in the lentils and the broth. Let the soup simmer over a low heat for 20 to 30 minutes, or until the lentils feel soft. Serve with a dab of soured cream in the soup.

Leek Soup

6 servings

5 large boiling potatoes
5 pints/3 l water
1 teaspoon salt
5 medium-sized leeks
1 small onion, finely chopped
2 oz/60 grams butter or margarine
1 oz/30 grams flour
½ pint/¼ l top of milk or evaporated milk
Generous pinch pepper
2 egg yolks
Optional garnishes (bacon bits, snipped parsley,
  grated cheese)

Peel and cut up potatoes. Boil in salted water about 10 minutes. Wash the leeks thoroughly and finely chop only the white portion.

Sauté leeks and onion slowly in hot butter or margarine until light golden brown. Sprinkle with flour and stir until flour is absorbed. Add enough of the potato cooking water to make a thin sauce, then turn sauce back into potatoes, stirring until well blended. Continue cooking until potatoes are soft enough to be puréed in a blender or food processor.

Return potatoes to soup pot and simmer about 5 minutes. Stir in cream or evaporated milk. Season and heat to boiling point. Beat egg yolks until frothy and spoon a little into each soup bowl. Ladle in hot soup and stir to blend in yolk. Sprinkle with garnish of your choice. Serve hot.

Fresh Mushroom Soup

6 servings

1 lb/450 grams fresh mushrooms
2 tablespoons vegetable oil
2 spring onions or shallots, finely chopped
2 pints/1¼ l chicken broth or bouillon
¼ teaspoon salt
½ teaspoon lemon juice
1 lemon, sliced

Wash mushrooms; pat dry on kitchen towel. Finely chop mushrooms, or chop in blender or processor.

Heat oil in frying pan and sauté onions about 3 minutes or until wilted. Add mushrooms; cook, stirring occasionally, about 5 minutes. Add broth, salt, lemon juice. Bring to the boil. Reduce heat to simmer and cook uncovered 30 minutes.

Blend finished soup in blender or processor or press through a coarse sieve, pressing hard on the mushrooms to extract all liquid. Reheat before serving. Garnish with lemon slices.

Chased Mushroom Cap Soup

4 servings

8 oz/225 grams large, white, firm, fresh
  mushrooms
½ lemon
1½ teaspoons lemon juice
1 oz/30 grams butter
2 to 3 tablespoons onion, finely chopped
1¼ oz/38 grams plain flour
1 pint/½ l vegetable broth
2 to 3 tablespoons Port wine
7 fl oz/200 ml double cream
About ½ teaspoon salt
Dash cayenne pepper or freshly ground white
  pepper

Choose the 12 largest, whitest and firmest of the mushrooms. Firmly hold the mushroom at the base of the stem. Hold on to the blade of a sharp vegetable knife with 4 fingers held close together under the blade and your thumb on top of the blade.

Place the middle part of the blade of the knife against the top of the mushroom cap. Let the top of your fingertips rest against the cap. Move the edge of the knife in a cutting half-arch movement toward yourself. The hold of your fingertips on the knife decides how deep a cut will be made. Continue cutting all around the mushroom.

Make sure that each cut starts at the top in the middle of the mushroom cap. Then cut off the stem of the mushroom and make a star on the top by pressing down with the tip of the knife so that you create 5 star points. Boil the caps in water so that they are just covered, together with the juice of ½ lemon.

Finely chop the remaining mushrooms and sprinkle the lemon juice over them. Sauté the chopped mushrooms together with the onion for a few minutes in the butter. Sprinkle with flour and add the broth, a little at a time. Add the cream and wine and simmer the soup so that it thickens, about 10 minutes.

Season the soup with salt and a dash of pepper. Serve in hot dishes with the chased mushrooms as garnish. The caps may be refrigerated for several days in their own juice or may even be frozen.

Charleston Okra Soup

6 servings

1 large beef soup bone
6 pints/3¼ l water
3 lb/1¼ kilos fresh okra, finely chopped
6 oz/175 grams bacon in the piece
8 large fresh tomatoes, peeled
2 medium onions, chopped
1 bay leaf
Salt and pepper, to taste

Wash beef bone and cook in water for 2 hours. Add okra, bacon, tomatoes, onions, bay leaf and salt and pepper to taste. Let cook another 2 hours. Add more water if needed. Remove bay leaf.

Onion Soup

6 to 8 servings

1½ lb/700 grams medium onions
1½ oz/45 grams butter
1 tablespoon oil
1 teaspoon salt
¼ teaspoon sugar
1½ oz/45 grams flour
4 pints/2¼ l boiling beef stock
¼ pint/140 ml dry white wine
6–8 thick slices French bread
Parmesan cheese to taste
6–8 slices Gruyère cheese

Cool the onions slowly with the butter and oil in a large heavy-bottomed, covered saucepan for 15 minutes. Uncover, raise heat to moderate and stir in the salt and sugar. Cook for 30 to 40 minutes, stirring frequently until onions have turned an even, deep golden brown. Sprinkle in the flour and stir for 3 minutes. Turn off heat. Blend in the boiling stock, add the wine and season to taste.

Simmer, partially covered, 30 to 40 minutes more, skimming occasionally. Set aside uncovered until ready to serve, then reheat, simmering.

Spoon soup into ovenproof bowls. Place bread on top, then Parmesan cheese and top with a slice of Gruyère. Place in oven until cheese melts and becomes bubbly.

Chased Mushroom Cap Soup

Parsley Soup

4 servings

½ oz/15 grams butter
1 oz/30 grams flour
1 teaspoon salt
1 pint/½ l milk
1 medium sized onion, finely chopped
¼ pint/140 ml cream
2 egg yolks
2 oz/60 grams parsley, finely chopped

Melt butter, add flour and salt gradually, then milk and onion. Cook until it starts to thicken, stirring constantly. Add the cream which has been mixed with the egg yolks. Cook 1 to 2 minutes longer. Remove from heat. Add parsley and serve hot. To serve cold, refrigerate after cooling. This is a good nourishing soup for hot or cold weather.

Fresh Pea Soup

6 servings

4 small onions, finely chopped
4 oz/115 grams butter
2 large potatoes, cut into cubes
2 lb/900 grams fresh green peas, shelled
3 teaspoons salt
1 pint/½ l milk
½ teaspoon pepper
¼ pint/140 ml single cream

Sauté the onions in half the butter in a saucepan over medium heat until tender, but not brown. Add the potatoes and 1 cup of boiling water in a saucepan and cover. Cook over medium heat until the peas are tender.

Place the potato mixture and the peas in a blender container and process until puréed. Pour the mixture into a large saucepan, then stir in the milk, remaining salt, pepper, remaining butter, and cream until blended. Place over low heat until heated through, adding more milk if soup is too thick.

One-Hour Black-Eyed Pea Soup

4 to 6 servings

10 oz/285 grams dried black-eyed peas
8 oz/225 grams ham, diced
1 large onion, diced
Dash of hot red pepper
½ teaspoon salt
2 pints/1¼ l water
4 fl oz/110 ml dry red wine (optional)

Combine all ingredients in large saucepan in order given. Bring to the boil, then reduce to simmer. Cook about 1 hour or until peas are tender. Add water if necessary.

Cream of Peanut Soup

10 to 12 servings

1 medium onion, chopped
2 sticks celery, chopped
2 oz/60 grams butter
1½ oz/45 grams flour
4 pints/2½ l chicken stock
1 lb/450 grams peanut butter
1 pint/½ l single cream
Chopped peanuts

Stir onion and celery in large pot with butter until vegetables are soft but not brown. Blend in flour, stir until smooth. Add chicken stock, still stirring, bring to the boil. (The onion and celery may be strained out at this point.) Remove from heat. Add peanut butter and cream; blend together until smooth. Return to low heat (do not boil) for 5 minutes.

Serve soup topped with chopped peanuts.

Potato Soup

10 servings

7 medium-sized potatoes
3 medium-sized onions
1½ oz/45 grams butter
2 pints/1¼ l milk
3 pints/2 l chicken stock
1 tablespoon salt
¼ teaspoon white pepper
5 rashers streaky bacon
½ pint/¼ l single cream
2 oz/60 grams chopped chives

Peel and slice the potatoes and onions. Melt butter in a large saucepan. Add the sliced onions and cook over low heat until tender but not brown. Add the

potatoes, milk, chicken stock, salt and pepper. Cover pan and cook over a very low heat for 1 hour.

Cut the bacon into small pieces and sauté until crisp. Remove from pan, drain and set bacon bits aside. After the soup has cooked for 1 hour, put in blender at high speed. Return it to a saucepan. Add cream and cook slowly until the soup is just hot but not boiling. Garnish with bacon bits and chives.

Green Potato Soup

4 servings

4 to 5 potatoes
1 onion
2 pints/1¼ l chicken broth
1 teaspoon salt
Black pepper
10 oz/285 grams finely chopped kale

Peel the potatoes and the onion; cut them into pieces. Bring the broth to the boil. Add the potatoes and onion. Cover and boil for about 25 minutes, or until the potatoes become mushy.

Add the kale. Cook a few minutes longer. Beat the mixture with a whisk so that the potatoes are mashed. Season and serve.

Sauerkraut and Hot-Dog Soup

6 to 8 servings

1 lb/450 grams lean beef
6 oz/170 grams lean bacon in the piece
3 pints/2 l water
2 medium onions, chopped
1 leek or 2 spring onions, sliced
1 clove garlic
2 carrots, cubed
3 stalks celery, cubed
1 lb/450 grams sauerkraut, rinsed well in cold
    water and drained
Salt and pepper to taste
4 Frankfurters, thickly sliced
Fresh dill leaves, chopped
Soured cream

Place beef, bacon, water, onions, garlic, carrots, celery, sauerkraut and seasonings in soup pot. Cover and cook about 2 to 3 hours.

Remove bacon and beef. Cube and return to soup. Add sausages and continue cooking until heated through. Serve soup hot, garnished with dill leaves and a spoonful of soured cream.

Spinach Soup

4 to 6 servings

2 lb/900 grams fresh spinach, cooked and
    chopped, or 20 oz/600 grams frozen chopped
    spinach
1 tablespoon lemon juice
1½ oz/45 grams butter
1½ oz/45 grams flour
1 pint/½ l milk
2 oz/60 grams Parmesan cheese, freshly grated
Pinch nutmeg
Salt and pepper to taste

Cook the spinach. Place the spinach and lemon juice in a blender and process until puréed. Melt the butter in a large saucepan, then stir in the flour to make a smooth paste. Add the milk gradually, stirring constantly and cook until thickened.

Stir in the cheese, nutmeg and spinach. Cook until heated through. Season with salt and pepper. More milk may be added if a thinner soup is desired.

Fresh Tomato Soup

6 servings

6 medium-sized tomatoes
1 onion, chopped
1 stalk celery, chopped
1 pint/½ l chicken broth
1 tablespoon tomato purée
½ teaspoon dried basil
¼ teaspoon freshly ground pepper
½ teaspoon salt
¼ pint/140 ml soured cream

Cut tomatoes into wedges; place in a large saucepan with all ingredients except cream. Simmer, uncovered, 30 minutes. Strain to remove tomato skins and seeds. Adjust seasonings. Garnish with spoonfuls of soured cream.

Tomato-Barley Soup

6 to 8 servings

2–4 knuckle or marrow bones
8 oz/225 grams barley, rinsed
1 carrot, sliced length-wise
8 pints/4½ l water
2 stalks celery, sliced
1 onion, whole
1 lb/450 grams tinned tomatoes, chopped
Salt to taste

Put bones in cold water in large pot and bring to the boil. Skim off fat. Reduce heat to simmer and add remaining ingredients. Cover and simmer 1½ hours.

Parsnip Soup

4 servings

1½ oz/45 grams butter
1 onion, chopped
12 oz/345 grams parsnips, peeled and finely sliced
½ oz/15 grams flour
2 pints/1¼ l vegetable stock
3 to 4 sprigs parsley
1 small bay leaf
Pinch thyme
Pinch nutmeg
Salt and pepper
¼ pint/140 ml cream
1 tablespoon chopped parsley
Croutons

Melt butter; cook onion and parsnips gently 5 to 6 minutes with a lid on pan to soften without browning. Remove from heat; sprinkle in flour. Then blend well. Pour on stock; mix well; add herbs and seasonings. Bring to the boil; simmer 20 to 30 minutes, until parsnips are tender. Remove bay leaf.

Put soup into electric blender or food processor and blend until smooth. Return soup to pan; adjust seasoning. Reheat, adding cream. Serve in soup cups sprinkled with chopped parsley and croutons.

Potato, Sausage and Cheese Soup

6 servings

4 medium potatoes, peeled and halved
1 medium onion, sliced
2 pints/1¼ l boiling water
3 oz/85 grams smoked sausage, diced
½ teaspoon thyme leaves
½ teaspoon marjoram leaves
1½ teaspoons salt
Pepper
1 oz/30 grams butter or margarine
4 oz/115 grams mature cheese, grated

Place potatoes and onion in half the boiling water and cook until tender. Do not drain.

Mash potatoes in the pot. Add sausage, thyme, marjoram, salt, pepper, butter and remaining boiling water. Simmer 10 minutes. Add grated cheese just before serving.

Spicy Tomato Soup

6 to 8 servings

1 oz/30 grams butter
2 medium onions, diced
2 pints/1¼ l fresh chicken stock
2 lb/900 grams tinned tomatoes, chopped
1 oz/30 grams fresh parsley, chopped, or 2
    tablespoons dried
2 bay leaves

1 teaspoon basil
1 teaspoon paprika
1 teaspoon sugar
¼ teaspoon ground cloves
¼ teaspoon nutmeg
¼ teaspoon pepper
Salt to taste
¼ pint/140 ml double cream, whipped (optional)

Sauté onion in butter in large, heavy saucepan over low heat for 5 minutes, or until onion is translucent.

Add remaining ingredients except salt. Cover and simmer at least 30 minutes. Discard bay leaves. Add salt, if desired. Garnish each serving with a spoonful of whipped cream, if desired.

Minted Courgette Soup

6 servings

6 small courgettes, trimmed and cut in cubes
1 large onion, chopped
1 teaspoon curry powder
½ teaspoon ground ginger
½ teaspoon dry mustard
1 pint/½ l chicken broth
3 tablespoons uncooked rice
½ pint/¼ l skimmed milk
2½ fl oz/75 ml plain yoghurt
½ pint/¼ l dry white wine
Salt and freshly ground pepper to taste
1 oz/30 grams fresh basil leaves
3 or 4 fresh mint leaves

Combine courgettes, onion and dry spices in saucepan. Add chicken broth and rice and bring to the boil. Cover and simmer about 45 minutes.

Purée mixture in a blender or food processor. Add milk, yoghurt, wine, salt, pepper and herbs and blend until smooth.

Garnish with a sprig of mint. Serve hot or cold.

Country-Style Chicken Soup

6 servings

1 small boiling fowl
4 pints/2¼ l water
8 oz/225 grams celery, chopped
8 oz/225 grams carrots, sliced
2 medium onions, sliced
1 small bay leaf or ½ teaspoon dill seeds
1 large potato, diced
2 teaspoons salt
¼ teaspoon pepper

Simmer chicken in water 1 to 1½ hours. Add celery, carrots, onions and bay leaf or dill. Simmer thirty minutes. Remove meat from the chicken carcass. Allow meat and vegetables to stand in broth overnight.

Fish Soup

Skim off excess fat; add potato and salt and pepper. Simmer 30 minutes longer. You can use left-over chicken to make this soup and omit letting it stand overnight.

Cream of Chicken Soup

8 servings

2 pints/1¼ l chicken stock
1 lb/450 grams celery, finely chopped
1 small clove garlic, crushed
2½ fl oz/75 grams single cream
Salt and freshly ground white pepper to taste
1 lb/450 grams cooked chicken, minced
8 oz/225 grams Parmesan cheese, finely grated

Pour the stock into a large saucepan and bring to the boil. Add the celery and garlic and simmer for 10 minutes or until tender. Pour into a blender or food processor and process until puréed, then return to the saucepan.

Add the cream, salt and pepper and bring just to boiling point. Stir in the chicken and cheese and heat, stirring, until the cheese is melted and the soup is well blended. Serve in soup bowls. A dash of whipping cream may be poured into the centre of each serving, if desired.

Chicken and Barley Soup

4 servings

4 pints/2¼ l water
2 lb/900 grams chicken wings, skinned
1 lb/450 grams tinned tomatoes
8 oz/225 grams celery, sliced
8 oz/225 grams onions, sliced
8 oz/225 grams carrots, sliced
2 oz/60 grams fresh parsley, chopped
6 tablespoons medium barley
1 bay leaf
¼ teaspoon dried marjoram

Bring water to the boil; add chicken wings. When boiling again, skim foam from surface. Add remaining ingredients. Cover and simmer 50 to 60 minutes.

Remove chicken wings and chill quickly. When cool enough to handle, remove meat from bones; return the meat to the soup. Before serving, skim fat from surface of soup and remove bay leaf.

Chicken and Ham Soup

4 to 6 servings

2¼ pints/1½ l clear chicken stock
1 glass dry white wine
2 slices cooked ham, minced
4 oz/115 grams fresh peas, lightly cooked
1 teaspoon fresh tarragon, chopped (or ½ teaspoon dried)
1 tablespoon parsley, chopped
1 to 1½ tablespoons gelatine for cold soup

If serving hot, heat clear chicken stock, adding at last minute a glass of white wine, ham which has had all fat removed, peas and herbs. Sprinkle with chopped parsley.

If serving cold and using chicken stock that is not already jellied, put gelatine to soak in ¼ pint/140 ml stock. When it has swollen, heat gently. Add to heated stock. Skim off any grease carefully; add white wine. Let cool in a bowl. When it is on the point of setting, add ham and peas; spoon into soup cups. Chill well; serve garnished with chopped parsley or watercress leaves.

Creamed Turkey Soup

4 to 6 servings

1 cooked turkey carcass
2 onions, sliced
1 carrot, sliced
1 tomato, chopped
2 stalks celery, chopped
2 sprigs parsley, chopped
1 bay leaf
1 teaspoon Worcester sauce (optional)
1 teaspoon salt
½ teaspoon pepper
1 oz/30 grams butter
1 oz/30 grams flour
½ pint/¼ l double cream or evaporated milk

Put broken-up carcass, vegetables and seasonings into a large pot or kettle with enough water to cover; bring to the boil. Cover and simmer 2 hours. Strain and skim the fat.

In a separate pan melt the butter. Stir in the flour until brown, then add a little of the soup and stir until smooth. Add to the pot and cook until thickened. Add the cream, stir and serve.

Scallop Bisque

6 to 8 servings

12 oz/345 grams cooked scallops
4 oz/115 grams celery, chopped
2 oz/60 grams onion, chopped
2 oz/60 grams butter
1½ oz/45 grams flour
1 teaspoon salt
Dash white pepper
1 pint/½ l milk
1 pint/½ l single cream
2 teaspoons lemon juice or 1 teaspoon curry powder

Drain scallops and chop. Sauté celery and onion in butter until tender, but not brown. Blend in flour, salt and pepper. Add milk and cream, stirring constantly. Cook and stir until sauce is smooth and has thickened.

Add chopped scallop meat and lemon juice or curry powder and heat.

Cream of Crab Soup

6 servings

2 pints/1¼ l single cream
2 pints/1¼ l milk
1 oz/30 grams butter
1 tablespoon parsley
1 lb/450 grams crabmeat, white part only
Seasoning to taste

Combine all ingredients and heat thoroughly. Do not boil!

Crab Soup

4 to 6 servings

3 pints/2 l beef stock
1½ lb/700 grams mixed vegetables, fresh, leftover or frozen (include chopped onions and celery, diced carrots, peas, lima or butter beans, cut runner beans, corn, okra and tomatoes; not cabbage or potatoes)
Seasoning to taste
1 lb/450 grams crabmeat (claw or white meat)
Claws and pieces of whole crab if available (either raw or cooked)

Heat stock in a large stock pot. Add vegetables and seasoning; simmer 1 hour. Add crabmeat and crab claws and pieces (if available) 30 minutes before serving. Simmer gently, to heat through and allow flavours to blend.

Serve hot in large soup bowls, with crusty rolls and butter as accompaniment.

Fine Fish Soup

Turkey and Corn Soup

4 to 6 servings

10 to 12 lb/5 kilos roast turkey carcass (broken up), drumstick and wing bones
4 pints/2¼ l water
1 medium onion, halved
2 inner sticks celery with leaves
1 large carrot, peeled
2 teaspoons salt
4 peppercorns
1 small bay leaf
9 oz/255 grams tinned cream-style sweet corn
12 oz/345 grams tinned whole kernel corn, undrained
Diced roast turkey leftovers

In a large saucepan, bring all the ingredients except the corn and turkey meat to the boil; cover and let bubble gently for 2 hours. Strain and reserve carrot. Dice carrot and reheat with broth, corn and turkey meat.

Quick Mussel Soup

4 servings

1 onion, chopped
1 leek, finely sliced
1 celery stalk, finely chopped
1 oz/30 grams butter
3 cloves garlic, crushed
1 teaspoon dried sage and salt mixed
3 oz/85 grams snipped parsley
20 fresh mussels
Liquid from the mussels
½ pint/¼ l white wine
1 pint/½ l fish broth
½ oz/15 grams butter
½ oz/15 grams flour
10 oz/285 grams salmon

Brown the onion, leek and celery in butter in a pot; then add the garlic, sage and parsley. Dilute with the mussel juice, wine and broth and bring to the boil.

Remove from the heat and make a liaison of equal parts butter and flour. Add this in small bits to the soup and stir until it becomes smooth. Heat the soup again. Add the mussels and pieces of salmon and serve immediately.

New England Clam Chowder

6 to 8 servings

2 pints/ 1¼ l tinned clams with liquid
3 slices salt pork, diced
2 small onions, finely chopped
2 medium potatoes, diced
1 bay leaf
½ pint/¼ l water
1½ pints/850 ml milk, scalded
1½ pints/850 ml single cream
2 oz/60 grams butter
Salt and freshly ground black pepper

Drain clams, reserving liquor, then chop coarsely. Fry salt pork slowly in a kettle until all fat is rendered. Add onions; sauté until golden. Add potatoes, bay leaf and water, then simmer until potatoes are tender.

Strain the reserved clam liquor, then stir into potato mixture with milk, single cream, butter and chopped clams. Add seasonings, then simmer 15 minutes.

Crab Chowder

10 servings

1 large onion, finely chopped
4 stalks celery, finely chopped
4 oz/115 grams butter
1 lb/450 grams crabmeat
2½ pints/1½ l milk
½ pint/¼ l single cream
1 lb/450 grams tinned cream of potato soup
1 lb/450 grams tinned sweet corn
3 tablespoons pimiento, diced
½ teaspoon salt
1 teaspoon dried dill
2 bay leaves
¼/140 ml dry vermouth

In a large pot, cook onion and celery in butter until soft. Add crab; stir and add milk, cream, potato soup, corn, pimiento, salt, dill and bay leaves. Mix well and heat over medium heat for 20 minutes—do not boil. Add vermouth and heat for 5 minutes more.

This soup can be reheated and stores well in refrigerator for 4 to 5 days.

Fish Soup

3 to 4 servings

10 oz/285 grams sole or cod fillets
½ oz/15 grams butter
1 oz/30 grams flour
2 pints/1¼ l fish stock
2 leeks (white part only)
About 1 teaspoon salt
¼ teaspoon white pepper
About 1 teaspoon ground fennel seed

Rinse the fish fillets and cut them in pieces.

Heat the butter and flour in a pot. Add the fish stock and bring to the boil, stirring constantly. Finely chop the leeks and add them to the soup. Season with salt, pepper and fennel. Add the fish and let it simmer 3 to 5 minutes, a little longer if the fish is frozen. Test to see if cooked by pricking it—it is done when soft. Fish should not cook longer than necessary. Serve the soup with French bread.

Fine Fish Soup

4 servings

2–3 lb/1–1¼ kilos whole white fish (cod,
  haddock, hake)
1 to 2 leeks
3 pints/2 l water
1 tablespoon salt
½ teaspoon white peppercorns
2 bay leaves
1 sprig thyme
Several sprigs parsley
2 potatoes, sliced
3 tomatoes, peeled and cut in pieces
1 to 2 cloves garlic, crushed
1 oz/30 grams butter or margarine
12 oz/345 grams raw prawns, shelled and
  deveined
¼ pint/140 ml white wine
Parsley and dill

Fillet the fish or ask the fishmonger to do so, saving the head, skin and bones. Put all the trimmings in a pot. Wash the leeks carefully and put the green part in the pot. Add water, salt, peppercorns, bay leaves, thyme and parsley. Let it boil, covered, for 20 minutes.

Sauté the potatoes, tomatoes and garlic in the butter or margarine for 5 minutes over low heat. Add the fish broth, which has been strained. Cut the fish fillets in pieces and let them simmer with the prawns and white wine for about 5 minutes. Sprinkle with parsley and dill and serve with hot French bread.

Red Fish Soup

4 servings

1 onion, chopped
1 green pepper, chopped
2 oz/60 grams celeriac, finely shredded
1 large clove garlic, crushed
2 tablespoons oil
1¼ lb/700 grams tinned tomatoes
1 tablespoon tomato purée
½ teaspoon basil, crumbled
1 bay leaf
½ teaspoon salt

Red Fish Soup

Pinch black pepper
8 fl oz/220 ml dry white wine
10 oz/285 grams cod fillet, cut into pieces
12 mussels with shells
4 oz/115 grams shelled raw prawns
Snipped parsley for garnish

Sauté the onion, green pepper, celeriac and garlic in oil over low heat for 5 minutes. Add the tomatoes and tomato purée. Stir in the seasonings. Let the tomato mixture simmer, covered, over low heat for about 30 minutes. Stir occasionally.

Add the wine, cod and mussels and simmer slowly for 7 minutes. Add the prawns. Simmer for another 5 minutes. Sprinkle with parsley and serve the soup piping hot with French bread.

Note: A more luxurious soup can be made if halibut, salmon and/or lobster are added.

Lobster Bisque

6 servings

1 large, freshly boiled lobster (or 2 small,
    preferably female, lobsters)
3 pints/2 l fish stock
1 small onion, sliced
1 carrot, sliced
2 stalks celery, sliced
1 bay leaf, 3 to 4 sprigs of parsley, tied together
Salt and pepper
3 oz/80 grams butter
1½ oz/40 grams flour
¼ teaspoon mace or nutmeg
½ pint/¼ l cream
3 to 4 tablespoons sherry (or brandy)
Paprika

Split freshly boiled lobster down back with a sharp knife; remove intestine, which looks like a long black thread down centre of tail. Also remove stomach sac from head and tough gills. Crack claws, remove meat and add this to tail meat. If lobster is female and there is red coral or roe, reserve this for garnish. Also reserve greenish curd from head.

Break up all lobster shells; put into a pan with fish stock. Add onion, carrot, celery, herbs, salt and pepper. Cover pan; simmer 30 to 45 minutes.

Meanwhile, cut lobster meat into chunks. Pound coral roe with 1 oz/30 grams butter to use as garnish and to colour soup. Melt 2 oz/50 grams butter in a pot; stir in flour until smoothly blended; cook a minute or two before adding strained lobster stock. Blend until smooth; then bring to the boil, stirring constantly. Reduce heat; simmer 4 to 5 minutes before adding lobster meat and curd. Remove herbs. Add mace or nutmeg; adjust seasoning. Add hot cream and the sherry (or brandy).

Serve in soup cups with a piece of the coral butter in each cup and sprinkle with paprika.

Mussel Soup

4 servings

About 48 fresh or frozen mussels
1 onion
2 shallots
8 fl oz/220 ml dry white wine
2½ fl oz/75 ml water
3 oz/85 grams snipped parsley
1 oz/ 30 grams butter
Pepper
Salt
1 clove garlic to rub into the sides of the soup
    dish

Allow 10 to 12 mussels per person. Wash them well and place in cold water.

Chop the onion and shallots and place in a thick-bottomed pot together with the wine, water, parsley, thyme and butter. Bring to the boil. Place the mussels in the pot and stir well; grind pepper over the pot. Cover the pot and shake well so that the mussels move around and change places with each other. Allow to boil for several minutes so that all the mussels have opened. Season the soup with salt and pepper.

Rub a garlic clove round the sides of a serving dish. Pour the mussels and broth into the dish. Remember, however, that there is sand at the bottom of the pot, so do not pour in all the broth. Sprinkle with snipped parsley and serve immediately.

Variations: Omit the parsley and use a smaller amount of wine. Instead, pour in double cream, ½ pint/¼ litre for 4 servings. Or, mix in 4 slices grated white bread before placing the mussels in the broth. Simmer for about 10 minutes and then add the mussels. The bread will somewhat thicken the soup.

Cream of Mussel and Saffron Soup

5 servings

1 dozen mussels
¼ pint/140 ml white wine
2 to 3 cloves garlic
Pinch oregano
½ medium potato, diced
1 leek, diced
1½ oz/45 grams butter
1 quart fish stock
Pinch saffron
2 cups double cream
Saffron strands

Wash mussels, then steam them in white wine, garlic and oregano. Pick mussels out of shell. Reserve liquor after straining through cheesecloth. Chop mussels very fine.

Lightly sauté potato, leek, onion and celery in butter. Add fish stock, chopped mussels and mussel juice. Cook until vegetables are very tender. Pass through a food mill.

Put puréed liquid back in pot. Add pinch saffron and cream and boil to reduce by about a quarter. If necessary, adjust thickness and seasoning. Strain through fine strainer. Garnish with saffron strands.

Bouillabaisse

Oyster Stew

4 servings

1 pint/½ l water
1 pint/½ l shelled raw oysters
½ pint/¼ l milk
½ pint/¼ l single cream
½ teaspoon salt
¼ teaspoon ground black pepper
½ teaspoon celery salt
¼ teaspoon paprika
¼ teaspoon Tabasco sauce
2 oz/60 grams butter or margarine

Oyster stew is best when cooked over water in a double boiler, so it does not boil or overcook. Fill the bottom part of the double boiler with 1 pint/½ litre of water and bring it to the boil.

Meanwhile, hold a strainer over a cold 8-inch/20-cm iron frying pan and pour the oysters into the strainer, so the liquid falls into the pan. After they have drained, sit the strainer of oysters over a medium-sized mixing bowl.

Put the frying pan with the oyster juice on top of the stove and bring to the boil. By this time the water in the bottom part of the double boiler should be boiling. Put the top section on the double boiler, then pour in the milk, cream, salt and pepper.

Next, add the strained oysters, celery salt and paprika to the liquid in the frying pan. Turn the heat down to medium and cook until the edges of the oysters start to curl (about 3 minutes).

Pour the oysters and juice into the cream and milk mixture in the top part of the double boiler. Put the lid on and cook for 3 minutes until the stew is hot. Do not boil. Add the Tabasco sauce and butter and stir.

Oyster Bisque

6 to 8 servings

2 pints/1¼ l fresh oysters
1½ pints/850 ml chicken stock
1 oz/30 grams fine breadcrumbs
3 oz/85 grams onion, finely chopped
1 cup celery, finely diced
Salt and white pepper to taste
2 pints/1¼ l milk, scalded
1 oz/30 grams butter
2½ fl oz/75 ml sherry

Drain the oysters and reserve the liquid. Chop the oysters. Pour the chicken stock into a soup kettle. Add the reserved oyster liquid, breadcrumbs, onion, celery, salt and pepper. Boil slowly, stirring frequently, for about 30 minutes.

Spin in the blender or food processor until onion and celery are puréed, then return to the soup kettle. Add the oysters and heat thoroughly, but do not overcook. Stir in the milk, butter and sherry and heat through. Serve immediately.

Chilled Prawn Soup

6 servings

1 medium cucumber
12 oz/345 grams prawns, cooked and chopped
1 tablespoon chopped fresh dill or 1 teaspoon
  dried
1 tablespoon prepared mustard
1 teaspoon salt
1 teaspoon sugar
2 pints/1¼ l buttermilk

Peel cucumber and slice in half lengthwise; scoop out seeds and discard. Finely dice the cucumber. Combine all the ingredients and chill for 2 hours or longer.

Prawn Soup

4 servings

1 lb/450 grams raw prawns, shelled, deveined
Cayenne pepper to taste
Salt to taste
1 oz/30 grams flour
2 tablespoons oil
1 large onion, finely chopped
1 clove garlic, finely chopped
1 pint/½ l water
8 oz/225 grams cooked rice
1 tablespoon fresh parsley, chopped

Sprinkle raw prawns generously with cayenne and salt; set aside. Stir flour and oil together over medium flame until dark. Brown onion and garlic in flour-oil mixture. Add prawns. When prawns are pink, add water. Cover; simmer about 45 minutes.

Five minutes before serving, add rice and parsley. Add additional seasonings if needed.

Bouillabaisse

6 to 8 servings

fish broth
1 pint/½ l dry white wine
1 pint/½ l fish stock
Shells from about 25 prawns
Bouquet garni

the fish
4 lb/1½ kilos whole fish, e.g. mullet and cod

remaining ingredients
1 carrot, peeled
1 large onion, finely chopped
1 leek, sliced (white part only)
2 tablespoons olive oil
1½ teaspoons saffron
1 teaspoon dried thyme
2 cloves garlic
½ pint/¼ l white wine, e.g. Muscadet
3 whole, skinned tomatoes, cut into small pieces
2 lb/900 grams fresh mussels
25 shelled prawns
½ pint/¼ l cream, firmly whipped
Finely chopped parsley
6 to 8 slices well drained, crisply fried bread

rouille
4 fl oz/110 ml mayonnaise
1 teaspoon concentrated tomato purée
2 to 3 cloves garlic, crushed
Salt
Paprika
Pinch cayenne pepper

Ask the fishmonger to give you 1 lb/450 grams of fresh fish fillet plus the heads, skin and bones of the fish.

Let broth ingredients, including the fish carcasses, come to the boil and simmer for 10 minutes, covered. Place the fillets in the broth, cooking them for 2 to 3 minutes. Remove the fillets carefully with a draining spoon. Refrigerate them in a little of the broth. Strain the rest of the broth.

Sauté the carrot, onion and leek in the oil. Mix with the saffron, thyme and the 2 crushed garlic cloves. Cover with half the white wine and let boil vigorously until only enough liquid remains to just cover the bottom of the pot. Add the tomatoes and the strained fish broth. Bring to the boil again, then add the mussels. Boil vigorously for about 5 minutes, or until all the mussel shells have opened. Remove most of the mussels from the shells, but leave a few in the shell to use for decorating the soup.

Thicken the soup with the whipped cream and let it start to simmer before carefully adding the pieces of fish, prawns and mussels with and without the shells. Bring to the boil again and let simmer before dishing out into individual, warmed bowls and garnishing with chopped parsley.

Serve with the fried bread and the rouille made in the following way: mix mayonnaise with the other ingredients and spice to taste. Spread over the slices of hot bread. Lay them in the soup and eat with a spoon.

Sherried Seafood Bisque

8 servings

2½ pints/1½ l water
5 medium-sized potatoes, peeled and diced
4 oz/115 grams onion, coarsely chopped
4 teaspoons Worcester sauce
1 clove garlic, crushed
½ teaspoon thyme leaves
½ teaspoon salt
12 oz/345 grams minced cooked mussels
1 lb/450 grams flaked, cooked fish
4 oz/115 grams medium-sized prawns, drained
2 tablespoons dry sherry
2 egg yolks
¼ pint/140 ml double cream

In a large saucepan, bring water to the boil. Add potatoes, onion, 2 teaspoons of the Worcester sauce, garlic, thyme and salt. Reduce heat and simmer uncovered 15 to 20 minutes or until potatoes are almost soft. Add mussels, fish, prawns, sherry and remaining 2 teaspoons Worcester sauce. Cook 5 minutes longer or until seafood is hot. Remove from heat. Combine egg yolks and cream; stir into fish mixture. Heat only until hot. Do not boil. Serve hot or cold. Garnish with paprika, if desired, or chopped chives.

Quick Bouillabaisse

4 servings

1 onion
1 oz/30 grams margarine
½ teaspoon paprika
3 pints/2 l fish stock
14 oz/400 grams tinned chopped tomatoes
Juice of ½ lemon
1 lb/450 grams frozen peas
1¼ lb/550 grams cod
2 teaspoons salt
1 clove garlic
4 fl oz/110 ml mayonnaise

Chop the onion and fry until transparent in margarine in a large saucepan. Dust with paprika, then add the fish stock. Bring to the boil and add the tomatoes.

Squeeze in the lemon juice and add the peas, fish and salt. Simmer for 5 minutes, or until the fish portions are just cooked.

Meanwhile, crush the garlic and add to the mayonnaise. Serve the hot soup with a spoonful of the garlic mayonnaise and hot, crusty bread.

Quick Bouillabaisse

Eggs and Cheese

Bacon and Egg Cake

4 servings

8 oz/225 grams bacon
6 eggs
½ oz/15 grams flour
½ teaspoon salt
¼ pint/140 ml milk or cream
3 tablespoons chives, finely cut

Cut each bacon rasher in half. Fry lightly, not too crisp. Drain; set aside. Remove all but about 1 tablespoon fat from pan.

Combine eggs, flour and salt in a bowl. Gradually add milk. Warm fat in a pan over moderate heat. Pour in egg mixture; turn heat to low. Do not stir—let eggs set firm. This takes about 20 minutes. When mixture is firm, remove from heat.

Arrange bacon rashers and chives on top. Serve directly from the pan.

Egg and Bacon Muffin Puffs

8 servings

½ pint/¼ l mayonnaise
1 egg white, stiffly beaten
8 muffins, split and toasted
8 hard-boiled eggs, sliced
Crispy bacon rashers, halved

Fold the mayonnaise into the egg white. Spread lightly on toasted muffin halves. Place a sliced egg on top of each muffin. Cover with mayonnaise mixture. Brown 1 minute under grill. Top with crispy bacon. Serve at once.

Baked Eggs

4 servings

4 eggs, separated
½ oz/15 grams butter
Salt and pepper
4 slices toast

Preheat the oven to 350°F/180°C/gas mark 4 and heat a baking dish. Melt the butter in the hot dish. Beat the egg whites until stiff; then arrange them on the pan in four "nests" by swirling with a spoon. Slide the egg yolks one at a time into the centres of the nests.

Place pan in oven and cook until egg whites have begun to colour and the yolks are set. Season and serve on buttered toast with a little butter on top.

Eggs Benedict

12 servings

6 muffins, split and toasted
1 lb/450 grams streaky bacon, thinly sliced and cooked
12 poached eggs
4 egg yolks
8 oz/225 grams butter, cut into bits
2 tablespoons lemon juice
¼ teaspoon salt
Dash of cayenne pepper
Dash of white pepper

On a large baking sheet, cover each muffin half with several rashers of bacon and a poached egg. Place in oven to keep warm. Over very low heat, beat egg yolks constantly, until they begin to thicken slightly. Beat in butter, bit by bit.

When thick, remove from heat and stir in lemon juice, salt and pepper. Cover poached eggs with sauce. Serve immediately.

Eggs in Bread Rings

10 to 12 servings

12 slices bread
Butter
12 eggs
Salt
Pepper

Cut a hole in the centre of each bread slice. Butter bread on one side, then toast.

In a pan, break an egg into each toast ring; season with salt and pepper. Cook until eggs are set, 12 to 15 minutes.

Curried Eggs

4 servings

8 eggs
1 large onion
½ oz/15 grams margarine
½ tablespoon mild curry powder
12 fl oz/350 ml chicken broth
½ teaspoon salt
¼ teaspoon black pepper
2½ teaspoons arrowroot
4 fl oz/110 ml double cream
Juice from ½ lemon

Hard boil the eggs for 10 minutes. Meanwhile, peel the onion and finely chop it. Melt the margarine in a saucepan. Add the curry powder and the onion. Cook the onion so that it slowly softens over low heat for several minutes. Add the chicken broth, salt and pepper and simmer for about 10 minutes.

Mix the cream with the arrowroot and lemon juice and fold into the sauce. Heat through quickly, then pour the sauce over the eggs, which have been shelled and cut in half. Sprinkle a little parsley on top if desired.

Southern Cheesed Eggs with Vegetables

5 to 6 servings

3 tablespoons oil
8 oz/225 grams green pepper, finely chopped
8 oz/225 grams red pepper, finely chopped
8 oz/225 grams courgette, finely chopped
8 oz/225 grams spring onion, finely chopped
1 lb/450 grams cooked sweet corn
½ teaspoon salt
½ teaspoon dill
8 eggs, beaten
8 oz/225 grams mature Cheddar cheese, grated
    pepper

Heat oil in a large frying pan and sauté pepper, courgets and onion in it until slightly softened. Stir in corn, salt, dill, eggs and cheese. Stir and cook until eggs are done. Sprinkle with pepper.

Chicken and Egg Scramble

4 to 5 servings

2 to 3 rashers bacon
2 oz/60 grams spring onions, sliced
1 clove garlic, finely chopped
½ teaspoon basil, ground
12 oz/345 grams tinned cream of chicken soup
8 large eggs, lightly beaten
6 oz/170 grams tinned chicken chunks
Freshly ground black pepper to taste
2 oz/60 grams pimiento, chopped

In a pan, cook bacon until crisp; remove and let drain on paper towel. Reserve 2 tablespoons of fat in the pan; discard rest of fat.

Add onions, garlic and basil to fat in pan and cook until vegetables are soft. In medium bowl, add soup to lightly beaten eggs and stir until mixed. Pour on top of onion mixture in pan and cook over low heat, lifting and turning with large spatula, until eggs are set but still moist. Break up chicken with hands and add to eggs with pimiento. Season to taste with pepper and crumble reserved bacon over all.

Creamed Eggs

4 servings

6 eggs, hard-boiled and shelled
1 oz/30 grams butter
½ oz/15 grams flour
¼ pint/140 ml milk
Salt and pepper
Tabasco sauce
Chopped parsley
Paprika
6 slices toast

Remove the egg yolks and dice the whites. Make a sauce with butter, flour, milk and seasonings. Stir the egg whites into the sauce.

Heap the mixture on toast slices. Put the yolks through a sieve and sprinkle over the egg white mixture. Dust with chopped parsley and paprika. Thin slices of baked ham may be browned in a pan and placed on top of the toast before the mixture is added. Creamed eggs are also good on rice, baked potatoes, broccoli or asparagus.

Devilled Eggs

6 servings

6 hard-boiled eggs, shelled
½ teaspoon salt
½ teaspoon dry mustard
¼ teaspoon pepper
3 tablespoons salad dressing, vinegar or single cream

Cut shelled eggs in half lengthwise. Slip out yolks; mash them in small bowl with fork. Mix in seasonings and salad dressing. Pile the egg mixture into the egg whites.

For a variation, mix in 2 tablespoons snipped parsley or 8 oz/225 grams grated cheese.

Hot Devilled Eggs

4 servings

1 oz/30 grams butter or margarine
½ green pepper, finely chopped
2 oz/60 grams celery, finely chopped
1 small onion, finely chopped
½ oz/15 grams flour
8 oz/225 grams tinned tomatoes
1 teaspoon salt
1 teaspoon Worcester sauce
2 drops Tabasco sauce
8 fl oz/220 ml cold milk
6 hard-boiled eggs, sliced
Breadcrumbs, mixed with melted butter or margarine

Heat butter or margarine and cook chopped vegetables in it until they are tender. Blend in the flour. Add tomatoes and seasonings and cook until thickened, stirring constantly. Stir the hot tomato mixture into the milk and carefully add the eggs.

Turn into a greased baking dish and top with crumbs. Dot with butter or margarine and bake at 375°F/190°C/gas mark 5 until the crumbs are brown and the mixture is hot, about 10 to 15 minutes.

Farmer's Breakfast

3 or 4 servings

4 medium sized potatoes
4 rashers bacon, cubed
3 eggs
3 tablespoons milk
½ teaspoon salt
4 tablespoons small cubes cooked ham
2 medium sized tomatoes, peeled
1 tablespoon chopped chives

Boil unpeeled potatoes 30 minutes. Rinse under cold water. Peel and set aside to cool. Slice potatoes. Cook bacon lightly in large frying pan. Add potatoes. Cook until lightly browned.

Meanwhile, blend eggs with milk and salt. Stir in cubed ham. Cut tomatoes into thin wedges, add to egg mixture. Pour over potatoes. Cook until eggs are set. Sprinkle with chives and serve at once.

Ham and Egg Patties

6 servings

1 lb/450 grams shortcrust pastry
12 oz/345 grams cooked ham, minced
2 hard-boiled eggs, chopped
Salt and pepper to taste
¼ teaspoon prepared mustard
2–3 tablespoons white sauce
Egg or milk to glaze

Roll out the pastry ¼-inch/½-cm thick and cut into rounds about 5 inches/12 cms across. Mix the ham with the eggs. Add salt, pepper, mustard and enough sauce to bind.

Divide the mixture evenly between the pastry rounds, moisten the edges and fold over. Press and crimp the edge, glaze with egg or milk and bake for about 25 minutes in a 425°F/220°C/gas mark 7 oven.

Curried Eggs

Grilled Corned Beef Hash with Eggs

8 servings

1½ lb/700 grams mashed potatoes
12 oz/345 grams corned beef, finely chopped
2 tablespoons tomato purée
Dash of pepper
4 eggs, beaten

Poached Eggs
8 eggs
Salt
Pepper

Combine potatoes, corned beef, tomato purée, pepper and eggs. Shape into 8 patties. Place on shallow dish and cover with cling film. Refrigerate overnight.

Place patties in non-stick pan. Cook about 4 minutes on each side or until heated thoroughly. Be careful when turning patties.

In a shallow pan, bring 2 inches/5 cms of water to simmer. Break eggs, 1 at a time, into cup. Transfer to pan by holding cup with egg on surface of water, gently pour egg into water. Cook 3 to 5 mintues, or until cooked to taste. Remove from water with draining spoon; sprinkle with salt and pepper.

Serve corned beef patties with the poached eggs.

Egg Hexel

4 servings

6 eggs
¼ pint/140 ml milk
¼ pint/140 ml cream
6 oz/170 grams baked ham, cut up
6 rashers bacon, cooked and chopped
2 oz/60 grams blanched chestnuts, chopped
3 small to medium onions, chopped
Salt and pepper
Pinch thyme

Beat eggs lightly with milk and cream. Add ham, bacon and chestnuts.

Brown onions in bacon fat. Pour off excess fat from pan. Add egg mixture, season and stir gently. Cover, cook well, serve with parsley garnishing.

Eggs in a Nest

4 servings

1 lb/450 grams cold mashed potato
5 tablespoons hot milk
4 oz/115 grams chopped ham or fried bacon bits
3 tablespoons parsley, chopped
4 eggs
Salt and pepper to taste
½ oz/15 grams butter

Soften mashed potato with hot milk. Add ham and parsley. Mix well. Place in greased baking dish. With back of tablespoon, form 4 large hollows on top. Break 1 egg into each hollow. Sprinkle with salt and pepper. Dot with butter. Bake at 325°F/163°C/gas mark 3 about 12 minutes or until egg whites are firm. Serve at once.

Scrambled Country Corn

4 to 6 servings

6 rashers lean bacon, diced
1 medium onion, chopped
1 green pepper, chopped
1 lb/450 grams corn kernels, fresh preferred but
    tinned may be used
1 large tomato, chopped
6 eggs
1 teaspoon Worcester sauce
1 teaspoon salt
Dash of freshly ground pepper

Cook bacon in deep pan until almost crisp. Pour off excess fat. Add onion, green pepper, corn and tomato. Sauté until onion is soft.

Beat eggs and seasonings in bowl until light and frothy. Add to vegetables. Stir until eggs are set.

Scrambled Eggs and Sausage

6 servings

8 oz/225 grams pork sausage meat
8 eggs
2½ fl oz/75 ml milk
1 teaspoon salt
¼ teaspoon freshly ground black pepper

Break up sausage meat in pan and sauté until cooked and brown. Drain off fat. Beat eggs, milk, salt and pepper together. Pour egg mixture over sausage; stir until eggs are cooked.

Soured Cream and Ham Savoury

4 to 6 servings

5 eggs, separated, whites beaten stiffly
½ pint/¼ l soured cream
¼ teaspoon salt
8 oz/225 grams cooked ham, finely chopped
1 oz/30 grams butter

Beat egg yolks until well mixed. Add half the cream and salt. Fold in stiffly beaten egg whites and ham.

Heat butter in medium sized flameproof casserole. Gently pour in egg mixture. Cook over low heat about 5 minutes. Place dish in 325°F/163°C/gas mark 3 oven; cook about 12 minutes more. Top should be golden brown and firm. Slice into wedges; garnish each slice with soured cream.

Roquefort Soufflé

4 servings

4 oz/115 grams Roquefort cheese
1½ oz/45 grams butter
1 oz/30 grams flour
4 fl oz/110 ml milk
5 eggs, separated
1 teaspoon potato flour
½ teaspoon salt
Pinch cayenne pepper
1½ tablespoons Armagnac

This soufflé is made best if the Roquefort is so dry that it can be grated. If this is not the case, freeze it for a short while so that it is easy to grate. Melt the butter, add the flour, then the milk, a little at a time, stirring constantly until the mixture becomes creamy. Remove from the heat and allow to cool for a few minutes.

Beat the egg yolks, one at a time, into the batter. Blend in the grated cheese, potato flour, cayenne pepper and the Armagnac.

Preheat the oven to 425°F/220°C/gas mark 7. Beat the egg whites into very stiff peaks and fold them extremely carefully into the soufflé batter without stirring too much. Grease and flour a soufflé dish and fill it with the batter. Flatten the surface of the soufflé with a knife.

Bake in the middle of the oven on a rack for about 25 to 30 minutes, or until the soufflé has risen to almost double its original height and has become a golden brown.

Top Hatters

6 servings

6 thick slices brown bread
12 tomato slices
3 egg whites
3 egg yolks
8 oz/225 grams mature cheese, grated
2 oz/60 grams cooked bacon, diced

Make toast and then brush with melted butter or margarine and place under grill until the butter is absorbed. Cut in half diagonally. Top each with a tomato slice and set aside for a moment.

Beat egg whites until stiff but not dry. Beat egg yolks until thick and lemon coloured. Fold egg yolks into egg whites, then fold in cheese and bacon. Place a spoonful of this mixture on each tomato slice. Return to the grill for a few minutes or until the topping is puffed and brown. Serve immediately.

Roquefort Soufflé

Spinach and Egg Bake

4 to 6 servings

2 oz/60 grams flour
Dash of cayenne pepper
1 teaspoon salt
2 oz/60 grams butter, melted
15 fl oz/425 ml milk
4 oz/115 grams breadcrumbs
1¼ lb/565 grams frozen chopped spinach, cooked and drained
2 hard-boiled eggs, shelled and thinly sliced
8 oz/225 grams Cheddar cheese, grated
1 rasher bacon, cut into 1-inch/2½-cm lengths

Add flour, cayenne and salt to melted butter. Gradually stir in milk over low heat until mixture is slightly thickened and smooth.

In 3-pint/2-litre greased baking dish, layer half of the breadcrumbs, half of the spinach, slices of 1 egg, one third of the sauce and half of the cheese. Repeat process with remaining spinach, egg, one third of the sauce and the cheese. Pour on rest of sauce. Top with rest of breadcrumbs, then bacon bits. Bake at 350°F/180°C/gas mark 4 for 40 to 45 minutes.

Eggs in Spinach Cups

8 servings

1¼ lb/565 grams frozen chopped spinach, cooked and drained
Small tin condensed cream of mushroom soup
¼ teaspoon onion salt
8 eggs
Paprika

Preheat oven to 325°F/163°C/gas mark 3.

Combine spinach, soup and onion salt. Grease 8 medium sized ramekins then line them with spinach. Break an egg into each cup. Bake 15 minutes; sprinkle with paprika.

Eggs Supreme

4 to 6 servings

8 oz/225 grams Cheddar cheese, grated
1 oz/30 grams butter
½ pint/¼ l single cream
½ teaspoon salt
Dash of freshly ground pepper
1 teaspoon prepared mustard
6 eggs, lightly beaten

Spread cheese in greased, 8-inch/20-cm square baking dish. Dot with butter.

Combine cream, salt, pepper and mustard. Pour half of cream mixture over cheese, followed by beaten eggs. Add rest of cream mixture. Bake at 325°F/163°C/gas mark 3 about 40 minutes or until set and firm.

Eggs in Toast Cups

6 servings

12 slices fresh bread, crusts removed
Melted butter or margarine
8 eggs
2 teaspoons salt
1 teaspoon pepper
2½ fl oz/75 ml double cream
Fried bacon bits (optional)

Preheat oven to 400°F/200°C/gas mark 6. Press bread slices into small yorkshire pudding moulds; brush with butter. Bake in oven 20 minutes.

Beat eggs until fluffy. Add salt, pepper, cream and bacon. Pour eggs into greased pan. Cook over low heat until set, lifting occasionally with spatula to let uncooked portion run underneath. Spoon into toast cups and serve immediately. Garnish with more bacon.

Mushroon-Stuffed Omelette

4 servings

12 oz/345 grams fresh mushrooms, sliced
4 tablespoons spring onions, finely chopped
½ oz/15 grams butter or margarine
¼ teaspoon salt
¼ teaspoon thyme
5 eggs, separated
2½ fl oz/75 ml water
½ teaspoon salt
Large pinch dry mustard
Pinch pepper
4 teaspoons oil

In a small pan, sauté mushrooms and onions in butter or margarine until both are tender. Add salt and thyme. Set mushroom mixture aside. Beat egg whites until stiff. In a separate bowl, beat yolks until thick. Stir water and seasonings into yolks and fold very carefully into whites.

Heat oil in a 10-inch/25-cm flameproof flan dish, making sure the sides and bottom are greased. When pan is hot, pour in egg mixture and cook over low heat until browned on the bottom (5 to 6 minutes). Lift the sides gently to check. Place in a preheated 325°F/163°C/gas mark 3 oven for 10 minutes or until the omelette has risen and centre is set.

Loosen omelette with a spatula and spread mushrooms gently over one side. Fold over the other side and slide out onto a serving platter. Serve immediately.

Turkey Roll Omelette

1 serving

2 eggs
2 tablespoons water
Pinch salt
Dash pepper
½ oz/15 grams butter
4 oz/115 grams turkey roll, diced
Choice of grated cheese, sliced mushrooms, spring onions or alfalfa sprouts
2 tablespoons soured cream or yoghurt

Mix eggs, water, salt and pepper with a fork. Heat butter in an 8-inch/20-cm omelette pan until just hot enough to sizzle a drop of water. Pour in egg mixture, which should set at edges at once. Carefully push cooked edges to centre so uncooked egg can flow to bottom. While top is still moist and creamy-looking, arrange turkey roll and other filling and turn out onto warm platter. Top with sour cream or yoghurt and any remaining diced turkey roll.

Cheese Griddle Omelette

2 servings

4 eggs, separated
White pepper to taste
4 oz/115 grams Parmesan cheese, freshly grated
Salt to taste
Butter

Beat the egg yolks until thick and lemon coloured, then stir in the pepper and cheese. Season with a very small amount of salt, as the Parmesan cheese imparts a salty flavour. Beat the egg whites in a large bowl until stiff peaks form. Push the egg whites to one side of the bowl, then turn the cheese mixture into the bowl next to the egg whites. Fold and cut the cheese mixture into the egg whites with a spatula until well blended.

Melt a small amount of butter on a griddle over medium-high heat. Spoon half the cheese mixture onto the hot griddle to form an oblong loaf, then repeat with remaining cheese mixture. Reduce heat to medium-low. Shape omelettes into neat ovals with a table knife and cook until bottoms are lightly browned and set. Turn the omelettes with a spatula and cook until lightly browned. Drizzle with melted butter.

Country Omelettes

12 servings

4 oz/115 grams butter
2 oz/60 grams green pepper, seeded and finely chopped
2 oz/60 grams onion, finely chopped
2 lb/450 grams chicken livers (about 24)
36 eggs
8 fl oz/220 ml single cream
Salt and pepper to taste
2½ fl oz/75 ml vegetable oil

Use 2 to 3 pans to make the omelettes quickly. Melt 2 oz/60 grams of the butter over medium heat. Add the green pepper and onion and sauté until soft. Set aside.

Melt the remaining butter in another pan and sauté the chicken livers, then chop them coarsely. Beat eggs and cream together; add salt and pepper.

Use 8 fl oz/220 ml egg mixture for each omelette. For each omelette, heat 1 teaspoon each butter and oil in a pan and add the eggs. Before the eggs begin to set, add 2 teaspoons green pepper and onion. When eggs begin to set, lift edges with spatula so uncooked egg will run to the bottom of the pan. When egg mixture is completely set, top with 2 to 3 tablespoons chopped chicken livers and fold omelette over. Serve immediately.

Cheese Pie

6 servings

pastry
5 oz/140 grams butter
10 oz/285 grams flour
3 tablespoons water

filling
8 fl oz/220 ml single cream
8 fl oz/220 ml soured cream
4 eggs
2 oz/60 grams grated Parmesan cheese
¼ teaspoon black pepper
1 teaspoon salt
½ teaspoon paprika
8 oz/225 grams mature Cheddar cheese, cubed
8 oz/225 grams Gruyère cheese, cubed
2 oz/60 grams onion, finely chopped

Combine all the pastry ingredients in a bowl. Mix the dough together using your fingertips until it is well blended. Let stand in a cool place for about ½ hour.

Preheat oven to 425°F/220°C/gas mark 7. Flatten the dough with the palm of your hand so that the bottom and sides of the tin are evenly covered. Make sure that the dough goes all the way up to the edge of the baking tin and that there are no holes in the dough. Place in the oven and bake the pie shell for about 10 minutes.

Meanwhile, mix together the cream, soured cream and eggs and beat well. Season with the grated Parmesan cheese, salt, pepper and paprika. Combine and lay out the 2 kinds of cheese in the pie case. Sprinkle the chopped onion on top. Finally pour the egg mixture over the cheese cubes and place the pie on a rack in the middle of the oven. Bake for 35 minutes. If the pie gets too dark, cover the top with a piece of foil.

Cottage Cheese-Corn Rolls

8 servings

1 lb/450 grams creamed cottage cheese
1 egg, lightly beaten
4 oz/115 grams fine dry breadcrumbs
2 tablespoons onion, finely chopped
1 12-oz/345-gram tin niblet corn with peppers and pimiento, drained
½ teaspoon salt
¼ teaspoon black pepper
½ teaspoon Worcester sauce
1½ oz/45 grams butter

Combine all ingredients except 1 oz/30 grams of the breadcrumbs and the butter. Divide mixture into

8 equal portions. Shape each portion as a cylinder or log and roll in crumbs until all surfaces are coated. Refrigerate at least ½ hour.

Heat butter in frying pan until bubbling. Place rolls in frying pan and fry, turning as needed, until golden brown. Serve with soured cream or tomato sauce.

Cheese Croquettes

3 to 4 servings

1½ oz/45 grams butter
1 oz/30 grams flour
8 fl oz/220 ml milk
12 oz/345 grams cheese (combine two hard cooking cheeses such as mature Cheddar, Gruyère or Parmesan), grated
2 egg yolks, beaten
Salt and pepper
Ground red pepper
1 whole egg, beaten
Breadcrumbs
Butter or oil for frying

Melt butter in large pan. Add flour and stir about 1 minute over medium heat. Add milk, stirring constantly, so mixture thickens without lumps. Add cheese and stir until it melts. Remove from heat, stir a little of the mixture into beaten egg yolks and then stir the yolks into cheese mixture. Season with salt and peppers and set aside to cool.

When cool and firm, shape portions into cylinders (or cut the mixture into squares or rectangles). Dip croquettes into beaten egg and then in breadcrumbs. Sauté in butter or deep-fry in hot fat (375°F/190°C) until golden. Serve with stewed tomatoes.

Ham and Cheese Pudding

6 servings

6 slices boiled ham, chopped
1 lb/450 grams cheese, grated
1 pint/½ l double cream
3 eggs, well beaten
1 teaspoon salt
Nutmeg for garnish

Preheat oven to 350°F/180°C/gas mark 4. Distribute the ham evenly over the bottom of 3 pint/2 litre greased casserole. Mix all ingredients except the nutmeg. Pour over ham. Sprinkle top lightly with nutmeg. Bake uncovered for 40 minutes or until set.

Small Cheese Pies with Green Pepper Sauce

Cheese Fritters

40 small fritters

1 egg, beaten
¼ pint/140 ml milk
1 teaspoon Worcester sauce
1 small onion, finely chopped
8 oz/225 grams biscuit mix
12 oz/345 grams cheese, diced
Fat for deep-frying
Redcurrant jelly

Mix egg, milk, Worcester sauce, onion, pepper and prepared biscuit mix in bowl. Blend well. Stir in cheese.

Preheat fat in pan. Drop mixture by teaspoonfuls into hot fat. Fry until golden brown. Drain on kitchen towel. Serve with a dish of redcurrant jelly for dipping.

Small Cheese Pies with Green Pepper Sauce

6 servings

1 pint/½ l milk
Nutmeg
Salt
Freshly ground pepper
4 oz/115 grams Gruyère cheese, freshly grated
3 egg yolks plus 2 whole eggs
Butter

sauce
1 oz/30 grams butter
1 medium onion, finely chopped
1 medium green pepper, finely diced
½ teaspoon paprika
8 fl oz/220 ml dry white wine
12 fl oz/350 ml double cream
Salt
Pepper

Bring the milk to the boil together with the spices. As soon as the milk begins to boil, stir in the cheese so that it will melt, at the same time removing the pot from the heat. Have the egg yolks and eggs next to the stove, already beaten together. Stir the boiled milk, by the spoonful, into the beaten eggs.

Grease 6 individual ramekins generously and pour the batter into them. Place in a pan of water (bain-marie) and bake for about 30 minutes in a 350°F/180°C/gas mark 4 oven.

For the sauce, sauté the onion and green pepper in the butter so that it becomes soft but not brown. Add the paprika and allow to bubble for a moment before adding the wine and the double cream. Let boil until only half the amount of liquid remains. Season with salt and pepper. Serve the sauce with the small cheese pies. This dish looks elegant if the pies are turned upside down out of the ramekins and served in a lake of sauce.

Ham and Cheese Rarebit

6 servings

½ oz/15 grams butter or margarine
1 oz/30 grams flour
½ pint/¼ l milk
1½ teaspoons Worcester sauce
½ teaspoon prepared mustard
Pinch salt
1½ lb/700 grams Cheddar cheese, grated
4 oz/115 grams tomato, diced
4 oz/115 grams ham, diced
1 egg, lightly beaten

In a medium saucepan, melt butter. Stir in flour. Gradually add milk, Worcester sauce, mustard and salt. Cook, stirring constantly, until thickened. Blend in cheese, tomato and ham. Cook and stir until cheese is melted. Mix in egg. Heat, but do not boil, stirring. Serve on toast triangles.

Cheese and Potato Omelette

2 to 4 servings

4 tablespoons vegetable or corn oil
2 medium sized potatoes, peeled and thinly sliced
Salt, if desired
Freshly ground pepper
6 eggs
6 oz/170 grams Gruyère cheese, finely diced
2 tablespoons parsley, chopped
2 tablespoons chopped chives (optional)
2 oz/60 grams butter

Heat the oil in a pan and add the potatoes. Add salt and pepper to taste. Cook, shaking the pan and redistributing the potatoes so that they cook on all sides, about 8 to 10 minutes, or until golden brown on the bottom and top. Drain well.

Beat the eggs in a mixing bowl and add salt and pepper to taste, cheese, potatoes, parsley and chives. Heat the butter in a non-stick pan and add the egg mixture, stirring. Cook until the omelette is done on the bottom. Invert the omelette onto a hot, round serving dish and serve.

Herb and Cottage Cheese Pie

6 servings

pie crust
3 oz/85 grams butter
Salt
6 oz/170 grams flour, sifted
1 egg yolk
1 tablespoon cold water

filling
2 leeks
1 oz/30 grams butter
8 oz/225 grams frozen or 1½ lb/700 grams fresh
  spinach
2 tablespoons parsley, chopped
2 tablespoons chives, chopped
Salt
Pepper
3 eggs, separated
5 oz/140 grams cottage cheese

First make the pie crust. Place the butter in a warm bowl and soften the butter with a wooden spoon. Add the salt to the flour and shape it into a pyramid in the bowl. Make a hole in the middle and fill it with the butter, egg yolk, another dash of salt and the water. Stir with a spoon. Dip your fingers in a small amount of flour and knead the dough. Add more water, if needed. Wrap the dough in a piece of waxed paper so that it is totally covered. Refrigerate. Remove the dough from the refrigerator 15 minutes before it is to be rolled out.

Cut the white part of the leeks into thin rings. Melt the butter in a frying pan and place the leek rings in the butter. Stir until they have become soft. Add the spinach and the herbs. Season well and mix. Add more melted butter if the mixture seems too dry. Let cool.

Roll out the dough and line a flan dish or 4 individual tart moulds with it. Cut away any extra around the edge with a sharp knife.

Preheat the oven to 375°F/190°C/gas mark 5. Cover a baking sheet with foil and place it in the oven. Place the herb mixture in the bottom of the moulds. Separate the egg yolks and the whites. Strain the cottage cheese through a sieve. Beat the egg yolks and the cottage cheese together and season well. Beat the whites into stiff peaks and fold them carefully into the cheese mixture. Pour into the moulds.

Bake for about 30 minutes until the pie has risen and become golden brown. Serve warm or cold.

Salads

Stuffed Apple and Jerusalem Artichoke Salad

6 servings

6 large red apples
Juice of 1 medium sized orange
3 medium sized Jerusalem artichokes
2 oz/60 grams celery, finely chopped
2 tablespoons walnuts, coarsely chopped
3 tablespoons mayonnaise
½ teaspoon celery salt

Remove the apple cores with a corer, then cut a thin slice about 1½ inches/4 cms in diameter from the stem end of the apple. Scoop out the apple pulp with the corer or a sharp knife, leaving a shell about ½ inch/1 cm thick. Chop the removed apple pulp coarsely and drop immediately into the orange juice to prevent discolouration.

Grate the artichokes coarsely and drop into the orange juice. Add the celery, walnuts, mayonnaise and celery salt. Then toss with a fork to mix well. Pack the salad mixture into the hollowed out apples and chill until serving time.

Apple Mould

6 servings

6 apples
1½ pint/850 ml water
8 oz/225 grams sugar
Red vegetable colouring
4 oz/115 grams crushed pineapple
2 oz/60 grams raisins
2 oz/60 grams chopped nuts
1 lemon-flavoured jelly

Peel and core the apples. Combine water, sugar and a few drops of red vegetable colouring. Drop apples in syrup and cook gently until apples are tender. Do not overcook so apples keep their shape. Remove apples from syrup and place each in a large cup.

Combine pineapple, raisins and nuts. Stuff centres of apples with this mixture. Make up jelly according to directions on package. When cool, pour over apples. Chill well until set. Turn out on crisp lettuce and serve with mayonnaise.

Apple and Bacon Salad

8 servings

8 oz/225 grams bacon
1 head lettuce, cut into bite-sized chunks
3 red apples
8 fl oz/220 ml garlic oil (place 2 or 3 cloves in oil, let stand overnight)
2 teaspoons lemon juice
4 oz/115 grams Parmesan cheese, grated
1 bunch spring onions, trimmed and sliced
4 oz/115 grams Parmesan cheese, grated
1 bunch spring onions, trimmed and sliced
4 oz/115 grams croutons
½ teaspoon coarsely ground black pepper
Pinch salt
1 egg, unbeaten

Cook bacon until crisp, drain on absorbent paper and break into small pieces. Quarter and core apples, but do not peel. Cut apples into thin slices and drop into garlic oil. Stir in lemon juice. Combine all ingredients in salad bowl. Toss until all traces of egg disappear.

Apricot Ring Mould

4 servings

1¼ lb/565 grams tinned apricots
½ pint/¼ l pineapple juice
1 envelope unflavoured gelatine
2 tablespoons water
3 oz/85 grams cream cheese
1 tablespoon whipped cream
½ small green pepper, blanched, finely chopped
Pinch paprika
Pinch salt
Watercress or lettuce

Drain apricots, finely chop about half of them and reserve rest. Mix ½ pint/¼ litre apricot syrup with pineapple juice. Heat to boiling.

Soften gelatine 5 minutes in water; dissolve in hot fruit juice. Add chopped apricots to half the gelatine; pour into small ring mould. Refrigerate until set. Chill remaining gelatine until it begins to thicken.

Blend cream cheese with cream. Add green pepper, paprika and salt; spread on firm gelatine. Cover with remaining thickened gelatine; set aside until firm. Turn out and fill centre with watercress and remaining apricots.

Melon and Ham Salad

Banana Mould

4 to 6 servings

1 packet pineapple-flavoured jelly
½ pint/¼ l hot water
½ pint/¼ l cream
4 large bananas

Dissolve jelly in hot water. When nearly cold, but before set, gradually stir in cream.

Peel bananas; mash with fork. Beat until light and smooth. Stir lightly but thoroughly into jelly and cream. Pour into glass dish; let set.

Note: If mixing is done before jelly is sufficiently cool, jelly, banana and cream will separate into layers.

Cranberry Salad

6 servings

1 lb/450 grams cranberries
1 orange, thinly sliced
½ pint/¼ l water
6 oz/170 grams sugar
1 envelope unflavoured gelatine
2½ fl oz/75 ml cold water
4 oz/115 grams seedless grapes, sliced
8 oz/225 grams celery, diced
2 oz/60 grams chopped nuts

Cook cranberries, orange and water in covered saucepan until cranberry skins pop open. Press through fine sieve. Add sugar and heat to boiling. Soften gelatine in cold water, add hot cranberries and stir until gelatine is dissolved. Chill until syrupy.

Add remaining ingredients and turn into a ring mould. Chill in refrigerator until firm. Turn out and garnish as desired.

Cranberry and Celery Mould

10 servings

1 lemon-flavoured jelly
½ pint/¼ l cold water
½ pint/¼ l boiling water
1½ lb/700 grams cranberries
1 whole orange, unpeeled
6 oz/170 grams chopped celery
1 apple, peeled, cored and diced
4 oz/115 grams chopped nuts
8 oz/225 grams sugar

Soften jelly in hot water; mix with cold water and stir until dissolved. Chill until syrupy. Pick over cranberries and put through food processor with unpeeled orange. Add celery, apple and nuts to cranberry mixture; cover with sugar and let stand while jelly cools. Stir fruit into jelly, pour into mould and chill until firm. Serve on salad greens.

Cinnamon-Spiced Orange Salad

Black Cherry Mould

4 to 6 servings

1 lb/450 grams tinned black cherries, stoned
1 packet lemon jelly
½ pint/¼ l hot water
4 oz/115 grams chopped nuts

Drain cherries; reserve ½ pint/¼ litre juice. Dissolve jelly in hot water. Add reserved cherry juice. Allow mixture to set slightly 1 hour in refrigerator. Add cherries and nuts. Pour into ring mould. Refrigerate several hours or overnight.

Turn out onto bed of crisp greens.

Grapes Waldorf

8 to 10 servings

8 oz/225 grams seedless grapes
8 fl oz/220 ml mayonnaise
¼ pint/140 ml soured cream
3 oz/85 grams sugar
Pinch salt
3 apples
1 lb/450 grams celery, chopped

8 oz/225 grams walnuts, coarsely chopped
Lettuce

Combine grapes, mayonnaise, soured cream, sugar and salt. Blend gently.

Core apples and cut into ½ inch/1 cm cubes. Immediately add to grape mixture. Mix in celery and walnuts. Cover and chill until serving time. Serve in lettuce-lined bowl.

Honeyed Salad

4 to 5 servings

4 dessert apples
4 oz/115 grams seedless raisins
2 oz/60 grams walnuts, chopped
12 oz/345 grams carrots, cooked and diced
Pinch of salt
1 tablespoon clear honey
3 tablespoons lemon juice

Peel, core and dice 3 apples. Combine with raisins, nuts and carrots. Add salt. Add honey and lemon juice blended together; toss lightly. Set aside in cool place about 1 hour.

Arrange in salad bowl or on platter. Garnish with remaining apple—unpeeled, cut into slices and brush with lemon juice.

Melon and Ham Salad

4 servings

1 melon, large enough for 4 servings
6 slices smoked ham
6 slices processed cheese
½ cucumber
2 tablespoons raspberry vinegar or red wine vinegar
2 tablespoons Dijon mustard
1 tablespoon snipped chives
Salt
Pepper
4 fl oz/110 ml oil
Lettuce

Cut the melon in half and scrape out the fruit with a spoon. Cut the fruit into wedges, peel them and cut them into thin slices. Arrange the slices on plates.

Cut the ham, cheese and cucumber into thin strips. Mix the vinegar, mustard, chives, salt and pepper—preferably in a blender. Then slowly drip the oil into the mixture while vigorously stirring. The dressing should be rather thick, but it can be thinned slightly with water if necessary. Blend with lettuce and place on plates with the slices of melon. Sprinkle snipped chives on top.

Orange and Onion Salad

6 servings

4 large oranges
1 Spanish onion, sliced
1 medium sized cucumber, sliced
1 small green pepper, peeled, seeded, chopped
4 fl oz/110 ml vegctable oil
2½ fl oz/75 ml wine vinegar
1 teaspoon sugar
½ teaspoon salt
Large pinch chilli powder

Peel oranges, remove as much white membrane as possible. Slice, remove seeds. Alternate layers of oranges, onion and cucumber in serving dish. Sprinkle with green pepper. Refrigerate.

Combine the oil, vinegar, sugar, salt and chilli powder and pour over salad. Refrigerate until serving time.

Cinnamon-Spiced Orange Salad

4 servings

8 oranges
About 2 oz/60 grams sugar
2 teaspoons cinnamon

Peel 7 of the oranges with a sharp knife, so that even the outer membrane around the orange fruit is removed. Slice the oranges.

Mix the sugar and cinnamon, put the sliced oranges and the sugar mixture in layers in a glass bowl. Squeeze the last orange and pour the juice over the fruit. Let stand in a cold place until the salad is to be served.

Valencia Salad

4 to 6 servings

6 oranges
1 pint/½ l water
6 oz/170 grams sugar

Brush the oranges with warm water. Peel them with a potato peeler and cut the peel into thin strips, or use an orange zester. Boil zest of orange strips in 1 pint/½ litre water with 2 oz/60 grams of sugar, and let them stand for several hours.

Melt 2 oz/60 grams sugar in a frying pan. Pour out onto greased aluminium foil when the sugar has melted and become golden brown. Leave to become firm. Then place the sugar in a plastic bag and hammer it into crumbs. Sprinkle the strips of peel and the crushed sugar over the orange salad before serving.

Valencia Salad

Stuffed Pears

6 servings

3 large ripe pears
Lemon juice
2 red dessert apples, cored and diced but not peeled
2–3 sticks celery, diced
8 oz/225 grams crabmeat
1 tablespoon onion, finely chopped
1 tablespoon parsley, chopped
French dressing
Lettuce

Wipe the pears but do not peel them. Cut in halves, remove the cores and scoop out some of the flesh. Brush the pear halves with lemon juice. Put the scooped-out flesh into a bowl and add apples, celery, crabmeat, onion and parsley. Add enough French dressing to moisten, mix well and check the seasoning.

Spoon into the pear halves, arrange on a bed of lettuce and garnish with thin slices of unpeeled apples brushed with lemon juice.

Summer Salad

6 to 8 servings

1 packet lemon-flavoured jelly
1 pint/½ l fizzy lemonade
12 oz/345 grams fresh plums, sliced
8 oz/225 grams fresh peaches, diced
Sweetened whipped cream
Chopped nuts

In saucepan, dissolve jelly in ½ pint/¼ litre of the lemonade which has been heated to boiling. Stir in remaining lemonade. Chill until slightly thickened.

Fold in prepared fruit; pour mixture into a 3-pint/2-litre mould. Chill until firm. To serve, turn out on platter; garnish with whipped cream and chopped nuts. Serve at once.

Raspberry Mould

8 to 10 servings

10 oz/285 grams frozen raspberries, thawed
3 packets raspberry jelly
1 pint/½ l boiling water
1 pint/½ l vanilla ice cream, softened
1 lb/ 450 grams tinned frozen fruit juice
4 oz/115 grams walnuts, chopped

Drain raspberries and reserve syrup. Dissolve jelly in boiling water; add ice cream by spoonfuls, stirring until melted. Stir in fruit juice concentrate and raspberry syrup. Chill in a 3-pint/2-litre ring mould until partially set. Add raspberries and nuts. Chill until firm. Turn out on platter.

Strawberry Salad

4 servings

Lettuce leaves
1 lb/450 grams fresh strawberries, hulled
1 orange, peeled and sliced
8 oz/225 grams pineapple chunks
4 fl oz/110 ml orange juice
4 fl oz/110 ml yoghurt
1 tcaspoon sugar

Arrange lettuce leaves, strawberries, orange and pineapple on serving platter or individual serving plates. Chill.

In small bowl, make a dressing by mixing together orange juice, yoghurt and sugar. Chill. Serve separately with the strawberry salad.

Strawberry Jelly Salad

8 to 10 servings

1 packet strawberry jelly
½ pint/¼ l boiling water
1¼ lb/565 grams sliced frozen strawberries, thawed
1 lb/450 grams tinned crushed pineapple, drained

8 oz/225 grams chopped pecans
2 medium sized ripe bananas, mashed
1 pint/½ l soured cream

Dissolve jelly in water; add sliced strawberries with liquid. Mix well. Add pineapple, pecans and bananas. Spread half the mixture in 13 × 9-inch/33 × 23-cm tin. Chill until firm.

Spread cream as one layer and then add remaining mixture on top. Chill well. Keeps for days in refrigerator.

Waldorf Salad

3 to 4 servings

¼ pint/140 ml mayonnaise
¼ pint/140 ml soured cream
1 tablespoon honey
12 oz/345 grams cooking apples, peeled, cored and diced
8 oz/225 grams celery, diced
4 oz/115 grams walnuts, coarsely chopped
8 oz/225 grams grapes, halved and seeded

Combine mayonnaise, soured cream and honey. Add apples. Mix well to prevent apple discolouring. Add celery, walnuts and grapes, mix lightly. Chill well before serving.

Fruit Bowl Salad

6 servings

2 red apples, cored and diced
1 pear, peeled, cored and diced
1 banana, peeled and sliced
8 oz/225 grams celery, diced
4 oz/115 grams walnuts, coarsely chopped
¼ pint/140 ml mayonnaise
2 tablespoons lemon juice
1½ teaspoons sugar
1½ teaspoons Worcester sauce

In a salad bowl, combine apples, pear, banana, celery and walnuts. Mix remaining ingredients. Pour over salad, toss gently. Serve in lettuce-lined salad bowl.

Fruit Salad

5 to 6 servings

1 ripe honeydew melon
1 small fresh pineapple
2 ripe pink grapefruits
3 kiwi fruits
Tinned papaya

Cut the melon in half and remove the seeds and peel. Cut the fruit into cubes. Slice the pineapple and cut away the peel edges. Cut the slices into smaller pieces. Peel the grapefruits with a knife, also cutting away the white membrane under the peel. Then cut the wedges of the grapefruit so that only grapefruit flesh gets into the salad.

Peel the kiwi fruits and slice them across. Turn papaya into a bowl.

Carefully mix the fruits together before serving.

Coleslaw

10 servings

1 large head cabbage
½ pint/¼ l mayonnaise
½ pint/¼ l soured cream
1 teaspoon prepared mustard
1 tablespoon lemon juice
Salt and pepper to taste
1 oz/30 grams sugar

Slice cabbage very thin. Mix other ingredients, stir into cabbage. Chill about 4 hours.

Peanut Crunch Slaw

6 to 7 servings

2 lb/900 grams white cabbage, shredded
8 oz/225 grams celery, diced

dressing
¼ pint/140 ml soured cream
¼ pint/140 ml mayonnaise
2 oz/60 grams spring onions, chopped
2 oz/60 grams green pepper, chopped
2 oz/60 grams cucumber, chopped

topping
4 oz/115 grams salted peanuts, coarsely chopped
½ oz/15 grams butter
2 tablespoons Parmesan cheese, grated

Combine cabbage and celery. Sprinkle with a little salt and pepper and set aside to chill.

Combine all ingredients for the dressing, season and chill.

Brown the peanuts in the butter and stir in the cheese. Toss the vegetables and dressing together and sprinkle the nuts and cheese on top.

Red Cabbage Slaw

4 servings

2 lb/900 grams red cabbage, finely shredded
8 oz/225 grams apple, chopped
2 oz/60 grams raisins
2 tablespoons onion, chopped
¼ pint/140 ml mayonnaise
½ teaspoon salt
Pinch ground cloves

In a large bowl, toss together all ingredients. Chill.

Mixed Green Salad

4 servings

½ head iceberg lettuce
2 green peppers, cleaned, seeded, cut into strips
4 small tomatoes, sliced
2 small onions, sliced, separated into rings
2 hard-boiled eggs, sliced
½ medium cucumber, peeled, seeded, cut into chunks

salad dressing
4 tablespoons olive oil
3 tablespoons tarragon vinegar
½ teaspoon salt
Large pinch freshly ground pepper
1 clove garlic, crushed
Large pinch crushed oregano
1 tablespoon fresh parsley, chopped

Wash lettuce, dry. Tear into bite-sized pieces and place in salad bowl. Add peppers, tomatoes, onions, eggs, olives and cucumber. Refrigerate.

Combine all dressing ingredients. Mix well. Toss salad at table with prepared dressing.

Fruit Salad

Avocado with Bacon and Roquefort Dressing

2 to 4 servings

1 avocado
Lettuce
Bacon
Roquefort cheese
Vinaigrette dressing (See index)
Parsley and chives

Cut the avocado in half, peel it and cut the halves into slices. Place on lettuce leaves. Cut the bacon into small pieces, fry them until crisp and then sprinkle over the avocado once they have drained completely. Mash the Roquefort cheese in vinaigrette dressing and drip it over the salad. Chop chives and parsley and sprinkle on top.

Salad with Oregano

4 servings

1½ lb/700 grams mixed salad greens such as cos, radicchio, lambs lettuce, cut into large, bite-sized pieces
4 oz/115 grams onion rings, thinly sliced
1 teaspoon dried oregano
1 tablespoon mustard
1 tablespoon shallots, finely chopped
2 tablespoons red wine vinegar
¼ pint/140 ml olive oil
Salt and freshly ground pepper to taste

Rinse the salad greens well and dry them in a salad spinner. Put the salad greens and onion rings in a salad bowl. Sprinkle with the oregano.

Put the mustard, shallots and vinegar in a mixing bowl. Gradually beat in the oil. Add salt and pepper. Pour the sauce over the salad and toss well.

Garden Salad

6 servings

3 ripe avocados, skinned and stoned and cut into ½-inch/1-cm chunks
3 ripe tomatoes, cut in sixths
1 medium sized Spanish onion, diced finely
1 teaspoon fresh or 2 teaspoons dried oregano
½ teaspoon fresh or 1 teaspoon dried basil
1 clove garlic, finely chopped
Juice of 1 lemon
½ teaspoon Worcester sauce

Mix ingredients together in a bowl. Pour clear vinaigrette dressing (see Index) over the salad and marinate for ½ hour before serving.

Serve on a bed of lettuce.

Marinated Vegetable Salad

6 servings

1 lb/450 grams cooked carrots, diagonally sliced
1 lb/450 grams cooked cauliflower florets
8 oz/225 grams cooked asparagus, diagonally sliced
15 fl oz/425 ml tomato or vegetable juice
2½ fl oz/75 ml red wine vinegar
1 tablespoon honey
1 teaspoon dry mustard
½ teaspoon dried dill, crushed
8 oz/225 grams radishes, sliced
1 small red onion, sliced

Cook carrots, cauliflower and asparagus just until fork tender—but not mushy.

In shallow dish, combine tomato juice, vinegar, honey, mustard and dill. Add cooked vegetables, radishes and onion. Cover. Chill 6 hours or more. Stir occasionally. Use draining spoon to serve.

Avocado Salad with Bacon

4 servings

8 rashers of bacon
3 to 4 ripe avocados
4 tender sticks celery
A piece of leek
3 to 4 hard-boiled eggs
2 tomatoes, cut in wedges

dressing
5 tablespoons oil
2 tablespoons tarragon vinegar
1 clove garlic, crushed
2 teaspoons Dijon mustard
1 teaspoon garlic salt

Mix the dressing together and adjust the seasonings. Fry the bacon in a dry pan until crisp. Place the bacon on kitchen towel so that the fat drains off. Divide the avocados in half and remove the stones. Peel the halves and cut them into slices.

Alternate in a salad bowl sliced avocado, celery, leek, bacon, egg slices and tomato wedges.

Mix the dressing ingredients together and adjust the seasonings. Shake up the dressing and pour it over the salad.

Hot Coleslaw

4 to 6 servings

2 tablespoons salad oil
2 lb/900 grams cabblage, shredded
½ teaspoon salt
½ teaspoon celery seeds
Large pinch pepper
2 tablespoons vinegar

Heat oil in medium sized pan. Add cabbage and seasonings, but not vinegar. Cover. Cook over medium heat about 3 minutes. Be sure to stir occasionally to mix flavours. Add vinegar and stir again.

Serve hot coleslaw at once.

Asparagus Salad Mould

4 servings

2 envelopes unflavoured gelatine
15 fl oz/425 ml water
1 tablespoon sugar
¼ pint/140 ml lemon juice
½ teaspoon salt
2 oz/60 grams pimiento, chopped

1 lb/450 grams tinned asparagus tips, drained
2 teaspoons onion, grated
8 oz/225 grams celery, chopped

Soften the gelatine in ¼ pint/140 ml water. Combine the sugar, ½ pint/¼ litre water and lemon juice in a saucepan and bring to the boil. Remove from heat, add the gelatine and salt and stir until dissolved. Chill until partially set.

Fold in the pimiento, asparagus tips, onion and celery and spoon into a 2-pint/1¼-litre ring mould. Chill until firm, then turn out onto a serving plate.

Green Beans with Mint

6 servings

1½ lb/700 grams fresh runner beans
4 tablespoons extra virgin olive oil
3 teaspoons lemon juice, freshly squeezed
3 tablespoons mint, freshly chopped
Pinch garlic powder
Pinch black pepper
Salt

Fantasy Salad

Steam runner beans just long enough to ensure that they are firm to the bite. Allow to cool. Place in a bowl and dress with the olive oil, lemon juice, mint, garlic powder and black pepper. Salt to taste. Toss gently.

Three-Bean Salad

6 to 8 servings

8 oz/225 grams red kidney beans, freshly cooked or tinned
8 oz/225 grams haricot beans, freshly cooked or tinned
8 oz/225 grams chickpeas, freshly cooked or tinned
6 oz/170 grams onion, finely chopped
½ teaspoon garlic, finely chopped
2 tablespoons parsley, finely chopped
1 small green pepper, seeded and coarsely chopped (optional)
1 teaspoon salt
Freshly ground black pepper
3 tablespoons wine vinegar
¼ pint/140 ml olive oil

If you plan to use tinned beans and chickpeas, drain them of all their liquid, wash them thoroughly under cold running water, drain again and pat dry with kitchen towel. If you plan to cook the beans yourself; soak the beans overnight in water, drain them, cover them with fresh water, then bring them to the boil. Boil them for 10 minutes and then simmer for 1½ hours until they are tender. 4 oz/115 grams of dry uncooked beans yields approximately 10 oz/ 285 grams cooked.

In a large bowl, combine the chickpeas, red kidney beans and haricots, onion, garlic, parsley and green pepper if you plan to use it. Add the salt, a few grindings of pepper and wine vinegar and toss the ingredients gently with a large spoon. Pour in the olive oil and toss again. This salad will be greatly improved if it is allowed to stand for at least 1 hour before serving.

Broccoli Salad

6 servings

1½ lb/700 grams fresh broccoli spears
2½ fl oz/75 ml vegetable oil
6 tablespoons cider vinegar
2½ fl oz/75 ml water
¼ pint/140 ml apple juice
Salt and pepper to taste
6 lettuce leaves
2 hard-boiled eggs, chopped

Cook the broccoli in a small amount of boiling, salted water until tender, then drain and cool. Place in a shallow dish. Place the oil, vinegar, 2½ fl oz/75

ml of water, apple juice, salt and pepper in a small bowl and mix well. Pour over the broccoli. Marinate in the refrigerator, carefully turning the broccoli occasionally, for at least 2 hours.

Place the broccoli in the lettuce leaves on individual salad plates, then sprinkle the eggs over the top. Garnish with tomato wedges.

Carrot Salad

10 to 12 servings

1 small onion, finely chopped
1 medium pepper, finely chopped
3 sticks celery, finely chopped
2 lb/900 grams tinned sliced carrots
8 oz/225 grams tomato soup, undiluted
8 oz/225 grams sugar
2½ fl oz/75 ml oil
8 fl oz/220 ml cider vinegar
1 tablespoon dry mustard
1 tablespoon Worcester sauce
Lettuce leaves, washed, drained

Add onion, pepper and celery to drained carrots, set aside. Put soup, sugar, oil, vinegar, mustard and Worcester sauce into small saucepan. Bring to the boil, so that all ingredients blend. Pour over vegetables. When cool, refrigerate to chill thoroughly, at least overnight.

Serve salad on crisp lettuce leaves.

Cauliflower Salad

8 servings

1 head cauliflower
2 oz/60 grams spring onions, finely chopped
4 oz/115 grams celery leaves, finely chopped
¼ pint/140 ml soured cream
¼ pint/140 ml vinaigrette dressing (see recipe below)
2 teaspoons caraway seed
Salt to taste
Lettuce leaves

Separate the cauliflower into florets and place in a large bowl, then chill. Place the onions, celery leaves, soured cream, vinaigrette, caraway seed and salt into a small bowl and mix until blended. Add the onion mixture to the cauliflower and mix well.

Line a salad bowl with lettuce, then place the salad in the bowl over the lettuce.

To make dressing: combine 2 teaspoons salt, ½ teaspoon freshly ground pepper, 1 teaspoon prepared mustard, ½ pint/¼ l olive oil, 2½ fl oz/75 ml red wine vinegar.

Pickled Corn Salad

4 to 6 servings

4 oz/115 grams onions, chopped
4 oz/115 grams green peppers, diced
4 tablespoons pimiento, chopped
3 oz/85 grams sugar
½ teaspoon salt
½ teaspoon celery salt
½ teaspoon dry mustard
¼ pint/140 ml cider vinegar
¼ pint/140 ml water
1½ lb/700 grams frozen whole kernel corn

Combine all ingredients except corn and bring to the boil. Lower heat, cover pan. Simmer 12 minutes, stirring occasionally.

Add frozen corn, raise heat. When boiling resumes, lower heat. Simmer until corn is just tender (20 or 3 minutes), drain. Serve salad hot, or refrigerate and serve on lettuce leaves.

Macaroni Salad

Carrot and Lentil Salad

2 servings

2 medium carrots, grated
1 medium tomato, chopped
1 tablespoon grated coconut
1 small bunch coriander leaves, chopped
1 tablespoon lentils, previously soaked in water
    for several hours or overnight
Salt to taste
1 tablespoon oil
1 teaspoon mustard seeds
Few drops lemon or lime juice

Mix together the carrots, tomato, coconut, coriander leaves, lentils and salt.

Heat oil. When it is hot, but not bubbling, add mustard seeds. When seeds start bubbling, add oil and seeds to salad. Add a few drops of lemon or lime juice.

Cucumbers in Soured Cream

4 servings

2 cucumbers
½ pint/¼ l soured cream
2 teaspoons onion, grated
1 tablespoon wine vinegar
½ tablespoon dill seed
1 teaspoon salt
Lettuce leaves

Peel the cucumbers, then slice paper-thin. Place in a bowl and chill well. Place the cream, onion, lemon juice, vinegar, dill seed and salt in a medium sized bowl and blend thoroughly. Add the cucumbers and toss lightly until coated.

Line a salad bowl with lettuce, then add the cucumber mixture.

Pepper Salad

6 servings

2 medium sized green peppers
3 large firm ripe tomatoes, thinly sliced
Salt and freshly ground pepper to taste
¼ pint/140 ml olive oil
1 to 2 tablespoons red wine vinegar
1½ teaspoons chopped chives
1½ teaspoons chopped parsley

Cut the peppers in half and remove the seeds and membranes. Cut into thin, lengthwise slices. Arrange the tomatoes and peppers in a serving dish and sprinkle with salt and pepper. Pour the oil evenly over all. Sprinkle the vinegar, chives and parsley over the top.

Cucumber Salad

4 to 6 servings

½ pint/¼ l water
4 oz/115 grams sugar
4 fl oz/110 ml white vinegar
2 large cucumbers, peeled and thinly sliced
4 tablespoons olive oil

Bring water, sugar and vinegar to the boil. Add cucumbers. Simmer 2 to 3 minutes. Remove from heat and add olive oil. Chill.

Potato Salad

6 to 8 servings

3 lb/1¼ kilos cooked potatoes, diced
3 or 4 spring onions, chopped
4 hard-boiled eggs, chopped
1 teaspoon celery seed
1½ teaspoons salt
Large pinch pepper
1 teaspoon curry powder
½ pint/¼ l soured cream
¼ pint/140 ml mayonnaise
2 tablespoons vinegar
Chopped parsley

Mix potatoes, onions, eggs and seasoning (except curry powder) together in bowl. Set aside to chill.

Mix curry powder with soured cream. Add mayonnaise and vinegar. When ready to serve, add to potato mixture. Toss together lightly, sprinkle with parsley. Serve cold.

German Potato Salad

10 servings

1lb/450 grams bacon
5 lb/2¼ kilo potatoes, boiled and sliced
1 large Spanish onion, chopped
3 oz/85 grams flour
¼ pint/140 ml vinegar
12 fl oz/350 ml water
4 oz/115 grams sugar
1 tablespoon salt
½ tablespoon pepper

Fry bacon until crisp. Crumble it and place in a bowl with potatoes and onion. Add flour to the pan with the hot bacon fat and mix. Add the remaining ingredients to the pan and mix thoroughly until sugar is dissolved and mixture thickens slightly.

Immediately pour contents of the pan over the potatoes, onion and bacon and mix thoroughly until most of the juice has soaked into the potatoes.

Fantasy Salad

Quantity Varies

Fresh spinach leaves
Lettuce
Sliced mushrooms
Finely shredded spring onions
Prawns or shredded crab
Finely chopped cucumber
Lime
Soy sauce
Vinaigrette dressing (See index)
Basil or mint leaves

This is an elegant, fresh salad with many different shades of green. Mix spinach with lettuce, mushrooms, spring onions, prawns or crab and cucumber.

Mix a small wedge of finely chopped lime (both the fruit and the peel) with the salad and drip a small amount of soy sauce on top. Garnish with leaves of basil or mint. Serve with vinaigrette dressing.

Rice Salad with Ham

Tomato Jelly Salad

6 servings

2 pints/1¼ l tomato juice
2 packets lemon jelly
1 teaspoon lemon juice
4 drops Tabasco sauce
3 sticks celery, finely chopped
5 spring onions, finely chopped
1 cucumber, finely chopped
7 radishes, finely chopped

Bring half the tomato juice to the boil. Add jelly and stir. Add the remaining cold tomato juice, then lemon juice and Tabasco and stir. Pour into glass bowl and refrigerate.

When beginning to thicken, add vegetables. Refrigerate until firm.

Hot Potato Salad

4 servings

3 large potatoes
2 tablespoons vinegar
1 teaspoon salt
Pepper to taste
8 oz/225 grams bacon, chopped
3 eggs, hard-boiled
2 oz/60 grams spring onions, chopped
Lettuce

Scrub the potatoes and cook in boiling salted water. Then drain, peel and dice potatoes. Add vinegar, salt and pepper.

Fry the bacon until crisp. Combine the potatoes, bacon, 2 tablespoons of the bacon fat, chopped eggs and onion and mix well. Serve hot on a bed of lettuce.

Sauerkraut Salad

6 servings

1 lb/450 grams tinned sauerkraut
8 oz/225 grams green pepper, chopped
8 oz/225 grams onion, chopped
1 small tin pimiento, chopped (optional)
8 oz/225 grams sugar
½ pint/¼ l white vinegar

Drain sauerkraut thoroughly. Add chopped vegetables, mix well. Bring sugar and vinegar to boiling point, but do not boil. This will thoroughly dissolve sugar. Pour over mixture. Toss thoroughly.

Chill in covered bowl in refrigerator for at least a few hours. Overnight is even better. This dish will keep well for several days.

Fresh Spinach Salad

6 servings

8 oz/225 grams raw spinach
2 oz/60 grams green pepper, chopped
4 oz/115 grams onion rings
1½ tablespoons fresh lemon juice
1 tablespoon salad oil
½ teaspoon tarragon leaves
½ teaspoon salt
Pinch ground black pepper
Hard-boiled eggs
Anchovies

Thoroughly wash spinach. Drain and wrap in a clean tea towel to absorb excess water. Tear leaves into bite-sized pieces and put into a salad bowl. Add chopped green pepper, onion rings, lemon juice, salad oil, tarragon leaves, salt and black pepper. Toss lightly. Garnish with hard-boiled eggs and anchovies.

Spinach and Mushroom Salad

6 servings

1 lb/450 grams fresh spinach
4 fl oz/110 ml red wine vinegar
8 fl oz/220 ml oil
2 eggs
2 teaspoons Dijon mustard
1 teaspoon dried tarragon
1 teaspoon parsley flakes
12 fresh mushrooms
6 pieces bacon, cooked and crumbled

Wash spinach thoroughly. In blender or food processor, combine red wine vinegar, oil, eggs, mustard, tarragon and parsley flakes. Blend until well mixed. Pour over spinach; add the sliced mushrooms and crumbled bacon.

Tomato, Avocado and Onion Salad

6 servings

6 large ripe tomatoes
4 ripe avocados, peeled and sliced
1 medium Spanish onion, cut into rings
Lemon juice (or lime juice)
Salt and freshly ground pepper
Olive oil

Slice tomatoes and arrange on a plate. Top with slices of avocado and onion rings. Squeeze a generous amount of lemon (or lime) juice over the top. Sprinkle with salt and pepper and top with a thin drizzle of oil.

Courgette Salad

4 to 6 servings

4 fl oz/140 ml oil
4 fl oz/140 ml lemon juice
1½ teaspoons salt
1½ teaspoons onion, grated
1 teaspoon dill
¼ teaspoon freshly ground pepper
4 medium courgettes, sliced
2 medium sized carrots, cut in very thin strips
4 oz/115 grams ripe olives, sliced
2 oz/60 grams pimiento, finely chopped
Webb's lettuce leaves

Combine oil, lemon juice, salt, onion, dill and pepper in a small covered jar. Shake well.

Mix courgettes, carrots, olives and pimiento in a large bowl. Toss gently. Add a little dressing and toss again. Cover and chill.

At serving, arrange lettuce leaves on serving plates. Spoon marinated vegetables onto lettuce leaves. Offer remaining salad dressing.

Seafood and Fresh Asparagus Salad

6 servings

1 lb/450 grams fresh asparagus
12 fl oz/350 ml vinaigrette dressing (see recipe below)
4 oz/115 grams fresh avocado strips
2 tablespoons fresh lemon juice
8 oz/225 grams boiled prawns
8 oz/225 grams cooked lobster chunks
8 oz/225 grams crabmeat
Fresh lettuce leaves

Cook the asparagus, then drain. Place in a shallow dish and add half the vinaigrette. Chill thoroughly. Combine the avocado and lemon juice in a small bowl and chill well.

Combine the prawns, lobster and crabmeat in a bowl and add the remaining vinaigrette, then chill. Arrange the lettuce leaves on a serving tray. Drain the prawn mixture and combine with the avocado, then place in the centre of the tray. Drain the asparagus and arrange at each end of the tray.

To make vinaigrette: combine 2 teaspoons salt, ½ teaspoon freshly ground pepper, 1 teaspoon prepared mustard, ½ pint/¼ litre olive oil and 2½ fl oz/ 75 ml red wine vinegar.

Festive Crab Salad

Mississippi Rice Salad

6 servings

1½ lb/700 grams rice, cooked and cooled
4 oz/115 grams onions, finely chopped
4 oz/115 grams sweet pickles, finely chopped
1 teaspoon salt
¼ teaspoon pepper
½ pint/¼ l mayonnaise
1 teaspoon prepared mustard
2 oz/60 grams tinned pimiento, diced
4 hard-boiled eggs, chopped

Blend all ingredients thoroughly. Chill. Serve on lettuce leaves.

Italian Tomato Salad

8 servings

6 large very ripe tomatoes, sliced
Salt
Sweet basil leaves
Olive oil

Arrange tomato slices on a large serving platter. Sprinkle with salt and basil. Drizzle olive oil over tomatoes and serve at room temperature or chilled.

Macaroni Salad

4 servings

14 oz/400 grams macaroni
4 tablespoons oil
1½ tablespoons vinegar
½ teaspoon salt
1 teaspoon thyme
4 oz/115 grams smoked sausage, cubed
About 8 oz/225 grams cheese, cubed
½ cucumber, cubed
White part of 1 leek, chopped
Tomatoes
Lettuce

Boil the macaroni according to the directions on the packet. Combine the oil, vinegar, salt and thyme. Pour the dressing over the hot macaroni. Let cool.

Mix the sausage, cheese, cucumber and leek with the cold macaroni. Season. Serve with tomatoes and lettuce.

Cold Pasta Salad

6 servings

8 oz/225 grams cold cooked medium pasta shells
1 or 2 tomatoes, diced
2 to 4 spring onions, diced
1 cucumber, peeled, seeded and diced
1 red onion, diced
1 Spanish onion, diced
2 green and/or red peppers
2 to 4 red potatoes, cooked and diced
5 oz/140 grams cold steamed broccoli, diced
6 oz/170 grams steamed green beans, diced
Fresh basil to taste
2 oz/60 grams parsley, finely chopped

dressing
2½ fl oz/75 ml low-acid vinegar (balsamic or similar)
¼ teaspoon Dijon mustard
Pinch oregano
½ teaspoon pepper
2 tablespoons apple juice

Toss all vegetables with cold pasta, adding more or less of each to taste. Mix dressing ingredients together, shake and pour over salad.

Variation: Dice or chop a skinned and boned chicken breast and poach in mixture of 2 tablespoons of white wine, 1 tablespoon lemon juice, 2 tablespoons water and lots of dried basil. Cover while cooking until poached through. Cool and add to salad.

Lobster and Wild Rice Salad

4 to 6 servings

2 lb/900 grams wild rice, cooked
1 lb/450 grams lobster meat, cooked and cut into bite-sized cubes
2 medium sized unblemished avocados
1 tablespoon lemon juice
4 oz/115 grams red onion, coarsely cubed
1 tablespoon German mustard
2½ tablespoons red wine vinegar
¼ pint/140 ml corn or vegetable oil
½ teaspoon garlic, finely chopped
Salt to taste, if desired
Freshly ground pepper to taste
2 tablespoons parsley, finely chopped

Put the rice in a mixing bowl; let cool and add the lobster.

Peel the avocados and slice in half. Remove stones. Cut the avocados into cubes and sprinkle with lemon juice to prevent discolouration. Add the cubes to the mixing bowl. Sprinkle with onion.

Put the mustard and vinegar in a small mixing bowl and beat lightly with a wire whisk. Gradually add the oil, beating briskly with the whisk. Add the garlic, salt, pepper and parsley. Pour over the salad and toss. Serve at room temperature.

Mussel Salad (lower right)

Rice Salad with Ham

4 servings

8 oz/225 grams rice
1½ tablespoons vinegar
½ teaspoon salt
¼ teaspoon black or white pepper
1 clove garlic, crushed
1 teaspoon tarragon (optional)
3 tablespoons oil
2 tablespoons water
1 lb/450 grams ham, cut into cubes
2 oz/60 grams parsley, finely chopped

Boil the rice according to the directions given on the packet. Mix together the vinegar, spices, oil and water and pour the dressing over the hot rice. Let stand until the rice becomes cold.

Mix the cold rice with the ham and the parsley.

Festive Crab Salad

4 servings

crab salad
4 meaty crabs
4 hard-boiled eggs
2 oz/60 grams celery, cut into ¼-inch/½-cm pieces

garnish
Lettuce
2 avocados, stoned
Mushrooms
Tomatoes
A small amount of vinaigrette dressing (See index)

dressing
8 fl oz/220 ml mayonnaise
2 tablespoons each snipped chives and parsley
2 tablespoons snipped dill
1 tablespoon capers, lightly chopped
1 clove garlic, crushed
Several drops Tabasco sauce
Lemon juice
1 teaspoon Worcester sauce
1 teaspoon chilli sauce

Lift away the shell of the crab and carefully remove the roe with a fork. Try to remove it in one piece, cut it into slices and place it decoratively on individual plates. Crack the claws and the legs with a nutcracker and scrape all the meat out into a bowl. Also scrape out as much of the rest of the crabmeat as possible.

Cut the eggs into pieces and mix with the crabmeat and the celery. Divide the salad up onto the plates and sprinkle with a small amount of snipped chives. Cut the lettuce, avocados, mushroom caps and to-matoes into slices and divide them up among the plates. Drip a small amount of vinaigrette dressing over the vegetables.

Mix all the dressing ingredients together and season to taste. It should be quite strong. Salt and pepper if necessary.

Mussel Salad

4 to 6 servings

40 mussels, fresh or frozen
4 fl oz/110 ml white wine
1 tablespoon shallot, finely chopped
Water
2½ fl oz/75 ml mayonnaise
½ lemon
1 tablespoon capers
1 tablespoon parsley, finely chopped
1 tablespoon chives, finely chopped
1 teaspoon dried tarragon
3 tomatoes
Salt
Pepper
1 drop Tabasco sauce
Lettuce leaves

Boil the mussels in the wine, water and shallots, covered, until they open. Remove the mussels from their shells. Save the largest shells, about 4 to 5 per person.

Chop the mussels and mix with the mayonnaise, juice from ½ lemon, capers and the herbs. Divide the tomatoes into wedges, remove the seeds and cut the tomato flesh into small pieces. Mix into the mussel mixture.

Season the salad to taste with salt, pepper and Tabasco. Fill the mussel shells and arrange them attractively on plates with leaves of lettuce.

Swedish Raw Spiced Salmon with Mustard Dressing

4 servings

mustard dressing
3 tablespoons mustard
2 tablespoons vinegar
1 teaspoon salt
¼ teaspoon black pepper
8 fl oz/220 ml oil
2½ fl oz/75 ml water
1 tablespoon sherry (optional)
2 oz/60 grams chopped dill

salad
½ head iceberg lettuce
¼ leek
1 cucumber
4 oz/115 grams fresh mushrooms

Mixed Green Salad and Swedish Raw Spiced Salmon

1 bunch radishes
6 oz/170 grams Gravadlax (raw spiced salmon)
1 lemon

Remove all the dressing ingredients from the refrigerator so that they become room temperature. This is especially important for the oil so that the dressing will "pull" together.

When the ingredients are at room temperature, mix the mustard, vinegar, salt and pepper; add the oil a drop at a time, while beating constantly. Finally add the water, sherry and chopped dill.

Finely shred all the salad ingredients. It is easiest to use a vegetable shredder on a food processor. Choose the fine cutter. Alternate all the ingredients on individual plates or on a large serving plate.

Immediately before serving, turn the slices of salmon very quickly in a piping hot pan and then place the slices on the salad. Squeeze with lemon juice.

The dressing is served with the salad, in generous proportions.

Chicken Salad Mould

6 servings

1 envelope unflavoured gelatine
2½ fl oz/75 ml cold water
½ pint/¼ l hot chicken broth
2 tablespoons green pepper, chopped
1 lb/450 grams cooked chicken, diced
1 tablespoon onion, chopped
8 oz/225 grams celery, chopped
8 oz/225 grams cooked rice
1 teaspoon salt
2½ fl oz/75 ml French dressing
¼ pint/140 ml mayonnaise

Combine gelatine and cold water, let stand 5 minutes. Add chicken broth and stir until gelatine is dissolved.

Place chopped green pepper in bottom of 4 pint/2¼ litre mould. Cover with 2 tablespoons of the gelatine, chill until firm. Combine remaining ingredients in remaining gelatine. Pour over firm green pepper and gelatine. Chill until firm. Turn out and serve on green salad.

Salmon Mould

6 servings

1 envelope unflavoured gelatine
2½ fl oz/75 ml water
1 lb/450 grams red salmon, skin and bones
   removed
½ pint/¼ l plain yoghurt
2½ fl oz/75 ml chilli sauce
4 oz/115 grams celery
2 tablespoons grated onion
2 tablespoons diced cucumbers
1 tablespoon prepared mustard
1 tablespoon lemon juice

Soften gelatine in water in small saucepan. Heat gently until dissolved. Combine salmon with yoghurt, chilli sauce, celery, onion, cucumbers, mustard and lemon juice. Blend in gelatine. Pour into 2 pint/1¼ litre mould and chill until firm.

Turn out onto lettuce leaves.

Prawn and Papaya Salad

4 servings

12 oz/345 grams cooked prawns, cut in chunks
¼ pint/140 ml mayonnaise
2 tablespoons lemon juice
Large pinch curry powder
1 tablespoon thin chopped chutney
Salt and pepper to taste
2 tins papaya
Lime wedges

Mix all the ingredients except the papaya and limes to make a prawn salad. Drain the papaya and heap with the prawn salad.

Garnish with lime wedges when ready to serve.

Chicken and Grape Salad

6 to 8 servings

1½ lb/700 grams cooked chicken, diced
8 oz/225 grams seedless white grapes, halved
8 oz/225 grams celery, diced
8 oz/225 grams blanched, salted almonds
12 oz/345 grams green pepper, diced
¼ pint/140 ml soured cream
1 tablespoon fresh lemon juice
¼ teaspoon tarragon (optional)
¼ teaspoon chervil (optional)
¼ teaspoon nutmeg
½ pint/¼ l mayonnaise

Combine ingredients and chill for several hours. Serve on lettuce and garnish with cantaloupe melon, peaches or strawberries.

Chef's Salad

8 servings

1 head Webb's lettuce
1 head cos lettuce
8 oz/225 grams cooked ham, cut into strips
8 oz/225 grams cooked chicken, cut into strips
4 hard-boiled eggs, sliced
1 tin anchovies
8 to 10 sweet pickles, sliced
Vinaigrette dressing (see Index)

Wash and drain lettuces; arrange on 8 salad plates. Spread remaining ingredients over tops of salad greens. Pour salad dressing over all; serve chilled.

Chicken Salad with Avocado Mayonnaise

Quantity Varies

Cooked chicken, skin and bones removed
Chopped walnuts
Chopped onion
Snipped parsley
Lettuce
Salt

Chicken Salad with Avocado Mayonnaise

Pepper
Paprika
Lemon
1 ripe avocado
Mayonnaise (homemade or shop bought mixed
    with a raw egg yolk)
Rosemary or oregano
Several whole walnuts

Cut the chicken into small pieces. Mix the chicken meat with the walnuts, parsley and onion. Place on a leaf of lettuce in an individual serving bowl. Lightly season with salt, pepper and paprika. Sprinkle with a little lemon juice.

Mash the avocado and blend it with mayonnaise, lemon juice, salt and freshly ground black pepper and a small amount of rosemary or oregano. Pour the avocado mayonnaise over the salad; garnish with several whole shelled walnuts and pieces of lettuce. Serve with warm French bread.

Wintry Turkey Salad

4 servings

1 lb/450 grams leftover turkey, chopped
2 oz/60 grams celery, cut in thin crescents
2 tablespoons pimiento, finely chopped
2 tablespoons capers
1 tablespoon spring onion, finely chopped
1 tablespoon parsley, finely chopped
¼ pint/140 ml mayonnaise
1 teaspoon Dijon mustard
Salt to taste
A few drops Tabasco sauce
½ lemon
Cos lettuce

Toss the ingredients together, except for the lemon and lettuce, adjusting seasoning. Squeeze lemon juice to taste.

To serve, arrange on lettuce leaves.

Smoked Turkey Salad

8 servings

8 oz/225 grams smoked turkey, diced
8 oz/225 grams Gruyère cheese, diced
2 cooked beetroots, diced
2 cold boiled potatoes, diced
1 pimiento, chopped
8 oz/225 grams cos lettuce, shredded
1 teaspoon chopped chives
French dressing
Watercress
Hard-boiled eggs

Combine all ingredients, adding enough French dressing to moisten. Season to taste and garnish with watercress and sliced hard-boiled eggs.

Blue Cheese Dressing

About 1 pint/½ litre

½ pint/¼ l mayonnaise
½ pint/¼ l plain yoghurt
1 tablespoon Worcester sauce
½ small onion, finely chopped
1 clove garlic, finely chopped
2 oz/60 grams blue cheese, crumbled

Combine all ingredients. Allow to stand overnight, if possible.

Creamy Garlic Dressing

½ pint/¼ litre

½ pint/¼ l mayonnaise
3 tablespoons skimmed milk
2 tablespoons cider vinegar
½ teaspoon sugar
¼ teaspoon salt
Large pinch pepper
1 clove garlic, crushed

Stir together all ingredients. Cover; chill.

French Dressing or Vinaigrette

14 fl oz/400 ml

2 teaspoons salt
½ teaspoon freshly ground pepper
1 teaspoon prepared mustard
½ pint/¼ l olive oil
2½ fl oz/75 ml red wine vinegar
1 teaspoon mixed herbs—for vinaigrette only

Place the salt, pepper and mustard in a medium sized bowl; then add several drops of vinegar, blending well. Add remaining oil and vinegar gradually, stirring constantly, until the total amount is used. Store in covered jar in refrigerator. Shake well before using.

Italian Dressing

14 fl oz/400 ml

½ pint/¼ l oil
4 fl oz/110 ml red wine vinegar
½ teaspoon salt
½ teaspoon dry mustard
¼ teaspoon paprika
Large pinch cayenne pepper
½ teaspoon oregano
½ teaspoon marjoram
½ clove garlic

Combine all ingredients and chill. Remove garlic before serving.

Curry Mayonnaise

12 fl oz/350 ml

½ pint/¼ l mayonnaise
3 tablespoons ketchup
2 tablespoons sweet pickle
1 teaspoon prepared French mustard
1 teaspoon curry powder

With a fork or a whisk, mix together all the ingredients. Store, tightly covered, in the refrigerator.

Lemon and Basil Dressing

½ pint/¼ litre

8 fl oz/220 ml olive oil
3 tablespoons lemon juice
2 cloves garlic, finely chopped
1 tablespoon finely chopped fresh basil or 1
    teaspoon dried leaf basil
1 teaspoon salt
Large pinch freshly ground pepper

Combine all ingredients in a small bowl or jar. Mix well. Cover. Refrigerate until ready to use. Serve with pasta salad.

Homemade Roquefort Dressing

18 fl oz/720 ml

½ pint/¼ l soured cream
2 tablespoons mayonnaise
2 tablespoons lemon juice
½ teaspoon Tabasco sauce
2 spring onions, chopped
4 oz/115 grams Roquefort cheese, crumbled
Salt

Mix together soured cream, mayonnaise, lemon juice and Tabasco sauce. Fold in spring onions and cheese. Salt to taste. Refrigerate several hours.

Soured Cream Dressing

12 fl oz/350 ml

½ pint/¼ l soured cream
2½ fl oz/75 ml lemon juice
1 teaspoon sugar
½ teaspoon salt
Cayenne pepper to taste
¼ teaspoon celery salt
½ teaspoon paprika
1 teaspoon dry mustard
¼ teaspoon garlic salt

Combine all ingredients in a small mixer bowl and beat until smooth.

Thousand Island Dressing

16 fl oz/440 ml

2 tablespoons chilli sauce
½ pint/¼ l mayonnaise
4 fl oz/110 ml milk
2 tablespoons sweet pickle relish
1 hard-boiled egg, chopped

Gradually stir chilli sauce into mayonnaise. Add milk, pickle relish and egg; stir until well blended. Chill. Serve on tossed green salad.

Chicken Cottage Loaf

Poultry

Apricot Chicken

4 servings

1 3lb/1¼ kilo chicken, cut up
2 oz/60 grams flour
½ teaspoon salt
½ teaspoon garlic powder
Large pinch ginger
1 tablespoon vegetable oil
8 fl oz/220 ml orange juice
2½ fl oz/75 ml honey
2 chicken stock cubes, crumbled
½ teaspoon rosemary, crushed
1 3-inch/7½-cm stick cinnamon
4 oz/115 grms dried apricots
4 oz/115 grams spring onions, sliced

Wash and dry the chicken. Mix the flour, garlic powder, salt and ginger. Roll chicken pieces in the flour mixture. Heat the oil in a large pan and add the chicken. Sauté until browned on both sides.

Combine the orange juice, honey, stock cubes and rosemary. Pour over the chicken. Add the cinnamon stick, apricots and onions. Heat to boiling. Reduce heat, cover and simmer for 25 minutes. Uncover and cook over medium heat 3 to 5 minutes, spooning sauce over chicken frequently until chicken is glazed.

Oven Barbecued Chicken

4 to 6 servings

1 2½–3 lb/1150–1350 grams chicken, cut into
   serving pieces
1 oz/30 grams butter
½ pint/¼ l ketchup
¼ pint/140 ml chilli sauce
1 teaspoon dry mustard
Dash Tabasco sauce
4 fl oz/110 ml vinegar

2 teaspoon Worcester sauce
3 oz/85 grams brown sugar
1 medium onion

Joint chicken; place in casserole dish with cover.

Place the rest of the ingredients in a saucepan; bring to the boil. Simmer 5 minutes, until all flavours blend. Pour sauce over chicken. If possible, marinate several hours. Cover casserole; bake at 350°F/180°C/gas mark 4 1½ hours. Uncover for last 15 minutes of baking.

Barbecued Chicken with Herb Butter

4 servings

¼ pint/140 ml dry white wine
2 tablespoons oil
Juice of ½ lemon
1 small onion, peeled and chopped
½ teaspoon tarragon
1 3 lb/1¼ kilo chicken

herb butter
4 oz/115 grams butter or margarine
4 tablespoons parsley, chopped
2 teaspoons rosemary

Combine wine, oil, lemon, onion and tarragon. Cut chicken into 8 pieces, put into wine mixture. Leave several hours, turn frequently. Drain.

Put herb butter ingredients into a small pan, heat just enough to melt the butter. Use half to baste the chicken; put the rest into the refrigerator to firm.

Brush the chicken with half the herb butter. Cook on rack over glowing charcoal. Baste several times. Cook until chicken is crisp and golden.

Cut the rest of the butter into pats and serve it on the chicken.

Lemon Chicken

6 to 8 servings

2 young medium chickens
4 oz/115 grams butter or margarine
1 clove garlic, crushed
1½ teaspoons salt
2½ fl oz/75 ml salad oil
2 tablespoons onion, finely chopped
½ teaspoon pepper
½ teaspoon dried thyme

Split chickens in half. Rinse in cold water and dry. Melt butter in a heavy pan. Brown chicken on both sides; combine rest of ingredients and pour the sauce over the chicken. Cover tightly. Cook over low heat about 40 minutes or until chicken is tender.

Beer Batter Chicken

3 to 4 servings

2 eggs, well beaten
7 fl oz/200 ml bitter or light ale
4 oz/115 grams flour
½ teaspoon salt
2 tablespoons oil or melted fat for frying
1 2½–3lb/1150–1350 grams chicken, cut into
   serving pieces

Combine eggs and beer. Slowly beat in flour, salt and 2 tablespoons oil until batter is smooth. Dip chicken into batter; drain. Drop into heated oil at 375°F/190°C and fry 15 to 20 minutes.

Chicken Casserole with Biscuit Topping

4 servings

filling
2 tablespoons vegetable oil
1 small onion, peeled and chopped
½ green pepper, finely chopped
6 oz/170 grams mushrooms, sliced
2 oz/60 grams cornflour
15 fl oz/425 ml milk
12 oz–1 lb/345–450 grams cooked chicken, cut
   into cubes

biscuit dough
8 oz/425 grams flour
1 teaspoon salt
2½ teaspoons baking powder
2½ oz/75 grams shortening
About 8 fl oz/220 ml milk

Heat the oil in a pan; add onion, green pepper and mushrooms and sauté for a few minutes. Add cornflour and cook for 1 minute, stirring constantly. Gradually add milk; stir until boiling, then add chicken and seasoning. Turn into a deep 8 to 9-inch/ 20 to 22-cm pie dish.

Sift flour, salt and baking powder together; cut in shortening with a pastry blender until mixture looks like coarse breadcrumbs. Using a fork, stir in enough milk to make a soft but not sticky dough. Knead lightly on a floured board, roll out about ½ inch/1 cm thick and cut into 1½-inch/3½-cm rounds with a pastry cutter. Place the rounds on top of the chicken mixture; brush with milk and bake for 10–15 minutes at 450°F/ 230°C/gas mark 8.

Chicken Cottage Loaf

6 servings

1 cottage loaf
1 oz/30 grams butter or margarine, melted
1 beaten egg

Filling
1 onion
½ oz/15 grams butter or margarine
8 fl oz/220 ml vegetable broth
3 juniper berries, crushed
½ teaspoon thyme
½ teaspoon salt
Large pinch black pepper
1 lb/450 grams cooked chicken meat
1 tin mushrooms (preferably Chanterelles)
4 oz/115 grams fresh mushrooms

Cut the lid off the bread and dig out well. (Save the bread and dry it to use as breadcrumbs.) Brush the bread, both inside and out, first with the melted butter and then with the beaten egg. Heat at 350°F/ 180°C/gas mark 4 for about 5 minutes.

Peel and thinly slice the onion. Brown it lightly in butter. Sprinkle with flour and cover with the broth. Add the seasoning and simmer over a low heat for a few minutes. Cut the chicken into pieces and stir into the sauce. Put aside.

Pour the liquid from the tinned mushrooms into a pot. Chop these mushrooms and add them to the liquid. Wipe any dirt off the fresh mushrooms. Slice and simmer them with the tinned ones until the liquid has been absorbed. Season, if desired, with salt and pepper.

Cover the bottom of the bread with half of the mushroom mixture. Place the chicken mixture over the mushrooms, and finally cover the chicken with the rest of the mushroom mixture. Cover with the 'lid' and warm the bread in the oven for another 7 to 10 minutes. Serve warm with a salad or fresh vegetables.

Brunswick Stew

4 to 6 servings

1 3–4 lb/1350–1800 grams boiling or roasting
  chicken
1 teaspoon salt
3 potatoes, sliced
1 large onion, sliced
8 oz/225 grams green lima beans
8 oz/225 grams tinned tomatoes (or 5–6 sliced
  fresh tomatoes)
1 oz/30 grams sugar
8 oz/225 grams corn niblets
1 tablespoon ketchup or Worcester sauce
2 oz/60 grams butter

Cut chicken into pieces and put it in a casserole
with enough boiling water to cover; add a little salt.
Simmer for about 45 minutes. Add sliced potatoes,
sliced onion, lima beans, tomatoes and sugar to casserole. Cook for 45 minutes, until beans and potatoes
are tender.

Remove as many bones as possible from the
chicken; add the corn. Cook for 10 minutes. Then
season to taste and add ketchup or Worcester sauce,
if desired. Add butter and stir well.

Flambéed Chicken with Cherries

4 to 5 servings

8 oz/225 grams tinned stoned cherries
2½ fl oz/75 mls port
1 3 lb/1¼ kilo chicken, quartered
1 tablespoon vegetable oil
2½ fl oz/75 ml brandy
8 fl oz/220 ml hot water
1 large onion, thinly sliced
½ teaspoon salt
Few grains pepper
1½ oz/45 grams cornflour

Drain cherries; reserve 2½ fl oz/75 ml syrup. Pour
reserved syrup and wine over cherries; cover. Marinate in refrigerator 2 hours.

Remove excess fat from chicken. Heat oil in a large
pan over moderately high heat; add chicken. Cook
until lightly browned on all sides. Remove from heat.
Pour brandy over chicken and ignite with match.
When flame goes out, add water, onion, salt and pepper. Cover and cook over moderately low heat 40 to
45 minutes, until chicken is tender. Remove chicken
to serving dish.

Pour juices into a measuring cup. Remove as much
fat as possible. Drain marinated cherries. Reserve liquid. Blend cherry syrup into cornflour; pour into a
pan. Add chicken juices; cook over moderate heat,
stirring constantly, until sauce is thickened. Add cherries. Cook 2 to 3 minutes to heat cherries. Pour over
chicken.

Chicken in Cider and Mustard

4 servings

1 spring chicken
¼ oz/8 grams margarine
1 large onion, peeled and thinly sliced
½ to 1 teaspoon salt
½ teaspoon black pepper
8 fl oz/220 ml apple cider
1 tablespoon Dijon mustard
½ teaspoon dried, or 2 sprigs fresh, thyme
8 fl oz/220 ml single cream

Divide the chicken into 6 to 8 pieces. Brown the
chicken on all sides in margarine. Add the sliced
onion, salt, pepper and cider. Mix the mustard and
thyme with the cream and pour it into the pot.

Mix thoroughly and let the chicken simmer for 30
to 35 minutes. Serve with chopped parsley, boiled
potatoes and tender boiled carrots.

Chicken in Cider and Mustard

Spiced Cranberry Chicken

4 servings

2 oz/60 grams flour
1 teaspoon salt
Large pinch pepper
6 chicken legs and thighs
Salad oil for frying
½ oz/15 grams cornflour
8 fl oz/220 ml cranberry juice
1 teaspoon ground nutmeg
1 teaspoon ground marjoram
1 tablespoon onion, finely chopped

In a paper bag, mix flour, salt and pepper together. Shake chicken pieces in seasoned flour mixture to coat. Brown chicken on all sides in hot oil. Cover tightly. Reduce heat and cook gently 20–30 minutes, turning occasionally, until tender. Drain on kitchen towel.

Mix brown sugar and cornflour together in a saucepan. Slowly stir in cranberry juice until smooth. Add cranberry sauce, spices and chopped onion. Cook over medium heat, stirring, until mixture comes to the boil. Spoon over top of chicken.

Creole Chicken

Creamed Chicken and Ham

4 servings

1 oz/30 grams flour or cornflour
1 oz/30 grams butter
8 fl oz/220 ml chicken stock
2½ fl oz/75 ml cream
4 oz/115 grams cooked chicken, diced
4 oz/115 grams cooked ham, diced
2 oz/60 grams celery, chopped
1 tablespoon parsley
1 egg, beaten
1 or 2 tablespoons sherry (optional)

Add flour to melted butter; stir until blended. Slowly stir in soup stock, then cream. When sauce is smooth and at boiling point, add chicken, ham, celery and parsley.

Mix 2 tablespoons of the sauce with the beaten egg. Reduce heat to low; return egg mixture to heat. Stir constantly until it thickens slightly. If desired, add 1 or 2 tablespoons sherry just before serving.

Chicken Snack

4 servings

2 oz/60 grams butter
1 oz/30 grams flour
½ pint/¼ l milk
8 mushrooms, sliced
4 tablespoons stock
1 lb/450 grams cooked chicken, chopped or
    diced
4 oz/115 grams cooked peas or corn niblets
5 thick slices white bread
½ pint/¼ l oil
1 tablespoon parsley, chopped

Melt 1½ oz/45 grams of the butter; blend in flour. Gradually add milk. When smooth, bring to the boil, stirring constantly. Boil 3 minutes, then cool slightly.

Cook mushrooms in stock 3 to 4 minutes. Add chicken and cooked vegetables. Add mixture to cream sauce and season well. Heat thoroughly; keep warm.

Remove crusts from bread; with a small pastry cutter, cut 4 crescent-shaped pieces from 1 slice.

Heat oil; add remaining butter. When foaming, fry bread slices and crescents until golden brown on both sides; drain on kitchen towel.

Arrange bread slices on a serving dish; spoon hot chicken mixture onto bread. Decorate with crescents and chopped parsley.

Creole Chicken

4 servings

1 2½ lb/1 kilo chicken
6 to 7 rashers of bacon
1½ oz/45 grams flour
1 tablespoon olive oil
6 oz/170 grams onion, sliced
1 clove garlic, chopped
2 to 3 celery sticks
1 green pepper, chopped
2 14–oz/400–gram tins chopped tomatoes
2 teaspoons thyme
1 teaspoon black pepper
¼ teaspoon cayenne pepper
1 bay leaf
Juice from ½ lemon

Divide the chicken into 8 pieces. Fry the bacon until brown and crispy in a large pan. Take out and let drain on a kitchen towel

Dredge the chicken pieces in flour and fry them in the bacon fat so that they become golden brown all over. Take them out of the pan. Pour the olive oil into the pan and add the onion and garlic. After about 5 minutes, add the celery and the green pepper.

After another 3 minutes, add the tinned tomatoes and the rest of the spices. Let the mixture come to the boil. Place the chicken pieces on the vegetable mixture, cover and let simmer for 30 minutes. Add a little water if the mixture becomes too dry.

Just before serving, add the lemon juice. Then sprinkle with the bacon, which can be slightly crumbled. Serve with rice.

Batter-Fried Chicken Breasts

4 to 6 servings

6 to 8 chicken breasts, boned
2 teaspoon salt
Dash pepper
1 egg, lightly beaten
¼ pint/140 ml milk
1 oz/30 grams flour
6 oz/170 grams flour for dredging chicken
Oil for deep-fat frying

Divide each chicken breast in half to make 12 to 16 pieces. Sprinkle each piece with salt and pepper.

Mix egg and milk in a shallow bowl or pie dish. Add flour and mix until very smooth. Dip each chicken piece in batter; dredge generously with flour. Put 4 or 5 chicken pieces into preheated 375°F/190°C oil; deep-fry 12 to 15 minutes or until chicken is golden brown on all sides. Drain on kitchen paper. Keep warm in a very low oven until all the chicken is fried.

Fried Chicken with Cream Sauce

4 to 6 servings

Salt, pepper and garlic salt
4 oz/115 grams flour
1 2½–3 lb/1–1¼ kilo chicken, cut into serving
    pieces
Fat for deep frying

cream sauce
1 oz/30 grams cornflour
8 fl oz/220 ml hot chicken broth
¼ pint/140 ml milk at room temperature
1 teaspoon salt
¼ teaspoon pepper

Mix seasonings with flour; coat each chicken piece.

Heat fat in a pan; fry the chicken, a few pieces at a time. Cook about 25 minutes per batch of chicken, so that pieces are crisp and crusty. Drain on kitchen towel; set on a warmed serving dish.

Pour off most of the fat in the pan; leave about 2 tablespoons.

Mix cornflour with chicken broth. Add to the hot fat, stirring constantly. Gradually add milk, salt and pepper. When slightly thickened, sauce is ready. Serve with the chicken.

Chicken Croquettes

4 to 6 servings

2 lb/900 grams cooked chicken, put through
  mincer
8 oz/225 grams celery, chopped
1 tablespoon onion, finely chopped
4 oz/115 grams butter
2 oz/60 grams flour
½ pint/¼ l milk
1 teaspoon salt
Generous dash of freshly ground pepper
1 egg, beaten with 1 tablespoon milk
4 oz/115 grams breadcrumbs
Oil for deep frying
2 tins cream of mushroom soup

Mix chicken and celery in a large bowl; set aside.
Sauté onion in butter in a small saucepan until onion
is softened. Blend in flour. Add milk and heat, stirring
constantly. When slightly thickened, add salt and pepper; simmer just 3 minutes. Add sauce to chicken and
celery and chill several hours.

Shape chicken into rolls about 3 inches/7½ cms
long. Dip rolls into egg; coat with breadcrumbs. Place
croquettes on a waxed-paper-lined baking sheet; chill
in refrigerator at least 3 hours.

Fry croquettes in deep fat, a few at a time, until
brown on all sides; drain on kitchen towel. Keep
warm in very low (250°F/120°C/gas mark ¼) oven
until ready to serve.

For a quick sauce, heat cream of mushroom soup
over low heat; stir until piping hot. If you prefer a
thinner sauce, add milk; stir until desired consistency
is reached.

Chicken in Crumb Baskets

6 servings

crumb baskets
5 oz/140 grams soft breadcrumbs
2 oz/60 grams onion, finely chopped
1 teaspoon celery salt
Pinch pepper
4 oz/115 grams melted butter or margarine

chicken filling
5 oz/140 grams butter or margarine
2½ oz/75 grams flour
¼ pint/140 ml single cream
15 fl oz/425 ml chicken broth
½ teaspoon salt
Pinch pepper
1 teaspoon Worcester sauce
8 oz/225 grams cooked peas
1½ lbs/700 grams cooked chicken, chopped

Mix the breadcrumbs with the onion, seasonings
and butter. Grease 6 individual casseroles and line
with the crumb mixture. Press into place. Bake in a
375°F/190°C/gas mark 5 oven for 15 minutes, or until
the crumbs are brown.

To make the filling, blend the flour in melted butter. Stir in the cream, broth and seasonings. Keep
stirring and cook until thickened. Then add the peas
and chicken. Serve the chicken mixture in the baked
crumb baskets.

Cucumber Stuffed Chicken

3 to 4 servings

1 2½ lb/1150 grams chicken
Salt
Pepper
3 tablespoons pink pepper, crushed
1 cucumber
1 tablespoon soy sauce
1 tablespoon fresh lemon juice
4 fl oz/110 ml dry white wine
1½ crumbled chicken stock cubes
¼ pint/140 ml double cream
1 oz/30 grams flour stirred into 2½ tablespoons
  single cream

Cucumber Stuffed Chicken

Remove the skin and the fat from the chicken. Salt and pepper the inside. Crush 2 tablespoons of the pink peppercorns. Peel the cucumber and cut into thin slices. Mix the cucumber slices with the crushed pepper. Stuff the chicken with the mixture and tie up the chicken with trussing string.

Mix together the soy sauce, lemon juice and the remaining 1 tablespoon of pepper, crushed. Brush the chicken in an ungreased, ovenproof dish that has a lid (preferably an earthenware dish) and pour the wine over the bird. Add the crumbled chicken stock cubes. Place the dish in a cold oven and set the temperature for 425°F/220°C/gas mark 7. Bake for about 1 hour after the oven has reached this temperature.

Remove the chicken from the dish, take away the string and remove the cucumber stuffing, which is to be added to the sauce. Allow the cucumber mixture to drain. Keep the chicken warm by wrapping it in aluminium foil and putting it back in the oven.

Strain the cooking juices and pour into a pot, making about ½ pint/¼ litre of gravy. Stir in the double cream and bring to the boil. Stir in the flour with a whisk. Add the well-drained cucumber mixture to the sauce, which should have a creamy consistency. This is not a thick sauce.

Chicken Florentine Au Gratin

4 servings

1 packet frozen spinach, unchopped
2 chicken breasts, skinned and boned
½ teaspoon salt
Dash grated nutmeg

cheese sauce

1 oz/30 grams margarine
2 oz/60 grams flour
32 fl oz/900 ml chicken stock
4 twists of ground black pepper from the mill
1 egg yolk
8 fl oz/220 ml single cream
6 oz/170 grams cheese (preferably strong cheese), grated

Cover an ovenproof dish with the thawed and well-drained spinach leaves. Cut the breast into bits but arrange so that they still look whole on top of the spinach leaves. Season with salt and nutmeg.

Melt the margarine in a saucepan on a low heat. Add the flour and make a roux for the sauce. Then add the chicken stock, turn up the heat and stir until the sauce comes to the boil. Reduce the heat again and cook for 3 minutes. Season with the black pepper.

Stir the egg yolk in the cream. Remove the saucepan from the heat and stir the egg mixture quickly into the sauce. Add the grated cheese and pour the sauce over the chicken meat and spinach leaves.

Bake in a preheated 425°F/220°C/gas mark 7 oven for 15 minutes. Serve with boiled rice or potatoes.

Fruit and Nut Stuffed Chicken Breasts

6 servings

6 oz/170 grams butter
8 oz/225 grams apple, diced
4 oz/115 grams nuts, coarsely chopped
4 oz/115 grams sultanas
1¼ lb/565 grams tinned crushed pineapple
4 oz/115 grams soft breadcrumbs, toasted
1 teaspoon salt
1 teaspoon cinnamon
½ teaspoon nutmeg
¼ teaspoon ginger
¼ teaspoon ground cloves
6 whole chicken breasts, boned

fruit sauce

1 oz/30 grams sugar
½ oz/15 grams cornflour
Large pinch salt
½ teaspoon cinnamon
¼ teaspoon nutmeg
Large pinch ginger
½ pint/¼ l orange juice
Pineapple and syrup reserved from stuffing
2 oz/60 grams sultanas
½ oz/15 grams butter
Sections and slivered peel of 1 orange

Melt 4 oz/115 grams of the butter in a pan; sauté the apple and nuts 10 minutes. Remove from heat. Add raisins, half the drained pineapple (reserve remaining pineapple), toasted breadcrumbs, ½ teaspoon salt, cinnamon, nutmeg, ginger and cloves.

Sprinkle inside of chicken breasts with ½ teaspoon salt. Spread the fruit stuffing on the inside of each breast; fold the sides over and fasten with skewers or string.

Place remaining butter in a 9 × 13-inch/23 × 33-cm baking tin lined with foil; place in moderate oven (375°F/190°C/gas mark 5) until melted, about 5 minutes. Place breasts top side down in the melted butter; return pan to oven and bake chicken 25 minutes. Turn chicken over and bake 20 minutes more.

Combine sugar, cornflour, salt, cinnamon, nutmeg and ginger. Stir in orange juice; add pineapple and pineapple syrup, sultanas, butter and slivered peel. Cook, stirring constantly, over medium heat until mixture comes to the boil and thickens. Add orange sections and heat. Serve with the chicken breasts.

Chicken Florentine au Gratin

Oven-Fried Chicken

4 to 5 servings

1 spring chicken, cut into serving pieces
2 oz/60 grams flour
Salt
Black pepper
Paprika
1 egg, beaten
Fine breadcrumbs
3 to 4 tablespoons oil

Preheat oven to 400°F/200°C/gas mark 6.

Toss chicken lightly in flour to which a little salt, pepper and paprika have been added. Brush with a beaten egg, then coat with breadcrumbs.

Heat oil in a roasting tin; put in chicken. Brush lightly with hot oil and bake about 30 minutes.

Glazed Chicken

4 servings

10 oz/285 grams apricot jam
6 chicken breasts
1 packet dried onion soup
1 pint/½ l water

Cover the chicken with the jam, then sprinkle on the onion soup. Pour the water round the chicken. Bake about 1 hour at 350°F/180°C/gas mark 4. Baste from time to time.

Honey Chicken

4 servings

2 oz/60 grams flour
1 teaspoon salt
3 or 4 chicken breasts, boned
2 oz/60 grams butter
2½ fl oz/70 ml honey
2½ fl oz/70 ml lemon juice
1 tablespoon soy sauce

Combine the flour and salt. Dip chicken in the flour-salt mixture. Melt butter and pour over chicken. Bake ½ hour at 350°F/180°C/gas mark 6. Mix the rest of ingredients and pour over chicken. Bake 30 minutes longer, basting often. Serve on rice.

Chicken and Beef Stew

8 to 10 servings

1 2–3 lb/1–1¼ kilo chicken, cut into small pieces
Salt and pepper to taste
1 lb/450 grams beef, cubed
2 tablespoons oil
1 teaspoon salt
8 oz/225 grams onions, chopped
1 green pepper, chopped
2 large tomatoes, peeled and diced
1½ teaspoons cayenne pepper
1 pint/½ l water
12 oz/345 grams peanut butter

Season chicken with salt and pepper; set aside.

Brown the beef cubes in hot oil in a large pan. Add salt, half the onions, half the pepper and tomatoes, cayenne and water. Simmer this gently for 30 minutes.

Mix ½ pint/¼ litre of cooking liquid with peanut butter to make a smooth paste. Add to pan, cook 15 minutes more. Add chicken pieces and remainder of vegetables. Simmer 30 minutes, until all is tender.

Chicken Hot Pot

4 to 5 servings

1 3 lb/1¼ kilo chicken
½ oz/15 grams flour
2 oz/60 grams butter or margarine
1 large onion, peeled and sliced
1 tin tomatoes (1 lb/450 grams)
2 teaspoons brown sugar
2 teaspoons prepared mustard
4 medium-sized potatoes, peeled and sliced
2 apples, peeled, cored and sliced

cream slaw
1 small head firm white cabbage, shredded
1 small green pepper, seeded and chopped
2 teaspoons prepared mustard
½ teaspoon paprika
2 teaspoons lemon juice
¼ pint/140 ml soured cream

Joint the chicken, dredge with flour mixed with a little salt and pepper and brown on all sides in the butter. Remove from the pan.

Lightly brown the onion in the remaining butter. Add tomatoes, sugar and mustard and heat gently. Arrange the potatoes in the bottom of a buttered casserole, season lightly and add the apples; cover with the tomato mixture. Put the chicken pieces on top; cover and cook in a 350°F/180°C/gas mark 6 oven for about 1½ hours.

Mix the cabbage and green pepper. Add the other ingredients to the cream, blend well and toss the cabbage and pepper lightly in the soured cream dressing. Serve with the chicken.

Orange Chicken

4 to 6 servings

3 lb/1¼ kilo chicken, quartered and skinned
4 teaspoons Dijon mustard (optional)
1 teaspoon salt
¼ teaspoon pepper
1 oz/30 grams butter
1 small onion, chopped
½ pint/¼ l orange juice
2 oz/60 grams brown sugar

Spread mustard on the meaty side of the chicken and sprinkle with salt and pepper. Place meaty side down in a 10x6 × 2-inch/25 × 15¼x4½-cm baking tin. Add butter, onion and orange juice. Bake in a preheated 375°F/190°C/gas mark 7 oven, for 20 minutes, basting after 10 minutes. Turn chicken over.

Stir the sugar into juices in the pan. Continue baking approximately 40 minutes, basting several times, until the chicken is golden brown and tender. Remove chicken and keep hot.

Pour the juice into a 2 pint/1¼ litre saucepan and boil gently, stirring often until reduced and thickened. Spoon this glaze over the chicken.

Jambalaya

6 servings

1 3 lb/1¼ kilo chicken, cut into serving pieces
Salt and pepper
3 tablespoons bacon dripping or vegetable oil
1 lb/450 grams celery, sliced
1 lb/450 grams spring onions with tops, sliced
8 oz/225 grams green peppers, chopped
8 oz/225 grams uncooked rice
1 pint/½ l boiling broth
1 teaspoon salt
½ teaspoon garlic salt
¼ teaspoon black pepper
¼ teaspoon red pepper

Season chicken with salt and pepper. Brown on all sides in dripping in a large pan. Remove chicken. Pour off all but 2 tablespoons of the dripping. Add celery, onions and green peppers. Sauté until tender. Stir in rice, broth and seasonings. Return chicken to pan. Cover and cook in the oven at 375°F/190°C/gas mark 5 for 30 minutes or until chicken is tender. Fluff with a fork.

Chicken in Lemon-Dill Butter

4 to 6 servings

4 oz/115 grams butter
2 tablespoons lemon juice
1 teaspoon salt
1 clove garlic, finely chopped
½ teaspoon paprika
1 tin sliced mushrooms, drained
1 tablespoon dill
3 lb/1¼ kilo chicken, cut into serving pieces

Melt the butter in a large pan. Add all ingredients, except the chicken. Bring to the boil. Add chicken, bring to the boil, but do not actually boil. Cover pan. Lower heat; simmer 30 minutes or until chicken is tender.

Remove chicken to a serving dish; serve with noodles or rice, covered with the remaining liquid.

Lemon and Garlic Filled Chicken

4 servings

8 chicken breasts
Salt
Pepper
3¼ oz/100 grams butter, at room temperature
3 cloves garlic, crushed
Juice of 1 lemon
2 tablespoons parsley, finely chopped
Flour
1 egg, beaten
Breadcrumbs
Oil

Fillet and pound the breasts so that they become quite thin. Salt and pepper them slightly. Mix the butter with the garlic, lemon juice, parsley, salt and pepper. Spread the butter mixture on the chicken breasts, fold in the edges and roll them together. Fasten with a toothpick.

First roll the breasts in flour, then dip them in a beaten egg. Finally roll in the breadcrumbs. Fry them rather slowly in hot oil until they have become golden brown and are cooked through.

Serve with peeled, seeded cucumbers, which have simmered slightly in the rest of the butter, and rice.

Chicken and Lobster Marengo

8 to 10 servings

2 lbs/900 grams boned chicken breasts, cut into bite-sized pieces
1 onion, sliced
1 clove garlic, crushed
¼ pint/140 ml olive oil
1 pint/½ l chicken broth (undiluted)
2 lbs/900 grams tinned or 5 medium-sized tomatoes, peeled and chopped
6 oz/170 grams celery, diced

1 bay leaf
2 tablespoons fresh parsley, finely chopped
Small teaspoon thyme
Small teaspoon basil
Small teaspoon tarragon
Salt and pepper to taste
1½ lb/700 grams fresh mushrooms
1 jar pearl onions
1 lb/450 grams cooked lobster meat (or prawns)
1 measure brandy

In a pan, brown the chicken, onion slices and garlic in olive oil. Set aside. In a saucepan, combine the broth, tomatoes, celery and bay leaf. Bring to the boil; cover and simmer about 30 minutes.

Add parsley, herbs, sherry, salt and pepper. Cook about 5 minutes more. Add mushrooms, pearl onions, chicken mixture, lobster and brandy. If sauce seems too thin, thicken it with a little flour and water.

Simmer until thickened and transfer to a casserole dish. Bake for 20 to 30 minutes at 350°F/180°C/gas mark 4. Serve on rice. This tastes better if served the next day.

Mint Julep Chicken

4 to 6 servings

3 oz/85 grams butter
4 whole chicken breasts, skinned and boned
2 oz/60 grams shallots, chopped
8 oz/225 grams mushrooms, sliced
Juice of ½ lemon
Salt and pepper to taste
2½ fl oz/75 ml whisky
½ pint/¼ l double cream
2 tablespoons mint, finely chopped

Melt 4 tablespoons of the butter in a pan; sauté the chicken breasts 1 minute on each side. Remove the chicken and keep it warm. Add shallots and cook for 3 minutes. Add the remaining 2 tablespoons of butter and sauté the mushrooms with lemon juice, salt and pepper for 3 minutes. Add the whisky and cream and bring to the boil

Put chicken breasts back in the dish, cover and cook for 10 minutes. If the sauce is too thin, remove the chicken and reduce the sauce, stirring, until it coats a spoon. Garnish with chopped mint.

Nut Coated Chicken

4 servings

8 oz/225 grams dry roasted, skinned peanuts,
  finely chopped
2 oz/60 grams fine dry breadcrumbs
1¼ teaspoons salt
½ teaspoon dried mixed herbs
Pepper to taste
4 drumsticks
4 wings
2½ fl oz/70 ml chicken broth

Mix peanuts, crumbs and seasonings together.

Dip chicken pieces in the broth, then in the peanut mixture; coat all over. Place in a single layer on a foil-lined pan. Bake at 400°F/200°C/gas mark 6 40 minutes or until tender. Do not turn chicken during baking.

Chicken and Oyster Casserole

4 servings

1 chicken, jointed
½ pint/¼ l water
¼ pint/140 ml vinegar
1 clove garlic
1 pinch dried thyme
1 bay leaf
1 teaspoon salt
1 pint/½ l oysters
1 oz/30 grams butter
½ oz/15 grams flour
2 tablespoons sherry
1 tablespoon parsley, minced
2 oz/60 grams breadcrumbs

Simmer the chicken in water and vinegar with garlic, thyme, bay leaf and salt for 30 minutes, or until tender. Cool and strip the meat from the bones, reserving liquid. Discard bones and skin and cut the chicken meat into bite-sized pieces.

Drain the oysters, adding oyster liquor to the liquid in which the chicken was cooked. In a frying pan, melt ½ oz/15 grams butter and stir in flour. Stir in the chicken and oyster liquid and simmer until slightly thickened. Add sherry and parsley; pour the sauce over the chicken and oysters in a large baking dish. Top with crumbs and the remaining tablespoon of butter; cut in small bits. Bake 15 minutes at 350°F/180°C/gas mark 4.

Lemon and Garlic Filled Chicken Breasts

Marinated Chicken

4 servings

2½ lb/1150 grams chicken

marinade
1 pint/½ l yoghurt
1 onion, peeled and sliced
2 teaspoons curry powder
1 teaspoon ginger
2 teaspoons paprika
1 teaspoon caraway seeds
1 to 2 cloves garlic, crushed

cucumber salad
1 pint/½ l yoghurt
½ cucumber
2 oz/60 grams chives, finely snipped
1 teaspoon salt
Black pepper

Divide the chicken in half. Mix all the marinade ingredients together. Place the chicken halves in a deep plate. Cover with the marinade. Refrigerate for 6 to 8 hours. Turn the chicken several times while it is marinating.

Preheat the oven to 350°F/180°C/gas mark 4. Place the chicken halves in an ovenproof dish. Pour the marinade over the chicken and brush the chicken well. Bake for about 45 minutes. Brush the chicken occasionally with the marinade while it is baking.

When making the cucumber salad, allow the yoghurt to drain through a coffee filter for about 15 minutes. Thinly slice the cucumber. Mix with the yoghurt. Add the chives; season with salt and pepper. Serve with brown rice.

Marsala Chicken

4 servings

1 chicken, cut into serving pieces
8 fl oz/220 ml Marsala (Port or Madeira can be used)
1 oz/30 grams butter
1 shallot, peeled and chopped
About 1 teaspoon salt
¼ teaspoon black pepper
8 fl oz/220 ml water
2 teaspoons flour
8 fl oz/220 ml double cream
Chopped walnuts

Marinated Chicken

Place the pieces of chicken in a freezer bag in a bowl. Pour the wine into the bag. Fold up the bag and refrigerate for 2 to 3 hours. Turn the bag occasionally while it is in the refrigerator. Remove the chicken but save the wine. Dry off the chicken.

Brown the pieces of chicken in a deep frying pan in a little butter. Add the shallot and lightly brown. Season with salt and pepper. Add the wine and water. Cover and cook the chicken for about 15 to 20 minutes, until the chicken is done. Place the pieces of chicken in a warm, deep dish.

Prepare the sauce by stirring the flour into the frying pan. Allow the sauce to boil for a few minutes, then add the cream.

Season to taste and possibly dilute the sauce slightly more. Pour over the chicken (if you prefer, strain the sauce before pouring it over the chicken). Sprinkle with the chopped nuts.

Chicken Delaware

6 servings

6 pieces chicken
2 oz/60 grams flour, mixed with salt, pepper and
  a pinch of cayenne pepper
1 egg
1 teaspoon oil
6 oz/170 grams fresh white breadcrumbs
2 tablespoons oil
3½ oz/100 grams butter
3 bananas, halved
6 rashers bacon

fritters
8 oz/225 grams tinned corn niblets
Salt and pepper to taste
1 egg, separated
2½ oz/70 grams flour
½ teaspoon baking powder
½ teaspoon curry powder
Fat for deep frying

tomato sauce
1½ oz/45 grams butter
1 onion, sliced
1 clove garlic, crushed
8 oz/225 grams tinned tomatoes
2 tablespoons mixed herbs
Salt and pepper to taste
1 teaspoon sugar
1 teaspoon paprika
¼ pint/140 ml cider or stock

Marsala Chicken

Roll chicken pieces in seasoned flour, then brush all over with egg beaten with oil. Coat well with fresh, white breadcrumbs. Heat oil and add 2–2½ oz/60–75 grams butter. When foaming, put in the chicken pieces and fry gently for 20–25 minutes, turning frequently until brown and crisp all over.

Meanwhile, prepare the corn fritters. Drain the corn and mix it with 1 egg yolk and seasoning. Sift flour, baking powder and curry powder together; stir into corn mixture. Just before frying, beat the egg white and fold it into the corn mixture. Heat the fat until very hot but not smoking. Drop the fritter mixture into the fat by tablespoonfuls and fry until light brown. Drain on kitchen towel. Keep warm.

Fry bananas in 1 oz/30 grams butter until golden brown. Keep warm. Cut bacon slices in half and roll up carefully. Thread onto skewers and grill until crisp all over. Keep warm.

Prepare tomato sauce: cook the onion and crushed garlic in melted butter for 5–6 minutes. Add tomatoes, herbs, seasoning, sugar, paprika and cider or stock. Bring to the boil, then strain or blend in an electric blender or food processor and serve hot with the chicken.

Quick Paella

4 to 6 servings

4 oz/115 grams bacon
½ onion, chopped
1 clove garlic
1 red or green pepper, cubed
1 pint/½ l chicken broth
¼ teaspoon saffron
Salt
Pepper
8 oz/225 grams rice
1 roast chicken, cut up into small pieces
4 oz/115 grams cooked shelled mussels
10 oz/285 grams frozen peas
About 20 large prawns with shells
Oil
Garlic powder
Lemon wedges

Cut the bacon into smaller pieces and brown them in a pot together with the onion, garlic and red or green pepper. Pour over the broth which has been flavoured with the saffron and season with salt and pepper. Bring to the boil. Add the rice and cover the pot. Simmer for about 25 minutes.

Warm the pieces of chicken in the rice mixture: add the mussels and peas. Dip the prawns in a little oil that has been seasoned with garlic powder and then salt. Sauté them quickly in a hot frying pan and then place them in and on top of the wedges.

Garnish with wedges of lemon.

Chicken and Peaches

6 servings

1 3½ lb/1½ kilo chicken or 6 to 8 chicken joints
1 oz/30 grams butter or margarine
1 tablespoon oil
1 large onion, peeled and sliced
1 green pepper, seeded and cut into strips
2 lbs/900 grams sliced tinned peaches
½ oz/15 grams cornflour
1 tablespoon soy sauce
3 tablespoons white wine vinegar
2 tomatoes, peeled and thickly sliced

Preheat oven to 375°F/190°C/gas mark 5.
Joint and skin chicken. Heat butter and oil in a pan. Brown chicken pieces on all sides. Cover; reduce heat. Cook about 10 minutes. Remove the chicken and arrange in a large casserole.

Sauté the onion and pepper in the remaining fat until the onion is soft. Drain the peaches; reserve syrup.

Mix cornflour smoothly with soy sauce and vinegar. Add ½ pint/¼ l peach syrup. Pour into a pan. Stir

until boiling; boil until clear. Add peaches and tomatoes. Pour pan contents over the chicken. Cover casserole and cook 30 to 40 minutes. Remove lid for the last 5 minutes. Adjust seasoning.

Serve with wild rice to which some cooked green peas and a few strips of red pepper have been added.

Chicken Pot Pie

6 servings

5 lb/2¼ kilo boiling chicken
3 pints/2 l water
2 teaspoons salt
1 small onion
1 carrot
1 stick celery
2 oz/60 grams flour
½ teaspoon onion salt
½ teaspoon celery salt
1 teaspoon thyme
Dash pepper
2 pints/1¼ l chicken broth
2 tablespoons sherry
1 egg white, slightly beaten
Pastry for pie crust

Place the chicken in a large pot and add water, 1 teaspoon salt, onion, carrot and celery. Simmer, covered, until tender, about 2½ hours. Remove chicken and cut the meat from the bones in large pieces. Refrigerate the chicken and broth to cool.

Combine flour, onion salt, celery salt, thyme, pepper and remaining salt with ¼ pint/140 ml cooled chicken broth. Mix until smooth.

Put 1½ pints/850 ml chicken broth in a pan; heat and add the flour mixture, stirring constantly to prevent lumps. Cook over medium heat, stirring, until mixture is thickened. Stir in sherry. Add chicken and blend well. Cool.

Pour filling into a 9-inch/22-cm deep pudding dish. Roll out pastry and brush underside with egg white. Cover filling with pastry and crimp edges. Cut vents in top. Freeze, then bake at 400°F/200°C/gas mark 6 for 45 minutes to an hour.

Chicken Biscuit Cobbler

8 servings

1 5 lb/2¼ kilo chicken, cut in serving pieces
2 small onions
1 teaspoon salt
¼ teaspoon pepper
Chicken giblets
2 oz/60 grams butter
2 oz/60 grams flour
1 pint/½ l chicken stock

2 oz/60 grams celery, diced
2 tablespoons parsley, chopped
1 onion, finely chopped

biscuit dough
6 oz/170 grams flour, sifted with 1½ teaspoons
  baking powder
Pinch of salt
½ oz/15 grams butter
2½ fl oz/75 ml milk

Place the chicken in a large pot; add water to cover and onions and cook until the chicken is tender, about 2½ hours. Season; remove the chicken from the broth and cut the meat from the bones.

Cook the giblets in salted water until tender; drain and mince. Melt the butter in a pan, then add flour and a little of the broth. Add the celery, parsley, onion, giblets and more chicken stock; cook all together for a few minutes. Season to taste.

Place the chicken in a buttered baking dish, pour the sauce over all, and drop teaspoonfuls of biscuit dough on top (not too close together) to make the crust.

To make the biscuit dough: sift the flour, baking powder and salt 3 times. Cut the butter into the flour, mix and stir in the milk.

Bake the pie in a 450°F/230°C/gas mark 8 oven for 15 minutes, or until the biscuit crust has browned.

Poached Chicken with Mushrooms

4 servings

4 whole chicken breasts, boned and skinned
½ pint/¼ l water
1 sprig fresh dill or 1 teaspoon dried dill
8 oz/225 grams fresh mushrooms, sliced
2 carrots, scraped and thinly sliced
½ teaspoon salt

Arrange the chicken breasts in a large pan. Pour water around the chicken. Add dill, mushrooms, carrots and salt. Cover and simmer gently for 15 to 20 minutes, until chicken is cooked through.

Quick Paella

Chicken and Oyster Pie

4 servings

12 oysters
1 oz/30 grams butter or margarine
1 large chicken breast, cut into strips
8 oz/225 grams mushrooms, sliced
Oyster liquor, made up to 2½ fl oz/75 ml with
    water
Pinch salt
Pinch cayenne pepper
Pinch sugar
¼ pint/140 ml single cream
1 teaspoon cornflour
Milk
1 egg yolk
1 8-inch/20-cm baked pastry case
Chopped parsley
1–2 pimientos (tin or jar)

Open the oysters and retain their liquor. Heat the butter in a sauté pan, add the strips of chicken and mushrooms and cook quickly for a few minutes. Heat the oyster liquor and water, put in the oysters and let stand for 7–8 minutes off the heat. Lift out into a bowl. Add the chicken, mushrooms, salt, cayenne pepper and sugar.

Stir all but 1 tablespoon of the cream into the oyster liquor; add the cornflour, mixed until smooth with a little milk. Stir until boiling and boil for 1 minute.

Mix the remaining 1 tablespoon cream with the egg yolk; stir a little of the hot sauce into the cream-yolk mixture, then return to the pan. Add all the other ingredients, check the seasoning and heat through. Pour into the warm pastry case, sprinkle with parsley and decorate with strips of pimiento.

Chicken in Apricot and Yoghurt Sauce

4 to 6 servings

4–6 chicken pieces, about 2 lb/900 grams or
    more
2 tablespoons oil
4 oz/115 grams butter
1 large onion, sliced
8 oz/225 grams dried apricots, chopped
½ teaspoon cinnamon
Salt and pepper to taste
Grated rind of 1 lemon
½ pint/¼ l yoghurt
12 oz/345 grams long-grain rice
2 tablespoons almonds

Heat the oil and 1 oz/30 grams of butter. When foaming, fry the chicken pieces until golden brown.

Remove and let cool. Cook onion in the same oil and butter until golden. Add apricots; sprinkle with cinnamon, lemon rind, salt and pepper. Remove bones from chicken pieces and shred meat. Mix yoghurt with onion mixture and soak chicken in this while rice is cooking.

Cook rice in boiling salted water for 10–12 minutes. Drain and rinse with boiling water. Dry for a few minutes. Heat 1½ oz/45 grams butter in thick pan or casserole; put half rice into pan and mix well with butter and seasoning. Spoon chicken mixture over rice and put remaining rice on top. Sprinkle with salt and pepper.

Melt the remaining butter and spoon over the rice. Cover the pan with cloth and a lid and cook gently for 15–20 minutes, until all the flavours are blended; the cloth absorbs extra moisture. (This process can be done in a 350°F/180°C/gas mark 4 oven but cloth should not be used.)

Brown slivers of almonds, sprinkle on top of the rice, and serve at once.

American Chicken Popovers

6 servings

4 oz/115 grams flour
½ teaspoon salt
2 eggs
½ pint/¼ l milk
1½ oz/45 grams butter or margarine
1 oz/30 grams flour
8 fl oz/220 ml chicken broth
8 oz/225 grams cooked chicken, cubed
2 oz/60 grams tinned mushrooms, drained and
    chopped
½ teaspoon salt or seasoned salt
Dash nutmeg
1 egg
2½ fl oz/75 ml cream
1 tablespoon sherry

Sift 4 oz/115 grams flour; measure and sift again with the salt. Beat eggs with a rotary beater until thick and lemon coloured; gradually add milk and ½ oz/15 grams melted butter. Stir in salted flour. Beat until mixture is smooth. Fill buttered ramekins a little less than half full. Bake in an oven preheated to 425°F/220°C/gas mark 7 about 40 minutes.

Meanwhile, melt the remaining 1 oz/30 grams butter and blend in 1 oz/30 grams flour; slowly add broth. Cook and stir until thickened. Add chicken, mushrooms, salt and nutmeg; heat through. Beat egg, cream and sherry together, then add to chicken mixture. Split sides of hot popovers and fill with creamed chicken.

Pot-Roast Chicken

4 servings

1 whole chicken
2 tablespoons vegetable oil
1 oz/30 grams butter or margarine
1 clove garlic, finely chopped
4 medium sized onions, quartered
4 medium sized potatoes, quartered
6 carrots, pared and cut in 2-inch/5-cm pieces
1 tin condensed chicken broth
1 soup tin water
1 teaspoon rosemary, crushed
½ teaspoon pepper
1 teaspoon salt

Using trussing string or heavy white thread, truss prepared chicken. Hook wing tips under back. Heat oil, butter and garlic in a heavy saucepan. Brown the chicken; remove from pot. Add onions, potatoes and carrots to pan drippings and sauté. Remove vegetables and reserve. Stir broth, water, rosemary and pepper into pan drippings.

Return the chicken to the pan; surround with vegetables. Baste with liquid; sprinkle vegetables with salt and cover. Cook at 350°F/180°C/gas mark 4 for 1 hour, basting twice with sauce, or until chicken is tender. Serve chicken and vegetables with sauce.

Chicken in Port

4 servings

1 spring chicken
1 oz/30 grams flour
1½ teaspoons salt
1 teaspoon paprika
Large pinch black pepper
½ oz/15 grams margarine
8 fl oz/220 ml Port
1 clove garlic, finely chopped
6 oz/170 grams mushrooms, sliced
4 fl oz/110 ml double cream

Cut the chicken into 8 pieces. Mix the flour, salt, paprika and pepper in a plastic bag. Dredge the chicken pieces in the bag.

Brown the chicken on all sides in the margarine. Add the port and let the chicken simmer for about 15 minutes.

Add the garlic, the mushrooms and the cream. Let simmer for another 10 minutes.

Chicken in a Potato Nest

4 servings

1 lb/450 grams cooked mashed potatoes
1 oz/30 grams butter or margarine
1 oz/30 grams flour
Salt to taste
½ teaspoon pepper
½ pint/¼ l chicken broth
2½ fl oz/75 ml double cream
3 oz/85 grams tinned sliced mushrooms
1 lb/450 grams cooked chicken, diced
2 tablespoons Parmesan cheese, grated

Line a buttered 8 to 9-inch/20 to 23-cm pie dish with the potatoes. Melt the butter in a pan, stir in the flour and seasonings. Add the broth gradually; stir until boiling. Add cream and mushrooms and cook for a few minutes.

Put the chicken into the prepared pie dish, cover with the sauce and sprinkle with the cheese. Bake in a 400°F/200°C/gas mark 6 oven for 25–30 minutes.

Chicken in Red Wine with Carrots and White Onions

4 servings

1 3½ lb/1½ kilo chicken, cut into serving pieces
3 tablespoons oil
1 clove garlic, finely chopped
¼ teaspoon thyme
Salt and pepper to taste
½ pint/¼ l dry red wine
2 sprigs parsley
12 small white onions, peeled
6 carrots, cut in 1-inch/2½-cm pieces

Wash the chicken and pat it dry. Heat the oil. Add garlic and cook briefly. Brown the chicken quickly on all sides. Add seasonings and red wine and simmer until nearly done (about 25 minutes).

Add vegetables and cook until tender.

Chicken Stew with Brandy

4 servings

1 2½ lb/1 kilo chicken or 2 small chickens
Olive oil
Butter
2½ fl oz/75 ml brandy
8 fl oz/220 ml white wine
12 fl oz/350 ml double cream
4 tomatoes, peeled, seeded and chopped into pieces
1 apple, cubed
10 green olives
10 small onions
Salt

Pepper
Tarragon
1 teaspoon curry paste
1 teaspoon chervil
1 teaspoon thyme
1 bay leaf
20 small mushroom caps
1 tablespoon parsley, chopped
Chopped chives

Cut the chicken into pieces. Brown the pieces in olive oil and a little butter. Pour off the fat when the pieces have become brown, add the brandy and flambé. Pour in the white wine. Add the tomatoes, apple, olives and onions to the stew. Season with salt, pepper, tarragon, curry paste, chervil, thyme and the bay leaf. Bake in a 350°F/180°C/gas mark 4 oven one hour or until the pieces are tender. Sauté the mushroom caps.

Remove the bay leaf. Transfer the chicken stew to a deep serving dish. Garnish with the mushroom caps and sprinkle with the parsley and chives. Serve with boiled noodles or rice.

Chicken Kebabs

Quantity Varies

Pieces of chicken liver wrapped up in bacon slices
Small pieces of chicken
Small onions
Tomato wedges
Pieces of pineapple
A couple of strips of green pepper

marinade

1 oz/30 grams brown sugar
1 tablespoon orange juice
1 teaspoon lemon juice
½ teaspoon ginger
8 fl oz/220 ml oil
Salt
Pepper
Pinch cayenne pepper

Alternate the meat and vegetables on a skewer. Combine the marinade ingredients and baste the meat and vegetables. Grill over charcoal or in the oven for 6 to 7 minutes on each side.

Serve with rice, preferably cooked in broth with chopped onion and seasoned with saffron. Also serve small bowls with the rest of the marinade with peanut butter sauce in them.

To make peanut butter sauce: beat together 12 fl oz/350 ml soured cream and 3 to 4 tablespoons chopped salted nuts. Spice with plenty of onion powder.

Summer Chicken with Fresh Tarragon

3 to 4 servings

1 2½–3 lb/1–1¼ kilo chicken
1 lemon
1 teaspoon salt
¼ to ½ teaspoon freshly ground black pepper
Several sprigs tarragon
1 oz/30 grams butter
Cream (optional)

Rub the chicken both inside and out with lemon, salt and pepper. Fill the chicken with sprigs of tarragon, perhaps even with a whole lemon and the butter. Bind the chicken together and sprinkle finely chopped tarragon on top.

Roast the chicken in a preheated 350°F/180°C/gas mark 4 oven on a rack over a roasting tin. Baste the chicken with water several times during baking. Cooking time varies, about 1 to 1¼ hours. When the drumstick can be turned in its joint, the chicken is done.

Stir a little water into the juice in the tin and bring to the boil. Add a little cream, if desired.

Chicken Kebabs

Chicken Surprise

5 servings

2 medium sized marrows
Butter
3 slices white bread, with crusts removed and cut into cubes
1 large egg
2½ oz/75 grams cheese, grated
Salt
Pepper
1 2½–3 lb/1–1¼ kilo chicken, cut into 4 pieces
Honey

Grate the washed and then dried marrows on the coarsest side of a grater. Sauté them in ½ oz/15 grams butter for 1 minute, making sure that they do not change colour. Then place them in a dish. Add the bread cubes, eggs, grated cheese, salt and pepper. Stir and season well.

Make a pocket between the skin and the meat on the chicken pieces by inserting your fingers. Place the bread filling into these pockets. Salt and pepper. Place the chicken pieces in a buttered oven dish and brush them with melted butter.

Bake them in the oven at 400°F/200°C/gas mark 6 for 50 minutes. Brush them with honey when 15 minutes remain of cooking time. Serve with fried potatoes, lightly cooked tomatoes and salad.

Chicken with White Wine

5 servings

About 3½ lb/1½ kilo chicken pieces
Salt
White pepper
1 tablespoon paprika
Butter
Oil
4 fl oz/110 ml cognac or whisky
1½ tablespoons Dijon mustard
4 oz/115 grams grated Cheddar cheese
12 fl oz/350 ml dry white wine
2½ fl oz/75 ml double cream
2 tablespoons grated cheese

Sprinkle salt, pepper and paprika over the chicken pieces. Brown them lightly in equal amounts of butter and oil. Pour warm cognac or whisky over them, flambé and allow them to burn out on their own.

Mix the mustard, cheese and wine and pour this mixture over the chicken. Allow to simmer slowly, covered, for 12 minutes. Strain the sauce, thicken it with the cream and pour it over the chicken again. Sprinkle with grated cheese.

Bake in oven at 450°F/230°C/gas mark 8 for 8 minutes. Serve with freshly cooked, butter-tossed spaghetti.

Chicken Breasts in Soured Cream

6 servings

8 oz/225 grams finely sliced smoked ham
6 chicken breasts, boned, skinned and split
6 rashers bacon, cut in half
2 tins condensed mushroom soup, undiluted
1 pint/½ l soured cream

Place the ham in the bottom of a casserole dish. Wrap each chicken piece in a piece of bacon, then place on the bed of ham. Mix the soup and cream together; pour over the chicken. Bake at 275°F/135°C/gas mark ½ 2½ to 3 hours.

Serve chicken on a bed of hot rice or mashed potatoes.

Stuffed Chicken Breasts

6 servings

½ oz/15 grams butter
12 oz/345 grams courgettes, chopped
1 tablespoon dill
Salt and freshly ground pepper to taste
6 chicken breast halves, boned, skinned and pounded thin
1 egg, beaten
Breadcrumbs

Melt butter in a large pan. Add the courgettes, dill, salt and pepper. Cook over medium heat until courgette is tender and loses moisture. Divide the courgette mixture among the chicken breast halves, using only enough filling so the chicken can be drawn up around it. Fold over the sides of the chicken to totally enclose the courgette. Secure with a toothpick.

Dip the chicken breasts in egg, then coat with breadcrumbs. Place in a lightly greased casserole and bake at 450°F/230°C/gas mark 8 about 15 minutes. Serve with boiled new potatoes and spinach.

Chicken Breasts with Celery Salad

4 servings

4 chicken breasts
1 lemon
Salt
Pepper
Butter
6 sticks celery
2 oz/60 grams walnuts, coarsely chopped
1½ oz/45 grams Roquefort cheese
4 fl oz/110 ml vinaigrette dressing (See index)
Lettuce
Snipped chives

Place the chicken breasts in a bowl with the juice from 1 lemon. Add salt and pepper. Allow the chicken to marinate while the salad is being made.

Cut the celery into small pieces and chop up the walnuts into fairly large pieces. Mash the cheese into the vinaigrette or mix it in a blender. Blend with the celery and the nuts. Place leaves of lettuce on individual plates or a large serving plate.

Fry the chicken breasts in butter. When they have become golden brown and are cooked through, cut them into slices and place them, warm, on the lettuce leaves. Place the salad on top of the chicken, sprinkle with snipped chives and decorate with watercress, if you have it on hand. Serve immediately while the chicken is warm.

It is also tasty to serve cold chicken leftovers, which have been sprinkled with lemon juice, in this manner.

Chicken or Turkey Cutlets in Tomato Sauce

4 servings

½ oz/15 grams butter or margarine
1 lb/450 grams chicken or turkey escalope
1 pint/½ l tomato juice
2 tablespoons onion, finely chopped
½ teaspoon dried savory
Salt or garlic salt to taste
Pepper to taste
Parsley

Melt butter in a non-stick pan. Add the chicken escalopes in a single layer. Cook over moderate heat, 1 to 2 minutes on each side, just until cooked through. Remove to a serving dish and keep warm. Drain pan.

Combine the remaining ingredients, except the parsley, in the pan. Raise heat to high and cook uncovered until juices are reduced by half. Pour the sauce over the escalopes and garnish with fresh parsley.

Curried Chicken Breasts

4 servings

1½ oz/45 grams flour
1 teaspoon salt
1 teaspoon curry powder
½ teaspoon crushed rosemary
4 chicken breasts
Margarine or butter

curry sauce
½ onion, chopped
½ oz/15 grams margarine or butter
1 small green apple, diced
1 clove garlic, crushed
1 to 2 teaspoons curry powder
1¼ oz/38 grams flour
½ pint/¼ l chicken stock
2½ fl oz/75 ml pineapple juice (from the tinned pineapples)
4 fl oz/140 ml cream
½ teaspoon salt

garnish
2 large bananas
1 tin pineapple slices in their own juice
Sliced red peppers
Roasted almond slivers

Mix the flour and spices together. Roll the chicken in the mixture. Brown in margarine in a frying pan. Place in a cooking pot. Add a little water and let simmer about 20 minutes.

For the sauce, sauté the chopped onion in margarine. Add the apple, garlic and curry. Sauté several

minutes. Sprinkle the flour on top. Pour in the stock and pineapple juice; boil several minutes. Beat in the cream. Season to taste with salt.

Peel the bananas. Divide them into bite-sized pieces. Roll them in the flour mixture you rolled the chicken in. Fry for several minutes in margarine. Pour the sauce onto a serving plate. Lay out the pineapple slices and place the chicken breasts over these. Garnish with banana pieces, sliced peppers and roasted almond slivers. Serve with boiled rice.

Baked Chicken Livers

4 servings

3 or 4 medium sized onions, sliced ¼ inch/½ cm thick
10 or 12 chicken livers
3 rashers streaky bacon
Salt and pepper to taste
¼ pint/140 ml sherry

Arrange onion slices in a flat, oblong casserole. Put 1 chicken liver on top of each onion; salt lightly. Cut each bacon rasher into quarters and place 1 quarter on each chicken liver. Sprinkle with salt and pepper. Pour sherry over all.

Cook at 350°F/180°C/gas mark 4 about 45 minutes or until bacon is crisp. Baste occasionally during cooking time. Serve 2 or 3 livers per portion.

Roast Capon with Orange Pecan Stuffing

6 to 8 servings

1 5 to 6 lb/2 kilo capon
2 oz/60 grams butter or margarine
8 oz/225 grams celery, thinly sliced
2 oz/60 grams onion, chopped
15 fl oz/425 ml water
6 slices white bread, toasted, cut in ½-inch/1-cm cubes
6 oz/170 grams oranges, segmented and chopped
3 oz/85 grams pecans, coarsely chopped
1 teaspoon orange rind, grated
1 teaspoon salt
½ teaspoon curry powder (optional)
Orange slices for garnish
Watercress for garnish

Wash, drain and dry the capon.

Prepare the stuffing: melt butter in a pan. Add the celery, onion and water; cook over moderate heat until the vegetables are tender. Combine the bread cubes, orange pieces, pecans, orange rind, ½ teaspoon salt and curry powder; mix. Add vegetables and mix carefully.

Sprinkle the remaining salt over the neck and body cavities of the capon. Stuff neck and body cavities loosely with the bread mixture. Skewer neck skin to back. Return legs and tail to tucked position. Place capon, breast side up, in an open roasting tin. Do not add water. Brush with melted butter or margarine. Cover the capon loosely with foil, crimping it to the edges of the dish. (Foil should not touch capon.) Place in a 325°F/165°C/gas mark 3 oven for about 3 hours. Remove the foil 45 minutes before the end of the roasting time to allow the bird to brown. Brush again with melted butter. Test and continue cooking if not done.

Roast Poussins with Savoury Stuffing

4 servings

4 poussins (about 1 lb/450 grams each)
8 thick slices white bread, crusts removed
1½ tablespoons parsley flakes
½ teaspoon salt
½ teaspoon dried sage and onion
¼ teaspoon freshly ground pepper
6 oz/170 grams butter
1 cup onions, finely chopped
4 chicken livers

Salt and pepper to taste
1½ oz/45 grams melted butter

Remove the giblets from the poussins; reserve the livers. Wash poussins and pat dry.

Cut the bread into ½-inch/1-cm cubes; place on a baking sheet. Bake at 350°F/180°C/gas mark 4 until golden, stirring occasionally. Remove from oven. Combine cubes with parsley, ½ teaspoon salt, sage and onion and ¼ teaspoon pepper; set aside.

Melt 6 oz/170 grams butter in a heavy pan. Add the onions and livers; cook until the livers are lightly browned and the onions tender. Remove livers; chop. Add the livers, onions and butter from the pan to the bread cube mixture; toss to mix well.

Salt and pepper poussins lightly. Pack tightly with stuffing; truss. Place in an ovenproof roasting tin, breast side up; brush with melted butter. Roast at 375°F/190°C/gas mark 5. Turn every 15 minutes and baste with butter and cooking juices. Cook a total of 45 minutes to 1 hour, until the juices run clear when the tip of a knife is inserted in the bird. Serve hot with wild rice and a green vegetable.

Summer Chicken with Fresh Tarragon

Poussins with Grapes

6 servings

6 poussins, 1–1¼ lb/450–565 grams each
4 oz/115 grams herb-seasoned croutons
4 oz/115 grams ripe olives, sliced
2½ fl oz/75 ml lemon juice
2½ fl oz/75 ml vinegar
2½ fl oz/75 ml vegetable oil
1 clove garlic, crushed
½ teaspoon dried thyme leaves
¼ to ½ teaspoon salt
Grape clusters

Dry the cavities of the birds. Mix the croutons and olives. Stuff each bird loosely with crouton-olive stuffing; fasten openings with skewers and lace shut with string. Place the birds, breast side up, in an ungreased, shallow roasting tin.

Mix lemon juice, vinegar, oil, garlic, thyme and salt; pour on birds. Bake uncovered in a 350°F/180°C/gas mark 4 oven for 2 hours, spooning the lemon mixture over the birds every 20 minutes.

Place on a warm serving dish. Garnish with grape clusters and parsley sprigs.

Poussins with Orange Sauce

4 servings

2 poussins, split in half
15 fl oz/425 ml orange juice
3 oz/85 grams orange marmalade
3 oz/85 grams redcurrant jelly
1 oz/30 grams cornflour
1 tin mandarin oranges (optional)

Roast birds in a 350°F/180°C/gas mark 4 oven for 45 minutes.

In a saucepan, combine the orange juice, marmalade and jelly. Heat, mixing until smooth. Add cornflour and stir until thick. Add drained mandarin oranges, if desired. Pour the sauce over the poussins and cook another 30–45 minutes.

Apricot Duck

4 to 6 servings

1 4–5 lb/1800–2250 grams roasting duck
1 lb/450 grams fresh apricots
1 orange
1 onion, finely chopped
Salt and pepper
2 to 3 tablespoons oil
3 tablespoons honey
10–15 fl oz/284–425 ml stock made with duck
   giblets
3 to 4 tablespoons apricot brandy

Chicken Surprise

Stuff the duck with half the stoned apricots and 3 strips of orange zest (the thin outer skin), onion and seasonings. Prick the skin of the duck with a fork to allow the fat to run out while cooking; season with salt and pepper.

Heat the oil in a roasting tin. When very hot, add the duck; baste all over with oil. Roast in a pre-heated 400°F/200°C/gas mark 6 oven; allow 20 minutes per pound. Half an hour before cooking is completed, spoon melted honey and juice of the orange over the duck. Ten minutes before the end of cooking, add the rest of the apricots to pan; heat through and brown slightly. Remove duck to warm dish; remove stuffing to bowl. Arrange roasted apricots around the duck.

Pour off fat from roasting pan. Put in stuffing; bring to the boil, stirring all the time. Taste for seasoning. Strain or blend in a blender or food processor. Return to heat and add apricot brandy. Serve at once with duck and apricots.

Duck in Brandy

4 to 6 servings

1 5–6 lb/2¼–2½ kilo duck
2 large onions, chopped
2 oz/60 grams parsley, finely chopped
1 bay leaf
½ teaspoon thyme
2 cloves garlic, crushed
3 measures brandy
1 pint/½ l red wine
2½ fl oz/75 ml olive oil or butter
12 oz/345 grams mushrooms, sliced
Salt and pepper

Clean the duck, then cut it into serving pieces. Place the duck pieces in a deep dish. Add onions, parsley, bay leaf, thyme, garlic, brandy and wine. Marinate at least 4 hours, preferably overnight.

Heat the oil; brown the pieces of duck about 15 minutes. Add marinade, mushrooms and seasonings. Cover tightly; simmer over low heat at least 1 hour.

Barbecued Game Birds

2 to 4 servings

2 plump game birds (partridge, grouse, quail etc.)
1 clove garlic
Salt
2 small onions, quartered
2 celery tops
2 sprigs parsley
2½ fl oz/75 ml olive oil
1 lemon, juice and grated rind
Dash Tabasco sauce
1 teaspoon onion juice
Large pinch thyme

Clean birds thoroughly and rinse in cold water; pat dry. Rub inside and out with garlic and salt. Insert an onion, celery top and parsley sprig into each cavity. Shake oil, lemon juice and rind, Tabasco sauce, onion juice and thyme in a wide-mouthed jar.

Place the birds on a rack in a covered roasting tin, roast in a 375°F/190°C/gas mark 6 oven until done to your liking, basting with sauce every 10 minutes, or grill over faintly glowing charcoal on an outdoor grill, turning and basting frequently until thoroughly done and tender.

Game Pie

4 to 6 servings

2 grouse (or other game birds)
8 oz/225 grams steak
8 oz/225 grams bacon
1 large onion, finely chopped
4–6 mushrooms
2 tablespoons chopped herbs
Salt and pepper
Pinch nutmeg
½ pint/¼ l red wine
½ pint/¼ l stock
8 oz/225 grams frozen puff pastry
1 egg

Cut the meat off the grouse (or other game birds), then cut the steak into small pieces and dice the bacon. Arrange them in layers with the onion, mushrooms, herbs and seasoning between each layer. Add ½ pint/¼ litre of red wine and enough stock to barely cover the meat. Cover with foil and bake very slowly in a pre-heated 325°F/163°C/gas mark 3 oven for about 1½ hours, until all meat is tender. Let cool completely.

Roll out the pastry and place a strip moistened with water, around the edge of the dish. Moisten the pastry strip and place a large piece of pastry on top. Press edges together. Cut off surplus and crimp edges. Make slashes in top to release steam and decorate with pastry leaves.

Put into a 425°F/220°C/gas mark 7 oven and bake for about 30 minutes. Serve hot or cold.

Fried Duckling

4 to 6 servings

1 3–4 lb/1¼–1½ kilo duckling, cut into serving pieces
4 oz/115 grams flour
2 teaspoons salt
¼ teaspoon pepper
2 oz/60 grams butter or margarine
Shortening
½ pint/¼ l water

Place 2 or 3 pieces of duckling in a paper bag with the flour, salt, pepper and paprika. Shake until thoroughly coated; repeat with the rest of the duckling pieces.

In a pan, heat the butter and enough shortening to make a ¼-inch/½-cm layer. Place the duckling in the hot fat, skin side down. Brown and turn. Add water and cover tightly.

Reduce the heat and cook slowly or bake in a 350°F/180°C/gas mark 4 oven about 1 hour. Uncover and continue to cook about 30 minutes, until duckling pieces are crisp on the outside.

Roast Goose with Apple-Sausage Stuffing

6 servings

12 oz/345 grams sausage meat
2½ oz/75 grams butter
1 medium sized onion, chopped
2 sticks celery, chopped
6 slices toasted white bread without crusts, cubed
1 large apple, peeled and chopped
½ teaspoon ground dried marjoram
3 teaspoons salt
½ teaspoon pepper
1 8 lb/3½ kilo goose
Juice of 1 lemon

giblet stock
Goose giblets and liver (including neck if available)
2 pints/1¼ l water
2 celery tops
1 small onion
2 cloves
Salt and pepper

gravy
3 oz/85 grams rendered goose fat or drippings
3 oz/85 grams flour
Salt and pepper
2 pints/1¼ l giblet stock

Fry the sausage in a heavy pan until well browned, breaking into bite-sized pieces as it cooks. Drain well; reserve. Melt butter in a pan. Add the onion and celery; cook until tender. Combine the sausage, onion, celery, butter, bread cubes, apple, marjoram, 1 teaspoon salt and pepper in a mixing bowl. Mix well and set aside.

Remove giblets from the goose; set aside. Remove and discard loose fat in body cavity; reserve for rendering, or discard. Wash goose well; pat dry. Rub the goose inside and out with the lemon juice and 2 teaspoons salt. Stuff neck cavity loosely; skewer shut. Spoon remaining stuffing into body cavity; truss. Be sure to tie wings and legs closely to the bird. Place the goose on a rack, breast side up; prick well on breast and thighs so that the fat will drain. Roast at 325°F/163°C/gas mark 3 for 3 to 3½ hours, or until a meat thermometer registers 185°F/85°C when inserted into the breast.

While the goose cooks, prepare the broth. Combine giblets, water, celery, onion and seasonings in a small saucepan; bring to the boil. Cover and simmer 30 minutes. Remove the liver; cook 30 minutes. Strain the broth and cool. Chop the liver and giblets; reserve.

Remove the goose to a serving dish when done; cover with a tent of aluminium foil while making the gravy. Combine goose drippings and flour in a medium sized saucepan; cook over low heat, stirring constantly, until lightly browned. Add salt and pepper. Slowly stir in giblet stock; cook, stirring constantly, over low heat until thickened. Add the reserved giblets and heat through.

Carve the goose. Serve with strained gravy and red cabbage or sauerkraut and apple sauce.

Roast Duck

2 to 4 servings

4–5 lb/2–2¼ kilo duck, fresh or frozen and thawed
Boiling water
Salt and pepper
2 small apples, oranges or lemons, or a combination, quartered

Remove the giblets and neck from inside the duck. Immerse the duck in boiling water for 1 minute. Remove, drain. Pat dry with kitchen towel. Sprinkle the cavity lightly with salt and pepper and stuff fruit into the cavity.

Truss the duck. Place on a rack in a roasting tin. Roast at 350°F/180°C/gas mark 4 for 30 minutes. Remove from oven. Pierce the duck all over (except breast) with a fork. Return duck to oven. Continue roasting, draining off the fat and piercing every 30 minutes, until the meat thermometer, placed in the meatiest part, reads 170°F/80°C, about 1½ to 2 hours. Remove and discard trussings and fruit. Cut the duck in half or quarters to serve.

For a crispier skin roast the duck at 450°F/230°C/gas mark 8 during the last 15 minutes of cooking.

Roast Goose with Giblet Stuffing

8 servings

1 9–11 lb/4–5 kilo goose with giblets, fresh if possible
1¼ pint/700 ml water
2½ oz/75 grams onion, sliced
2 oz/60 grams celery, diced
2 chicken stock cubes
Salt and pepper to taste
4 oz/115 grams butter
4 oz/115 grams onion, finely chopped
4 oz/115 grams celery, finely chopped
2 tablespoons parsley, chopped
1 tablespoon dried sage and onion
5 slices bread, without crusts, cubed
¼ pint/140 ml milk
1 oz/30 grams cornflour

Put the water, sliced onion, diced celery, stock cubes, salt, pepper and goose giblets, neck and liver if desired, into a small saucepan. Bring to the boil. Reduce heat. Simmer until tender. Remove from heat. Drain and reserve broth. Chop the meat from the neck, giblets and liver.

Meanwhile, melt butter in a large saucepan. Add the onion, celery, parsley, sage and onion, salt, pepper and half of the giblet meat. Stir to blend. Cover and simmer 12 minutes. Stir in bread cubes and milk, toss well.

Rinse the goose and pat dry. Pull off all inside fat. Rub inside and out with salt and pepper. Fill breast cavity loosely with stuffing. Put on a rack in a large roasting tin, breast side down. Cover with aluminium foil and roast at 400°F/200°C/gas mark 6 for 1 hour.

Remove the foil. Turn goose breast side up, lower heat to 350°F/180°C/gas mark 4 and continue roasting 2 hours, uncovered. Remove goose from oven and prick surface area all over with a fork. Return to oven and continue roasting 1 more hour until browned and drumsticks move easily. The internal temperature of the breast should register about 175°F/80°C. Transfer to a warm serving dish. Let stand 15 minutes before carving; temperature should increase slightly.

Pour off fat from the roasting tin drippings. Dissolve cornflour in reserved giblet broth. Deglaze. Cook and stir over medium heat until thickened. Add remaining chopped giblet meat. Taste and adjust seasonings.

American Pheasant

4 servings

1 pheasant
Salt and pepper
8 oz/225 grams butter
6–8 oz/170–225 grams fresh white breadcrumbs
Pinch cayenne pepper
4 tomatoes, halved and seasoned
4 rashers bacon
8 flat mushrooms

Cut the pheasant open along its back with a sharp knife. Remove backbone. Open it out and flatten with a heavy rolling pin. Season with salt and pepper. Melt butter in a large pan and, when hot, sauté pheasant on both sides. Remove from heat.

Cover the pheasant well with the breadcrumbs and sprinkle with a little cayenne pepper. Heat the grill and grill slowly so that the crumbs do not become too brown before the bird is cooked. Test with a skewer in the thickest part of the leg. At the same time grill the tomatoes. Also grill the bacon and mushrooms, filled with butter and seasonings.

When the pheasant is cooked serve it on a dish surrounded by grilled accompaniments.

Chicken with White Wine

Quail on Toast

4 servings

4 quail, split
2 oz/60 grams flour
½ teaspoon salt
Pinch pepper
2 oz/60 grams butter or margarine
½ pint/¼ l boiling water
1 pint/½ l single cream
4 fl oz/110 ml sherry
Buttered toast

Roll each piece of quail in flour seasoned with salt and pepper. Brown in butter on all sides. Pour boiling water over and cover. Let simmer until tender (15 to 20 minutes). Remove lid. Add cream and sherry and simmer for 10 minutes.

Place birds on pieces of buttered toast. Taste sauce for seasoning and pour it over the quail.

Chicken Breasts with Celery Salad

Sautéed Pheasant with Herbs

4 servings

2 lb/900 grams pheasant, cleaned and cut into
   serving pieces
Salt to taste
Freshly ground pepper to taste
1 oz/30 grams butter
2 whole cloves garlic, peeled
1 bay leaf
2 sprigs fresh thyme or ½ teaspoon dried thyme
8 fl oz/220 ml dry white wine
1½ oz/45 grams cold butter
2 tablespoons parsley, finely chopped

Sprinkle the pheasant pieces with salt and pepper.
Heat the butter in a pan and add the pieces, skin side
down. Cook about 2 or 3 minutes until the skin is
golden brown. Turn the pieces and continue cooking
about 3 minutes more. Add the garlic, bay leaf, thyme
and wine. Cover and cook 20 minutes or until the
pheasant is tender,

Transfer the pheasant pieces to a serving dish.
Swirl the cold butter into the pan sauce. Pour and
scrape the sauce (including garlic and thyme) over
the pheasant and serve sprinkled with chopped parsley.

Roast Guinea Fowl

4 servings

2 2–3 lb/900–1300 grams dressed guinea fowl
1½ teaspoons salt
1 lemon, quartered
4 rashers bacon, sliced

Rub birds inside and out with salt and lemon
wedges. Insert an onion in each one. Place bacon
over the backs of the birds. Roast in a 325°F/163°C/
gas mark 3 oven for 40 minutes, backs up. Turn birds
over in roasting tin and rearrange bacon over the
breasts of the birds. Cook 35 to 45 minutes or until
tender.

Squabs Stuffed with Almonds and Raisins

4 servings

4 tender squabs or baby pigeons
8 oz/225 grams cooked rice
2 onions, cooked
1½ oz/45 grams butter
3–4 tablespoons peeled, flaked almonds
1 tablespoon chopped herbs
4 tablespoons raisins

2–3 tablespoons sherry
4 rashers streaky bacon
2–3 tablepsoons oil
1–2 teaspoons flour
¼ pint/140 ml red wine
¼ pint/140 ml stock

Boil the rice until tender. Drain and let cool. Cook the onions, until soft, in the butter. Add the almonds and cook until all are golden brown. Add the rice to the pan. Cook for 1 minute then remove from heat. Add chopped herbs, raisins that have been soaking in sherry and seasonings. Stuff mixture into the pigeons.

Tie a slice of streaky bacon around the breast of each bird. Heat oil in a 400°F/200°C/gas mark 5 oven. Add the birds and baste thoroughly. Roast in the oven for about 35–40 minutes, basting and turning every 10 minutes. Remove the bacon for the last 15 minutes, to brown the breast. Remove to a serving dish and keep hot.

Pour off the oil and sprinkle flour into the roasting tin. Blend with the drippings and add wine and stock. Stir until smooth and boiling, add seasonings, pour into a sauce-boat.

Barbecued Turkey

10 to 12 servings

4 oz/115 grams onion, chopped
1 oz/30 grams butter
15 fl oz/425 ml ketchup
2 oz/60 grams soft brown sugar
1 clove garlic, crushed
1 lemon, thinly sliced
2½ fl oz/75 ml Worcester sauce
2 teaspoons prepared mustard
1 teaspoon salt
¼ teaspoon freshly ground pepper
1 12 lb/5½ kilo fresh or frozen turkey
2–3 tablespoons barbecue salt

Sauté the onion in butter, in a small saucepan, until lightly browned. Add remaining ingredients, except the turkey and barbecue salt. Simmer 20 minutes. Remove lemon slices. Store this barbecue sauce in a jar, in a refrigerator, if not to be used immmediately.

Thaw turkey if frozen. Rinse and pat dry.

Start a charcoal fire 20 to 30 minutes before cooking turkey, allowing about 5 lb/2½ kilos charcoal to start the fire. During the cooking period push burning charcoal to the centre and add more brickettes as needed around the edge.

Sprinkle the cavity of the turkey with barbecue salt. Insert a spit rod in front of its tail and run it diagonally through the breast bone. Fasten tightly with spit forks at both ends. Test for balance and adjust spit rod if necessary. Insert a meat thermometer into the thickest part of the thigh. Make sure the thermometer does not touch the bone or spit rod and that it will clear the charcoal as the spit turns.

Brush off grey ash from the coals and push coals to back of fire. Place a drip pan made of heavy duty foil directly under the turkey in front of the coals. Attach spit and start it rotating. Cook 25 minutes per lb/450 grams or to about 185°F/85°C on the meat thermometer. Baste frequently with barbecue sauce during the last 30 minutes of cooking.

Turkcy, Ham and Oyster Casserole

6 to 8 servings

4 oz/115 grams butter or margarine
1 oz/30 grams flour
1 pint/½ l milk
½ teaspoon salt
Large pinch pepper
¼ teaspoon dry mustard
1 lb/450 grams cooked turkey, diced
8 oz/225 grams cooked ham, chopped
1 pint/½ l oysters, preheated in juice
1½ lb/700 grams mashed potato
Paprika

Melt the butter in a saucepan. Stir in the flour and blend. Add milk, salt, pepper and mustard. Cook over a low heat, stirring, until smooth and thickened. Add turkey, ham and oysters.

Pour the mixture in a greased 3-pint/2-litre casserole. Make a border around the casserole with mashed potatoes and sprinkle with paprika. Bake in a 350°F/180°C/gas mark 4 oven for 30 minutes.

Baked Turkey Hash

2 servings

12 oz/345 grams turkey, diced
1 medium sized onion, diced
1 medium sized potato, diced
1 pimiento, diced
2 medium sized carrots, coarsely grated
1 teaspoon salt
2 teaspoons parsley, finely chopped
¼ teaspoon dried sage and onion
¼ pint/140 ml seasoned thin gravy

Combine all the ingredients except the gravy. Mix lightly to distribute seasoning evenly throughout the mixture. Blend in gravy and stir until all ingredients are moistened. Spoon into a greased 2-pint/1¼-litre casserole. Cover and bake in a 350°F/180°C/gas mark 4 oven for 45 minutes. Remove lid and continue to bake uncovered for 15 minutes. Serve with reheated extra gravy.

Turkey Gratin

4 to 6 servings

1–1½ lb/450–700 grams cooked turkey, chopped
1½ oz/45 grams butter
1 onion, chopped
2–3 large mushrooms, chopped
1¼ oz/38grams flour
15 fl oz/425 ml turkey or chicken stock
½–1 lb/225–450 grams cooked vegetables (peas, beans, corn, chopped carrots, pimiento, etc.) or 8 oz/225 grams cooked noodles
3–4 tablespoons double cream
1 tablespoon chopped parsley and thyme
4–5 tablespoons Cheddar cheese, grated

Melt the butter and cook the onion until tender. Add the mushrooms and cook for 1 minute. Sprinkle in flour and blend well. Add the stock and bring to the boil, stirring constantly. Add the chopped turkey and any available cooked vegetables or cooked noodles. Stir well into the sauce. Add cream and herbs.

Turn into a buttered baking dish and sprinkle thickly with grated cheese and a little paprika. Grill until crisp and brown all over. Serve with cooked noodles, rice or potatoes.

Turkey Fricassée

4 servings

3 oz/85 grams butter
1½ oz/45 grams flour
15 fl oz/425 ml mixed turkey stock and milk
½ teaspoon onion powder
1 tablespoon parsley, chopped
1 tablespoon thyme
1 tablespoon powdered bay leaf
¼ teaspoon mace
2 egg yolks
3–4 tablespoons cream
1 lb/450 grams cold turkey meat
4 rashers bacon, cut in half
8 mushroom caps

Melt half the butter. Add flour and pour on mixed stock and milk. Blend well. Bring to the boil, stirring constantly. Simmer for a few minutes. Then add onion powder, herbs and seasonings. Beat egg yolks with a little cream. Add a little sauce then add the egg yolk to the sauce. Do not allow to boil.

Cut the cold turkey in slices. Place it in a buttered, ovenproof dish. Cover with buttered greaseproof paper and heat in a preheated 325°F/163°C/gas mark 3 oven for 10 to 15 minutes. Spoon the sauce over the turkey and return to oven for 10 minutes, being careful not to boil the sauce.

Meanwhile, roll up the bacon rashers and put them on skewers. Grill until crisp. Put the mushrooms into a buttered dish with seasoning and a pat of butter on each. Cook in the oven for 15 minutes at the same time as the turkey. Arrange mushrooms around the sides of the dish and bacon rolls down the centre. Serve hot, with rice or mashed potatoes.

Curried Chicken Breasts

Meat

Boiled Beef and Carrots

6 servings

3–4 lb/1½–2 kilos silverside of beef
1 large onion, stuck with 2 cloves
4–6 small onions, whole
6 peppercorns
1 bay leaf
Some parsley stalks
Sprig of thyme
8–10 medium sized carrots
2 small turnips
3 sticks celery
8 oz/225 grams flour
8 oz/225 grams suet
3 tablespoons parsley, chopped
½ tablespoon thyme
½ tablespoon marjoram

Put the beef, large onion, peppercorns, bay leaf, parsley stalks, sprig of thyme, enough water to cover meat and a little salt in a large pot. Bring to the boil slowly; remove any scum that rises to the surface, put a lid on the pot and simmer for 1 hour.

Peel and quarter the carrots and turnips length-ways. Remove the herbs and the single onion from the pot; add the carrots, turnips, celery and small onions. Simmer for another hour.

Sift the flour with a pinch of salt. Mix in finely shredded suet, parsley, thyme, marjoram and pepper. Mix in enough water to make a light dough. Divide the dough into pieces about the size of a small walnut, rolling it between your hands. Bring the liquid the meat has been cooking in to the boil. Drop the dumplings into the boiling liquid, cover the pot and cook them for about 15–20 minutes.

Serve the beef on a large dish surrounded by the vegetables and dumplings and serve the cooking soup in a separate sauceboat.

Vegetable-Stuffed Beef

6 servings

2 lb/900 grams sirloin beef, boned out but left flat
2 oz/60 grams butter or margarine
4 oz/115 grams onion, finely chopped
4 oz/115 grams carrot, finely chopped
4 oz/115 grams celery, finely chopped
8 oz/225 grams apple, chopped, peeled and cored
2 tablespoons parsley, chopped
1 teaspoon salt
½ teaspoon ground sage
½ teaspoon marjoram
1 large slice fresh bread, cubed
18 fl oz/500 ml water
2 teaspoons cornflour

Lay the meat flat on a board; trim any excess fat; score the top side with a sharp knife. In a large flame-proof casserole melt 1½ oz/45 grams of butter; sauté the onion, carrot and celery until tender, about 5 minutes. Add the apple, parsley and seasonings; cook 3 minutes longer. Add the bread cubes; mix well.

Spread the stuffing on the unscored side of the meat, leaving a 1-inch/2½-cm margin all around. Roll up lengthwise; tie in several places with string. In the same casserole, melt the remaining butter; brown the meat on all sides. Add 15 fl oz/425 ml of water. Cover and cook in a 350°F/180°C/gas mark 4 oven for 1½ hours or until the meat is tender.

Remove the meat to a heated serving dish; remove the string. Blend the cornflour and remaining water together; add to the drippings in the casserole. Cook, stirring, until the gravy is thickened. Slice the meat into ½-inch/1-cm slices. Serve with hot gravy.

Brisket in Beer

4 to 6 servings

3½ lb/1½ kilos brisket of beef
1 teaspoon seasoned salt
1 teaspoon paprika
1 clove garlic, crushed
½ pint/¼ l chilli sauce
15 fl oz/425 ml light ale
1 onion, sliced
4 medium sized potatoes

Trim the excess fat from the brisket. Sprinkle seasoned salt, paprika and garlic over both sides of the brisket.

Place the meat in a shallow roasting tin and roast on a high heat for 20 minutes. Turn the brisket and continue on a high heat for another 20 minutes. Reduce the heat to 350°F/180°C/gas mark 4. Add the chilli sauce, beer and onion; cover tightly and bake for 1 hour.

Meanwhile peel the potatoes and cut them into 1-inch/2½-cm thick slices. Add the potatoes to the brisket and continue cooking, covered, 1 hour or until tender. Carve the meat diagonally across the grain into thin slices. Serve the cooking juices with the carved roast.

Barbecued Brisket

4 to 6 servings

1 onion, diced
1 clove garlic, chopped
2 lb/900 grams brisket, cut into 1-inch/2½-cm pieces
8 oz/225 grams mushrooms, sliced
¼ pint/140 ml beef stock
¼ pint/140 ml barbecue sauce
½ oz/15 grams cornflour (optional)

Place the onion, garlic and mushrooms in a heavy baking dish. Top with the meat; add the stock and barbecue sauce. Bake at 300°F/150°C/gas mark 2 about 3 hours, until the meat is tender. Remove the fat from the resultant gravy.

For a slightly thickened gravy, remove ½ pint/¼ litre liquid from the pot; mix with the cornflour. Return to the pot; stir until slightly thickened. Serve the brisket with hot buttered noodles or rice.

Fillet Steak Provencale

Fillet Steak with Garlic Butter

Braised Salt Beef

8 to 10 servings

4–5 lb/1800–2250 grams salt beef
2 bay leaves
5 peppercorns
2 sprigs parsley
1 bunch celery, cut in chunks
1 small onion, sliced
Whole cloves
1 oz/30 grams butter or margarine, melted
1 tablespoon prepared mustard
2 oz/60 grams brown sugar
4 fl oz/110 ml ketchup
3 tablespoons vinegar
3 tablespoons water

Rinse the beef and place it in a large pot. Add enough cold water to cover, bay leaves, peppercorns, parsley, celery and onion. Cover and simmer about 45 minutes per lb/450grams or until tender. Drain.

Place the meat in a shallow baking dish. Stick a few whole cloves in it and season. Combine the remaining ingredients; cook over medium heat until well blended. Pour this over the meat and bake in a 350°F/180°C/gas mark 4 oven 30 minutes, basting with the liquid several times.

Barbecued Rump Steak

8 servings

3 lb/1¼ kilos rump steak, ½–2 inches/1 cm–5 cms thick
4 fl oz/110 ml wine vinegar
2½ fl oz/75 ml ketchup
2 tablespoons soy sauce
1 teaspoon salt
2 teaspoons Worcester sauce
1 teaspoon prepared mustard
¼ teaspoon ground garlic
¼ teaspoon pepper

Trim the fat from the meat. Place the meat in a clear plastic bag; set in a deep bowl. Mix the vinegar, ketchup, soy sauce, salt, Worcester sauce, mustard, garlic and pepper; pour the sauce over the meat. Close the bag. Marinate 2–3 hours at room temperature or overnight in the refrigerator. Turn the bag occasionally to distribute the marinade. Remove meat from the bag; reserve the marinade. Place the meat in a grill pan and grill 6–8 inches/15–20 cm from the heat, about 50–60 minutes. Turn the meat every 10 minutes. Baste with marinade the last 15–20 minutes.

Beef in Spicy Sauce

6 to 8 servings

3 tablespoons oil
3–3½ lb/1¼–1½ kilos boned, rolled beef
3 tablespoons Worcester sauce
½ teaspoon salt
1½ oz/45 grams butter or margarine
2 cloves garlic, halved
Water
8 oz/225 grams onion rings, sliced

In a large, heavy, ovenproof pan, heat the oil until very hot. Pat the meat dry and add it to the dish. Brown it well, about 3 minutes on each side. Pour off the oil.

Combine the Worcester sauce and salt; brush it over both sides of the meat. Spread ½ oz/15 grams of the butter over the meat. Place the garlic around the meat. Bake, uncovered, in a preheated 350°F/180°C/gas mark 4 oven 15 to 20 minutes for medium rare or longer if a more well done piece is desired. Remove the steak from the dish; keep warm. Pour off and measure the drippings, discarding the garlic.

Add water to the drippings to make up to 8 fl oz/220 ml. Set aside.

Melt the remaining butter. Add the onions and sauté 5 minutes. Add the reserved drippings. Bring to boiling point. Slice the meat and serve with sauce.

Beef Hash

4 servings

1 lb/450 grams cooked beef, chopped
4 small potatoes, cooked and chopped (about 1 lb/450 grams)
1 medium sized onion, chopped
1 tablespoon parsley, chopped
½ teaspoon salt
Large pinch pepper
2 oz/60 grams cooking fat

Mix the beef, potatoes, onion, parsley, salt and pepper. Heat the fat in a 10-inch/25-cm pan over medium heat until melted. Spread the beef mixture evenly in the pan. Fry, turning frequently, until browned, 10 to 15 minutes.

Pot Roast

Fillet Steak Provencale

6 servings

2 tablespoons oil
1 oz/30 grams butter
6 thick tomato slices
4 cloves garlic, crushed
6 aubergine slices, sliced lengthwise
6–12 thin slices fillet steak
Salt
Pepper

Heat the fat in a pan and sauté the tomatoes and garlic over medium heat for 8 to 10 minutes, turning the tomatoes from time to time. Remove the tomatoes to a heated dish and sauté the aubergine in the same pan until tender and lightly browned on both sides. Place the tomatoes back in the pan. Season with salt and pepper. Keep very warm.

Heat another pan. Sprinkle both sides of the steak slices with salt and pepper and sauté them 1 minute on each side. Serve the meat on a heated dish surrounded with aubergine and tomato.

Sirloin Steak Grill

8 servings

2 lb/900 grams sirloin steak
½ pint/¼ l salad oil
½ pint/¼ l dry red wine
4 tablespoons soy sauce
2 tablespoons spring onions, chopped
1 clove garlic, chopped
1 teaspoon salt
¼ teaspoon pepper

Place the meat in a shallow dish; combine the remaining ingredients and pour them over the meat. Marinate at least 4 hours. Grill 5 to 7 minutes on each side 3 inches from the heat; baste frequently. Slice thinly on the diagonal.

Fillet Steak with Garlic Butter

4 servings

8 to 10 potatoes
1 oz/30 grams butter or margarine
1½–2 lb/700–900 grams fillet steak in the piece
½ oz/15 grams butter or margarine
½ teaspoon salt
Black pepper
Water
2 tomatoes

garlic butter
2 oz/60 grams butter
2 cloves garlic

Preheat oven to 450°F/230°C/gas mark 8. Peel and slice potatoes and spread them out in a greased, ovenproof dish. Season with salt; dot with butter. Cover with foil and place in the centre of the oven for 15 minutes. Remove the foil and cook for an additional 30 minutes, moving them around gently from time to time.

Trim any long tendons from the meat. Melt the butter in a frying pan or casserole and brown the meat slowly on all sides. Season with salt and pepper. Lower the heat and cook, covered, for 10 to 15 minutes. Lift out the meat and leave to stand for a short while. Add a little water to the pan juices and stir. Pour gravy over the potatoes.

Carve the meat into slices when the potatoes are ready and arrange on a serving plate. Cut the tomatoes in half and use as a garnish.

Make the garlic butter: melt the butter in a saucepan and add the crushed garlic. Pour the garlic butter over the meat, potatoes and tomato. Up to this stage, the dish can be prepared in advance.

Shortly before serving, place the dish on the top shelf of the oven at 450°F/230°C/gas mark 8 and heat through.

Roast Beef with Nobis Sauce

Old Fashioned Beef Mould

4 to 6 servings

1 lb/450 grams steak
8 oz/225 grams bacon
6 oz/170 grams fresh breadcrumbs
Grated nutmeg
1 tablespoon Worcester sauce
1 egg
1 oz/30 grams butter
1 oz/30 grams flour
½ pint/¼ l milk
2 teaspoons English mustard (more if strong
   flavour desired)
1 tablespoon white wine vinegar
Dash Tabasco sauce
Salt and pepper

Mince the beef and bacon and combine with the breadcrumbs, nutmeg and Worcester sauce. Mix with the beaten egg. Pack the mixture into the top of a well greased double boiler, covering with a double layer of greaseproof paper or foil. Tie the paper on tightly and steam for 2 hours.

To make a mustard sauce: melt the butter. Remove the pan from the stove and add flour and milk. Bring to the boil, stirring continuously. Boil for 2 minutes. Add the mustard, mixed with vinegar and a dash of Tabasco, and seasoning to taste.

Turn out the meat mould and serve with the mustard sauce.

Beef Pot Pie

4 servings

1 medium sized onion, peeled and chopped
1½ lb/700 grams stewing steak
1 oz/30 grams flour
Salt and pepper
1 teaspoon crushed thyme
2 teaspoons dill
½ pint/¼ l dry red wine
1½ pint/850 ml beef stock
8 oz/225 grams fresh mushrooms, thickly sliced
Pastry for pie crust, unbaked

Sauté the oil in a heavy pan, remove it and set to one side. Trim, cube and dredge the meat in flour seasoned with salt and pepper. Brown the cubes in hot oil on all sides, a few cubes at a time, adding more oil as needed.

Return the beef and onions to the pan and add the thyme and dill. Add the wine, cover and simmer for 3 minutes. Add the stock and mushrooms and stir well. Simmer, uncovered, for 1 hour or until the beef is tender and the gravy has thickened.

If a thicker gravy is desired, blend ½ oz/15 grams of flour with ¼ pint/140 ml water and add, a little at a time, until the gravy reaches the desired consistency.

Cool to room temperature. Turn into a pie dish and cover with a pastry top and bake in a moderate oven until the pastry is golden.

Rib Roast

10 to 16 servings

8 lb/3½ kilo aitchbone of beef
Salt and pepper

Stand the roast, fat side up, on a wire rack in a shallow roasting tin. Add no water but insert a meat thermometer into the middle of the joint making sure the point is touching only meat. Roast, uncovered, in the oven at 325°F/163°C/gas mark 3 until the thermometer registers 140°F/60°C for rare, 160°F/71°C for medium and 170°F/77°C for well done. Cook for about 23 to 25 minutes per lb/450 grams for rare, 27 to 30 minutes for medium and 32 to 35 minutes for well done.

Remove the roast from the oven and place it on a large, warm serving dish. Slice as desired. Season with salt and pepper.

Roast Beef with Nobis Sauce

8 servings

4 lb/1800 grams sirloin of beef
2½ teaspoons salt
½ to 1 teaspoon freshly ground black pepper

Preheat oven to 375°F/190°C/gas mark 5. Season the meat on all sides with salt and pepper. Stick a meat thermometer into the joint so that the tip of the thermometer is in the middle of the roast. Place the meat in a roasting tin and put in the oven. Cook 1 to 1¼ hours. Serve with Nobis sauce (see below).

Nobis sauce

4 servings

1 egg
2½ to 3 teaspoons vinegar
½ teaspoon salt
¼ teaspoon black pepper
1 teaspoon light French mustard
1 tablespoon snipped chives
¼ to ½ clove garlic, crushed

Boil the egg for 3 minutes exactly. Break open the egg and scrape out the insides with a spoon into a bowl. Alternate adding drops of vinegar and oil while beating constantly so that the sauce is well blended before adding the next drops. The sauce should thicken to the consistency of mayonnaise.

Season with salt, pepper, mustard, chives and garlic and refrigerate before serving.

Hungarian Goulash

Pot Roast

6 to 8 servings

2½ lb/1¼ kilos silverside of beef
Salt
Pepper
7 pints/4 l strong beef stock
12 leeks (white part only)
6 carrots, cut into pieces
6 medium onions, peeled
12 potatoes, all the same size, peeled
2 fresh fennel bulbs, well trimmed and sliced
Cauliflower
24 Brussels sprouts
Parsley

Place the stock in a large pot. Add the carrots and onions when it starts to boil. Cook for several minutes, then add the leeks and fennel.

Boil the potatoes and cauliflower separately in salted water. Do the same with the Brussels sprouts.

Tie the beef up well, leaving a long piece of string hanging from the meat. Season with salt and pepper. When all the vegetables are cooked, remove them with a draining spoon and keep them warm. Place the meat in the simmering stock and let it simmer

until it feels done, about 7 to 10 minutes per lb/450 grams. Pick up the meat and cut a slice to see if it is pink inside. Add more stock, if necessary. The meat should be pink on the inside.

When the meat is done, take it out of the liquid and remove the string. Cut into thin slices.

Meanwhile, place the vegetables in the meat liquid and make sure that they become well heated. Place the ingredients in a large, deep serving bowl and pour the liquid over them. Serve immediately. On the table, you should have different kinds of mustard, pickles, grated horseradish, a peppermill and coarse salt.

Leftover cooking broth makes an excellent soup for the next day.

Savoury Pot Roast

8 servings

1 4lb/1800 grams pot roast
½ teaspoon salt
¼ teaspoon pepper
1 oz/30 grams flour
2 oz/60 grams butter
3 onions, sliced
3 carrots, peeled and sliced
2 sticks celery, sliced
¼ pint/140 ml tomato sauce
1 pint/½ l water
1 bay leaf
¼ pint/140 ml red wine

Wipe the meat with a damp cloth. Combine the salt, pepper and flour. Rub the seasoned flour on the meat.

Melt the butter in a large pan. Brown the meat on all sides. Add the onions; brown. Add the carrots, celery, tomato sauce, water, bay leaf and red wine. Cover and simmer 3 hours.

Slice the meat. Serve with cooking juices, accompanied by rice or potatoes.

Sweet and Sour Pot Roast

8 to 10 servings

1 oz/30 grams shortening
5 lb/2½ kilo pot roast
4 oz/115 grams onion, sliced
½ pint/¼ l vinegar
6 oz/170 grams brown sugar
¼ teaspoon nutmeg
½ teaspoon salt

Melt the shortening in a heavy saucepan. Brown the meat in the melted fat. Remove the meat. Add the onions and cook until soft. Return the meat to the saucepan. Add the remaining ingredients. Cover and simmer over low heat until the meat is tender, about 3½ hours. If desired, thicken the liquid with a butter and flour liaison and cook 5 minutes.

Hungarian Goulash

4 servings

1 to 1½ lb/450 to 700 grams trimmed stewing steak
4 to 5 onions
14 oz/400 grams tinned tomatoes
1 to 2 cloves garlic, crushed
1½ teaspoons salt
¼ teaspoon black pepper
1 teaspoon thyme
About 1 tablespoon paprika
2 oz/60 grams tomato paste
Water (optional)

Cut the meat into sugar-cube size. Peel and cut the onions into large pieces. Mix the meat, onions, tomatoes with juice and spices together in a pot.

Simmer, covered, for about 45 minutes or until the meat feels tender. Add water, if necessary, while simmering. Season to taste and serve with boiled potatoes or rice.

Steak with Seasoned Butter

6 servings

1 lb/450 grams butter
Pinch white pepper
1 tablespoon parsley, finely chopped
2 tablespoons lemon juice
1 tablespoon fresh horseradish
1 teaspoon sugar
½ teaspoon dry mustard
1 tablespoon onion, finely grated
6 individual steaks of your choice

Soften the butter at room temperature for 1 hour. Transfer to a small mixing bowl. Add all the other ingredients, except the steaks. Cream the mixture with the back of a spoon, then beat until mixed thoroughly.

Preheat the grill. Spread seasoned butter over one side of each steak. Place under the grill, butter side up. Cook as preferred. Remove from the grill and spread seasoned butter on the other side of each steak. Return to the grill until cooked to your liking.

Serve the steaks with toast spread with the remaining seasoned butter. Leftover butter may be refrigerated for later use.

Beef and Aubergine Pie

Roast Ribs with Garden Vegetables

4 servings

3 lb/1¼ kilos beef ribs
1 teaspoon salt
¼ teaspoon pepper
1 lb/450 grams carrots, cleaned and halved
1 lb/450 grams potatoes, peeled and halved
8 oz/225 grams fresh green beans
4 small white onions
15 fl oz/425 ml beef broth
2 tablespoons horseradish
2 teaspoons prepared mustard
1 oz/30 grams cornflour
2½ fl oz/75 ml water

Trim excess fat from the meat. Place the meat in a 13×9×2-inch/33×23×5-cm roasting tin; sprinkle with salt and pepper. Roast uncovered in a 350°F/180°C/gas mark 4 oven 2 hours; drain the fat. Add the next 4 ingredients. Mix the broth, horseradish and mustard; pour over meat and vegetables. Cover with foil; bake 1 to 1½ hours longer or until tender.

Arrange the meat and vegetables on a serving dish; keep warm. Strain the broth; remove excess fat. Add water, if necessary, to make 1 pint/½ litre and return to the roasting tin. Mix cornflour and 2½ fl oz/75 mls cool water; stir into the tin. Bring to the boil over medium heat, stirring constantly and boil 1 minute. Serve this gravy with meat and vegetables.

Barbecued Ribs

4 servings

4 lb/1800 grams beef ribs
2 teaspoons salt
½ teaspoon pepper
8 oz/225 grams tomato purée
2½ fl oz/75 ml ketchup
2 oz/30 grams brown sugar
2½ fl oz/75 ml vinegar
2 tablespoons prepared mustard
4 oz/115 grams onion, chopped
1 clove garlic, crushed
1 tablespoon chilli powder

Place the meat in a covered frying pan and cook slowly for 1½ hours, turning occasionally. Season with salt and pepper. Combine the tomato purée, ketchup, brown sugar, vinegar, mustard, onion, garlic and chilli powder in a saucepan and simmer 5 minutes. Remove each rib from the pan, dip in sauce to coat all sides and place on a grill, brushing with sauce and turning occasionally for 20 to 30 minutes, or until done.

Beef Stew

6 servings

3 tablespoons corn oil
2 lb/900 grams stewing steak, cut in 2-inch/5-cm cubes
1 beef stock cube
2 teaspoon salt
1 bay leaf
¼ teaspoon dried thyme leaves, crushed
2¼ pints/1¼ l water
6 carrots
12 small white onions
1 oz/30 grams cornflour

In a pan, heat the corn oil over medium heat. Add the meat, brown on all sides. Add the next 4 ingredients and 2 pints/1¼ litres of the water. Cover; bring to the boil. Reduce the heat and simmer 1½ hours. Add the carrots and onions. Simmer ½ hour or until tender.

Mix the cornflour and remaining water, stir into the stew. Bring to the boil, stirring constantly; boil 1 minute.

Mince with Green Peppers

Beef Bourgignon

6 to 8 servings

2½ lb/1¼ kilos stewing steak
1½ oz/45 grams butter
½ teaspoon coarsely ground black pepper
2 teaspoons salt
2 large onions, chopped
6 cloves garlic, crushed
6 oz/170 grams belly of pork
2½ fl oz/75 ml brandy
2 tablespoons tomato paste
1 oz/30 grams flour
½ pint/¼ l water
1 bottle Burgundy
1 carrot, cut into pieces
1 piece celeriac
2 teaspoons thyme
1 bay leaf
1 sprig parsley
Soy sauce
25 small onions
10 oz/285 grams fresh mushrooms
Noodles with butter

Cut the meat into 1½-inch/3½-cm cubes and brown it in butter in a hot stew pan. Add salt and pepper. Add the onions to the stew together with the garlic cloves. Add belly of pork, diced.

Flambé with the brandy. Add the tomato paste, flour, water and wine. Stir in the pieces of carrot and celeriac and the thyme, bay leaf and parsley. Place over low heat and simmer, uncovered, for 2 hours. Add a little more water if necessary.

When the meat is done, remove it from the stew and place in a serving dish. The sauce may be thickened using a flour and butter liaison and should be allowed to boil for another 5 minutes. Flavour with a few tablespoons of soy sauce and strain it over the meat.

Boil the small onions for several minutes, peel them and glaze them with a few spoonfuls of the sauce before serving. Brush the mushrooms and brown them in butter. Cook the noodles, rinse them quickly in cold water and reheat quickly with butter. Serve the onions, mushrooms and noodles with the stew.

Hunter's Stew

8 servings

3 lb/1¼ kilos stewing steak, cubed
2 pints/1¼ l water
8 peppercorns
8 whole cloves
2 whole bay leaves
2 teaspoons salt
1 teaspoon marjoram
3 lb/1¼ kilos chicken, cubed
2 medium sized onions, peeled and cut into rings
5 large carrots, peeled and sliced
2 sprigs parsley, chopped
4 sticks celery, chopped
3 leeks, chopped
½ teaspoon white pepper
3 sprigs dill, chopped
½ bunch parsley, chopped

Cover the meat with water; bring to the boil. Tie the peppercorns, cloves and bay leaves in a cloth bag; drop into the boiling meat. Sprinkle 1 teaspoon of salt and marjoram over, simmer 2 hours in a covered saucepan. Add the chicken; simmer, covered.

Put the butter into a pan. Add the vegetables, 1 teaspoon salt and pepper; sauté over low heat until tender. Take the herb bag out and discard. Remove the meat from the liquid. Add the sautéed vegetables to the meat stock; simmer until tender. Add the meat. Pour into a serving dish; sprinkle with chopped dill and parsley.

Mince and Pasta

Beef and Aubergine Pie

6 servings

2½ lb/1¼ kilo stewing steak
Butter for frying
1 oz/30 grams flour
1 teaspoon salt
¼ teaspoon black pepper
1 large onion, chopped
1 large aubergine, sliced and peeled
4 oz/115 grams fresh mushrooms
1 tin chopped tomatoes
12 fl oz/350 ml beef broth
2 cloves garlic, crushed
2 teaspoons marjoram
3 to 4 tablespoons red wine
2 to 3 teaspoons arrowroot, mixed with a little
   water
Stuffed olives, cut in half
Snipped parsley
8 oz/225 grams frozen pastry crust, just thawed
1 egg, beaten

Cut the meat into 1¼-inch/2½-cm cubes, dredge in flour and brown in butter in a frying pan. Season with salt and pepper. Place the meat in a stew pan. Brown the onion, aubergine and mushrooms, each separately, in the frying pan and place them in the stew pan. Pour over the crushed tomatoes and broth. Bring to the boil and season with the garlic and marjoram.

Simmer the stew for about an hour, or until the meat feels very tender. Season with red wine toward the end of the simmering time. Thicken with the arrowroot, which has been mixed with a little water, so that the stew has a fine consistency. Pour into a pie dish. Garnish with sliced olives and snipped parsley.

Roll out the pastry into a ¼-inch/½-cm thick crust. Brush the edges of the dish with a beaten egg. Place the pastry on top. Press well on to the edges of the dish, make a hole in the crust for the steam to escape and place in a 400°F/200°C/gas mark 6 oven for about 20 to 25 minutes.

Mince with Green Peppers

8 servings

1¼ lb/565 grams minced beef
1¼ oz/38 grams butter or margarine
3 onions, peeled and chopped
2½ teaspoons salt
½ teaspoon ground black pepper
2 to 3 tablespoons tomato paste
4 to 5 green peppers
1½ to 2 tablespoons snipped fresh thyme (or 1½
   teaspoons dried thyme)

Dash cayenne pepper (optional)
1 small beef stock cube (optional)

Brown the meat in a little butter or margarine in a large frying pan. Stir so that the meat crumbles into little pieces. Peel and chop the onions and brown them with the meat toward the end of the browning process.

Turn the meat and onion into a stew pan. Add the tomatoes, salt, pepper and tomato paste. Cover and simmer over fairly low heat for 10 minutes.

In the meantime, remove the seeds and membranes from the peppers. Cut into thin strips then divide the strips into pieces. Add the peppers and the thyme to the stew. Simmer the stew for another 5 to 8 minutes so that the peppers become somewhat soft.

Adjust the seasoning if necessary; melt a stock cube in the stew, if desired, or if the stew has a weak flavour. Serve with boiled new potatoes.

Mince and Pasta

4 servings

2 large onions
1 small piece celeriac
12 oz/345 grams minced beef
About 1 teaspoon salt
¼ teaspoon white or black pepper
2 teaspoons paprika or chilli powder
1 stock cube
3 tablespoons tomato paste
About 8 fl oz/220 ml water
Pasta (shells or penne)

Peel and chop the onions and cut the celeriac into small cubes. Brown the meat in a pan while stirring, so that it crumbles evenly. Sauté the onion and celeriac with the meat when the meat is almost all brown. Season and add the stock cube, tomato paste and water. Stir well and simmer for several minutes.

Prepare the pasta according to the directions on the packet (make enough for 4 servings). Add the cooked pasta to the stew.

Meatballs in Vegetable Stew

4 servings

3 onions, peeled and sliced
6 potatoes, peeled and quartered
2½ oz/75 grams celeriac, cut in small cubes
2 to 3 carrots, thinly sliced
14 oz/400 grams tinned, chopped tomatoes
4 fl oz/110 ml vegetable broth
2 tablespoons tomato paste
1 teaspoon salt
½ teaspoon lemon pepper
¼ teaspoon cayenne pepper
1 green pepper, seeded and cut in strips

1 red pepper, seeded and chopped
1 leek, finely chopped

meatballs
10 oz/285 grams minced veal or beef
½ oz/15 grams breadcrumbs
4 fl oz/110 ml milk
½ teaspoon salt
Large pinch pepper
1 egg

yoghurt salad
1 pint/½ l natural yoghurt
¼ fresh cucumber
1 clove garlic, crushed
¼ teaspoon salt
Large pinch pepper

Place the onion, potatoes, celeriac and carrots in a pot. Add the crushed tomatoes, broth, tomato paste and spices and simmer until the vegetables begin to feel soft. Add the peppers and leek.

Mix the meatball ingredients together and shape them into small balls. Add them to the vegetables and let them simmer for the final 5 minutes.

Serve with yoghurt salad. To make the salad, drain the yoghurt for abut 2 hours in a paper coffee filter.

Grate the cucumber coarsely and press as much liquid out of it as possible. Mix it with the yoghurt just before serving. Season with the garlic, salt and pepper.

Beef Barbecue

4 servings

1 lb/450 grams minced beef
4 oz/115 grams onions
4 oz/115 grams green pepper (optional)
2½ fl oz/75 ml ketchup
1 tablespoon vinegar
1 oz/30 grams sugar
1 tablespoon Worcester sauce
8 oz/225 grams tomato purée

Brown the beef, onions and green peppers; set aside. Put the remaining ingredients in a large saucepan and simmer. Add the beef mixture to this. Simmer for 1 hour.

Meatballs in Vegetable Stew

Swiss Steak

6 servings

2 lb/900 grams rump steak, cut into 6 pieces
1 oz/30 grams flour
1¼ teaspoons salt
3 tablespoon oil
4 oz/115 grams onion, chopped
1 lb/450 grams tinned plum tomatoes, broken up
4 tablespoons Worcester sauce
6 carrots, halved lengthwise and cut in thirds
2 green peppers, cut into 1-inch/2½-cm pieces

Dredge the meat with flour mixed with half the salt. Pound the flour into both sides of the meat with the edge of a heavy plate.

In a large, heavy pan heat the oil. Add the meat and brown well on both sides. Add the onion; sauté until soft. Stir in the tomatoes and 2 tablespoons of the Worcester sauce. Cover; reduce heat and simmer 45 minutes.

Add the carrots and green peppers. Cover and cook 45 minutes longer or until the vegetables and meat are tender. Stir in the remaining 2 tablespoons of Worcester sauce and ½ teaspoon of salt.

Barbecued Meatballs

3 to 4 servings

meatballs
1 lb/450 grams minced beef
3 oz/85 grams breadcrumbs
¼ pint/140 ml milk
4 oz/115 grams onions, chopped
1 teaspoon salt
½ teaspoon pepper
½ teaspoon oregano
1 egg

barbecue sauce
10½ oz/300 grams tinned tomato purée
2½ fl oz/75 ml molasses
2 oz/60 grams brown sugar
2½ fl oz/75 ml vinegar
1 teaspoon sweet basil

Combine the meatball ingredients; form into 1-inch/2½-cm balls. Brown in a pan; drain.

Combine the sauce ingredients; simmer, covered, in the meat pan about 15 minutes to allow flavours to blend.

Cabbage Surprise

4 servings

1 small head of cabbage
½ teaspoon salt per ½ pint/¼ l of water
2 oz/60 grams round-grained rice
1 stick celery, thinly sliced
1 onion, finely chopped
5 oz/140 grams minced stewing steak
5 oz/140 grams minced pork
1 clove garlic, crushed
1 egg
14 oz/400 grams tinned chopped tomatoes
1½ teaspoons salt
½ teaspoon black pepper
¼ teaspoon garlic salt
1 oz/30 grams parsley
4 fl oz/110 ml vegetable broth

Remove the outer leaves of the cabbage head. Rinse the cabbage head and cut a cross in the root. Place the cabbage in boiling salted water—it should be totally covered—and simmer for 10 minutes. Pour off the water and let the cabbage cool enough so that the leaves can be turned out, one by one, into a water lily. (See picture.)

Boil the rice. Mix the rice, celery and onion in a large bowl and add the meat together with the garlic, egg, half of the chopped tomatoes, spices and parsley. Blend well.

Cabbage Surprise

Gorgonzola Hamburgers

Spoon the meat mixture in between the leaves of cabbage. Start in the middle and fold up the leaves as you go along. Tie the cabbage head up into a parcel using fine string and place in a stew pan.

Mix the rest of the chopped tomatoes with the broth. Pour it over the cabbage and simmer for 2 hours, so that the cabbage becomes cooked all the way through. Baste the cabbage now and then with the broth. This dish may be prepared in advance, as it is easy to warm up.

Pink Pepper Hamburgers

4 servings

1½ lb/700 grams minced beef
5 tablespoons onion, finely chopped
2 eggs
½ pint/¼ l double cream
Salt
Pepper
2 tablespoons plus ½ teaspoon pink pepper
Butter or margarine for frying
12 fl oz/350 ml strong meat broth
1 teaspoon French mustard
1 to 2 teaspoons soy sauce

Mix the meat, onions, eggs, half the cream, salt and pepper together. Blend to an even mixture. Crush the pink peppercorns. This spice has a very mild flavour, which is why so much is needed.

Shape the meat into 8 hamburgers. Sprinkle with 2 tablespoons ground pink pepper and flatten the hamburgers with your hands, pressing in the pepper.

Brown the hamburgers in the butter or margarine in a large frying pan. Decrease the heat and add the broth, a little at a time. Let the hamburgers simmer in the gravy until they are done. Remove the hamburgers.

Mix the mustard and the remaining cream in the cooking juices. It should not be boiling. This sauce will first look as though it has curdled but it will become the right consistency after it comes to the boil. Season with soy sauce and ½ teaspoon pink peppercorns which have been crushed. The sauce should have a creamy consistency and a fairly strong flavour.

Place the hamburgers back into the sauce and let it come to the boil.

Gorgonzola Hamburgers

Amount varies

Minced beef
Salt
Pepper
Minced onion
Soda water
1 tablespoon Gorgonzola cheese for each
    hamburger
Oil

Blend minced beef with salt, pepper, onion and a little soda water. Fold so that all becomes well mixed.

Shape the meat into hamburgers. Make a hole in the middle of each one and fill it with Gorgonzola cheese. Press the meat around the cheese so that it thoroughly covers the cheese and brush with oil.

Grill the hamburgers for about 10 minutes on each side and serve with a mixed salad.

Green Pepper Hamburgers

4 servings

1½–2 lb/700–900 grams mince
1 teaspoon salt
1 egg
2½ fl oz/75 ml water
1¼ fl oz/38 ml double cream
1 to 1¼ tablespoons dried or preserved green
    peppercorns or 1 tablespoon coarsely ground
    black pepper
About 1 oz/30 grams butter

sauce
About 4 fl oz/110 ml beef broth
4 fl oz/110 ml double cream
½ tablespoon mustard

Mix the meat with salt. Add the egg and moisten with the water and cream. Mix well.

Pound the dried peppercorns or chop the preserved ones. Make 8 hamburgers. Dredge them in the pepper, making sure it gets evenly spread. Push in the pepper so that it goes into the meat.

Sauté the hamburgers in a little butter in a frying pan. Place on a warm dish.

Make the sauce by pouring the broth and cream into the frying pan. Add the mustard. Let simmer for a few minutes.

Meat Croquettes

4 servings

1 lb/450 grams boiled potatoes, mashed
1 small onion, finely chopped
1–1½ lb/450–675 grams cooked mince
1 tablespoon chutney
1 tablespoon chopped herbs
½ teaspoon salt
Large pinch white pepper
Tomato purée (optional)
1–1½ oz/30–45 grams flour
2 eggs, beaten
Dry white crumbs
Fat for deep frying
Bunch of parsley

Mix the potatoes and onion with the meat, chutney, herbs and seasonings. Add a little tomato purée if the mixture is too dry. Put the mixture on a floured board. Make into a long roll; cut into sections about 1 inch/2½ cm thick and 3 inches/7½ cm long. Roll in seasoned flour. Brush all over with egg; roll in breadcrumbs.

Deep-fry in smoking-hot fat until well browned; drain. Serve with parsley fried in deep fat a few seconds.

Green Pepper Hamburgers

Beef Hedgehog

4 to 6 servings

1 lb/450 grams minced beef
8 oz/225 grams ham (or bacon), chopped
5–7 tablespoons oil
1 small onion, finely chopped
1 oz/30 grams flour
½ pint/¼ l strong beef stock
3 oz/85 grams fresh breadcrumbs
1 egg
2 tablespoons ketchup (or 1 tablespoon soy
  sauce)
2 tablespoons chopped mixed herbs, mainly
  parsley
2 lb/900 grams potatoes
1 oz/30 grams butter or margarine
½ pint/140 ml milk
12 pickling onions
12 small button mushrooms

Mix the mince and chopped ham in a bowl. (If using bacon, chop and cook for a few minutes before adding the beef.) Heat 3–4 tablespoons of oil in a fairly large pan. Cook the onion with the lid on the pan for 5 minutes. Add the mince and ham. Mix in the flour and blend well. Add the stock and bring to the boil, stirring all the time. Cook for a minute or two; then cool slightly. Add the breadcrumbs, then the beaten egg and sauce. Mix well, adding herbs and seasoning to taste.

Butter a loaf tin or oval baking dish well and turn the meat mixture into it. Cover with a lid or foil and bake for about 1 hour.

Peel and boil the potatoes; drain and dry them before mashing. Beat in butter and enough milk to make a dryish mixture. Season well and keep warm. Heat 2–3 tablespoons of oil and cook pickling onions for about 10 minutes sprinkling with a little sugar to help the browning. Remove and keep warm. Add the button mushrooms to the pan and cook these for 3–4 minutes.

When the beef roll is cooked, turn it onto an ovenproof dish, reserving any juice to make gravy. Coat the meat roll all over with an even layer of mashed potato and mark with a fork. Press the onions and mushrooms into the potato in rows to represent the hedgehog's spines. Then return the roll to the oven for 15 minutes or until golden brown.

Pink Pepper Hamburgers

Mazetti

10 to 12 servings

2 lb/900 grams minced beef
1½ lb/700 grams celery with leaves (about ½
  bunch), finely chopped
1 lb/450 grams onions, chopped
2 cloves garlic, finely chopped
1 tablespoon water
1 8 oz/225 grams packet medium fine noodles
2 tins condensed tomato soup
6 oz/170 grams tinned mushrooms and liquid
2 teaspoons salt
½ teaspoon pepper
1 lb/450 grams Cheddar cheese, grated

Brown meat in a pan, then add the celery, onions, garlic and water. Cover and cook until the vegetables are tender. Remove from the heat.

Cook the noodles according to packet directions; drain. Combine the noodles and beef mixture; add the soup, undrained mushrooms, salt and pepper. Spread the mixture in a 6 pint/3½ litre casserole. Sprinkle with cheese on top. Place in a cold oven. Bake uncovered at 250°F/120°C/gas mark ¼ about 1 hour, until bubbly. This dish may be refrigerated up to 24 hours, or frozen before cooking.

Corn Rolls

4 servings

12 oz/345 grams minced beef
1 large yellow onion, chopped
14 oz/400 grams tinned chopped tomatoes
3 to 4 tablespoons tomato paste
6 to 8 fresh corn cobs
1 green pepper, chopped
Garlic salt
Black pepper
1 pint/½ l beef stock

Place the mince and onion in an ungreased pan; brown. Add the chopped tomatoes and tomato paste and let simmer for 25 minutes, stirring occasionally.

Remove the husks and keep to one side. Scrape the corn from the cob and add it to the mince mixture. Cut the pepper into small bits and add. Season and let simmer a few minutes.

Rinse the corn husks. Use several for each roll. Place a spoonful of the mince mixture in the centre of a husk. Roll into a tight parcel and fasten with a toothpick. Place the corn rolls together in a shallow pan. Pour boiling stock over the rolls. Cover and simmer for 15 minutes. Turn and baste after 7 minutes.

Beef Loaf

8 servings

6 oz/170 grams soft breadcrumbs
8 fl oz/220 ml milk
2 lb/900 grams minced beef
2 teaspoons salt
Large pinch pepper
1 medium sized carrot, peeled and grated
1 small onion, peeled and chopped
2 eggs, beaten
2½ fl oz/75 ml ketchup
3 oz/85 grams brown sugar
2 tablespoons prepared mustard

Put the breadcrumbs in a large bowl and pour milk over them. Stir in the mince, salt, pepper, carrot, onion and beaten eggs. Mix thoroughly with a spoon or fork. Lightly shape the meat mixture with your hands to make an oval loaf. Put in a shallow roasting tin, such as a 13 × 9 × 2-inch/33 × 23 × 5-cm tin. Gently smooth the loaf to make it even and neatly shaped. The loaf will be juicier if the mixture is not handled too much.

Mix the ketchup, brown sugar and mustard; spread over the loaf. Bake at 325°F/163°C/gas mark 3 for 1½ hours. Remove the meatloaf from the oven. Loosen

Corn Rolls

the bottom of the loaf from the tin and lift it with a wide spatula onto a warm dish. Slice to serve.

Bacon and Mince Rolls

4 servings

1 lb/450 grams minced stewing steak
1 tablespoon onion, chopped
1 tablespoon parsley, chopped
3 tablespoon double cream
½ teaspoon salt
Pepper
4 oz/115 grams thin sliced bacon
Juice from 1 orange
About ½ pint/¼ l beef broth
2 tablespoons red wine
1 tablespoon blackcurrant juice or jelly
1 teaspoon thyme
1 teaspoon arrowroot mixed with a little water
1 teaspoon lemon juice (optional)
Orange peel
Finely chopped parsley

Mix together the meat, onion, parsley and cream. Season with salt and pepper and form into rolls. Wrap the rolls up in thin bacon slices.

Fry the stuffed bacon slowly in a frying pan until evenly brown. Add the orange juice, broth, red wine and currant juice or jelly. Season with thyme, salt, pepper and lemon juice. Thicken with the arrowroot mixed with a little water. Simmer for 4 to 5 minutes. Heat up thin strips of orange peel in the sauce. Sprinkle with parsley when serving.

Western Meatballs and Frankfurters

6 servings

1 lb/450 grams minced beef
1 egg, slightly beaten
1 oz/30 grams dry breadcrumbs
1 medium sized onion, grated
1 teaspoon salt
8 fl oz/220 ml chilli sauce
1 oz/30 grams redcurrant jelly
2 tablespoons lemon juice
6 fl oz/170 ml water
1 lb/450 grams frankfurters, cut diagonally in ½-inch/1-cm slices

Mix the mince, egg, crumbs, onion and salt together. Shape the mixture into small balls. Place the chilli, redcurrant jelly, lemon juice and water in a large pan. Heat; add the meatballs and simmer until the meat is cooked.

Just before serving, add the frankfurters and heat.

Bacon and Mince Rolls

Mince Gratin with Mushrooms

4 servings

1 aubergine, peeled
1 teaspoon salt
About 12 oz/345 grams fresh mushrooms, rinsed
    and chopped
½ oz/15 grams margarine
1 lb/450 grams minced beef
1 teaspoon salt
Black pepper
2 teaspoon paprika
10 oz/285 grams boiled rice
1 onion, finely chopped
1 green pepper, cubed
8 fl oz/220 ml broth
About 8 oz/225 grams grated cheese

Cut the aubergine into slices and place on the bottom of a greased, ovenproof dish. Season with salt. Sauté the mushrooms in margarine until the liquid has soaked back into the vegetables. Place the mushrooms over the aubergine.

Mix the mince with salt, pepper and paprika. Add the boiled rice, which has been allowed to become cold, and the onion. Add the green pepper and the broth. The beef should be rather loose in consistency.

Spread the meat out in the dish. Sprinkle with the grated cheese. Place the dish in a preheated 350°F/180°C/gas mark 4 oven for about 30 minutes, or until the meat is cooked through.

Devilled Lamb Chops

4 to 5 servings

1½–2 lb/700–900 grams rack of lamb
Salt and pepper
Butter or margarine
1 onion, peeled and chopped
2 oz/60 grams celery, finely chopped
1 clove garlic, crushed
10 oz/285 grams tinned tomato soup
1 tablespoon Worcester sauce
1 tablespoon lemon juice
2 tablespoons sherry
1 oz/30 grams brown sugar
2 teaspoons prepared mustard

Trim and cut the meat into chops and arrange in a buttered casserole. Sprinkle with salt, pepper, onion, celery and garlic. Cover and cook for about 20 minutes. Remove any excess fat.

Heat the tomato soup; add all the other ingredients and mix well. Adjust seasoning. Pour the sauce over the chops. Cover and cook in a preheated 350°F/180°C/gas mark 4 for about 1 hour, basting occasionally.

Serve with chutney.

Porcupine Meatballs

4 servings

1 lb/450 grams minced beef
2 oz/60 grams uncooked rice
2 oz/60 grams onion, finely chopped
1 teaspoon salt
Pinch pepper
1 egg
10 oz/285 grams tinned condensed tomato soup
¼ pint/140 ml water
1 teaspoon Worcester sauce

Combine the mince, rice, onion, salt, pepper and egg in a bowl. Mix lightly but well. Shape the mixture into 24, 1-inch/2½-cm meatballs.

Blend the tomato soup, water and Worcester sauce in a 10-inch/25-cm pan. Cook over medium heat until the mixture boils, about 3 minutes. Add the meatballs to the simmering sauce, spooning sauce over all. Return the mixture to the boil. Reduce heat to low. Cover and simmer 45 minutes, turning meatballs once or twice during cooking.

Bitter-Sweet Lamb Casserole

4 to 6 servings

2–2½ lb/900–1150 grams rack of lamb
2 tablespoons oil
3 tablespoons vinegar
¼ pint/140 ml tinned orange juice
2 teaspoons Worcester sauce
½ teaspoon salt
Pinch freshly ground pepper
Pinch dry mustard
Pinch paprika
½ teaspoon celery seed
½ teaspoon basil
½ teaspoon oregano
3–4 cloves
2 teaspoons sugar
Cooked rice or noodles

Trim and cut the meat into chops; brown it in hot oil and place in a casserole with ½ pint/¼ litre of water and the vinegar. Cover and cook in a 350°F/180°C/gas mark 4 oven for 1 hour.

Put the orange juice, Worcester sauce, seasonings and flavourings into a small pan and simmer, uncovered, for 10 minutes. When the meat has cooked for 1 hour, stir in the orange juice mixture and cook for another hour.

Serve with rice or noodles.

Stuffed Green Peppers

6 servings

6 green peppers
1 lb/450 grams minced beef
Margarine or oil for frying
1 whole garlic, peeled and chopped
Salt
Pepper
1 tin chopped tomatoes
2 to 3 teaspoons mixed herbs (oregano, basil and
  chervil)

Boil the green peppers in salted, boiling water for 10 minutes. Cut a lid off of each pepper and let the peppers drain. Remove the seeds.

Brown the minced beef and garlic cloves in margarine for about 10 minutes. Season with salt and pepper and pour the mixture into a pot with the chopped tomatoes. Simmer for 5 minutes. Season by adding oregano, basil and chervil, according to your taste. Serve with boiled potatoes or rice.

Stuffed Meatloaf

4 to 5 servings

1 lb/450 grams lean minced beef
1 lb/450 grams dry breadcrumbs
4 oz/115 grams carrot, grated
2 oz/60 grams plus 1 tablespoon onion, finely
  chopped
2 eggs, beaten
$\frac{1}{4}$ pint/140 ml milk
$2\frac{1}{4}$ teaspoons salt
1 teaspoon Worcester sauce
Pinch pepper
4 oz/115 grams tinned mushrooms, drained
1 oz/30 grams butter
8 oz/225 grams soft breadcrumbs
1 tablespoon parsley, chopped
$\frac{1}{2}$ teaspoon sage and onion

Combine the mince, breadcrumbs, carrot, 2 oz/60 grams of the onion and eggs. Add the milk, 2 teaspoons of salt, Worcester sauce and pepper. Place the mixture on a double thick square of greased aluminium foil. Shape into a 14×18-inch/35×45-cm rectangle.

Chop and sauté the mushrooms and remaining 1 tablespoon of onion in butter over medium heat. Add the remaining ingredients. Spread the mushroom stuffing over the meat: roll up the foil starting with the long side. Press the overlapping edge into the roll to seal. Bring the foil edges together in a tight double fold on the top. Fold ends up, using tight double folds.

Place the wrapped meatloaf on a rack in a shallow pan. Bake in a 375°F/190°C/gas mark 5 oven 1 hour.

Open the foil: continue baking for 15 more minutes, or until the loaf browns.

Grilled Lamb Chops with Asparagus

6 servings

5 tablespoons olive oil
1 clove garlic, finely chopped
2 oz/60 grams butter
$\frac{1}{2}$ teaspoon tarragon
$\frac{1}{2}$ teaspoon rosemary
1 tablespoon fresh parsley, chopped
6 double lamb chops
Salt and pepper to taste
1 lb/450 grams carrots, peeled and julienned
$3\frac{1}{2}$ oz/100 grams butter
24 spears asparagus

Combine the olive oil and garlic; set aside. Cream the butter with tarragon, rosemary, and parsley. Cut a slit along the back, fatty edge of the lamb chops and stuff with a little of the butter mixture, dividing it equally among the chops. Brush the chops with the olive oil mixture and place on a rack over a baking sheet. Grill 2 inches/5 cm from the source of heat Brown both sides, cooking a total of 10 minutes for rare, 15 for medium, and 20 for well done. Transfer to a warm dish. Season with salt and pepper.

Put the carrots in a saucepan. Add salt and pepper to taste and 1 oz/30 grams of butter. Cover and simmer until tender. Toss with $\frac{1}{4}$ oz/7 grams of butter. Wash the asparagus, carefully scraping sand out from the sides. Steam for about 8 minutes: pat with 1 oz/30 grams of butter and season with salt and pepper.

To serve put 4 asparagus spears on each plate. Place the lamb chop on top and serve the carrots next to the chop.

Pan-Fried Lamb Slices

8 to 10 servings

1 leg of lamb
2 or 3 medium sized onions, peeled and sliced
  into rings
4 or more tablespoons oil for frying
Salt and pepper to taste

With a sharp knife, cut the lamb into $\frac{1}{2}$-inch/1-cm steaks. Brown the onion rings in oil in a large pan. Drain and set aside to keep warm. Sauté slices in the same oil; season with salt and pepper.

To serve, arrange the meat on a dish. Cover the slices with drained onions.

Mini Lamb Rolls

a toothpick.

Brown the rolls on all sides in the butter and then place them in a greased, ovenproof dish. Add the onions. Pour in the hot broth, cover and place in the oven for about 1 hour. Add the rest of the celeriac stalks about 15 minutes before the end of baking. Serve with boiled potatoes sprinkled with snipped parsley or chives.

Lamb and Cheese Rolls

6 servings

1 lb/450 grams cooked lamb, cubed
8 oz/225 grams Gruyère cheese, grated
5 oz/140 grams celery, diced
3 tablespoons onion, grated
1 teaspoon salt
2½ fl oz/70 ml mayonnaise
2 tablespoons chilli sauce
6 French rolls, about 6 inches/15 cm long
Butter or margarine

Toss together the lamb, cheese, celery, onion and salt in a mixing bowl. Combine the mayonnaise and chilli sauce and stir into the lamb mixture, mixing thoroughly.

Slightly hollow out the centre of the rolls. Spread lightly with butter or margarine and fill with the lamb mixture. These may be served immediately or wrapped in foil and heated in the oven until the cheese melts.

Mini Lamb Rolls

4 servings

About 2½ lb/1150 grams thin breast of lamb
Salt
Pepper
1 bunch parsley
1 bunch chives
1 teaspoon salt
¼ teaspoon ground black pepper
½ teaspoon thyme
1 large piece celeriac
2 medium sized onions, cut into large pieces
About ½ pint/¼ l broth
½ oz/15 grams butter

Preheat oven to 400°F/200°C/gas mark 6. Remove bones from the lamb breast. Cut away the largest membranes and cut straight across where the bone sits, making 3 to 4-inch/7½ to 9-cm wide strips. Cut these strips down the middle.

Salt and pepper the meat. Chop the chives and parsley, mix with the thyme and sprinkle the mixture evenly over the meat.

Cut the celeriac into ½-inch/1-cm strips. Place one strip on each piece of meat. Roll the meat strips up tightly into mini rolls and fasten them securely with

Lamb and Potato Casserole

4 servings

1 oz/30 grams flour
Salt and pepper
4 large lamb chops (loin)
2 oz/60 grams butter or margarine
8 oz/225 grams onions, peeled and sliced
1 small clove garlic, crushed
4 tomatoes, peeled and sliced
1 to 2 sprigs fresh, or pinch dried, rosemary
1 lb/450 grams potatoes, peeled and sliced
3 to 4 tablespoons broth or water

Mix the flour with a little salt and pepper and dredge the chops well. Heat 1½ oz/45 grams of the butter in a sauté pan. Brown the chops on both sides and remove from the pan. Add the onion and garlic to the remaining fat and cook until softened.

Arrange the meat, onion, tomatoes, rosemary and potatoes in layers in a casserole, seasoning each layer lightly and finishing with the potatoes. Add the broth or water and dot with the remaining butter. Cover and cook for about 2 hours. About 15 minutes before the end of cooking, remove the lid and allow the potatoes to brown.

Rolled Leg of Lamb

6 to 8 servings

1 4–7 lb/2–3 kilo leg of lamb, boned, trimmed of
   fat, rolled and tied.
1 teaspoon salt
½ clove garlic, finely chopped
¼ teaspoon pepper
½ small bay leaf, crushed
¼ teaspoon ground ginger
¼ teaspoon dried thyme
¼ teaspoon dried sage
¼ teaspoon dried marjoram
1 teaspoon lemon juice
1 tablespoon olive oil

With a sharp knife, cut small but deep slashes in
the lamb, distributing them evenly.

In a small bowl, mix the salt, garlic, pepper, bay
leaf, ginger, thyme, sage and marjoram together. Fill
the slashes with this herb mixture, then rub the surface of the lamb with lemon juice and olive oil.

Place the lamb on a rack in a roasting tin. Roast in
a preheated 325°F/163°C/gas mark 3 oven for 20 minutes per lb/450 grams, or until it reaches the desired
degree of cooking. Make a gravy from the drippings
in the roasting tin.

Lamb Chops Marinated in Beer

2 to 4 servings

½ pint/¼ l light ale
4 fl oz/110 ml salad oil
1 clove garlic, finely chopped
1 tablespoon lemon juice
1 tablespoon sugar
½ teaspoon salt
Pinch pepper
4 lamb chops

In a shallow baking dish, combine the beer, oil,
garlic, lemon juice, sugar, salt and pepper. Add the
lamb chops, cover and refrigerate overnight. Remove
the chops from the baking dish, drain and grill 6 to
8 minutes each side or until done. Delicious with
grilled apple rings.

Herb Spiced Leg of Lamb

Herb Spiced Leg of lamb

8 servings

1 6 lb/2½ kilo leg of lamb
2½ fl oz/75 ml vegetable oil
2 teaspoons salt
1 teaspoon thyme
1 teaspoon marjoram
1 teaspoon black pepper

Rub the oil and spices into the lamb. While the oven is heating, let the meat stand so that it can absorb the seasonings. Preheat the oven to 350°F/180°C/gas mark 4.

Stick a meat thermometer into the thickest part of the meat, but not touching the bone. Cook until the thermometer registers 160°F/71°C. The meat should still be pink at the centre after about 2 hours cooking. Leave it to stand for about 10 minutes before carving.

Lamb with Dill

4 servings

About 2½ lb/1150 grams lamb on the bone—
    shoulder or breast.
Water
2 teaspoons salt per 2 pint/1¼ l water
Dill stalks
6 white peppercorns
2 unpeeled cloves garlic
1 small carrot, cut into small pieces
1 leek or onion, cut into small pieces

sauce
1½ oz/45 grams butter or margarine
2½ oz/75 grams flour
1½ to 2 pints/1 to 1¼ l broth
3 tablespoons snipped dill
1 tablespoon fresh lemon juice
1 egg yolk
2½ fl oz/75 ml cream

Place the lamb in a large saucepan. Pour over as much water as needed to cover the meat. Add salt and bring to the boil. Skim well and add dill, pepper, garlic, carrot and leek or onion. Let the meat simmer over a low heat until tender, about 1 to 1½ hours.

To make the sauce: melt the butter in a small saucepan and stir in the flour. Dilute with the cooking liquid. Allow to boil for several minutes then season with dill and lemon juice.

Remove the pan from the heat and add the yolk, which has first been beaten together with the cream. The sauce should not boil again or it will curdle.

Slice up the meat and serve it with the sauce, boiled potatoes and vegetables.

Lamb with Dill

Lamb Pie with Sweet Potato Topping

6 servings

1 lb/450 grams cooked lamb, cut into 1-inch/2½-
    cm cubes
½ pint/¼ l rich lamb gravy
½ pint/¼ l stock
12 small cooked white onions
1 lb/450 grams peas
8 oz/225 grams celery, diced
¼ teaspoon thyme
¼ teaspoon ground allspice
Salt
Pepper
1 lb/450 grams sweet potatoes, mashed
¼ pint/140 ml milk
¼ teaspoon baking powder
1 tablespoon brown sugar

Combine the lamb, gravy, stock, onions, peas, celery, thyme and allspice. Season to taste with salt and pepper. Turn the mixture into a 5-pint/2½-l greased casserole or 6 individual greased casseroles. Bake uncovered in a preheated oven at 400°F/200°C/gas mark 6 for 15 minutes.

Beat together the potatoes, milk, baking powder,

½ teaspoon salt and brown sugar. Arrange the mixture on top of the casserole. Return to the oven and continue cooking for another 15 to 20 minutes or until the topping is heated through and lightly browned.

Lamb Stew

4 servings

1½–2 lb/700–900 grams lamb on the bone— shoulder or breast
8 small onions
4 tomatoes, cut into pieces
About 1 teaspoon salt
½ teaspoon black pepper
1–2 cloves garlic, crushed
Slightly less than 1 teaspoon thyme
2 oz/ 60 grams parsley, chopped
2 oz/ 60 grams snipped chives
10–15 fl oz/285–425 ml broth
½ oz/15 grams flour
4 fl oz/ 110 ml soured cream

Cut the meat into pieces and brown them in a small amount of butter in a frying pan. Pour into a stew pan. Peel and brown the onions and mix them with the meat. Add the tomatoes, season and pour in the broth. Cover and simmer until the meat is tender, about 45 minutes.

Stir the flour into a small amount of water and mix into the stew together with the cream. Simmer for another 5 to 10 minutes. Season to taste. Serve with boiled potatoes.

Lamb with Vegetables

10 servings

1 large onion, chopped
1 large carrot, sliced
2 large leeks, sliced
Butter or oil
1 large, meaty lamb roast
1 tin consommé plus 1 stock cube
Water
Salt
Pepper
Mustard seeds
Bay leaf
Sprigs of parsley

Brown the onion, carrot and leeks in butter or oil in a thick-based stewing pot. Insert a cooking thermometer in the well trimmed lamb. Place the meat on the vegetables and cover with the consommé, stock cube and enough water to come more than half way up the meat. Salt lightly, season with pepper, mustard seeds, bay leaf and sprigs of parsley. Cover and cook slowly until the thermometer registers 150

Lamb with Vegetables

to 160°F/65 to 71°C. Remove the lamb, wrap in aluminium foil and keep it warm.

Strain the juice and simmer it so that it becomes a thick gravy. Then mix in more mustard seeds to make a strong sauce.

Serve the lamb with fried potato and apple sauce.

Roast Best End of Lamb

4 servings

1 2½ lb/1150 grams best end of neck
Salt and freshly ground pepper to taste
2 tablespoons vegetable oil
1 tablespoon soy sauce
1 tablespoon tomato purée
1 clove garlic, crushed
Salt and pepper

Sprinkle the meat with salt and pepper. Place it on a rack in a roasting tin, meat side down, and cook in a preheated oven at 350°F/180°C/gas mark 4 for 30 minutes. Turn the joint and cook for a further 30 minutes.

Combine the oil, soy sauce, tomato purée, garlic, salt and pepper in a small bowl and brush over the meat. Cook for a further 30 minutes. Cut the chops into serving portions.

Lamb Fricassee

Lamb Fricassee

4 servings

About 2½ lb/1150 grams lamb on the bone,
    shoulder or breast.
Water
1 teaspoon salt per pint/½ l of water
10 white or black peppercorns 1 carrot, cut into
    pieces
1 leek, cut into pieces
Sprigs of dill

sauce
1 oz/30 grams butter or margarine
1 oz/30 grams flour
1 pint/½ l broth
1 egg yolk
2½ fl oz/75 ml double cream
2 oz/60 grams dill, finely chopped
Pressed lemon juice (optional)

Place the meat in a pot. Measure and pour in
enough water to cover the meat. Add the salt and
bring to the boil. Skim well and add the peppercorns,
vegetables and dill. Simmer over a low heat until the
meat is tender, about 1 to 1½ hours.

To make the sauce: melt the butter in a saucepan

and stir in the flour and then the broth. Let the sauce
boil for a few minutes.

Remove the pan from the heat and stir in the egg
yolk which has been mixed with the cream. The
sauce should not be allowed to boil again as it will
curdle. Season with dill and lemon if desired. Slice
the meat and serve it with the sauce, boiled potatoes
and vegetables.

Lamb with Horseradish

4 servings

4 large pieces lamb fillet
2 tablespoons oil
1 teaspoon paprika
1 large onion, peeled and sliced
8 oz/225 grams mushrooms, sliced
½ pint/¼ l water
1 tablespoon prepared horseradish
1 teaspoon parsley, chopped
¼ teaspoon dried rosemary
¼ teaspoon sweet basil
¼ teaspoon oregano
½ pint/¼ l soured cream

Heat the oil in a heavy pan. Sprinkle the lamb with
paprika and then brown it with the onion in the oil.
Add the mushrooms and cook for a few minutes
more; then remove all ingredients to a casserole.

Add ½ pint/¼ litre water to the pan drippings, deglaze and bring to the boil. Pour into the casserole.
Add horseradish, herbs and seasonings. Cover and
cook in a preheated oven at 325°F/163°C/gas mark 3
for 1½ hours, or until the meat is tender.

Remove the lamb from the casserole and cut up
the meat. Stir the cream into the casserole and adjust
the seasoning. Put the meat back and leave just long
enough for it to reheat.

Lamb and Sausage Roll

4 servings

3 lb/1¼ kilo boned breast of lamb
Salt
Pepper
8 oz/225 grams pork sausage meat
1 oz/30 grams lard
¼ pint/140 ml ketchup
8 fl oz/220 ml water
4 oz/115 grams onion, chopped

Rub the lamb with the pepper and spread with the
sausage meat. Roll lengthways and tie or fasten with
skewers. Sauté the roll in hot lard until browned.

Combine the ketchup, water and onion and pour
it over the lamb. Cover and simmer about 1½ hours
until the meat is tender and the sausage meat cooked
through. Add more water during the cooking as

needed. Skim off the fat and slice the roll. Serve with the sauce.

Sweet Shoulder of Lamb

4 servings

1 4–5 lb/2–2¼ grams shoulder of lamb, presliced and tied into an oblong
Salt
Pepper
1 apple, thinly sliced
4 fl oz/110 ml redcurrant jelly
1 tablespoon lemon juice
4 oz/115 grams seedless raisins soaked in 2 tablespoons water
2 oz/60 grams onion, finely chopped

Place the lamb in a roasting tin. Sprinkle generously with salt and peper. Cook in a preheated oven at 325°F/163°C/gas mark 3 for 1½ hours. Press rows of apple slices between the meat slices.

Bring the remaining ingredients to the boil in a small saucepan. Brush them over the lamb. Return the lamb to the oven for 30 minutes or until a meat thermometer registers 160°F/71°C for medium, or 170°F/75°C for well done, brushing occasionally with sauce. Remove the strings, separate the lamb slices from the bone and serve with the remaining sauce.

Baked Glazed Ham

4 to 6 servings

2–3 lb/1–1¼ kilos tinned ham
2 tablespoons honey
Grated rind of 1 orange
1 teaspoon mustard powder
4 tablespoons brown sugar
¼ pint/140 ml cider or pineapple juice
½ oz/15 grams butter
1 small tin pineapple rings
Sugar to dust
6–8 tinned cherries

Scrape the jelly off the ham and reserve it. Place the ham in a roasting tin. Melt the honey and spread it over the ham. Mix the orange rind, mustard and brown sugar together and sprinkle over the meat. Pour the cider over the ham. Add the jelly from the ham. Cook in a preheated oven at 400°F/200°C/gas mark 6 for 30 minutes. Baste after 15 minutes.

Melt the butter in a frying pan. Sprinkle the pineapple slices with sugar then brown them in butter on both sides. Serve around the ham with cherries in the centre of each ring.

Use the liquid from the roasting tin to make a sauce: add water and a squeeze of lemon if too sweet.

Grilled Ham with Raisin and Cranberry Sauce

4 to 5 servings

1½–2 lb/700–900 grams 1-inch/2½-cm thick gammon steaks
Few cloves
4 oz/115 grams brown sugar
1 oz/30 grams cornflour
15 fl oz/425 ml cranberry juice
4 fl oz/110 ml orange juice
4 oz/115 grams raisins

Score the gammon rind at 2-inch/5-cm intervals and insert 2 or 3 cloves.

Mix the sugar and cornflour with the cranberry juice and put in a pan. Add the orange juice and raisins and bring to the boil. Stir constantly until the mixture thickens.

Put the gammon steaks on a barbecue over charcoal away from the hottest part. Cook about 15 minutes. Turn the steaks, brush liberally with the glaze and cook for 10 more minutes. Turn again and brush the other side with glaze.

These steaks can also be cooked on a grill.

Lamb Stew

Ham Hocks in Sauerkraut

4 servings

3 large ham hocks
1 lb/450 grams sauerkraut
1 large onion, sliced into thin rings
1 tablespoon sugar
¼ teaspoon black pepper

Cover the ham with water. Simmer 1 hour. Drain.
Add the sauerkraut, onion, sugar and pepper and place on the stove again and simmer 1½ to 2 hours, until the meat falls off the bone.

Spicy Ham Loaf

6 servings

1½ lb/700 grams minced cooked ham
2oz/60 grams fine breadcrumbs
2 oz/60 grams onions, finely chopped
2 tablespoons green pepper, finely chopped
½ teaspoon dry mustard
Large pinch allspice
Large pinch ground cloves
2 eggs, lightly beaten
¼ pint/140 ml milk

Combine the ham, breadcrumbs, onion, green pepper, mustard, allspice and cloves. Add the eggs and milk and mix until combined. Pack the mixture into a 2-pint/1¼-litre loaf tin. Bake in a 350°F/180°C/gas mark 4 oven for 45 minutes. Turn out and serve hot.

Southampton Ham

20-24 servings

1 10–12 lb/4½–5 kilo uncooked ham
3–3½ pint/2–2¼ l cold water (2½ pint/1½ l cold water plus 1 pint/½ l dry sherry) (optional)

Soak the ham overnight or for about 8 hours in water to cover. Rinse the ham under running water. Place it in a roasting tin and add the water or water and sherry. Cover tightly with foil. Put the ham in 475°F/245°C/ gas mark 9 oven and cook for 15 to 20 minutes. Turn off the oven and leave the door shut. The entire cooking time of the ham the oven door must remain closed at all times to retain the heat necessary to cook the ham.

Leave the ham in the oven for 3 hours and then turn the heat back on to 475°F/245°C/gas mark 9. Cook the ham 20 to 25 minutes, turn the heat off again and allow the ham to sit in the oven undisturbed for another 3 hours or overnight.

To make this a simple one day affair soak the ham in the morning. About 6.00 pm begin the first phase of cooking; at about 9.30 pm turn the heat back on to complete the cooking. Turn off the oven and leave the ham undisturbed in the oven until the next morning. At this time the rind and excess fat can be trimmed away and the ham glazed, if desired. Be sure to carve it wafer thin.

Note: do not attempt to use this cooking method with a ham larger than 12 lb/5 kilo.

Ham with Sweet Potatoes

5–6 servings

1½ lb/700 grams ham, sliced
1½ lb/700 grams raw sweet potatoes, sliced
1 oz/30 grams sugar
½ pint/¼ l hot water
½ oz/15 grams drippings or other fat

Cut the ham into pieces for serving. Brown the meat lightly on both sides and arrange the pieces to cover the bottom of a casserole.

Spread the sliced sweet potatoes over the meat and sprinkle with sugar. Add the hot water to the dripping in the frying pan and pour over the sweet potatoes and meat.

Cover the casserole and cook at 325°F/163°C/gas mark 3 until the meat and sweet potatoes are tender, basting the potatoes occasionally with the gravy. Towards the end of cooking time remove the lid and let the top brown well.

Pork with Cider

4 servings

1½ lb/700 grams lean pork, cut into
    1-inch/2½-cm cubes
1 oz/30 grams flour
4 fl oz/110 ml vegetable oil
15 fl oz/425 ml apple cider or apple juice
2 carrots, sliced
1 small onion, sliced
½ teaspoon rosemary
1 bay leaf
1 teaspoon salt
½ teaspoon pepper

Thoroughly dredge the pork with the flour. Heat the oil in a large frying pan. carefully add the pork and cook until browned on all sides. Remove the meat and drain on kitchen towel. Place in a casserole.

Drain the oil from the pan. Pour in the cider. Heat and deglaze the pan. Add the carrots, onion, rosemary, bay leaf, salt, pepper and hot cider to the casserole. Cover. Cook in 325°F/163°C/gas mark 3 oven for 2 hours, until the meat is tender. Remove the bay leaf.

Pork or Veal with Artichoke Hearts

4 servings

4 artichokes
4 loin of pork steaks or 4 veal chops
2 teaspoons salt
Black pepper
1 oz/30 grams margarine
4 slices cheese
8 fl oz/220 ml chilli sauce
1 to 2 tablespoons grated horseradish

Twist off the stalks of the artichokes and remove the outer leaves. Place the artichokes in lightly salted, boiling water. Cover and boil for 30 to 40 minutes. They are ready when the leaves come off easily. Remove the leaves from the artichokes. Place them in a pot with the cover on so that they will keep warm. Save the artichoke hearts.

Brown the meat on both sides in margarine. Add salt and peppr. Sauté until the meat is cooked all the way through. Place an artichoke heart on each slice of meat. Cover with a slice of cheese. Place a lid on the frying pan. Allow the cheese to melt.

To make the sauce: mix the chilli sauce with the grated horseradish. Place the meat on plates, putting the artichoke leaves decoratively around each slice. Dip the leaves in the sauce.

Loin of Pork with Cabbage in Beer Sauce

6 servings

1 head cabbage
8 cloves garlic
5 oz/140 grams butter
2½ lb/1150 grams loin of pork
¼ teaspoon black pepper
½ to 1 teaspoon salt
8 fl oz/220 ml stout
8 fl oz/220 ml beef broth
½ teaspoon caraway seeds

Rinse the cabbage. Cut away the larger stalks and shred the leaves. Quickly place the cabbage in boiling water, let the water come to the boil again, remove the cabbage right away and dip it in cold water so that it remains an attractive green. Drain. Parboil the garlic cloves separately but in the same way.

Trim the pork and place in a deep frying pan. Sprinkle it with pepper and brown all around in some of the butter. Cover and cook until it registers 170°F/75°C on a meat thermometer. Sprinkle with salt. Remove meat from pan.

Pour beer and broth into the frying pan. Add the cabbage, peeled garlic cloves and caraway seeds. Bring to the boil and season to taste.

Remove the pan from the heat, push the cabbage

Pork or Veal with Artichoke Hearts

over to one side and add the rest of the butter, by dabbing it into the sauce so that the mixture becomes slightly thickened. Cut up the meat and place it on top of the cabbage. Serve with potatoes.

Ham and Potato Cakes

4 to 6 servings

8 oz/225 grams mashed potatoes
8 oz/ 225 grams cooked ham, chopped
1 egg, lightly beaten
2 oz/60 grams onion, finely chopped
¼ teaspoon dry mustard
¼ teaspoon white pepper
Flour for coating
Fat for frying

Mix the potatoes, ham, egg, onion and seasonings together. Form into flat cakes about 3 inches/7½ cms in diameter. Dip each cake lightly in flour, coating both sides. Set aside.

Melt the fat in a frying pan. Lightly brown each cake on both sides. Dry on kitchen towel. Put on a warming plate in the oven until all are cooked and ready to serve.

Pork, Apples and Sauerkraut

4 servings

4 pork chops, ½-inch/1-cm thick
1 oz/30 grams butter
1 teaspoon salt
Large pinch pepper
1 tablespoon prepared mustard
1 tablespoon horseradish
2 lb/900 grams tinned sauerkraut, drained
2 medium sized apples, chopped
4 oz/115 grams onion, chopped
1 teaspoon caraway seeds.

Brown the pork chops in the butter and pour off the excess fat. Season the chops with salt and pepper.

Combine the mustard and horseradish and spread over the chops. Combine the sauerkraut, apples, onion and caraway seeds and place in a 4-pint/2¼-litre casserole. Arrange the chops on top of the sauerkraut and apple mixture. Cover and bake in a pre-heated 350°F/180°C/gas mark 4 oven for 30 minutes. Remove the lid and cook for a further 30 minutes.

Barbecued Pork Tenderloin

8 servings

2 whole pork tenderloins
1 oz/30 grams butter or margarine
2 oz/60 grams flour
2½ fl oz/75 ml vinegar
½ teaspoon salt
½ teaspoon dry mustard
2 teaspoons celery seed
1½ teaspoons chilli sauce
¼ pint/140 ml ketchup
1 oz/30 grams sugar
2 tablespoons paprika
Pepper

Cut each tenderloin lengthwise and crosswise. This will make 8 pieces. Melt the butter in a pan. Coat the meat with flour and brown in the hot butter. Combine the remaining ingredients and pour over the meat. Cover and simmer over very low heat for about 2 hours.

Baked Stuffed Pork Chops

4 servings

2 oz/60 grams butter or margarine
4 oz/115 grams onion, finely chopped
2 tablespoons celery, finely chopped
¼ pint/140 ml water, stock or tinned broth
4 slices white bread made into croutons
4 pork chops, 1½-inch/3½-cm thick, cut with
  pockets
Salt
Pepper

Melt the butter in a medium sized saucepan over a low heat. Add the onions and celery. Cook, stirring frequently, until tender. Add the water. Bring to the boil. Remove the pan from the heat. Add the croutons, tossing lightly until evenly moistened.

If necessary extend the pocket in each pork chop to the bone. Fill with the crouton mixture. Fasten the edges with wooden toothpicks. Place the stuffed chops, flat side down, in a shallow roasting tin. Ensure they are not touching and sprinkle with salt and pepper. Cover the tin tightly with foil.

Cook in a 350°F/180°C/gas mark 4 oven for about 55 minutes. Remove the foil and cook about 30 minutes more or until the chops are browned and tender.

Smoked Pork Loin with Rice

4 servings

8 oz/225 grams long grain rice
1 teaspoon salt
1 pint/½ l meat stock (from cubes)
14 oz/400 grams tinned sweet corn
About 1½ lb/700 grams smoked pork loin, cut in
  6 to 8 slices
14 oz/400 grams tinned, peeled, tomatoes
1½ teaspoons sage or basil
½ teaspoon white pepper
½ teaspoon garlic salt (optional)

Place rice, salt and stock in a wide shallow pan and bring to the boil. Simmer slowly, covered, for about 15 minutes. Drain the sweet corn and mix with the rice. Place the pork slices in a ring on top of the rice. Finally, place the tomatoes and some of the liquid in the centre.

Mix the sage, pepper and garlic and sprinkle this mixture over all the ingredients in the pan. Cover and simmer gently for 5 to 8 minutes more. Serve immediately.

Spareribs and Sauerkraut

4 servings

2 lb/900 grams pork spareribs
1 teaspoon salt
2 lb/900 grams sauerkraut

Divide the spareribs into serving portions. Wipe them with a cold, damp cloth and sprinkle with salt. Put the ribs in a deep saucepan and cover with cold water. Bring to the boil. Cover. Reduce the heat and simmer for 30 minutes.

Add the sauerkraut. Bring to the boil, reduce the heat and simmer, uncovered, for 30 minutes more. Serve hot.

Pork Loin with Cabbage in Beer Sauce

Breaded Pork Escalopes

4 servings

12 pork escalopes
Salt to taste
Freshly ground pepper to taste
1 egg
3 tablespoons water
¼ pint/140 ml plus 1 tablespoon corn, peanut or
    vegetable oil
1 oz/30 grams flour
4 oz/115 grams fine fresh breadcrumbs
1½ oz/45 grams butter (optional)
Lemon wedges for garnish

Pound each escalope lightly with a cutlet bat. Arrange on a flat surface and sprinkle with salt and pepper on both sides.

In a dish combine the egg, water, 1 tablespoon oil, salt and pepper. Beat well to blend. Put the flour in a second dish and the breadcrumbs in a third. Dip the escalopes in flour to coat thoroughly, shaking off excess. Then dip each one in the egg mixture and then in the crumbs to coat well. Pat to help the crumbs adhere.

Heat about half the oil in a large, heavy pan and add a few escalopes to fill the pan without overlapping. Cook about 5 minutes on one side until golden brown. Turn and cook about 5 minutes or slightly longer on the other side. Transfer to a warm dish. Continue adding oil and pork until all are cooked.

Heat the butter until lightly browned and pour over the meat. Serve with lemon wedges.

Grilled Marinated Spareribs

4 servings

2½ lb/1150 grams pork spareribs, preferably
    thinly cut so that they take less time to grill.

marinade
14 oz/400 grams tinned, crushed pineapple
1 tablespoon vinegar
1 tablespoon soy sauce
2 tablespoons oil
1 teaspoon salt
1 teaspoon ginger
Juice from 1 orange or 4 fl oz/110 ml orange
    juice

Mix all the marinade ingredients together. Place the ribs in a thick plastic bag. Pour in the marinade and fasten the bag tightly. Place in the refrigerator for at least 3 hours, preferably overnight.

Place the ribs under the grill. Grill about 20 minutes for thinly sliced ribs, 40 minutes otherwise. Turn occasionally. Make sure the ribs are not too near the heat, as they can easily burn without being thoroughly cooked inside. Baste with the marinade.

Boil the rest of the marinade and serve as a sauce. Serve the ribs with baked potatoes and corn on the cob.

Garlic-Spiced Pork Loin with Green Pepper Sauce

6 servings

2½ lb/1150 grams fresh pork tenderloin
6 cloves garlic, sliced lengthways
1½ oz/45 grams butter
½ teaspoon coarsely ground black pepper
½ teaspoon salt
8 oz/225 grams frozen puff pastry
1 egg

mushroom filling
4 oz/115 grams smoked ham
5 to 6 shallots
1 lb/450 grams fresh mushrooms
½ oz/15 grams butter
½ teaspoon salt
Large pinch coarsely ground black pepper

green pepper sauce
4 shallots, chopped
1 teaspoon dried green peppercorns, crushed
4 fl oz/110 ml red wine vinegar
½ pint/¼ l beef broth
8 fl oz/220 ml double cream
½ oz/15 grams flour
2 tablespoons soy sauce
Salt
1 teaspoon whole green peppercorns
Butter

Trim the meat well. Make tiny holes in it with a sharp knife and stick garlic cloves into the holes. Sauté the pork in butter until golden brown on all sides. Season with salt and pepper. Do not overcook—the meat should just be done, which takes about 7 to 8 minutes. Leave to cool.

Finely chop the ham, shallots and mushrooms for the filling. The mushrooms may be chopped in a food processor if they are done quickly and in several batches. Melt butter in a large frying pan and add the chopped ingredients. Let them sweat and then become dry. Salt and pepper and leave to cool.

Thaw the puff pastry. Roll out until large enough to cover both the meat and the filling.

Spread the filling over the dough. Place the meat pieces one on top of the other in the centre of the filling. Spoon the filling up onto the meat and onto its sides.

Wrap up the dough, pinching the seams together well. Trim off extra pastry. Decorate the parcel with stripes or squares or with a flower and leaves made with the remaining puff pastry. Everything up to this point may be prepared in advance. Keep refrigerated.

Preheat the oven to 400°F/200°C/gas mark 6. Brush the dough with beaten egg and bake in the middle of the oven for 20 to 30 minutes.

To make the green pepper sauce: place the shallots in a pot together with the green peppercorns and vinegar. Simmer until the vinegar has almost totally evaporated. Add the broth and bring to the boil.

Strain the shallots and beat in the cream, flour and soy sauce. Simmer, stirring continuously, for a few minutes. Season with salt and finally mix in a teaspoon of whole green peppercorns and a dab of butter. Serve the sauce piping hot.

Garlic-Spiced Pork Loin with Green Pepper Sauce

Texas Pork Chops

2 servings

1 tin condensed oxtail soup
8 oz/225 grams cooked rice
2 tablespoons green pepper, finely chopped
2 tablespoons ripe olives, sliced
4 pork chops, 1-inch/2½-cm thick
1 lb/450 grams tinned tomatoes
1 medium sized onion, sliced
1 medium sized clove garlic, crushed

Combine 2½ fl oz/75 ml of soup, rice, green pepper and olives. Trim excess fat from the chops. Slit each chop from the outer edge toward the bone, making a pocket; stuff with the rice mixture and fasten with toothpicks.

In a pan, brown the chops; pour off the fat. Add the remaining ingredients. Cover and cook over low heat 1¼ hours. Stir now and then to break up the tomatoes. Uncover and cook to desired consistency.

Pork Chops and Sweet Potatoes

4 servings

4 pork chops
Salt and pepper to taste
1 oz/30 grams flour
1 oz/30 grams butter
4 oz/115 grams redcurrant jelly
¼ pint/140 ml orange juice
1 tablespoon lemon juice
1 teaspoon dry mustard
1 teaspoon paprika
½ teaspoon ground ginger
3–4 medium sized sweet potatoes, boiled, sliced

Season the chops with salt and pepper; coat with flour. Brown on both sides.

Melt the butter in a small saucepan. Add the remaining ingredients, except the sweet potatoes, stirring constantly, to make a sauce.

Arrange the sweet potatoes and pork chops in an ovenproof dish. Pour most of the sauce over the potatoes and chops; keep the remainder for basting while baking. Bake, uncovered, at 350°F/180°C/gas mark 4 for 45 minutes.

Pork Loin with Gorgonzola

4 servings

1 onion, with butter to sauté
½ oz/15 grams flour
1 tin broth
4 fl oz/110 ml double cream
Tarragon
French mustard

Pork Loin with Gorgonzola

Salt
Black pepper
Gorgonzola cheese, according to taste
3 peppers, preferably 2 different colours
1½ lb/700 grams pork loin, finely trimmed
Butter
A few drops of sherry, port or brandy
2 oz/60 grams chopped walnuts

Chop the onion and sauté it in butter in a small pan. Sprinkle the flour into the pan. Alternate beating in the cream with 4 fl oz/110 ml broth and let the mixture simmer until it has a pleasant sauce consistency. Season with tarragon, mustard, salt and a little black pepper. Finally, add a large dab of Gorgonzola cheese. Let it melt while stirring constantly. Season with tarragon, mustard, salt and a little black pepper. Finally, add a large dab of Gorgonzola cheese. Let it melt while stirring constantly. Season to taste. Let the sauce stand and thicken on the side of the stove.

Slice the peppers and simmer them in the rest of the broth until they are almost soft. Then let the liquid reduce to half the original amount.

Grease an ovenproof dish. Pour in the reduced broth, mixed with a little wine. Place the pork, which has been cut into several pieces, on a bed of the soft peppers. Season the meat lightly and dab on a little butter. Place high up in a hot oven 2 to 3 minutes. Lower the rack and open the oven door a little so that the temperature quickly sinks to 350°F/180°C/gas mark 4. Total time in the oven: about 8 minutes for pink meat, otherwise longer. Cut the meat up into thinner slices and place it back on the peppers.

Keep the sauce ready and warm. Just before serving, add the nuts and swirl the thick sauce over the pork slices. The dish can be garnished with watercress if desired.

Japanese Pork Loin

4 servings

About 1 lb/450 grams thick pork loin

marinade
4 fl oz/110 ml oil
2 tablespoons soy sauce
2 onions, chopped
¼ teaspoon black pepper
1 clove garlic, crushed
1 tablespoon vinegar
5 coriander seeds

Trim and cut the loin into thick (½-inch/1¼-cm) slices. Mix the marinade ingredients together. Place the pork in a greased tin and cover with the marinade. Let stand in a cool place for about 24 hours.

Preheat oven to 400°F/200°C/gas mark 6. Place the tin with the meat and the marinade in the oven for about 20 minutes if pink and juicy meat is desired, somewhat longer if the meat is to be well done. Baste several times with the marinade while baking. Serve immediately with rice mixed with sliced mushrooms or raisins.

Pork Roast with Cranberry Stuffing

6 servings

1 6–7 lb/2½–3 kilos pork loin roast
Salt and pepper
Sage and onion, dried
½ pint/¼ l boiling beef broth
4 oz/225 grams butter
1 8 oz/225 grams packet stuffing
4 oz/115 grams cranberries, chopped
1 small red apple, unpeeled, cored and diced
2 oz/60 grams celery, finely chopped
2 oz/60 grams parsley, shopped
1 large egg

Have the butcher saw off the chine of the roast. Place the meat, rib ends up, on a cutting board. Holding the meaty side of the roast with one hand, and

starting 1 inch/2½ cms from one end of roast and ending 1 inch/2½ cms from the other end, cut a slit between the meat and rib bones almost to the bottom of the roast. With your fingers, pull the meaty part slightly away from the ribs to form a pocket. Sprinkle the inside of the pocket and outside of the roast with salt, pepper and dried sage and onion.

Pour boiling broth into a large pan off the heat. Add butter; over very low heat stir until melted. Remove from the heat. Add the bread stuffing mixed with hot water, cranberries, apple, celery and parsley; mix well.

Beat the egg until thick and pale-coloured; mix with the stuffing. Spoon the stuffing into the pocket in the roast; put any leftover stuffing into a small baking tin. Roast the pork on a rack in a shallow roasting tin in a 350°F/180°C/gas mark 4 oven 35 minutes per pound/450 grams. About half an hour before the roast is ready, put the baking dish of extra stuffing in the oven to heat.

After the roast has been removed to a hot serving dish, pour off the fat in the roasting tin. Spoon some drippings over the top of the stuffing in the roast and some over the small baking dish of extra stuffing.

Japanese Pork Loin

Pork Pie

6 servings

1 medium sized head of cauliflower
1 tablespoon oil
2 small onions, peeled and very finely chopped
1 clove garlic, crushed
1½ lb/700 grams tinned tomatoes
Pinch thyme
Salt and pepper
¼ teaspoon paprika
1½ oz/45 grams flour
1½ lb/700 grams cooked pork, diced
Pastry to top a 9-inch/23-cms pie

Cook the cauliflower until just tender in boiling, salted water. Drain and divide into small florets.

Heat the oil in a pan; add the onion and garlic and sauté for a few minutes. Add the tomatoes, thyme, salt, pepper and paprika. Simmer for 10 minutes, then press through a sieve. Blend the flour with a little cold water; add it to the sauce and stir until boiling.

Put the pork and cauliflower into a deep dish (about 4 pints/2¼ litres) and pour the sauce over them. Cover with the pastry and bake for about 25 minutes in a preheated 450°F/230°C/gas mark 8 oven or until the crust is well browned.

Pork Stroganoff

4 servings

1½ lb/700 grams shoulder of pork
4 onions
Butter or margarine for frying
Salt
Pepper
18 fl oz/500 ml strong beef broth
2 tablespoons tomato paste
15 fl oz/425 grams soured cream
1 to 2 teaspoons soy sauce

Cut the meat into strips. Peel and slice the onions. Brown the meat in the butter in a stew pan. Add salt and pepper. Add the onions so that they also become brown.

Decrease the heat and gradually add the beef broth. Add the tomato paste. Simmer the meat and the onions in the gravy for about 25 minutes, or until the meat is tender and thoroughly cooked. Cover the pan when simmering the meat.

Remove from the heat and stir in the cream. Bring to the boil and add the soy sauce. This dish should have a rich and rather strong taste. Serve with rice.

Muckalica

4 servings

2 lb/900 grams boneless loin of pork
1 oz/30 grams butter or margarine
2 green peppers, seeded and cubed
2 onions, chopped
4 tomatoes, chopped
4 pepperoni (fresh), cubed
2 teaspoons soy sauce
1¼ teaspoons salt
½ teaspoon black pepper
8 fl oz/220 ml soured cream
1 onion, chopped

Trim the meat by cutting away any extra pieces of fat, then cut the meat into strips. Brown it well in the butter. Mix the green peppers, onions, tomatoes, and pepperoni with the meat, decrease the heat and add the soy sauce, salt and pepper. Cover and simmer for about half an hour. If the stew begins to look dry, add 2½ fl oz/75 ml water.

Serve with soured cream, chopped raw onion and boiled rice.

Smoked Pork Loin

Barbecued Pork Ribs

6 servings

15 fl oz/425 ml ketchup
15 fl oz/425 ml water
8 fl oz/220 ml chilli sauce
¼ pint/140 ml vinegar
6 tablespoons Worcester sauce
3 oz/85 grams light brown sugar
3 tablespoons fresh lemon juice
1 tablespoon paprika
3¼ teaspoons salt
1 clove garlic, crushed
5 lb/2¼ kilos pork ribs in the piece
½ teaspoon pepper
Thin slices of onion and lemon (optional)

Combine the ketchup, water, chilli sauce, vinegar, Worcester sauce, brown sugar, lemon juice, paprika, 2¼ teaspoons of salt and garlic in a large saucepan. Heat to boiling; reduce heat. Simmer 30 to 45 minutes, until the sauce is good basting consistency.

Cut the meat into 3 to 4 rib portions. Sprinkle with 1 teaspoon of salt and pepper. Put it on a rack in a shallow baking tin. Bake at 450°F/230°C/gas mark 8 for 30 minutes. Remove the meat from the rack; drain off excess fat.

Put the ribs in a baking tin, meaty side down; brush with sauce. Reduce the oven temperature to 300°F/150°C/gas mark 2, bake 30 minutes. Turn the ribs meaty side up; brush with sauce. Top each rib with an onion slice. Bake about 1 hour, brushing frequently with some remaining sauce, until the ribs are tender and nicely browned. Add lemon slices to the ribs during the last half hour of baking. Serve the remaining sauce on the side.

Roast Pork with Oranges

6 servings

4 lb/1800 grams pork loin roast
1 teaspoon sage
Salt and pepper
½ pint/¼ l water
Juice of 1 orange
¼ pint/140 ml sherry
1 tablespoon redcurrant jelly
Grated rind of 1 orange
3–6 oranges, peeled and sectioned

Rub the pork with sage, salt and pepper. Put it on a rack in a shallow roasting tin. Add the water. Roast at 325°F/163°C/gas mark 3 for 2 hours or until a thermometer registers 170°F/75°C.

About 45 minutes before the meat is done, pour off the fat; leave the cooking juices. Pour orange juice and sherry over the meat. Spread jelly over the meat; sprinkle with orange rind. Baste a few times. When

Grilled Marinated Spareribs

done, put the meat on a dish; surround it with oranges.

Savoury Pork in Sweet Potato Nests

4 servings

1 lb/450 grams sweet potatoes, mashed
Milk
½ oz/15 grams butter or margarine, melted
12 oz/345 grams cooked pork, finely chopped
8 oz/225 grams peas
¼ pint/140 ml pork gravy
½ teaspoon salt
Large pinch thyme

To the mashed sweet potatoes, add enough milk to make the mixture smooth and easy to shape. Divide in mounds on a baking sheet. Make a well in the centre of each mound with the back of a spoon. Brush with melted butter.

Combine the remaining ingredients in a baking dish. Place the pork mixture and sweet potato mounds in a 350°F/180°C/gas mark 4 oven for 15 to 20 minutes. Spoon over the pork into the sweet potato nests and serve at once.

Rolled Pork Shoulder with Ham and Cheese

4 servings

¼ oz/8 grams butter
8 thin slices of lean pork shoulder, about 1 lb/450 grams
4 oz/115 grams smoked ham, in thin slices
5 to 6 slices cheese
½ teaspoon salt
¼ teaspoon black pepper
½ to 1 teaspoon crushed sage (optional)
Tomato halves (optional)

Grease a roasting tin, placing a wide strip of butter along the middle of the tin. Place the shoulder slices in the middle of the roasting tin. The slices should be placed in a row, slightly overlapping. Sprinkle with most of the salt, pepper and sage, if desire. Place the ham and cheese on top.

Roll up the meat, first from one side and then from the other, so that it becomes a long roll. Fasten with toothpicks. Salt.

Bake in the middle of a preheated 350°F/180°C/gas mark 4 oven until a toothpick goes easily through the meat, about 45 minutes. Toward the end of the baking time, brush the roll with a small amount of the gravy and fat which has collected in the bottom of the tin. If you wish, place tomato halves around the meat when 15 minutes of the baking time remains.

Cut the roll up into slices and serve with boiled potatoes. Lightly salt and pepper the tomatoes.

Swedish-Style Pork

4 servings

1¼ lb/565 grams lean, boned pork shoulder
1 tablespoon soy sauce
1 tablespoon oil
Black pepper
1½ lb/700 grams par-boiled potatoes, diced
1½ oz/45 grams butter
1 onion, finely chopped
1½ teaspoons salt
4 raw egg yolks (optional)

Cut the meat into small cubes and mix with soy sauce, oil and black pepper. Sauté the potatoes in 1 oz/30 grams of the butter in a large frying pan until soft and browned, about 10 minutes. Cook the onion with the potatoes for the last 3 to 4 minutes. Season with about 1 teaspoon salt.

Finally, sauté the meat quickly in butter in a large, very hot pan—cook about 3 to 4 minutes. Season the meat with ½ teaspoon salt.

Serve the meat and potatoes with a raw egg yolk, if desired.

Sausage and Apple Casserole

4 to 6 servings

15 slices white bread, cubed
1 lb/450 grams sausage meat
1 large onion, diced
1 green pepper, diced
¼ pint/140 ml water
2 large apples, peeled, cored and chopped
1 teaspoon salt

Use stale white bread for the cubes, or stale them by putting the bread in a 250°F/120°C/gas mark ¼ oven for 10 minutes. Brown the sausage in a large pan. Cook until there is no trace of pink in the meat. Add the onion and green pepper; cook for 2 minutes more. Stir in the bread cubes, water, apples and salt. Mix together until evenly moist.

Turn out the cooked mixture into a well-greased casserole. Cook in a 350°F/180°C/gas mark 4 oven 30 minutes or until the top crusts.

Baked Smoked Sausage and Rice

6 servings

1 lb/450 grams smoked sausage
12 oz/345 grams onion, chopped
¼ pint/140 ml ketchup
1 oz/30 grams brown sugar
1 teaspoon prepared mustard
½ teaspoon salt
¼ teaspoon ground black pepper
1½ lb/700 grams cooked rice

Simmer the sausage in water to cover for 10 minutes. Remove the sausage and cut it in 1½-inch/3-cm pieces. Combine with the remaining ingredients. Turn into a greased, shallow 4 pint/2¼ litre casserole. Bake, uncovered, at 350°F/180°C/gas mark 4 for 20 to 25 minutes.

Barbecued Hot Dogs

4 to 6 servings

2 oz/60 grams onion, chopped
2 teaspoons sugar
1 teaspoon paprika
¼ teaspoon salt
Large pinch pepper
4 fl oz/110 ml ketchup
4 fl oz/110 ml water
3 tablespoons vinegar
2 teaspoons Worcester sauce
1 lb/450 grams Frankfurters

Combine all the ingredients and pour the sauce over the sausages in a baking dish. Bake at 400°F/200°C/gas mark 6 for 30 minutes.

Muckalica

Breast of Veal with Herb Stuffing

6 servings

herb stuffing

3 rashers bacon
1 medium sized onion
4 oz/115 grams tinned mushroom pieces
2 oz/60 grams fresh parsley, chopped
1 tablespoon fresh dill, chopped
1 teaspoon dried tarragon leaves
1 teaspoon dried basil leaves
8 oz/225 grams lean mince
2 oz/60 grams dried breadcrumbs
3 eggs, beaten
4 fl oz/110 ml soured cream
½ teaspoon salt
¼ teaspoon pepper

veal

3–4 lb/1350–1800 grams boned breast of veal
½ teaspoon salt
¼ teaspoon pepper
1 tablespoon vegetable oil
1 pint/½ l hot beef broth
1 oz/30 grams cornflour
¼ pint/140 ml soured cream

Prepare the stuffing: Dice the bacon and onion. Cook the bacon in a pan until partially cooked. Add the onion; cook 5 minutes.

Drain and chop the mushrooms; add to the pan. Cook 5 minutes; remove from the heat. Let cool; transfer to a mixing bowl. Add the herbs, mince, crumbs, eggs and soured cream; mix thoroughly. Season with salt and pepper.

With a sharp knife, cut a pocket in the veal; fill it with the stuffing. Close the opening with toothpicks. (Tie with string if necessary.) Rub the outside with salt and pepper.

Heat the oil in a heavy saucepan; place the meat in the pan. Bake in a preheated 350°F/180°C/gas mark 4 oven about 1½ hours; baste occasionally with beef broth. When done, place the meat on a preheated serving dish.

Pour the rest of the beef broth into the pan; scrape any brown particles from the bottom. Bring to a simmer. Thoroughly blend the cornflour with the cream; add to the pan drippings, stirring. Cook and stir until thick and bubbly. Slice the veal breast. Serve the sauce separately.

Pork Stroganoff

Hot Dogs in Batter

6 servings

4 oz/115 grams cornmeal
2 oz/60 grams flour
1 teaspoon salt
½ teaspoon pepper
¼ pint/140 ml milk
1 egg, beaten
2 tablespoons oil
12 Frankfurters
Fat or oil for deep frying

Mix the cornmeal, flour, salt and pepper in a bowl. Add the milk, egg and oil. Stir until smooth. Dip the sausages into batter; drain over a bowl. Fry in deep fat 2 to 3 minutes, until golden brown, turning once. Remove from the fat; drain.

Frankfurter and Bean Casserole

4 to 6 servings

2 lb/900 grams baked beans
2½ fl oz/75 ml ketchup
2½ fl oz/75 ml molasses
2 oz/60 grams onion, finely chopped
1½ teaspoons prepared mustard

¼ teaspoon Worcester sauce
1 lb/450 grams Frankfurters

Combine all the ingredients except the sausages and place them in a 3 pint/1½ litre casserole. Slash the top of the sausages in 3 or 4 places and arrange them on top of the bean mixture. Bake in a 350°F/180°C/gas mark 4 oven for 25 to 30 minutes.

Sausage and Apple Toads

6 to 8 servings

1 lb/450 grams sausages
3 apples, peeled, cored and sliced
2 tablespoons sugar
3 oz/85 grams butter or margarine
4 oz/115 grams flour
1 teaspoon salt
1 egg, beaten
Milk

Grease a large baking tin. Place the sausages in a pan; prick each sausage with a fork. Cover with water; bring to the boil. Simmer 5 minutes; drain off the water. Brown the sausages; place in the baking tin. Spread apple slices over the meat. Sprinkle the apples with sugar.

Mix the butter and flour; add the salt. Stir in the egg and enough milk to make a stiff dough. Spread the dough over the apples, using your fingers. Brush with butter (or some of the egg). Make a hole in the centre for the steam to escape. Bake 25 to 30 minutes in a 400°F/200°C/gas mark 6 oven.

Veal Chops with Rosemary

6 servings

6 veal chops
Flour
1 large clove garlic, crushed
1 oz/30 grams butter
2 tablespoons olive oil
Rosemary to taste
Salt and freshly ground pepper

Dust the veal chops lightly with flour. Set aside on a paper towel. Add the garlic to the melted butter and oil in a sauté pan large enough to hold all the chops without crowding or overlapping. When the oil begins to sizzle, add the chops and sauté quickly on both sides until well browned.

When the chops have browned on first side, sprinkle with rosemary. Season to taste with salt and pepper. Cover the pan and let the chops cook until cooked through. Do not overcook or chops will dry out and toughen. Serve with some of the garlic butter spooned on each chop.

Veal with Onions

6 servings

2 onions
1 oz/30 grams butter
6 carrots, sliced
2 oz/60 grams butter, additional
2½ lb/1150 grams stewing veal
Salt and pepper
¼ pint/140 ml water
½ oz/15 grams flour (optional)

Peel the onions and slice into rings. Sauté the onion rings in 1 oz/30 grams of butter until brown. In a large, covered pan, melt 2 oz/60 grams of butter until light brown. Add the sautéed onions, carrots, veal and salt and pepper to taste. Mix well; add the water. Mix; cover and simmer over low heat for 30 minutes.

Serve over rice or noodles. If a thicker sauce is desired, mix 1 tablespoon of flour with 3 tablespoons of cold water and add to sauce; mix to thicken.

Braised Liver and Vegetable Rings

6 servings

1½ lb/700 grams lambs liver
1 oz/30 grams flour
2½ teaspoons salt
Large pinch pepper
1 oz/30 grams cooking fat
4 medium sized turnips, thinly sliced
4 medium sized carrots, thinly sliced
1 large onion, sliced
¼ teaspoon marjoram
¼ pint/140 ml water
Paprika

Cut the liver in 6 serving-size pieces. Combine the flour, 1 teaspoon salt and pepper; dredge the liver slices. Brown the liver in the cooking fat and remove from the pan. Pour off the drippings. Add the turnips, carrots and onion to the pan and sprinkle with 1½ teaspoons salt and marjoram.

Place the liver on top of the vegetables; add the water, cover tightly and cook slowly 20 minutes or until done. Place the liver and vegetable on a serving dish and sprinkle with paprika.

Rolled Pork Shoulder with Ham and Cheese

Piccata with Rice and Saffron Sauce

pint/3 litre casserole. Add the tomatoes, onions and mixed vegetables. Bake covered in a 350°F/180°C/gas mark 4 oven for 45 minutes.

Meanwhile, whip the sweet potatoes, butter and milk until fluffy. When the veal is tender, spoon sweet potato in mounds over the casserole. Bake uncovered 15 minutes or until the potatoes are heated through.

Piccata with Rice and Saffron Sauce

4 servings

8 escalopes of pork or veal

batter
2 to 3 eggs
6 oz/170 grams grated Parmesan cheese
2½ tablespoons water
½ teaspoon paprika
½ teaspoon salt
Large pinch white pepper
1 oz/30 grams flour
1–1½ oz/30–45 grams butter

saffron sauce
18 fl oz/500 ml soured cream
Pinch saffron, crushed
½ teaspoon salt
About ½ oz/15 grams butter

Beat each escalope out flat.

Mix the eggs, cheese, water and spices into a batter. Pour the flour out on a plate and dredge the meat in the flour. In the meantime, heat a large frying pan to medium temperature.

Lightly brown the butter in the pan. Dip the meat in the egg batter, turning so that both sides get covered and place in the frying pan. Sauté 1 to 2 minutes on each side, making sure that the pan does not get too hot. Cook in several batches if the pan is not large enough.

Make the saffron sauce. Bring the cream to the boil. Season with the saffron and the salt. Boil the sauce for several minutes and then beat in ½ oz/15 grams cold butter.

Serve the piccata on warm plates with a pool of saffron sauce and with rice as a side dish. Allow 2 escalopes per person.

Veal Stew with Sweet Potatoes

6 servings

1 lb/450 grams veal, thinly cut
1 oz/30 grams flour
2 tablespoons salad oil
1 clove garlic, crushed
10 oz/285 grams condensed tomato soup
½ pint/¼ l beef broth
1 teaspoon salt
1 teaspoon paprika
2 bay leaves
4 tomatoes, peeled and quartered
2 medium sized onions, sliced
12 oz/345 grams frozen mixed vegetables, partly thawed
1 lb/450 grams sweet potatoes, mashed and seasoned
1 oz/30 grams butter or margarine, melted
4 fl oz/110 ml milk

Cut the veal into 1-inch/2½-cm strips. Dredge in flour. Brown in hot oil with garlic. Combine with the tomato soup, broth and seasonings. Turn into a 5

Veal Schnitzel with Spinach and Sherry Sauce

2 servings

10 oz/285 grams frozen spinach
8 oz/225 grams asparagus tips
½ teaspoon salt
Pinch pepper
Pinch garlic powder
¼ teaspoon crushed basil
2 veal cutlets
1 oz/30 grams butter
1½ teaspoons soy sauce
1 teaspoon arrowroot or cornflour
2 tablespoons sherry

Cook the spinach in its own juice over medium heat. When tender, drain and reserve the liquid. Cook the asparagus tips in ¼ pint/140 ml boiling salted water for 4 to 5 minutes. Drain and combine the liquid with the spinach broth.

Combine the spices; rub half of them into the cutlets and season the spinach with the rest.

Heat a nonstick pan, add the butter and sauté the cutlets, 1 to 2 minutes on each side. Place the cutlets on a heated dish along with the asparagus and the spinach. Cover with foil and keep warm while making the sauce.

Boil the vegetable broth until it measures approximately 12 fl oz/350 ml. Add the soy sauce. Mix the thickener with the sherry and add it to the broth, stirring constantly. Bring to the boil and season with salt and pepper. Pour the sauce around the meat and serve immediately.

Marinated Liver

4 servings

15 fl oz/425 ml red wine
1 teaspoon thyme
4 to 6 slices calves' liver
4 tomatoes
1 small onion
1 tablespoon olive oil
8 oz/225 grams celery, cut in strips
½ teaspoon basil
1½ teaspoons salt
1½ oz/45 grams flour
¼ teaspoon black pepper
½ oz/15 grams butter or margarine

Mix the wine and thyme in a bowl. Place the liver slices in the mixture and marinate for 1 hour in the refrigerator.

Dip the tomatoes in boiling water, then peel. Remove the seeds and cut the tomatoes into large pieces. Peel and finely chop the onion. Heat the oil in a small saucepan and lightly sauté the onion. Add the tomato pieces, celery, basil and ½ teaspoon of the salt. Simmer for a few minutes.

Dry off the liver. Dredge the slices in flour that has been mixed with the remaining salt and pepper. Brown the butter in a frying pan and sauté the liver slices for about 3 minutes on each side.

Divide the tomato mixture over the liver slices and serve immediately.

Autumn Stew with Tongue

Rabbit Stew

6 servings

4–5 lb/1800–2250 grams rabbit, fresh or frozen
   and thawed
2 oz/60 grams bacon fat or butter
1½ oz/45 grams flour
1 pint/½ l chicken stock
1 pint/½ l dry white wine
1 clove garlic, crushed
2½ tablespoons tomato paste
Salt
Pepper
1 teaspoon tarragon
1 bay leaf, crushed
½ teaspoon thyme
3 tablespoons soured cream

Have the butcher cut the rabbit into serving pieces. Heat the fat; brown the rabbit pieces on all sides. Sprinkle with flour; blend in well. Add the stock, wine, garlic, tomato paste and seasonings. Simmer, covered, over low heat 1½ hours. Transfer the meat to a warm serving dish.

Reduce the sauce if necessary. Stir in the soured cream; heat, but do not let the sauce boil. Pour the sauce over the rabbit.

Autumn Stew with Tongue

4 servings

1½ lb/700 grams tongue
Water
1 bay leaf
10 white peppercorns
1 lb/450 grams potatoes
1 leek
4 oz/115 grams celeriac
2 carrots
1 teaspoon mustard seeds
2 oz/60 grams snipped green herbs

Place the tongue in a pot and pour over enough water so that it is just covered. Add the bay leaf and the peppercorns. Cover and simmer over low heat for about 1 hour. Test to see if the tongue is done by pricking it with a toothpick. If the toothpick goes easily through, the meat is done.

Remove the cooked tongue from the pot and skin it while still warm. Place the meat back in the broth.

Peel and prepare the vegetables by cutting them into pieces. Cut the celeriac into thinner pieces. Place all the vegetables and spices in a pot and cover with enough broth to cover the vegetables. (Add more broth, if necessary.)

Cut the tongue into strips or cubes. Return to the pot and cover. Cook for about 15 minutes or until the potatoes and vegetables feel soft. Add the mustard

Marinated Liver

seeds and sprinkle with the snipped herbs (parsley, dill etc.) just before serving.

Venison Loaf

8 to 10 servings

2 lb/900 grams minced venison
2 lb/900 grams pork sausage
2 medium sized onions, finely chopped
6 oz/170 grams golden, packet, breadcrumbs
½ pint/¼ l evaporated milk
3 eggs, lightly beaten
1 pint/½ l barbecue sauce
1 teaspoon salt
½ teaspoon freshly ground pepper

Place the venison, sausage, onions and crumbs in a large bowl and mix well. Add the milk, eggs, half the barbecue sauce, salt and pepper and blend well. Chill for 15 minutes.

Shape into 2 loaves, then place the loaves in a large, greased baking tin. Bake in a preheated 350°F/180°C/gas mark 4 oven for 30 minutes. Spoon the remaining barbecue sauce over the loaves and bake for 45 minutes longer.

Fish and Shellfish

Soused Herrings

3 to 4 servings

6 herrings, split and boned
Salt and pepper
1 tablespoon pickling spice
1 bayleaf
1 onion, thinly sliced
15 fl oz/425 ml vinegar and water, in equal
    proportions

Have herrings split and boned. Season cut surface
and roll up from head to tail. Pack in a deep dish or
casserole. Set oven to 325°F/163°C/gas mark 3.

Put pickling spice and bayleaf into a pan with
onion, vinegar and water. Add salt and bring to the
boil. Cool, then pour over the herrings. The liquid
should just cover them. Cook in the preheated oven
for about 1 hour. Serve the herrings cold.

Fried Herrings

4 servings

8 herrings, topped, tailed and backbone removed
2 eggs
2 tablespoons water
8 oz/225 grams seasoned flour
Fat for frying

Flatten out fish. Beat the eggs and water together.
Dip the fish in the egg mixture, then in the flour to
coat.

In a heavy, preferably cast-iron, pan heat about ½-
inch/1-cm deep of fat. Fry the herrings until they are
a crusty golden brown, turning once. Drain and serve
very hot with wedges of lemon.

Parmesan Baked Halibut with Courgette

Pike with Tomato and Anchovy

Cod with Clam and Mushroom Sauce

4 servings

1½ lb/700 grams cod fillets
Butter or margarine

clam and mushroom sauce
1½ oz/45 grams butter or margarine
1½ oz/45 grams flour
15 fl oz/425 ml plain yoghurt
8 oz/225 grams tinned minced clams, undrained
4 oz/115 grams mushrooms, sautéed in butter
Salt and freshly ground black pepper to taste
Fresh dill leaves for garnish

Sauté the fish in butter or margarine in a large pan until the fish can be separated into flakes with a fork.

Prepare the sauce. Melt the butter in a saucepan. Add the flour; stir to form a smooth paste. Add the yoghurt; heat and stir over moderate heat just until the mixture comes to the boil and is thickened. Add the clams, mushrooms and salt and pepper. Reheat briefly.

Place the fish on a warm serving dish. Ladle the sauce over the fish. Serve at once garnished with sprigs of dill.

Red Mullet with Fennel and Lemon

4 servings

4 red mullet, cleaned
Salt
Pepper
4 tablespoons oil
1 shallot, finely chopped
2 heads of fennel
1 lemon
1 oz/30 grams butter
Chopped parsley

Trim the mullet and make 3–4 diagonal slits on each side of the fish. Season and marinate in oil and shallot while preparing fennel.

Cut fennel into thick slices and blanch 2–3 minutes; drain well. Remove peel and pith from lemon and cut flesh into segments. Sauté fennel in butter until just tender, season and add lemon and parsley.

Brush grill rack with oil and pre-heat grill. Remove mullet from marinade and grill for 8–10 minutes, brushing with oil if necessary during cooking. Serve with fennel and lemon on a hot dish.

Salt Cod with Pork

4 to 6 servings

1 lb/450 grams salt cod
4 large red or yellow onions, finely sliced
8 fl oz/220 ml white vinegar
8 fl oz/220 ml water
2½ oz/75 grams sugar
Salt and pepper to taste
12 oz/345 grams lean salt pork, finely diced
4 lb/1800 grams medium sized potatoes

Cover the cod with cold water and let it soak overnight. Drain and rinse well.

Combine the onions, vinegar, water, sugar, salt and pepper in a bowl and let stand for about 2 hours before serving time.

Place the diced pork in an iron pan and cook slowly over medium to low heat until golden brown.

Peel the potatoes and cut them in half, then place in a 10 pint/5½ litre pan. Place the cod over the potatoes and add enough water to cover. Cover and bring to the boil. Reduce the heat and simmer for about 40 minutes or until the potatoes are tender.

Pour the diced pork and fat into a gravy boat. This is the sauce. Drain the potatoes and cod and arrange on a serving dish. Spoon the pickled onions over the potatoes and cod.

Lemon Haddock

4 to 6 servings

2 lb/900 grams thick haddock fillet
½ lemon, thinly sliced
Salt and pepper
2 tablespoons lemon juice
1 tablespoon parsley, chopped
3 spring onions, diced, including green part
4 oz/115 grams butter, melted

Score the fish with a sharp knife. Lay the lemon slices in the slits. Add the remaining ingredients to the melted butter; simmer 3 minutes.

Place the fish in an ungreased oven dish. Pour the sauce over the fish. Bake the fish about 20 minutes, or until the fish is flaky. Baste several times with the sauce while the fish is cooking.

Poached Haddock with Mussels

6 servings

2 lb/900 grams haddock, cod or other thick fillets
4 lb/1800 grams mussels in shells (about 48)
½ pint/¼ litre dry white wine
½ pint/¼ litre water
1 small onion, sliced
½ teaspoon salt
¼ pint/140 ml whipping cream
2 oz/60 grams margarine or butter

Dash white pepper
Dash nutmeg
2 tablespoons parsley, chopped

Cut the fillets into serving-size portions.

Clean the mussels in cold water; scrub the shells with a stiff brush, rinsing thoroughly several times. Combine the wine, water and onion in a large pan; bring to a simmer. Add the mussels. Cover and steam about 5 minutes or until the shells open. Remove the mussels from the shells; set aside.

Strain the cooking liquid into a large pan. Add the fillets and salt. Cover; simmer 8 to 10 minutes or until the fish flakes easily. Transfer the fillets to a warm dish; keep warm.

Reduce the cooking liquid to ¼ pint/140 ml. Stir in the whipping cream, the margarine or butter, pepper and nutmeg; simmer until the sauce thickens slightly. Add the mussels and parsley; heat. Spoon the mixture over the fillets.

Sole Fillets in Orange Sauce

Parmesan Baked Halibut with Courgette

6 servings

1½ lb/700 grams fillets of halibut
1 pint/½ l fish stock
1 courgette

sauce
8 fl oz/220 ml stock from the above
2½ fl oz/75 ml dry white wine
4 fl oz/110 ml double cream

garnish
2½ oz/75 grams Parmesan cheese, freshly grated
2½ oz/75 grams white bread
1 egg yolk plus 4 fl oz/110 ml double cream

Boil the fish stock in a shallow, large pan and poach the fish fillets in the stock for 2 to 4 minutes. Then place them on a large, ovenproof plate or on individual serving plates.

Thinly slice the courgette and prepare the slices by placing them in salted boiling water, letting the water come to the boil again, draining off the water and finally cooling off the slices in cold water.

Prepare the sauce by mixing the stock, wine and

Festive Cold Sole Plate

cream in a pan. Bring the sauce to the boil, then let simmer until it has a thick, creamy consistency. Pour the sauce over the fish. Mix the cheese and white breadcrumbs together and cover the entire dish with them.

Preheat oven to 450°F/230°C/gas mark 8. Beat the egg yolk and cream together and sprinkle drops of this mixture over the crumb mixture, using a fork to mix it in. Finally sprinkle a little more Parmesan cheese on top and bake in the oven until the dish has browned.

Pike with Tomato and Anchovy

4 servings

About 3 lb/1¼ kilos pike fillets
½ teaspoon salt
Freshly ground white pepper
8 oz/225 grams sieved tomatoes
2 oz/60 grams onion, finely chopped
2 oz/60 grams anchovy fillets, chopped
1 teaspoon chervil or thyme
6 oz/170 grams mild Cheddar cheese, grated
2 tablespoons grated Parmesan
½ pint/¼ l fish stock
2 oz/60 grams butter
About 2 oz/60 grams parsley, chopped

Grease an ovenproof dish and place the fish on it with the flesh side facing up and the belly parts slightly overlapping. Season well with salt and a few turns of the pepper mill. Combine the tomatoes, onion, anchovies and thyme or chervil in a bowl. Divide the tomato mixture evenly over the fish. Blend the 2 cheeses and sprinkle over the tomato mixture.

Bring the stock to the boil and pour it carefully around the fish. Place the dish in a preheated 450°F/230°C/gas mark 8 oven for 15 to 20 minutes. Then carefully pour off most of the liquid into a saucepan and beat in the butter and the chopped parsley. Heat the sauce and pour around fish on a serving dish. Serve with freshly boiled potatoes or boiled rice.

Sole Fillets in Orange Sauce

4 servings

2½ fl oz/75 ml soy sauce
½ teaspoon ground ginger
1 teaspoon salt
Juice of 2 oranges
1 lb/450 grams sole fillets
1 large onion, chopped
½ oz/15 grams margarine
4 leaves Chinese cabbage, finely shredded
2½ fl oz/75 ml water
¼ oz/8 grams arrowroot or cornflour
Pepper

Mix the soy sauce, ginger, salt and orange juice in a bowl. Cut each fillet into 3 strips lengthwise and place in the mixture.

Fry the onion in the margarine in a large pan, then add the cabbage. Lift out the fish and stir arrowroot or cornflour into the soy sauce mixture and pour this over the fish. Cover and allow to come to the boil while shaking the pan. Season with salt and pepper and serve with boiled rice.

Festive Cold Sole Plate

6 servings

4 bay leaves
1 teaspoon whole allspice
2–3 lb/900–1350 grams sole fillets
½ bottle dry white wine

sauce
12 fl oz/350 ml whipped cream
1 jar lumpfish roe
3 tablespoons chilli sauce
Several dashes of tabasco
About 6 oz/170 grams snipped dill
1 large tin clams
Prawns to taste, but at least 14 oz/400 grams with
   the shells still on
Lemon slices

Place the bay leaves and the allspice in a piece of gauze and tie it together into a little spice bag. Thaw the fish, if frozen, and place it with the wine and the spice bag in a pot. Simmer for 10 minutes.

Remove the spice bag and allow the fish to become cold in the wine. (The fish may be prepared in advance up to this step and then refrigerated overnight.) Pour off the wine and place the fish on a serving plate.

Whip the cream. Mix in all the ingredients except the clams and the prawns. Pour off the clam juice from the tin. Shell the prawns. Add both clams and prawns to the mixture, saving a few prawns with which to garnish the dish.

Pour the sauce over the fish and garnish with prawns, lemon slices and sprigs of dill.

Baked Salmon

6 servings

1 5 lb/2¼ kilos salmon (whole or piece), scaled
   and fins removed
Salt and pepper
Flour
3 oz/85 grams butter, melted
1 large onion, finely chopped
1 clove garlic, crushed
1 tablespoon Worcester sauce

Sole Pie

2 tomatoes, peeled, drained of juice, seeded and
   chopped, or tinned tomatoes, drained
2½ fl oz/75 ml (approximately) single cream
½ oz/15 grams butter and ½ oz/15 grams flour,
   kneaded together, if necessary
Lemon wedges
Parsley

Rub the salmon inside and out with salt and pepper, dredge with flour and put it into a well-greased narrow baking tin. Bake in a preheated 425°F/220°C/gas mark 7 oven for 15 minutes, then add the butter, onion, garlic, Worcester sauce and tomatoes and reduce heat to 375°F/190°C/gas mark 5. Bake for 30 minutes longer, basting frequently. A meat thermometer, inserted into the thickest part of the fish, should reach 160°F/70°C.

Remove the fish to a hot dish and keep warm. Add a little cream, about 2½ fl oz/75 ml, to the sauce in the pan and stir well until smooth. If sauce is too thin, thicken with the butter kneaded with flour. Garnish the fish with lemon wedges and parsley and serve the sauce in a separate dish.

Sole Pie

6 servings

pastry

5 oz/140 grams flour
3½ oz/100 grams butter or margarine
2½ oz/75 grams cottage cheese

filling

1 lb/450 grams fillet of sole
1½ oz/45 grams flour
1 teaspoon dried parsley
1 teaspoon tarragon
½ teaspoon salt
8 oz/225 grams frozen broccoli, thawed and
   drained

sauce

½ oz/15 grams flour
6 oz/170 grams crushed tomatoes
½ teaspoon French mustard
2 oz/60 grams grated mild Cheddar cheese
¼ teaspoon salt
Large pinch nutmeg

Mix the pastry dough and refrigerate it for 30 minutes. Roll out the dough and line a pie plate with it. Prick with a fork and bake in a 400°F/200°C/gas mark 6 oven for 7 minutes.

If the fish fillets are large, they should be cut up into smaller pieces. Dredge with the flour, which has been mixed with the spices and salt. Lightly dry the broccoli with kitchen towel. Alternate the fish and the broccoli in the baked pastry case. Bake the pie for another 10 minutes.

Mix the flour for the sauce in a little of the crushed tomatoes, to avoid lumping. Add the rest of the ingredients. Divide the sauce evenly over the fish and bake the pie for another 10 minutes or until the pie has an attractive colour. Serve hot or slightly warm.

Note: the pie can also be made from leftover, cooked fish. Bake the pastry case so that it is almost done. Cover the fish with the sauce, right from the beginning. Fish that is already cooked can easily become dry if it stays in the oven too long.

Poached Salmon

8 to 10 servings

Water to fill fish kettle halfway
1 pint/½ litre dry white wine
2 tablespoons peppercorns
1 tablespoon salt
2 onions, sliced
¼ pint/140 ml white wine vinegar
8 oz/225 grams celery tops
5–6 lb/2¼–2½ kilos whole salmon (or one that
   fits the fish kettle)
Lemon slices

Place all of the ingredients in the kettle except the salmon and boil for 15 minutes. Strain the mixture (it is now called a court bouillon) and let it cool to room temperature.

Wash the salmon, make sure the scales are removed and trim the fins. Place the salmon in the kettle to size it. If the fish is a bit too long, trim off a little of the tail. If your fish is much too long, use 2 kettles and cut the fish in half. Join the fish together after it is cooked, hiding the seam with a garnish of lemon slices.

Measure depth of the thickest part of the fish with a ruler. After measuring the fish, wrap it in cheese cloth. Put in the kettle and place over high heat. When the court bouillon comes to the boil, begin timing the cooking. The fish should cook for 10 minutes per inch of thickness. A 2-inch/5-cm thick fish would cook for 20 minutes, a 2½-inch/6-cm thick one for 25 minutes. Work out the time to the minute and remove the fish promptly.

Place the fish on a warm dish and remove the skin. Under the skin is a brownish fatty layer than can be lifted off the fish to reveal the coppery flesh beneath.

Salmon Slices in Herb Sauce

4 servings

1¼ fl oz/38 ml water
8 fl oz/220 ml dry white wine
4 tablespoons olive oil
2 cloves garlic, chopped
6 to 8 slices fresh salmon (2 lb/900 grams)
Salt
Pepper
4 fl oz/110 ml double cream
2 tablespoons parsley, chopped
1 rounded teaspoon each of oregano, basil, thyme
   and tarragon
4 fl oz/110 ml soured cream

Simmer the water, wine, oil and garlic together. Salt and pepper the salmon slices; then place the fish in the pan. Cover and simmer for about 10 minutes. Pick up the fish with a draining spoon and place it in a deep, warm plate.

Mix the cream with the salmon broth and let it boil vigorously for a few minutes, uncovered, before adding all the herbs. After a few minutes, beat in the cream and season with salt, pepper and perhaps a little stock cube, crumbled. Serve immediately with boiled rice and a green salad.

Sole in Vermouth Sauce

Fillets of Whiting with Orange

4 servings

8 whiting fillets
15 fl oz/425 ml fish stock
2 navel oranges
Juice of 1 lemon, strained
1½ oz/45 grams butter
4 fl oz/110 ml sherry
½ pint/¼ l double cream
Salt and pepper
½ teaspoon paprika
3 egg yolks, well beaten
½ pint/¼ l white wine
1 shallot, finely chopped

Wash the fillets in cold water and dry on kitchen towel. Strain and heat the fish stock.

Wash the oranges and, with a sharp knife or a potato peeler, remove only the orange part of the rind. Cut it in thin slivers and cover immediately with strained lemon juice. With a sharp knife cut off the remaining white pith from the oranges and cut between sections to extract the pulp in neat, crescent-shaped pieces.

Melt 1 oz/30 grams of butter in the top part of a small double boiler over boiling water. Add the sherry. When hot, stir in the double cream. Season to taste with salt and pepper and the paprika. Cook for a minute or two, then pour the hot mixture over the egg yolks, stirring hard. Return to the top of a double boiler and cook, stirring constantly, until the sauce is smooth and thick like custard, about 2–3 minutes. Remove the top pan and set it aside to keep warm.

Put the white wine in a shallow enamel pan, add the shallot, the remaining butter, the fish stock and the prepared orange peel, drained of lemon juice. Season lightly to taste with salt and pepper and lay the fillets on this bed. Poach very gently until opaque, about 15 minutes, turning the fillets over once when half done. Transfer the fillets gently to a hot dish and keep warm.

Reduce the stock in the fish pan to a third of its original quantity by boiling rapidly. Add this gradually to the egg sauce, place over hot water and stir constantly until warm, not hot. Pour the sauce over the fish, garnish with the orange sections and serve at once accompanied by tiny boiled potatoes.

Crab Stuffed Salmon Trout

4 servings

2½ oz/75 grams onion, finely chopped
1½ oz/45 grams butter
8 oz/225 grams crabmeat, picked over
2 oz/60 grams fresh breadcrumbs
1 oz/30 grams fresh parsley, chopped
2½ fl oz/75 ml double cream
¼ teaspoon thyme
3–4 lb/1350–1800 grams salmon trout, cleaned
   for stuffing
Salt and pepper
4 fl oz/110 ml dry white wine mixed with 2½ oz/
   75 grams melted butter

Sauté the onion in butter until golden. Remove from the heat and mix in the crabmeat, breadcrumbs, parsley, cream and thyme. Sprinkle the cavity of the fish lightly with salt and pepper. Stuff the fish and skewer edges securely.

Place the fish in a greased baking tin. Pour the wine-butter mixture over the fish. Bake, uncovered, in a 400°F/200°C/gas mark 6 oven for 30 minutes, or just until the flesh is opaque. Baste frequently with the wine sauce.

Mackerel Algérienne

4 servings

4 mackerel
Salt and pepper
½ lemon
Chopped parsley

salpicon
½ oz/15 grams butter
1 shallot, finely chopped
1 red or green pepper
12 oz/345 grams tomatoes
1 clove garlic, crushed with ¼ teaspoon salt
1 teaspoon paprika

Split and bone the mackerel. Wash and dry. Place the mackerel in an ovenproof dish. Add salt and pepper and a little lemon juice. Bake in a preheated oven at 350°F/180°C/gas mark 4 for about 20 minutes.

To prepare the salpicon: shred the pepper, blanch and refresh. Skin the tomatoes, de-seed and slice. Melt the butter, add the shallot and cook until soft. Add the tomatoes, garlic and paprika. Stew slowly to a pulp then add the pepper. Continue cooking for 2–3 minutes.

Spoon salpicon over the fish and serve with thin slices of lemon and chopped parsley.

Deep Fried, Batter Coated Sole

4 servings

1 egg
4 oz/115 grams flour
Salt to taste, if desired
½ pint/¼ l beer, at room temperature
1 egg white
1½ lb/700 grams small fillets of sole
Vegetable oil for deep-frying

Put the egg in a mixing bowl and beat it briskly until foamy. Add the flour and salt and stir together until blended. Beat in the beer. Beat the egg white and fold it in. Let stand until ready to use.

Meanwhile, split the fillets lengthwise in half. There may be a small bone line running down the centre of each fillet. If so, trim it away and discard it. Cut the sole pieces crosswise in half. Add the fish to the batter and stir to coat.

Heat the oil in a deep-fryer. Add the fish pieces. When brown on one side, turn with a draining spoon and continue cooking until crisp and brown all over. Cooking time is about 2 or 3 minutes. Drain on kitchen towel. Serve with tomato or tartar sauce.

Fillet of Turbot with Tomato Butter

Salmon Cakes

4 servings

1 lb/450 grams tinned salmon
2 oz/60 grams onion, chopped
2½ fl oz/75 ml oil
4 fl oz/110 ml salmon liquid
1½ oz/45 grams dry breadcrumbs
1 teaspoon parsley, chopped
½ teaspoon mustard

Drain and flake the salmon. Save the liquid. Cook the onion in oil until soft. Add the eggs, pepper, breadcrumbs, parsley, mustard and onion to the salmon. Use enough liquid to keep the mixture together. Form into 4 or 8 cakes. Fry or grill.

Grilled Mackerel

4 to 6 servings

4–6 whole boned mackerel
Watercress
Lemon slices

Place the fish on a greased grill tray. Spread with melted butter; sprinkle with salt and pepper. Grill 20 to 25 minutes, depending on the size and turning after 10 minutes. Remove to a hot dish. Garnish with watercress and lemon slices.

Devilled Roes

4 servings

½ lb/¼ kilo soft herring roes
4 slices toast
2 oz/60 grams anchovy butter
1 oz/30 grams seasoned flour
Clarified butter, for frying
1 oz/30 grams butter
2 teaspoons lemon juice
Dash tabasco sauce
Paprika

Wash the herring roes, put them in a colander and pour over a jug of boiling water, drain well. When cool, roll them in seasoned flour and fry in the clarified butter until brown and crisp.

Place on toast, spread with the anchovy butter and cut in half.

Heat 1 oz/30 grams butter in the pan until brown, then add lemon juice and tabasco. Pour the mixture over the roes while still bubbling hot. Dust with paprika and serve very hot.

Sole in Vermouth Sauce

4 servings

4 large sole fillets
Salt
Pepper

Easy-to-Bake Fish

1 tablespoon shallot, finely chopped
About 3½ oz/100 grams butter
1½ oz/45 grams white breadcrumbs
8–10 fl oz/220–285 ml dry vermouth
1 beef stock cube stirred into 1 tablespoon hot
    water
Beurre manié (½ oz/15 grams butter blended
    with ½ oz/15 grams flour)
1 tablespoon parsley, chopped

Season the fish with salt and pepper. Grease a roasting tin or ovenproof dish and sprinkle it with half the shallots. Then place the fish fillets in the dish so that they look like a whole fish. Brush the top side with melted butter—use a generous amount. Then sprinkle with the breadcrumbs in an even layer.

Carefully pour a small amount of butter over the crumbs. Pour in enough vermouth to cover the bottom of the dish. Place in a 450°F/230°C/gas mark 8 oven and bake until the sole is golden brown with a crispy surface. This usually takes about 15 minutes but can vary depending on the size of the fish.

In the meantime, make the sauce. Pour the rest of the vermouth in a pan with the rest of the shallots and the broth. Allow this to boil until a little more than half remains. Thicken with a small amount of beurre manié. Remove from the stove and slowly stir in the butter in nut-sized pieces until 8 fl oz/220 ml of sauce has been made.

Place the pan in hot water (or over a double boiler) so that it remains warm. Should there be any vermouth left in the bottom of the roasting tin when the fish is done, add this also to the sauce. Season with pepper. Add the chopped parsley.

Place the fish on a serving plate or on individual plates. Pour a small amount of sauce around the fish and pour the rest onto a warm sauce boat. Serve with small, boiled potatoes.

Fillets of Sole with White Grapes

6 to 8 servings

6 oz/170 grams white seedless grapes
½ pint/¼ l dry white wine
3 lb/1350 grams sole fillets
2¼ oz/68 grams butter
Juice of 1 lemon
3 bay leaves
2 small shallots, peeled and sliced
12 white peppercorns
1 oz/30 grams flour
¼ pint/140 ml milk, warmed
¼ pint/140 ml double cream
Salt
Cayenne pepper

Peel the grapes and soak them immediately in the white wine. Wash the sole fillets and pat dry. Butter a large, flat, ovenproof glass or enamel dish with about ¼ oz/8 grams butter. Lay the fillets in the dish. Pour ¼ pint/140 ml of cold water, the strained lemon juice and the white wine, in which the grapes have been soaking, over the fillets. Cover the grapes and put them aside until ready to use.

Scatter the bay leaves, shallots and whole peppercorns over the fish. Dot with 1 oz/30 grams of butter. Bake in a preheated 350°F/180°C/gas mark 4 oven until the fish is opaque throughout, about 25 minutes, basting occasionally. When done, remove the fish from the oven and carefully strain the juices into a small pan. Keep the fish warm while making the sauce.

Make a white roux by cooking 1 oz/30 grams of butter and the flour together over a very low heat, stirring constantly with a wooden spoon. Cook very slowly for 5 minutes, then gradually add the strained juice reserved from the fish. Continue cooking for about 5 minutes longer. Remove from the heat and stir in the warm milk. Put the pan back on the heat and bring to the boil, stirring vigorously, then grad-

Fish in Foil with Tomato Filled Courgette

ually add the cream. Do not allow the sauce to boil after the cream has been added. Season to taste with salt and a very small pinch of cayenne. Add the grapes to the sauce and pour over the fish. Serve at once.

Fried Trout

6 servings

6 small trout
½ pint/¼ l milk
½ teaspoon celery salt
½ teaspoon onion salt
½ teaspoon garlic salt
¼ teaspoon black pepper
3 oz/85 grams flour
12 rashers bacon
3 oz/85 grams butter or margarine
1 lemon

Clean and split the trout; remove the heads and tails. Dip the fish in milk. Combine the seasonings and sprinkle them over the fish. Dip the fish in flour.

Fry the bacon until crisp; drain. Add butter to the bacon fat; heat. Fry the fish gently in the hot fat until crisp and brown. Serve the fish garnished with bacon and lemon.

Swordfish Kebabs

6 to 8 servings

2 lb/900 grams swordfish
¼ pint/140 ml olive oil
8 fl oz/220 ml lemon juice
2 oz/60 grams onion, finely chopped
2 teaspoons salt
½ teaspoon freshly ground pepper
1 teaspoon paprika
12–16 bay leaves
2 tablespoons parsley, chopped

Rinse the fish and pat it dry. Cut the fish into 1½-inch/4-cm cubes. In a casserole dish mix 2½ fl oz/75 ml of olive oil, 2½ fl oz/75 ml lemon juice, the onion, 1½ teaspoons salt, the pepper, paprika and bay leaves. Toss the fish in the mixture, then cover and marinate in the refrigerator 6–8 hours. Turn and baste the fish frequently.

Drain and divide the fish among 6 or 8 skewers, putting a couple of bay leaves on each skewer. Grill 15 minutes, or until the fish is browned and tender, turning the skewers so as to be sure to brown all sides evenly.

Mix the remaining oil, lemon juice, salt and parsley together. Serve in a sauceboat.

Steamed Swordfish with Herbs

4 to 6 servings

2 slices swordfish, about 1 inch/2½ cm thick
  (about 2½ lb/1125 grams)
Coarse salt
Freshly ground pepper
Extra virgin olive oil
Fresh lemon juice
Fresh basil and parsley, chopped
Dried oregano

Arrange the swordfish in a single layer on one of two round, heavy porcelain plates. Sprinkle with salt and pepper and trickle olive oil over both slices of the fish; then sprinkle with lemon juice, basil, parsley and oregano, placing one slice on top of the other. Cover with the second plate and set on a steamer in a large stockpot over boiling water. When the fish is white, it is done.

The fish can be served hot, cold or at room temperature.

Fillets of Sole with Crayfish Stuffing

6 servings

4 oz/115 grams soft breadcrumbs
1 crayfish tail, cooked, shelled and finely chopped
3 tablespoons olive oil
Salt
1 oz/30 grams and 1 teaspoon parsley, finely chopped
1 tablespoon onion, finely chopped
Pinch oregano
6–8 toasted almonds, crushed
6 fillets sole
2 spring onions, finely chopped
1 clove garlic, crushed
2 medium sized tomatoes, peeled, seeded and chopped
2 tablespoons sherry

Combine the breadcrumbs, crayfish, 2 tablespoons of oil, ¼ teaspoon salt, 1 oz/30 grams of parsley, onion, oregano and almonds. Place 1–1½ tablespoons of the mixture on each fillet and roll up. Place on individual squares of foil with the overlapped side of the fillet underneath.

Combine the spring onions, garlic, tomatoes and sherry, remaining parsley and oil and salt to taste. Spoon some over each stuffed fillet. Crimp the edges of the foil together to seal. Bake in a 350°F/180°C/gas mark 4 oven for 25–35 minutes.

Fish au Gratin on a Bed of Broccoli

Fish Kebabs, Two Different Ways

Grilled Buttered Trout

2 servings

1 2 lb/900 gram trout
2½ fl oz/75 ml oil
¼ teaspoon pepper
Butter
Lemon slices
Parsley

Split the trout into 2 fillets; remove the backbone. Wash thoroughly; remove all traces of blood or membrane.

Preheat the grill about 10 minutes. Oil the preheated grill pan.

Brush the fish with oil mixed with pepper. Amount of oil required will be about 2½ fl oz/75 ml with ¼ teaspoon pepper. Place the trout on the grill pan, skin side up, about 2 inches/5 cm below the heat. After 5 minutes, the skin should be turning brown; baste. Cook until the skin is well browned, then turn the fish flesh side up. Baste again; cook until the flesh side is well browned. Remove to a hot dish; butter the top of the fish.

Garnish with lemon slices and parsley.

Baked Fish in Wine

3 servings

1 lb/450 grams white fish fillets
1 tablespoon parsley, chopped
1 tablespoon lemon juice
1 teaspoon seasoned salt
3 tablespoons olive oil
1 medium sized onion, thinly sliced
1 clove garlic, crushed
1 large tomato, chopped
3 slices lemon
2 tablespoons white wine

Arrange the fish in an 8-or 9-inch/20-or 22½-cm square baking dish. Sprinkle with parsley, lemon juice and seasoned salt.

Heat the oil in a small pan; fry the onion and garlic until soft.

Top the fish with the onion mixture, including the oil from the pan. Arrange tomatoes on top of the onion mixture; place the lemon slices on top of the fish. Pour wine over all; bake at 350°F/180°C/gas mark 4 oven for 30–35 minutes or until the fish flakes with a fork.

Trout with Lemon and Parsley

4 to 8 servings

4 8–10 oz/225–285 gram trout
¼ pint/140 ml milk
1 oz/30 grams flour
Salt and freshly ground pepper
¼–½ pint/140 to 285 ml vegetable oil
Juice of 1 lemon
4 oz/115 grams butter
8 lemon slices, seeded
1 oz/30 grams parsley, finely chopped

Put the trout in a shallow dish and add the milk. Turn the fish in the milk. Drain the trout one at a time, but do not pat dry. Blend the flour with salt and pepper to taste. Dip each trout in the mixture and shake off any excess flour.

Heat ¼ pint/140 ml of oil in a pan (or use 2 pans, with ¼ pint/140 ml oil in each). Fry 2 trout at a time in 1 pan, or cook all 4 in 2 pans. The oil must be quite hot when the trout are added.

When the trout are browned on one side, about 2 to 3 minutes, turn them. Spoon the oil over the trout as they cook. An 8 oz/225 grams trout should be cooked in about 8 minutes (total cooking time, about 1 minute per 1 oz/30 grams).

When all the trout are cooked, transfer them to a serving dish. Squeeze the juice of a lemon over the trout.

Heat the butter in a clean pan, swirling it around until it foams. Continue cooking, swirling it around, until the butter turns brown. Pour this over the trout. Garnish each trout with 2 lemon slices topped with finely chopped parsley.

Texas Tuna

4 servings

10 oz/285 grams tinned tuna in oil
6 oz/170 grams onion, chopped
4 oz/115 grams celery, chopped
8 fl oz/220 ml ketchup
8 fl oz/220 ml water
½ oz/15 grams sugar
1 tablespoon vinegar
1 tablespoon Worcester sauce (optional)
1 teaspoon prepared mustard
¼ teaspoon salt
Pepper to taste

Drain and flake the tuna, but save the oil and put it in a saucepan. Cook the onion and celery in tuna oil until soft but not brown.

Add the remaining ingredients, except the tuna, and simmer uncovered about 10 minutes. Fold in the tuna and heat.

Serve on noodles, spaghetti, toast or rice, or make hot sandwiches on rolls.

Fillet of Turbot with Tomato-Butter

4 servings

onion in wine
1 large onion
½ pint/¼ l red wine
2½ fl oz/75 ml red wine vinegar
1 oz/30 grams butter
Salt
Pepper
1 tablespoon honey

tomato-butter
7 to 8 medium-large tomatoes
4 fl oz/110 ml double cream
2 oz/60 grams butter
Salt
Pepper

fish
4 turbot fillets
1 tablespoon oil
Salt
Pepper
Cayenne pepper
Snipped parsley

Shred or finely chop the onion. Place in a pot with the wine and vinegar, cover and simmer for 10 minutes. Then simmer uncovered so that all the liquid evaporates. Add the butter and seasonings and stir until the butter has melted. Add the honey and mix well. This may be done in advance and then reheated.

Boil and peel the tomatoes; remove the seeds from 3 of the tomatoes. Cut the 3 seeded tomatoes into small pieces, cover and refrigerate. Strain the other tomatoes into juice and bring it to the boil together with the cream. Simmer, uncovered, until reduced by a third. Add the butter and season carefully.

Dredge the fish fillets in the oil; add salt, pepper and a dash of cayenne pepper. Heat up the tomato-butter sauce and the onion in wine. Grill the fish 2 to 3 minutes on each side. Carefully warm up the refrigerated tomatoes in the tomato sauce. Divide the onion onto 4 warm plates. Place a fish fillet on each bed of onions and pour the decorative tomato sauce around the onion. Sprinkle with parsley and serve immediately.

Three Kinds of Fish in Red Wine Sauce

Tuna Pie

6 servings

pastry base
8 oz/225 grams cooked brown rice
4 oz/115 grams whole-wheat flour
2½ oz/75 grams sunflower kernels
2 tablespoons wheat germ
1 teaspoon salt
Pinch pepper
4 fl oz/110 ml salad oil
4 fl oz/110 ml milk

filling
4 eggs
15 fl oz/425 ml milk
14 oz/400 grams tinned tuna in vegetable oil
8 oz/225 grams frozen chopped broccoli, thawed
4 oz/115 grams Gruyére, coarsely grated
4 oz/115 grams celery, chopped
4 oz/115 grams carrot, chopped
1 teaspoon salt
Pinch pepper

Mix the cooked rice, flour, sunflower kernels, wheat germ, salt and pepper in a bowl. Stir in the oil and milk. Roll out the dough between 2 pieces of waxed paper to a 10-inch/25-cm round. Remove the top piece of waxed paper and turn into a 9-inch/22½-cm flan dish. Remove the second piece of waxed paper. Make a rim on the edge of the crust. Bake in a 400°F/200°C/gas mark 6 oven for 20 to 25 minutes, until lightly browned. Cool.

Beat the eggs with milk. Add the tuna, broccoli, cheese, celery, carrot, salt and pepper; mix well. Turn into the baked pastry case. Bake in a 350°F/180°C/gas mark 4 oven for 1 hour or until the tip of a knife inserted in the centre comes out clean. Let stand 10 minutes before serving.

Fried Sardines

6 servings

18 fresh sardines, cleaned and boned
1½ teaspoons salt
¼ teaspoon pepper
2 oz/60 grams flour
1 oz/30 grams cornflour
½ pint/¼ l water
1 egg yolk, lightly beaten
1 egg white, beaten until stiff
Fat for deep-frying

Sprinkle the fish with 1 teaspoon of salt and pepper; set aside.

Combine the flour, cornflour and ½ teaspoon of salt. Blend the water and egg yolk together; stir into the flour mixture until smooth. Fold in the egg white.

Dip the fish into the batter; deep-fat fry at 350°F/

180°C 2 to 3 minutes, until the fish is golden brown. Drain on kitchen towel.

Baked Fish with Cucumber Sauce

4 servings

½ cucumber, peeled, seeded and coarsely grated
½ teaspoon salt
½ pint/¼ l plain yoghurt
1 teaspoon fresh dill, chopped
¼ teaspoon freshly ground black pepper
1–1½ lb/450–700 grams fish fillets
Fresh parsley leaves

Prepare the sauce. Sprinkle the grated cucumber with salt; let it stand 20 minutes to withdraw some of the water present. Drain away the accumulated water; combine the cucumber with the salt, yoghurt, dill and pepper.

Place the fish on a lightly greased baking sheet. Bake at 425°F/220°C/gas mark 7 for 10 minutes for each 1-inch/2½-cm of thickness, or until the fish can be separated into flakes with a fork.

Place the fish on a warm dish. Ladle the sauce over the fish; garnish with fresh parsley leaves.

Quick Paella

Easy-to-Bake Fish with Cheese and Tomatoes

4 servings

1½ lb/700 grams haddock or cod fillets
¼ oz/8 grams butter
½ oz/15 grams flour
1 teaspoon salt
1 tablespoon squeezed lemon juice
2 tablespoons chopped dill
6 oz/170 grams grated cheese
2½ fl oz/75 ml milk
2 to 3 tomatoes

Rinse the fish and let the water totally drain off. Grease a shallow casserole and sprinkle flour on the bottom. Place the fish in the pan. Salt and sprinkle with lemon juice. Add the dill and grated cheese. Cover with the milk.

Bake in the middle of a preheated 425°F/220°C/gas mark 7 oven for about 20 minutes or until the fish is a good colour. Cut the tomatoes into cubes and spread them over the top of the fish.

Fish in Foil with Tomato Filled Courgette

4 servings

A whole haddock, cod or pike (3–3½ lb/1350–1575 grams)
2 teaspoons salt
Dill
Parsley stalks
1 sheet of aluminium foil
2 large courgettes
2 teaspoons salt per 2 pints/1¼ l water
1 lb/450 grams tomatoes
1 small carrot, finely grated
2 onions, finely chopped
2 tablespoons tomato paste
½ teaspoon black pepper
½ teaspoon salt
½ teaspoon tarragon
1 oz/30 grams chopped parsley

Clean the fish, but let the head and fins remain. Rub salt into the fish and fill the cavity with dill and parsley. Place the fish on a sheet of aluminium foil. Place a ruler next to the fish and measure the back at the thickest spot.

Make a tight parcel with the foil around the fish and place it in a baking tin in the oven. If the fish is 1½ inches/4 cm thick, it will take 30 minutes to bake; 2½ inches/6¼ cm thick, 40 minutes; and 3 inches/7½ cm thick, 50 minutes. Increase or decrease by 5 minutes for every ¼ inch/½ cm.

Peel the courgette along 4 lines with spaces in between, so that the peel remains on the gaps in between. Cut lengthwise into halves and take out the seeds. Place in salted, boiling water and boil for 10 minutes. Remove from the water and drain well.

Scald the tomatoes in the same water and peel. Cut the tomatoes into 4 pieces and place them in a saucepan together with the carrot, the onions, the tomato paste, the pepper, salt and tarragon. Boil for about 4 minutes.

Place the courgette halves on an ovenproof plate and pour the tomato mixture into the courgettes. Place the plate over the fish and let it sit there during the last 20 minutes of the fish baking time.

Serve the fish in the foil, surrounded by the tomato-filled courgettes. Sprinkle with parsley.

Island Fish Stew

Spicy Shellfish Stew

Grilled Fish with Fresh Tomatoes

4 servings

2 medium sized tomatoes, coarsely chopped
2 tablespoons onion, finely chopped
½ teaspoon dried basil leaves, crushed
½ teaspoon salt
Dash pepper
1¼ lb/565 grams fish fillets
1 oz/30 grams butter or margarine, melted

Stir the first 5 ingredients together. Brush both sides of the fish with butter or margarine. Arrange the fish on a rack in the grill pan. Top with the tomato mixture.

Grill 4 inches/10 cm from the heat 4 to 6 minutes, or until the fish flakes easily.

Fish Crumble

4 servings

1½ lb/700 grams cooked white fish, flaked
3 hard-boiled eggs, roughly chopped

crumble mixture
1½ oz/45 grams butter
3 oz/85 grams flour

2 oz/60 grams cheese (grated)
Salt and pepper

béchamel sauce
1 pint/½ l flavoured milk
½ oz/15 grams flour
½ oz/15 grams butter

Set the oven to 350°F/180°C/gas mark 4.

To make the crumble: rub the butter and flour together, then add the cheese and salt and pepper. Put mixture to one side.

Make the béchamel sauce. Then mix the fish with the chopped eggs. Blend this mixture with the sauce and turn into an ovenproof dish.

Cover the mixture with crumble topping and put in the oven for about 20 to 30 minutes to brown.

Fish with Herb Sauce

4 servings

1½ lb/700 grams fresh fish fillets
1 to 2 tablespoons lemon juice
4 tomatoes, peeled and sliced
Salt and pepper
1 rasher lean bacon, diced
1 small onion, chopped
¼ pint/140 ml plain yoghurt
½ oz/15 grams flour
1 tablespoon parsley leaves, chopped
1 tablespoon chives, chopped
1 teaspoon dried dill (optional)
½ teaspoon tarragon
½ teaspoon chervil
1 tablespoon dried breadcrumbs

Sprinkle the lemon juice over the fish; set aside. Line the bottom of a greased, shallow casserole dish with the tomato slices. Season with salt and pepper. In a small pan, combine the bacon and onion. Cook until the onion is golden.

Combine the yoghurt, flour and herbs. Season to taste with salt and pepper.

Place the fish fillets on top of the tomatoes, pour the yoghurt sauce over the fish; cover with the bacon-onion mixture and sprinkle breadcrumbs over all. Cover; bake at 350°F/180°C/gas mark 4 for about 20 minutes, or until the fish can be separated into flakes with a fork. Serve at once.

Fish Au Gratin on a Bed of Broccoli

4 servings

½ lb/225 grams frozen broccoli
1½ lb/700 grams fresh or frozen fish fillets-cod, haddock etc.
1 teaspoon salt
10 oz/285 grams coarsely grated cheese
3 tablespoons breadcrumbs
3 oz/85 grams finely shredded leek or snipped chives
2 to 3 tablespoons milk or cream

Prepare the broccoli according to directions on the packet. Place it in a greased, ovenproof dish. Cut the fish fillets in slices. Place the fish over the broccoli. Sprinkle with salt.

Mix the grated cheese with the breadcrumbs and the leek or chives. Combine the mixture with milk or cream.

Dab the cheese mixture over the fish. Bake in a preheated 425°F/220°C/gas mark 7 oven for 20 to 30 minutes, or until the fish is done. Serve with sliced or mashed potatoes.

Shellfish Rice Feast

Pan Fried Fish

6 servings

6 fish fillets
1 teaspoon salt
Pinch pepper
1 egg
1 tablespoon milk
4 oz/115 grams breadcrumbs

Wipe the fish. Beat the egg lightly and blend in the milk. Dip the fish in the egg and roll it in crumbs.

Place the fish in a heavy frying pan which contains a thin layer of melted fat, hot but not smoking. Fry at moderate heat. When the fish is brown on one side, turn carefully and brown the other side. Cooking time is about 10 minutes, depending on the thickness of the fish. Drain on kitchen towel. Serve immediately.

Fish Kebabs, Two Different Ways

4 servings

1 lb/450 grams firm fish fillets
Salt
Pepper
4 oz/115 grams mushrooms
6 rashers of bacon, cut in squares
5 tomatoes
Oil

crayfish kebabs
25 grapes
12 crayfish tails
4 tomatoes
Oil
Salt
Black or white pepper

Cut the fish into 1 × 1 × ½-inch/2½ × 2½ × 1¼-cm cubes. Lightly salt and pepper the fish cubes. Divide each tomato into 8 pieces.

Alternate the fish, mushrooms, bacon and tomato pieces on a skewer, making 4 skewers in all. Baste with oil before grilling for 10 to 15 minutes. Turn the skewers several times.

To make 4 skewers of crayfish kebabs, take the seeds out of the grapes without cutting them in two. Cut each tomato into eight pieces. Alternate the grapes, crayfish tails and tomatoes on a skewer. Baste with oil, salt and pepper lightly and grill until slightly brown (4 to 8 minutes). Turn several times.

French-Style Clams

Mustard Grilled Fish Fillets

3 to 4 servings

1½ lb/700 grams mackerel fillets
Oil
2 tablespoons mayonnaise
1 tablespoon Dijon mustard
Chopped parsley
Ground pepper

Lay the fillets on a lightly greased grill or dish in one layer. Brush lightly with oil. Combine the remaining ingredients and spread them on the fish. Grill for 3–8 minutes, or until the topping is browned and the fish flakes lightly with a fork. The length of grilling time depends on the thickness of the fillets.

Poached Fillet of Fish

4 servings

1½ pints/850 ml water
2 very thin, round slices ginger crushed with the side of a meat cleaver
2 spring onions, stalks only, cut into 2-inch/5-cm lengths

1 lb/450 grams fish fillets, cut into 1½-inch/4-cm squares
1 tablespoon wine
2½ teaspoons soy sauce
1 teaspoon sugar
½ teaspoon sesame oil
1 tablespoon oil
½ tablespoon ginger, crushed
2 further stalks spring onions, chopped

Put the ginger and spring onion stalks into a pot containing the water. Bring the water to the boil and boil for 3 minutes. Gently add the fish slices. When the water begins to boil again, remove the fish slices immediately and set on a dish. Keep warm.

Combine the wine, soy sauce, sugar and sesame oil to form the sauce. Set within easy reach.

Heat the oil in a pan over high heat until hazy. Put in the crushed ginger and fry for 10 seconds. Put in the chopped spring onions and stir-fry another 10 seconds. Pour in the sauce and heat until bubbly. Then pour the sauce over the fish slices and serve hot.

Crayfish Timbales

Fish Fillets in Soured Cream

4 to 6 servings

1 lb/450 grams fish fillets
Salt and pepper to taste
Dash tabasco sauce
½ pint/¼ l soured cream
2 tablespoons dill pickle, finely chopped
2 tablespoons onion, finely chopped
2 tablespoons green pepper, chipped
1 tablespoon parsley, chopped
1 tablespoon lemon juice
¼ teaspoon dry mustard
¼ teaspoon sweet basil
Paprika

Place the fish in a greased baking dish. Sprinkle generously with salt and pepper.

Mix the rest of the ingredients, except the paprika, together. Pour the mixture over the fish. Use a generous amount of paprika on top. Cover. Bake at 325°F/163°C/gas mark 3 for 45 to 60 minutes, until the fish flakes when tested with a fork. Serve at once.

Seafood Jambalaya

6 servings

1½ oz/45 grams margarine
6 oz/170 grams green pepper, chopped
2 oz/60 grams celery, chopped
3 oz/85 grams onion, chopped
2 oz/60 grams fresh parsley, chopped
1 lb/450 grams tinned tomatoes, chopped
1 pint/½ l chicken stock
½ teaspoon salt
Pinch pepper
½ teaspoon chilli powder
2 bay leaves
1 lb/450 grams cooked rice
1 pint/½ l oysters, drained
½ lb/225 grams white fish, cut in chunks
1 lb/450 grams crabmeat, cartilage removed

Sauté the green pepper, celery and onion in margarine 5 minutes in a large saucepan. Add the parsley, tomatoes, water, stock and seasonings; simmer over medium heat 30–40 minutes.

Add the rice, oysters and fish and simmer 10 minutes. Add the crabmeat and simmer 5 more minutes.

Quick Paella

4 servings

1 lb/450 grams white fish, fresh or frozen
1 onion
1 oz/30 grams margarine
1 teaspoon curry powder or ½ envelope saffron
8 oz/225 grams long-grain rice
1 pint/½ l chicken broth
1½ teaspoons salt
8 oz/225 grams frozen peas
4 oz/115 grams red pepper, frozen
10 oz/285 grams frozen prawns in shells

If the fish is frozen, place it in lukewarm water. Chop and fry the onion until transparent in the margarine in a large frying pan. Dust the onion with curry powder or saffron and stir in the rice. Add the chicken broth; cover the pan and simmer for 10 minutes.

Cut the fish into pieces, season with salt and press them into the rice which will have expanded and absorbed most of the liquid. Place the peas, red pepper and prawns on top of the rice, cover and cook for 10 more minutes.

Serve in the pan or in a large dish and garnish with lemon wedges. Serve with a green salad.

Three Kinds of Fish in Red Wine Sauce

4 to 6 servings

4 to 6 pieces each: eel, pike and perch—cleaned, trimmed and skinned or scaled

marinade
8 fl oz/220 ml olive oil
2 teaspoons salt
2 cloves garlic, crushed
1 shallot, chopped

red wine sauce
2 shallots, chopped
½ oz/15 grams butter
¼ teaspoon black pepper, coarsely ground
2½ fl oz/75 ml brandy
1 tomato, boiled, peeled and cut into pieces
1 oz/30 grams flour
½ bottle red wine
About 8 fl oz/220 ml broth from cooking the fish
Butter

for the fish
1 pint/½ l fish stock

Mix the marinade ingredients together in a plastic bag. Place the prepared fish pieces in the bag. Tie a knot and place in the refrigerator overnight. For best results, turn the bag several times while the fish is marinating.

The sauce may be prepared while the fish is marinating. Sauté the shallots and pepper in butter. Add the brandy and flambé. Add the tomato, flour and wine. Allow the sauce to boil vigorously until the amount has decreased by a third. Strain the sauce.

Everything may be prepared in advance up to this point.

Bring the fish stock to the boil in a wide pan. Add the fish and let it simmer in several batches until it is just done. Remove the pieces with a draining spoon and keep them warm.

Now beat about 8 fl oz/220 ml of the fish broth into the sauce. Season to taste. Add a dab of butter and pour into a wide, attractive serving dish.

Place the fish pieces in the sauce. Garnish with mushroom caps sautéed in butter and small toast triangles fried in butter and garlic.

Stuffed Crayfish

Lobster Mousse in Avocado Sauce

Island Fish Stew

4 servings

About 1 lb/450 grams cod or haddock
1 small tin clams in water
2 pints/1¼ l fish broth
1 tin whole peeled tomatoes
Salt
Freshly ground pepper
4 to 6 potatoes, peeled and boiled
¼ lb/115 grams fresh prawns, shelled
Dill

Cut the fish into large cubes. Drain the clams, reserving their juice. Mix the clam juice, fish broth and the juice from the tin of tomatoes and simmer together for about 10 minutes. Add the fish cubes and simmer in the broth for several minutes. Season with salt and freshly ground pepper.

Add the boiled potatoes, clams, prawns and tomatoes and simmer for several more minutes. Chop the dill and sprinkle it over the stew.

Serve with crispy, warm French bread.

Seafood Rolls

6 servings

¼ pint/140 ml mayonnaise
2½ fl oz/75 ml soured cream
2 teaspoons lemon juice
¼ teaspoon dill
10 oz/285 grams tinned prawns, crab or tuna, flaked
4 oz/115 grams celery, finely chopped
12 small rolls, split and buttered

Combine the mayonnaise, soured cream, lemon juice and dill. Mix with the seafood and celery. Fill the rolls with the mixture. Wrap and chill.

Spicy Shellfish Stew

4 servings

1 tablespoon curry paste
2 tablespoons oil
1 lb/450 grams frozen prawns
2 green peppers, finely shredded
2 cloves garlic, crushed
2 tablespoons chilli sauce
½ teaspoon salt
1 tin crushed tomatoes
Pinch cayenne pepper
8 fl oz/220 ml soured cream

Heat the curry paste in hot oil while stirring constantly. Sauté the prawns on all sides in this, but only for a short time so that the flesh does not become tough; it should be just cooked through. Remove the fish from the pan and place on a plate.

Sauté the shredded peppers in the same oil. Add the garlic, chilli sauce, salt and crushed tomatoes. Stir and season with cayenne pepper, a few grains at a time, constantly testing. Cover and allow the mixture to simmer until the green peppers feel soft. Then blend in the prawns and the cream. Slowly bring the mixture to the boil and check the seasoning.

Serve with rice or freshly boiled noodles.

Shellfish Kebab

4 servings

12 large scampi in their shells
8 scallops, white part only, cubed
About 8 slices leek
Freshly squeezed lime juice
Oil
Salt
Pepper

Curry Creamed Mussels

Push the scampi, scallops and leeks onto skewers. Brush each skewer with a little oil and a few drops of lime juice. Add salt and pepper. Cook on the skewers for 3 to 4 minutes on each side over a hot grill.

This kebab may also be fried in butter in a frying pan on top of the stove.

Serve with Indonesian soy sauce and lime wedges.

Prawn Chop Suey

4 servings

6–8 oz/170–225 grams prawns shelled
4 tablespoons oil
1 large carrot, shredded
1 large onion, sliced
1 sweet pepper, shredded
2 sticks of celery, sliced
8 oz/225 grams tinned bean sprouts

topping
1 large egg
1 tablespoon oil
Salt and pepper

Heat 3 tablespoons of oil in a large frying pan and add the onion, pepper, carrot and celery. Lightly cook over a medium heat. Add the prawns and drained bean sprouts. Mix in well and heat through. Turn mixture into a round serving dish.

Wipe out the pan, reheat with remaining oil.

To prepare topping: beat egg with oil, season and pour into pan. Cook slowly until egg is set, turn it with a slice and cook for a further 30 seconds. Place topping out on prawn chop suey and serve hot.

Shellfish Rice Feast

5 to 6 servings

8–10 oz/225–285 grams long-grain rice
1 onion (optional), finely chopped
½ oz/15 grams butter
About 1¼ pints/630 ml fish broth
3 oz/85 grams snipped dill
1 teaspoon crushed tarragon (optional)

mushrooms
¼ to ½ lb/115 to 225 grams fresh mushrooms
½ to 1 oz/15 to 30 grams butter
About ½ tablespoon squeezed lemon juice
Salt
1 jar black lumpfish roe
¼ pint/140 ml soured cream

curried prawns
1¼ lb/565 grams prawns
½ oz/15 grams butter
1 to 1½ teaspoons curry

garlic mussels
8 oz/225 grams cooked, shelled mussels
½ oz/15 grams butter
1 clove garlic, crushed

Sauté the rice and the onion, if desired, lightly in butter. Cover with the broth. Boil the rice for 20 to 25 minutes according to the directions on the packet. Mix the dill and perhaps the tarragon with the rice. Transfer to a heated bowl.

While the rice is cooking, rub the mushrooms clean and sauté in butter over rather low heat for 5 to 8 minutes. Season with the salt and lemon. Alternatively the mushrooms can be placed in a warm bowl and covered with aluminium foil.

Place the lumpfish roe and the cream in separate bowls, or in a bowl together. Shell the prawns. Drain the mussels. Melt butter for the prawns and the mussels in separate pots just before serving. Add the curry powder to the prawns and crush the garlic for the mussels. Add the prawns and mussels to their individual pots. Sauté lightly and place them in warm bowls.

Place all the dishes on the table and let diners help themselves to whichever side dishes they want.

Sweet and Sour Prawns

4 servings

16 Pacific prawns, or 1 lb/450 grams small
    prawns
Oil
Chopped garlic
Chilli sauce
Tomato ketchup

½ oz/15 grams cornflour in 2 tablespoons water
8 oz/225 grams fried rice
8 oz/225 grams tinned bean sprouts

Thaw out and drain prawns well.

Fry prawns in oil in a deep pan for 6 minutes, turning constantly. Add the garlic and, after a few minutes, the chilli sauce and tomato ketchup. Heat thoroughly and thicken with the cornflour.

Continue to cook 2–3 minutes, then serve with fried rice into which the drained bean sprouts have been stirred.

French Style Clams

4 servings

1½ lb/700 grams tinned clam meat in water
3½ oz/100 grams butter, melted
3 oz/85 grams tinned sprats, herrings or
    anchovies
2 oz/60 grams parsley, finely chopped
8 fl oz/220 ml soured cream
3 to 4 small cloves garlic, crushed
½ teaspoon salt
¼ teaspoon black pepper
2 oz/60 grams fresh breadcrumbs
3 oz/85 grams grated cheese

Drain the clams. Spread them out in a deep, ovenproof dish. Mix the melted butter with the drained, mashed sprats, parsley, soured cream, garlic, salt and pepper. Divide the mixture up evenly over the clams.

Mix the grated cheese and breadcrumbs together and sprinkle over the dish. Cook at 450°F/230°C/gas mark 8 for about 10 minutes or until the top has browned. Serve with crisp, warm bread and butter.

Crab Cakes

4 servings

2 lb/900 grams crabmeat
½ pint/¼ l mayonnaise
2 oz/60 grams breadcrumbs
1 teaspoon mustard
2 dashes Worcester sauce
1 whole egg
1 teaspoon parsley, chopped
Juice of ½ lemon

Remove the cartilage from the crabmeat.

Combine the mayonnaise with all other ingredients, except the crabmeat. Add the mayonnaise mixture to the crabmeat. Form into 8 round 5-oz/140-gram balls and bake at 450°F/230°C/gas mark 8 until golden.

Crab Imperial

8 servings

1 green sweet pepper, finely chopped
1 medium sized onion, finely chopped
2 teaspoons dry mustard
2 teaspoons prepared horseradish
2 teaspoons salt
½ teaspoon freshly ground white pepper
2 eggs, beaten
½ pint/¼ l mayonnaise
3 lb/1150 grams crabmeat
Paprika

Combine the green pepper, onion, mustard, horseradish, salt, white pepper and eggs and mix well. Blend in the mayonnaise thoroughly, then fold in the crabmeat.

Spoon the crabmeat mixture into 8 large, cleaned crab shells or ramekins. Coat with additional mayonnaise and sprinkle generously with paprika. Arrange the crab shells in a shallow, rectangular baking tin. Cook in a preheated oven at 350°F/180°C/gas mark 4 for 15 to 20 minutes until heated through.

Crab Norfolk

8 servings

1 oz/30 grams clarified butter
3 oz/85 grams prosciutto ham, cut into julienne strips
4 spring onions, finely chopped
8 fl oz/ 220 ml Madeira
3 lb/1150 grams crabmeat, picked clean of shells
Chopped parsley
4 oz/115 grams butter
8 parsley sprigs

Heat a large flameproof casserole and grease it with the clarified butter. Drop in the ham and onions. Turn once and add the Madeira. The temperature is right if the Madeira flames. If the alcohol is not burned off, allow the Madeira to reduce for 1 minute. Add the crabmeat.

Bring the ham and onions to the top of the casserole. Sprinkle with chopped parsley and dot with cold butter. Place in an oven at 400°F/200°C/gas mark 6 for 2 minutes until the butter melts and mixture is hot.

Spoon carefully into 8 ramekins. Garnish with parsley sprigs.

Herb-Marinated Mussels with Walnuts

Crab Casserole

4 servings

1 lb/450 grams crabmeat
1 oz/30 grams butter
1 green pepper, chopped
1 bunch spring onions, chopped
½ oz/15 grams flour
½ pint/¼ l milk
3 tablespoons Parmesan cheese, grated

Carefully pick over the crabmeat to remove any shell pieces, then set aside. Melt the butter and sauté the pepper and onions in it until softened. Sprinkle with flour and slowly stir in the milk. Stir over a low flame until the mixture thickens slightly.

Stir in the crab and place in a 2-pint/1¼-litre ovenproof dish. Sprinkle with Parmesan cheese and brown quickly under the grill.

Sautéed Crab Flakes

6 to 8 servings

5 oz/140 grams butter
1 teaspoon salt
Pinch pepper
2 oz/60 grams parsley, chopped
2 tablespoons brandy
2 lb/900 grams crabmeat, picked over
Pinch nutmeg
Parsley and lemon wedges

Melt the butter in a large saucepan or chafing dish. Add the salt, pepper, parsley, brandy and nutmeg. Stir in the crabmeat, trying not to break up the lumps, and sauté slowly for 5 to 8 minutes, or until the crabmeat is heated.

This dish may be served on toast or on its own. Garnish with parsley and lemon wedges.

Soft Shell Crabs

4 to 6 servings

2 oz/60 grams butter
2 tablespoons lemon juice
6 to 8 soft shell crabs, cleaned
½ oz/15 grams flour or cornflour
2½ fl oz/75 ml water

Heat the butter and lemon juice in a medium sized pan. Cook the crabs over medium heat until brown, 5 minutes per side. Remove the crabs to a heated serving dish.

Mix the cornflour and water. Add to the cooking juices, stirring until slightly thickened. Pour the sauce over the crabs. Serve at once.

Crayfish Timbales

4 servings

2½ lb/1150 grams frozen crayfish or small lobsters
1 oz/30 grams butter
2½ fl oz/75 ml tomato paste
1 tablespoon brandy
4 fl oz/110 ml water
8 fl oz/220 ml double cream
4 fl oz/ 110 ml dry white wine
1 envelope gelatine
Salt
Pepper
Sprigs of dill

Clean the thawed crayfish. Place the tails and the meat from the claws in a plastic bag in the refrigerator. Sauté the shells in a covered saucepan in butter and simmer for a few minutes. Add the tomato paste and stir. Pour in the brandy, remove from the heat and flambé.

Return to the stove and pour in the water, cream and wine. Cover and simmer for a further 10 minutes. Strain this sauce.

Dissolve the gelatine in a little cold water then stir it into the sauce, stirring constantly. Season with pepper and a little salt if desired. If the sauce is too strong, add more cream.

Cut the crayfish meat into small pieces, saving some of the larger tails for garnishing. Add the pieces to the sauce. Mix well and pour the mixture into 4 individual moulds. Refrigerate for at least 6 hours and allow to set.

Before turning out of the moulds dip them for a second in hot water. Garnish with dill and crayfish tails.

Lobster Mousse in Avocado Sauce

4 servings

1 boiled lobster, 12 oz to 1lb/345 to 450 grams
1 envelope gelatine
2½ fl oz/75 ml fish broth
1 tablespoon dry sherry
48 fl oz/220 ml whipping cream
¼ teaspoon salt
Large pinch white pepper
Pinch cayenne pepper
1 teaspoon lemon juice

avocado sauce
1 large, ripe avocado
1 teaspoon lemon juice
4 fl oz/110 ml soured cream
2½ fl oz/75 ml water
¼ teaspoon salt
Large pinch white pepper

Marinated Mussels

Clean the lobster, saving the meat from the claws for garnish. Chop the rest of the meat.

Soak the gelatine in cold water for 5 minutes. Dissolve in boiling fish stock.

Using a blender or food processor, mix the lobster meat with the broth and sherry until it becomes a smooth purée. Refrigerate the purée. Whip the cream and fold it into the purée. Season with the spices.

Pack the mousse into a mould, cover with cling film and refrigerate until it is time to serve. Remove the mousse by using a spoon that has been dipped in cold water.

Scoop out the avocado flesh and mix it with the other avocado sauce ingredients until smooth. Serve with the mousse.

Herb-Marinated Mussels with Walnuts

4 servings

25 to 30 fresh mussels
4 pints/2¼ l water
1 tablespoon salt
½ tablespoon vinegar

marinade
1 large clove garlic, crushed
The white part of a small leek, chopped
2 tablespoons walnuts, chopped
4 to 5 tablespoons dill, finely chopped
½ lemon
1 teaspoon vinegar
Salt
Pepper
4 to 5 tablespoons oil

Clean and rinse the mussels. Place them in boiling water with salt and vinegar until they have all opened, about 5 to 7 minutes. Drain and allow to cool. Remove the upper part of the shell.

Combine the marinade ingredients. Drip the marinade over the mussels and refrigerate for several hours before serving, so that the mussels soak in the flavour of the marinade. The mussels will look very decorative if they are served on a plate that has first been covered with crushed iced or coarse rock salt.

Serve with warm French bread.

Lobster Boats

4 servings

8 oz/225 grams cooked lobster meat
24 fresh mushrooms, approximately $1\frac{1}{2}$ inches/ $3\frac{1}{2}$ cm in diameter
$2\frac{1}{2}$ fl oz/75 ml condensed cream of mushroom soup
1 oz/30 grams fine, soft breadcrumbs
2 tablespoons mayonnaise or salad cream
$\frac{1}{4}$ teaspoon Worcester sauce
Dash pepper
Grated Parmesan cheese

Drain the lobster meat. Remove any remaining shell or cartilage. Chop the lobster meat. Rinse the mushrooms in cold water. Dry them and remove the stems.

Combine the soup, crumbs, mayonnaise, seasonings and lobster. Stuff each mushroom cap with a tablespoon of the lobster mixture. Sprinkle with cheese.

Place the mushrooms in a well-greased $15 \times 10 \times 1$-inch/$38 \times 25 \times 2\frac{1}{2}$-cm ovenproof dish. Cook in an oven at 400°F/200°C/gas mark 6 for 10 to 15 minutes, or until lightly browned.

Crab Ramekins

4 servings

1 teaspoon tomato purée
1 glass sherry
10 fl oz/285 ml tinned consommé
8 oz/225 grams white crab meat

Mix the tomato purée with the sherry and gently stir in the consommé. Lift the crabmeat with a fork into the ramekin dishes; this is to make sure that the crabmeat does not get tightly packed.

Spoon over the prepared consommé mixture and put in refrigerator for at least 1 hour to set.

Stuffed Crayfish

10 servings

12 crayfish or small lobsters
1 3 lb/$1\frac{1}{4}$ kilo perch ($1\frac{1}{2}$ lb/700 grams perch fillet)

stock
Crayfish shells and trimmings from the fish
1 oz/30 grams butter
2 tablespoons brandy
2 small carrots
2 shallots
4 oz/115 grams celeriac
4 sprigs parsley
1 bay leaf
$\frac{1}{2}$ teaspoon thyme

1 bottle dry white wine
2 pints/$1\frac{1}{4}$ l water

fish paté
3 egg whites
24 fl oz/660 ml double cream
1 teaspoon salt
$\frac{1}{4}$ teaspoon white pepper
$\frac{1}{4}$ teaspoon ground nutmeg

sauce
Cooking liquid
14 fl oz/400 ml double cream
$\frac{1}{4}$ teaspoon cayenne pepper
Salt to taste

Shell the crayfish carefully. Delicately remove the "stomach," which is situated right behind the eyes, and throw it away. The upper part of the shell and the tailmeats should be in one piece. Also try to retain the long antennae. The claws, legs and rest of the shell should be saved for the stock. (See illustration. The upper shells/heads are filled with paté.)

Rinse the upper shells well and place them in the refrigerator together with the tails.

Clean the perch and cut into fillets. Save the trimmings for the stock. Place the fillets in the refrigerator.

Crush or coarsely chop the crayfish shells, claws etc. Sauté these in butter in a large pan. Add the brandy and flambé.

Peel and finely chop the carrots, shallots and celeriac. Sauté them together with the shells for several minutes. Add the sprigs of parsley, the bay leaf, the thyme, white wine and water. Cover and boil for about 20 minutes. Strain and then allow the stock to thicken, uncovered, until slightly more than half the original amount of liquid remains. Up to this point the dish can be prepared in advance.

To make the fish paté: put the fish fillets through a food processor. Add the egg whites, one at a time, beating constantly. Add the cream, a small amount at a time. Season with salt, white pepper and nutmeg.

Spoon the paté into the clean, cold upper crayfish shells and place them closely together in a wide pan. Cover with the stock and simmer for 5 to 7 minutes, until the paté has become white. Remove the shells from the pan and keep them warm under a sheet of aluminium foil.

To make the sauce: add cream to the stock and let it simmer until it starts to thicken. Thicken with $\frac{1}{4}$ oz/8 grams butter mixed with $\frac{1}{4}$ oz/8 grams flour, if necessary. Season with cayenne pepper and salt to taste.

Place the tails in the bottom of a copper pan or serving dish with sides. Place the filled upper shells on top, with the antennae sticking up. Carefully pour the hot sauce over the dish. Heat well on the stove or in the oven for about 5 minutes at a very high temperature.

Curry Creamed Mussels

4 servings

2 onions
8 fl oz/220 ml dry white wine
2½ fl oz/75 ml water
2 oz/60 grams snipped parsley
Pinch thyme
2½ oz/75 grams butter
About 48 mussels, in the shells
1 teaspoon curry powder
Juice of ½ lemon
2 egg yolks
8 fl oz/220 ml double cream
1 carrot
½ fennel
1 leek
½ celeriac
Salt
Pepper

Finely chop one of the onions and place it in a heavy bottomed pan with the wine, water, parsley, thyme and 1 oz/30 grams of the butter. Bring to the boil. Add the mussels and stir well. Cover the pan and shake well so that the mussels move around. Boil for several minutes, until all the mussels have opened. Remove the mussels from their shells. Save the mussels for later, but discard the shells.

Strain the liquid. Cut the carrots, fennel, leek and celeriac into thin strips and finely chop the remaining onion. Place the rest of the butter in a 4-pint/2¼-litre pan.

Add the vegetables and simmer for a few minutes over a low heat. Salt and pepper slightly. Pour over the mussel liquid and simmer so that the vegetables become soft but not mushy. Remove the vegetables with a draining spoon and put them in a bowl.

Beat the egg yolks and the cream together in a bowl. Carefully beat in the hot liquid. Pour the mixture back into the pan. Place over a medium heat and thicken, if desired, with a little beurre manié (½ oz/15 grams butter mixed with ½ oz/15 grams flour). Season with curry powder, lemon, salt and pepper. Adjust the seasoning if necessary with more wine or a fish stock cube. Fold in the mussels and the vegetables. The consistency should be rather thick and creamy.

Prawn Croquettes

Spoon into individual serving dshes. This may also be served on toast with cheese on top and cooked until golden brown.

Oyster Puffs

3 servings

4 eggs, separated
2 oz/60 grams spring onions, finely chopped
¼ teaspoon freshly ground white pepper
1 teaspoon salt
1 oz/30 grams flour, sifted
2 oz/60 grams ground almonds
12 oz/345 grams oysters, drained and chopped

Combine the beaten egg yolks, onions, pepper, salt, flour and almonds in a medium sized bowl. Beat the egg whites until very stiff and fold them with the oysters into the egg yolk mixture. Drop this oyster mixture by tablespoonfuls into 375°F/190°C hot fat in a deep-fryer and fry until golden brown. Drain on kitchen towel.

Prawn Omelette Sandwiches

Place the onion, wine, water, parsley, thyme and butter in a heavy saucepan. Bring to the boil. Place the mussels in the pot and stir well. Cover the pot and shake well so the mussels move around. Boil for several minutes, until all the mussels have opened. Cool. Remove mussels from their shells.

Mix the marinade ingredients together. Add the mussels and mix well. Let stand for several hours.

Cut the tomatoes into 4 wedges, then slice into thin pieces. Cut the leek into thin rings, sprinkle with the snipped parsley. Sprinkle the rest of the marinade over the salad. Serve with marinated mussels.

Oysters Baltimore

4 to 6 servings

4 rashers bacon
18 oysters
3 tablespoons chilli sauce
1 tablespoon Worcester sauce
6 tablespoons double cream
½ teaspoon tarragon
2 tablespoons lemon juice
1 teaspoon salt
¼ teaspoon pepper

In a medium sized pan, fry the bacon until crisp. Set the bacon aside to drain, then crumble it into bits.

Pour off all but 1 tablespoon of fat from the pan. Add the oysters with their liquid. Cook, uncovered, over a medium heat until most of the cooking juices are absorbed.

Mix the remaining ingredients and add to the oysters. Simmer no more than 5 minutes to blend all flavours. Add extra seasonings if desired. These oysters are delicious served on hot buttered toast. Garnish with crumbled bacon.

Marinated Mussels

4 servings

About 48 mussels (10 to 12 per person)
1 onion, finely chopped
8 fl oz/220 ml dry white wine
2½ fl oz/75 ml water
1 oz/30 grams snipped parsley
Pinch thyme
1 oz/30 grams butter

marinade
4 tablespoons olive oil
2 tablespoons dry white vermouth or white wine
2 tablespoons shallot, finely chopped
1 tablespoon snipped parsley
2 tablespoons mixed herbs: tarragon, thyme, basil
   etc
Salt
Pepper

salad
1 tomato per person
1 leek
Lettuce
Snipped parsley

Fried Oysters

6 to 8 servings

50 prime oysters
3 or 4 beaten eggs
1 packet golden breadcrumbs
1 teaspoon salt

Take the oysters right out of their liquor without draining. Dip them in the crumbs, then set aside on a board in a cool place. (Do not pierce the oysters with a fork—lift them with a draining spoon.) Dip the oysters in the egg, then in the crumbs again and set aside. Fry them quickly in deep, hot fat. Drain on kitchen towel. Serve at once.

Grilled Scallops

6 servings

1½ lb/700 grams fresh scallops
2 tablespoons honey
2 tablespoons prepared mustard
1 teaspoon curry powder
1 teaspoon lemon juice
Lemon slices

Rinse the scallops and pat them dry with kitchen towel. Combine the honey, mustard, curry and lemon juice.

Place the scallops on a grill pan and brush with the honey mixture. Grill on a high heat 8 to 10 minutes or until lightly browned. Turn the scallops and brush with the remaining sauce. Grill 8 to 10 minutes longer. Garnish with lemon slices.

Dill Scallops in Lemon Butter

4 to 6 servings

1½ lb/700 grams scallops
2 oz/60 grams dry breadcrumbs
4 oz/115 grams butter or margarine
¼ teaspoon salt
Dash pepper
Dash paprika
1 tablespoon parsley, chopped
2 teaspoons dill
3 tablespoons lemon juice

Coat the scallops well in breadcrumbs.

Melt 2 oz/60 grams of butter in a pan. Add the salt, pepper and paprika. Sauté the scallops slowly until evenly browned, about 8 minutes. Remove them to a heated dish. Add the remaining butter to the pan with the parsley, dill and lemon juice. Stir until hot. Pour over the scallops. Serve at once.

Prawn Omelette Sandwiches

4 servings

omelette mixture
2 large eggs
2 tablespoons double cream
Salt
Pepper
Butter

filling
About 1–1½ lb/450–700 grams shelled prawns
6 rounded teaspoons garlic butter

bread
6 slices white bread
Butter for the bread
Parmesan cheese for garnish
Dill for garnish

Deep Fried Prawn with Rhode Island Sauce

Beat the omelette ingredients together. If you want a light omelette, whip the cream before adding it to the eggs. Make the omelette "pancakes" as thick as possible, frying them only on one side in a well-greased pan. Place them so that they can cool separately.

Cut out rounds of bread of the same size. Spread butter on the slices and place the prawns on top. Put a dab of garlic butter on each sandwich and cover with the omelette so that the baked side is facing upward. The omelette will then sink down around the prawns.

Place the sandwiches in a small roasting tin at room temperature and wait for your guests to arrive. Sprinkle Parmesan cheese over the sandwiches and place them under the grill for about 5 minutes, or until the cheese has become golden brown, the bread is thoroughly warm, and the garlic butter has begun to melt. Remove from the oven and garnish with dill before serving.

Prawn Croquettes

4 to 6 servings

8 oz/225 grams shelled fresh prawns, chopped
½ pint/¼ l thick béchamel sauce (see below)
3 egg yolks
Pepper
Salt (optional)
Dash nutmeg
Flour
1 egg beaten
Breadcrumbs
Oil for deep-fat frying
Lemon
Parsley

Make a thick béchamel sauce and mix in the chopped prawns. Let boil for just a second and remove from the heat. Stir in the egg yolks, and season with pepper and perhaps a small amount of salt. Season with a dash of nutmeg.

Pour the mixture onto an oiled plate and let it cool. It is best to allow the mixture to sit in the refrigerator overnight. The mixture should be really cold or it will be difficult to form the croquettes.

Divide the mixture into small piles and shape them into croquettes the size of wine bottle corks. Roll them in flour. Then dip them in beaten egg. Roll in breadcrumbs. Fry them in smoking oil until they become golden brown in colour. Remove with a draining spoon and let them drain on a piece of kitchen towel.

Serve the croquettes piled on top of each other in a pyramid shape on a plate, and serve with lemon and a bunch of deep-fat fried parsley.

Béchamel sauce: Melt 1½ oz/45 grams butter in top of a double boiler over boiling water; stir in 1½ oz/45 grams flour with a wooden spoon until smooth. Add 1 pint/½ litre milk gradually stirring constantly; check until sauce is thick. Stir in salt and pepper. Remove top of double boiler from water.

Strain sauce through a fine sieve; use as desired. Pour any remaining sauce into a small bowl. Cover top of sauce with a circle of wet waxed paper; refrigerate for future use. Makes 1 pint/½ litre.

Deep Fried Prawns with Rhode Island Sauce

4 servings

batter
2½ fl oz/75 ml tepid beer
2½ fl oz/75 ml tepid water
2 tablespoons oil
1½ oz/45 grams flour
1 teaspoon salt
1 egg white, stiffly beaten

prawns
2½ lb/1150 grams king size, unshelled prawns
1½–2 pints/850–1135 ml oil for deep frying

Rhode Island sauce
8 fl oz/220 ml mayonnaise
1 tablespoon tomato paste
1 tablespoon dry sherry
¼ teaspoon garllc powder
½ teaspoon salt
3 to 6 dashes tabasco sauce
¼ pint/140 ml soured cream
Parsley
Lemon wedges

Mix all but the egg white of the batter ingredients. Beat until smooth. Let stand and soak. Meanwhile shell the prawns. Beat the egg white into stiff peaks and fold it carefully into the batter. Stir only as much as is necessary. This is so the prawns will be as crispy as possible.

Heat up the oil so that it is about 350°F/180°C or until a little cube of white bread quickly becomes golden brown. Another sign that the oil is at the right temperature is if you can just see small smoke rings.

Mix the prawns in the frying batter and put them carefully, one by one, into the oil. Do not put too many into the oil at one time. They easily bunch together and cause the oil to lose its heat. It is, therefore, best to deep-fry in several batches. Drain by placing them on folded kitchen towel.

Make the Rhode Island sauce by mixing together the mayonnaise tomato paste, sherry, garlic powder, salt and tabasco sauce. Mix until smooth then add cream.

Finally, when everything else is done, deep-fry the parsley. The parsley should be dry and well drained, and all the stems should be removed. Carefully drop a fistful of parsley in the hot oil and fry it for several seconds until it becomes dark green in colour. Serve the prawns with the sauce, parsley and lemon wedges.

Prawns in Oriental Sauce

5 to 6 servings

3 lb/1350 grams prawns
2 tablespoons oil
1 pint/½ l water
1 oz/30 grams butter
2 teaspoons curry
1 large onion, chopped
2 to 3 cloves garlic
½ oz/15 grams flour
12 fl oz/350 ml prawn liquid, see method
2 tablespoons tomato paste
4 drops tabasco

Prawns in Oriental Sauce

1 large green pepper
1 large red pepper
8 fl oz/220 ml soured cream
1 tablespoon brandy (optional)

Shell the prawns and place them in the refrigerator. Save the shells. Sauté the shells in a pan with oil until they start to look dry and turn white. Add the water and let the shells boil for 6 to 7 minutes. Strain the liquid.

Melt the butter in a pan, add the curry powder and then the onion. Sauté until the onion has become soft. Crush the garlic over the mixture.

Sprinkle with the flour and stir. Dilute with the prawn liquid; let it come to the boil while stirring, then add the tomato paste and the tabasco sauce. Simmer for 5 to 6 minutes.

Take the seeds out of the peppers and slice them into fine strips. Store them in a cool place in clingfilm. Everything up to this point can be made in advance.

Bring the sauce to the boil and add the peppers. Stir in the cream and brandy if desired. Simmer 4 to 5 minutes. The peppers should just have become soft. Season. Add the prawns and heat until they become warm. Note: the prawns should not be boiled or they will become tough.

Serve with rice and a green salad.

Steamed Prawns

4 servings

8 fl oz/220 ml water
2½ fl oz/75 ml vinegar
1 tablespoon seafood seasoning
1½ lb/700 grams king prawns with shells
1 lemon

Wipe the prawns dry with kitchen towel. Put the water, vinegar and seafood seasoning into the saucepan and place over medium-high heat. After it boils, add the prawns (with shells) to the pan. Cover the pan, leaving the lid about ½ inch/1¼ cm open to let some steam escape. Cook the prawns until they turn bright pink, 4 to 5 minutes. Then using the lid to hold the prawns drain the pan of liquid.

Cut the lemon into 4 pieces. When the prawns are cool enough to handle, peel and devein them and serve with the lemon quarters.

Prawns with Tomatoes and Cheese

Prawn Tarragon with Pimiento Rice

4 servings

1 oz/30 grams butter, melted
1½ oz/45 grams flour
1 tin prawn bisque
¼ pint/140 ml chicken broth
¼ pint/140 ml Sauterne
2 tablespoons lemon juice
½ teaspoon tarragon
½ teaspoon pepper
½ teaspoon salt
½ teaspoon onion powder
1¼ lb/565 grams prawns, shelled and deveined

pimiento rice
8 oz/225 grams onion, chopped
1 oz/30 grams butter
1 to 1½ lb/450 to 700 grams boiled rice
2 oz/60 grams pimiento, diced

Blend the butter and flour in a saucepan until smooth, then stir in the soup broth, Sauterne, lemon juice, tarragon, pepper, salt and onion powder. Cook

over medium heat until thickened, stirring constantly. Add the prawns and cook for 5 to 10 minutes longer or until they turn pink. Turn into a heated serving dish.

Sauté the onion in butter in a saucepan until tender but not brown. Stir in the rice and pimiento and simmer, stirring frequently, until heated through.

Prawns with Tomatoes and Cheese

4 servings

1 tin tomatoes (whole tomatoes)
2 tablespoons plus 4 fl oz/110 ml olive oil
About 2 oz/60 grams snipped parsley
15 large prawns
½ lb/225 grams soft whipped cream cheese
1½ oz/45 grams butter
Black pepper
Tabasco sauce
Salt (optional)

Prepare the sauce at least 8 hours in advance so that it has time to pull together. Pour off the juice from the tomatoes. Chop the tomatoes into large pieces; mix the pieces with the juice and 2 tablespoons of the oil in the pot. Simmer, uncovered, for 15 minutes. Let cool.

Remove the shells from the prawns but leave the outer tip of the tail.

Grease a shallow ovenproof dish, pour in the tomato sauce and place the prawns in the sauce with the tails facing up. Cover with parsley, the soft cheese and the butter in small dabs. Grind a fair amount of pepper over the dish and add a few drops of tabasco sauce. Drip the rest of the oil over the dish and place under the grill until the prawns are cooked and the dish has become golden brown. Serve with rice.

Vegetables

Asparagus Delight

4 servings

9 oz/255 grams tinned asparagus or about 20
   fresh asparagus, cooked and cooled
8 fl oz/220 ml soured cream
1 jar red caviar

Place a pile of about 5–6 asparagus on each plate. Mix together the cream and red caviar. Dab it over the asparagus.

Baked Asparagus

4 servings

16 fat asparagus
Salt and freshly ground pepper
Sweet butter
1 lemon, cut into wedges

Cut the asparagus to fit a large, flat, ovenproof serving dish. With a vegetable peeler, lightly peel the heavy stalk to within 3 or 4 inches/8 or 10 cm of the tip. Rinse the asparagus in cold water and arrange it in the dish, gently shaking off only the excess water.

Sprinkle with salt and pepper and dot generously with butter. Cover the dish tightly with foil. Bake the asparagus at 350°F/180°C/gas mark 4 for 20 minutes or until it is tender but crisp. Serve with lemon wedges.

Asparagus with Dill

4 servings

1½ lb/700 grams asparagus spears, about 2
   bunches
Salt to taste
½ oz/15 grams melted butter
1 tablespoon dill or parsley, finely chopped

Using a peeling knife, scrape the sides of the asparagus, leaving about 2 inches/5 cm of the tops unscraped. Cut about 1 inch/2½ cm off the bottom of the asparagus stalks. Heat water in the bottom of a vegetable steamer and when it comes to the boil place the asparagus in the top of the steamer. Cover and let steam 5 minutes.

Transfer the asparagus to a warm serving dish and sprinkle with salt, butter and dill.

Home Baked Beans

8 to 10 servings

1 lb/450 grams dried haricot beans
12 oz/345 grams lean salt pork
2 tablespoons molasses
5 tablespoons dark brown sugar
Boiling water
1 teaspoon dried English mustard
2 cups boiling water

Put the beans in a strainer and wash them under cold running water. Put them in a bowl and cover with cold water. Soak overnight. Drain. Then cover, in a saucepan, with fresh water and heat slowly, keeping the water below boiling point. Cook until the skins burst open when a few beans are held on the end of a spoon and blown on.

Scald the pork by frying it briefly on all sides. Score the pork rind. Put the pork in ovenproof casserole with the drained beans. Cover.

Dissolve the sugar and molasses in boiling water. Add mustard to the cold water and stir into a paste. Add the paste to the molasses mixture and stir. Add the beans and pork. Add enough extra boiling water to cover the beans. Cover the casserole and bake at 250°F/120°C/gas mark ¼ for about 8 hours. Check every 2 hours to make sure the beans are covered with water.

Stuffed Avocado au Gratin

4 servings

4 ripe avocados
1 packet Hollandaise sauce
Milk and a little butter
4 to 6 ham slices, slivered
Grated Gruyère cheese

Cut a "lid" off the avocados leaving tle botton part, which is to be filled. Remove the stone. Loosen the avocado flesh and cut it into pieces.

Dilute the sauce powder with milk and a little butter. Add the ham and avocado pieces. Divide the mixture among the 4 larger avocado halves. Place them on aluminium foil or a baking sheet on an oven rack. Cover them with a generous amount of cheese. Cook at 450°F/230°C/gas mark 8 about 15 minutes.

Banana Casserole

4 to 6 servings

6 ripe bananas
4 oz/115 grams orange sections
4 oz/115 grams sugar
2 tablepoons orange juice
2 tablepoons lemon juice
Pinch salt

Peel the bananas and cut them lengthways. Place them in a buttered dish.

Remove the membrane from the oranges and arrange them on top of the bananas. Sprinkle sugar over the bananas. Add the orange and lemon juices, to which salt has been added.

Cook at 300–350°F/150–180°C/gas mark 2–4 for 30 to 45 minutes.

Baked Beans with Apples

10 servings

2 lbs/450 grams dried haricot beans, soaked overnight
4½ pints/2½ l water
1 lb/450 grams salt pork, diced
3 cooking apples, peeled, cored and coarsely chopped
1 medium sized onion, chopped
3½ oz/100 grams brown sugar, firmly packed
8 oz/225 grams molasses
3 teaspoons dry mustard
3 tablespoons vinegar
½ teaspoon pepper

Place the soaked beans and the salt pork in a stewing pan and cook until the beans are tender, about 1 hour.

Pour the bean mixture into an ovenproof casserole, add the remaining ingredients and cook, cov-ered, 6 hours in a 300°F/150°C/gas mark 2 oven. Add more warm water during cooklng if necessary.

Pinto Beans

10 to 12 servings

6 pints/½ l water
1 lb/450 grams dried pinto beans, washed
1 lb/450 grams tinned tomatoes
1 large onion, chopped
8 rashers bacon, cut in 2-inch/5-cm lengths
8 oz/225 grams celery, sliced
1½ teaspoons salt
1 teaspoon ground cinnamon
6 oz/170 grams sugar
3 tablespoons vinegar

Put the water and the beans in a large stewing pan and simmer, covered, for 4 hours, or until the beans are tender. Add the rest of the ingredients.

Place the mixture in a large casserole. Cover and cook in a 350°F/180°C/gas mark 4 oven for 2 to 3 hours, or until done. Add water if necessary.

Butter Beans

4 to 6 servings

2 lbs/450 grams small butter beans
¼ pint/140 ml water
1 oz/30 grams bacon dripping
1 teaspoon seasoned salt
1 onion, cut in half
½ teaspoon pepper
1 clove garlic (optional)
1 teaspoon salt
2 teaspoons cornflour
½ oz/15 grams butter

Put all the ingredients, except the cornflour and butter into a saucepan. Cook until the beans are tender, about 10 minutes. Remove the onion and garlic. Drain the beans, reserving the liquid. Slightly thicken the liquid with cornflour. Add butter and mix well. Pour over the beans. Serve at once.

Fresh Green Beans with Cherry Tomatoes

6 servings

1 lb/450 grams fresh green beans
1¼ teaspoons salt
1½ oz/45 grams butter
½ teaspoon sugar
Pinch freshly ground pepper
1½ tablespoons fresh parsley, chopped
8 cherry tomatoes, halved

Wash the beans, remove the tips, and cut them into 1-inch/2½-cm pieces. Place the beans in a saucepan with 1-inch/2½-cm of boiling water and 1 tea-

Asparagus Delight

spoon of salt. Cook 5 minutes. Cover. Cook over medium heat 10 to 15 minutes, until just crisp and tender. Drain, if necessary. Add the butter, sugar, pepper, remaining salt and parsley. Toss lightly until the butter is melted and beans are coated. Place in a serving bowl and garnish with cherry tomatoes.

Ham Flavoured Green Beans

6 servings

1½ lbs/450 grams green beans, broken into short pieces, or 1¼ lbs/565 grams frozen cut green beans
2 small onions, quartered
½ stick celery, sliced
About 2 oz/60 grams cooked ham, cut into bite-sized pieces
2 teaspoons salt
Pepper to taste
¼ pint/140 ml water
½ oz/15 grams butter or margarine

Put the beans in a large stewing pan. Add the remaining ingredients and simmer until the beans are tender, 12 to 20 minutes

Green Beans with Dill

6 servings

8 oz/225 grams onion, chopped
3 tablespoons butter or margarine
½ pint/¼ l water
¼ pint/140 ml chilli sauce
½ teaspoon dill
1 oz/30 grams cornflour
2 tablespoons water
1½ lb/700 grams cooked or tinned green beans

Sauté the onion in melted butter in a saucepan until transparent. Stir in the water, chilli sauce, and dill.

Mix the cornflour and water together and add to the onion mixture. Cook, stirring, until thickened.

Combine the sauce and beans.

Baked Lima Beans in Cream

4 to 6 servings

10 oz/285 grams tinned lima beans
½ teaspoon seasoned salt
Freshly ground pepper to taste
8 fl oz/220 ml milk or cream

Put the beans into a greased 2-pint/1¼-litre casserole. Sprinkle the seasoning over the beans. Pour milk on top. Cover the casserole and cook in a 350°F/180°C/gas mark 4 oven for 20 minutes. Stir once. Reduce heat to 300°F/150°C/gas mark 2 and cook for 20 minutes more. When the beans are tender, the dish is ready to be served.

Baked Broccoli

8 servings

1 large egg
¼ pint/140 ml mayonaise
12 oz/345 grams tinned cream of mushroom soup
1¼ lb/565 grams frozen chopped broccoli, cooked and drained well
1 medium onion, finely chopped
8 oz/225 grams Gruyère, grated and packed loosely
2 oz/60 grams fine dry breadcrumbs, mixed with 1 oz/30 grams butter
Paprika

Stir the eggs lightly with a whisk. Blend together the mayonnaise and soup. Stir in the cooked broccoli, onion, and cheese. Pour into a 1-pint/½-litre baking dish. Sprinkle with the breadcrumb mixture and top with paprika. Bake in a preheated oven at 350°F/180°C/gas mark 4 until hot and the sides begin to bubble, about 35 minutes.

Fresh Lima Beans in Parsley Sauce

4 servings

3 lb/1¼ kilo fresh lima beans
Salt and white pepper
1 oz/30 grams butter or margarine
¼ pint/140 ml cream
1 tablespoon parsley, chopped

Cut off the outer edge of each lima bean pod with scissors. Shell them into a small saucepan and cover with boiling water. Add 1 teaspoon of salt and cook until tender, 20 to 25 minutes unless the beans are very small. Drain well and return to pan. Heat with butter and cream. Season to taste with salt and pepper. Serve in individual bowls and sprinkle with parsley.

College Beetroot

4 to 5 servings

1 1-lb/450-gram jar sliced beetroot
1 oz/60 grams cornflour
2 oz/60 grams sugar
2½ fl oz/75 ml cider vinegar

Drain the beetroot, saving 2½ fl oz/75 ml liquid. In a 2-pint/1¼-litre saucepan stir together the cornflour and sugar. Gradually stir in the beetroot juice and vinegar. Cook over a medium heat, stirring constantly, until thickened. Add the beetroot and heat gently.

Beetroot with Orange Sauce

6 servings

2 oz/60 grams sugar
1 teaspoon salt
1 oz/30 grams cornflour
4 fl oz/110 ml orange juice
2 tablespoons lemon juice
½ oz/15 grams butter or margarine
1½ lb/700 grams beetroot, cooked, sliced, drained

Mix the sugar, salt and cornflour well. Stir in the orange juice. Cook until thickened stirring constantly. Remove from the heat and stir in the lemon juice and butter. Pour the sauce over the beetroot, stir carefully. Heat and serve.

Pickled Beetroot

makes 2 pints

4½ lb/2 kilo beetroot
Water
1 piece horseradish for pickling

for pickling
1 pint/½ l vinegar
1¼ pint/710 ml water
½ tablespoon salt

10 oz/285 grams sugar
10 white peppercorns
8 whole cloves
5 allspice corns

Brush and rinse the beetroot well, without damaging the skins or root tips. Boil in water until almost soft. Rinse under cold running water. Pull off the skins.

Prepare the pickling liquid by boiling together the vinegar, water, salt, sugar and spices.

Place the beetroot in the liquid and boil until soft. Then put the beetroot and liquid in earthenware or glass jars. Put small pieces of horseradish on top.

Variation: Boil large beetroots until partially soft. Peel them and cut into slices. Place in jars with the horseradish on top. Pour the hot liquid over the beetroot.

Marinated Broccoli

10 servings

3 lb/1¼ kilo broccoli, cut in strips
½ pint/¼ l cider vinegar
1 tablespoon sugar
1 tablespoon dill
1 tablespoon pepper
1 tablespoon salt
1 tablespoon garlic salt
15 fl oz/425 ml vegetable oil

Combine all the ingredients and pour them over the broccoli. Marinate overnight in the refrigerator, shaking occasionally. Serve cold. Before serving, pour off some of the marinade.

Broccoli and Potato Casserole

4 servings

10 oz/285 grams frozen broccoli, chopped
2 oz/60 grams butter
1 small onion, finely chopped
2 medium sized potatoes
Salt and pepper to taste

Cook the broccoli as directed. Drain. In a small pan, melt the butter and add the onion and cook gently until yellowed.

Peel the potatoes and steam or cook in boiling water until tender. Drain and put through a food processor. With a fork or spoon, mix the broccoli, onion and salt and pepper with the potatoes. Cover and reheat over boiling water.

Sautéed Broccoli

4 servings

1 lb/450 grams fresh young broccoli
Boiling salted water
3 tablespoons olive oil

1 clove garlic, peeled, chopped
Salt and pepper

Remove any dry, woody stems from the broccoli. Trim all discoloured parts and dead leaves. Separate into small spears and peel the stalks with a vegetable peeler. Cook 3 to 5 minutes in 1-inch/2½-cm of boiling salted water. Drain thoroughly. Heat the oil with the garlic and toss the broccoli in the oil for 1 minute. Season.

Brussels Sprouts

6 servings

3 lb/1¼ kilos Brussels sprouts
1 oz/30 grams butter
2½ fl oz/75 ml lemon juice
½ pint/¼ l soured cream
1 oz/30 grams fresh parsley, finely chopped
½ teaspoon salt
¼ teaspoon pepper
Sliced stuffed olives (optional)

Stuffed Avocado au Gratin

Wash and trim the sprouts removing any loose or yellow leaves. Cut a cross in the stems so the sprouts will cook faster. Soak the sprouts in cool, salted water.

Melt the butter in a pan over medium heat. Drain the sprouts, then add them to the pan. Cover and sweat about 10 minutes, shaking the pan occasionally.

Add the lemon juice and sweat 2 minutes more. Then add the rest of the ingredients, except the olives. Heat, but do not boil. Serve topped with sliced olives, if desired.

Creamy Brussels Sprouts and Peppers

4 servings

1½ lb/700 grams Brussels sprouts
2 red peppers
¼ onion, chopped
1 bay leaf
2 tablespoons oil
1 potato, cubed
2½ fl oz/75 ml stock
1 oz/30 grams butter
½ teaspoon salt

Clean and trim the Brussels sprouts, cut the large ones in half. Cut the peppers into ½-inch/1¼-cm pieces. Sauté the onion in oil with a bay leaf until the onion is soft. Add the pepper pieces and stir briefly. Add the stock and sweat all the vegetables until just tender.

Sweat or boil the potato cubes separately and purée them in a blender with butter, salt and some of the juice from the vegetables. Stir together with the sprouts and peppers.

Dutch Cabbage

6 servings

2½lb/1150 grams cabbage, shredded
4 rashers bacon, diced
½ teaspoon salt in 4 pints/2¼ l boiling water
1 oz/30 grams brown sugar
1 oz/30 grams flour
4 fl oz/110 ml cider vinegar
¼ pint/140 ml water
1 small onion, finely chopped
Salt and pepper to taste

Cook the cabbage in 4 pints/2¼ l of boiling, salted water for 7 minutes.

Meanwhile, fry the bacon pieces and set aside. Add the sugar and flour to the bacon fat. Blend over low heat. Add the remaining ingredients and bacon pieces. Cook and stir until thickened and smooth. Pour over the drained, cooked cabbage in a casserole dish.

Fruity Red Cabbage

6 to 8 servings

1 head of red cabbage
1½ oz/45 grams margarine
4 fl oz/110 ml red wine
4 fl oz/110 ml water
1 onion
4 whole cloves
2 teaspoons salt
½ teaspoon black pepper
8 to 10 plums, stoned and cut into pieces.
1 large cooking apple, peeled, cored and cubed

Rinse the head of cabbage. Divide it into 4 parts. Remove the core. Shred the cabbage.

Heat the margarine in a pan.

Quickly stir the cabbage and heated margarine together in a large pot. Add the wine and water.

Peel the onion and halve it. Stick 2 cloves into each half. Place them in with the cabbage, adding the salt and black pepper. Let this come to a boil. Cover and let simmer about 15 minutes. Add the plums and apple. Let the cabbage boil, covered, for another 30 to 45 minutes, until it is soft. Remove the onion with cloves.

This can be frozen and kept for several months.

Sauerkraut

4 servings

to make sauerkraut
6½–7 lb/3–3¼ kilos cabbage
2 cooking apples
3 tablespoons coarse salt
2 teaspoons caraway seeds
10 dried juniper berries (optional)

to cook sauerkraut
14 oz/400 grams sauerkraut
1 pint/½ l broth or pork dripping
1 onion, stuck with 1 clove
1 teaspoon caraway seeds

To make sauerkraut:

Clean and rinse the cabbage. Put aside several whole leaves. Separate the head of cabbage and take away the core. Shred the cabbage into fine pieces.

Core the apples and cut them into thin slices.

In a deep flameproof casserole, layer the shredded cabbage with the salt, apple slices, caraway seeds and, if desired, the juniper berries. Pound each layer hard so that the cabbage becomes juicy. Cover with the whole cabbage leaves. Place a plate with something heavy on it over the mixture. Let the cabbage stand for 3 to 4 days at room temperature and then in a cool place.

After about 14 days the cabbage is ready to be cooked. It will keep for several months if stored in a cool place, such as a refrigerator vegetable compartment.

To cook sauerkraut:

Rinse it and let it drain. Place it in the broth with the onion and caraway seeds. Let simmer until soft, about 30 to 45 minutes. Season as desired.

Carrot Fritters

6 to 8 servings

1 bunch carrots or 2 lb/900 grams tinned, sliced carrots
1 egg
1 oz/30 grams sugar
1½ oz/45 grams flour
Salt and pepper to taste
1 teaspoon baking powder
Deep fat for frying

If using raw carrots, cook them in a small amount of water until very tender. Mash the carrots. Add the egg and sugar. Next add the flour, salt, pepper and baking powder and stir until well blended.

Drop by spoonfuls into deep fat (375°F/190°C). The fritters will brown quickly when the fat is the right temperature. Drain on kitchen towel. Keep warm until all are finished. Serve at once.

Glazed Carrots

4 to 6 servings

10 to 12 small young carrots, washed and trimmed
1 oz/30 grams margarine
1 oz/30 grams brown sugar
1 oz/30 grams honey
2 tablespoons fresh mint

Cook the carrots in a small amount of boiling, salted water for 10 minutes. When tender, drain and set aside.

Melt the margarine in a medium sized pan. Add the sugar and honey and blend. Add the carrots and cook 3 or 4 minutes over a low heat, stirring so each carrot is glazed. Sprinkle with mint.

Carrot Pudding

6 to 8 servings

4 oz/115 grams brown sugar
1 egg, beaten with 1 tablespoon water
1 lb/450 grams carrots. grated
12 oz/345 grams
½ teaspoon bicarbonate of soda
½ teaspoon nutmeg
1 teaspoon baking powder
½ teaspoon salt
½ teaspoon cinnamon

Cream the shortening and sugar. Add the rest of the ingredients and mix well. Pour the mixture into a greased ring mould or loaf tin. Refrigerate overnight. Remove 30 minutes before baking. Bake at 350°F/180°C/gas mark 4 for 1 hour.

Carrots with Walnuts

8 servings

2 lb/900 grams carrots, peeled and cut in sticks
15 fl oz/425 ml water
½ teaspoon salt
12 oz/345 grams butter or margarine, melted
2 teaspoons honey
½ teaspoon salt
¼ teaspoon coarse pepper
2 tablespoons lemon juice
¼ teaspoon lemon peel, grated
4 oz/115 grams walnuts, coarsely broken

Cook the carrots in salted water until tender. Drain.
In a saucepan, combine the remaining ingredients, except the walnuts, and heat. Pour this sauce over the carrots. Mix in the walnuts.

Cauliflower and Chestnut Casserole

6 servings

1 medium sized cauliflower
Boiling water
1¼ teaspoons salt
1 oz/30 grams butter or margarine
1 lb/450 grams chestnuts (see instructions below)
¼ teaspoon white pepper
2 tablespoons hot water

Break the cauliflower into florets. Place in a saucepan with 1 inch/2½ cms of boiling water and 1 teaspoon of salt. Bring to the boil and cook uncovered 5 minutes. Cover and cook 5 minutes longer. Drain.
Put a layer of cauliflower in a buttered casserole, cover with a layer of prepared chestnuts, dot with butter or margarine and sprinkle lightly with white pepper mixed with the remaining ¼ teaspoon salt.
Continue until all the ingredients are used. Add 2 tablespoons of hot water. Cover and cook in a preheated 350°F/180°C/gas mark 4 oven for 30 minutes.
To prepare the chestnuts: Prick them with a fork or split the top end in a cross slit.
Place in a saucepan, cover with cold water and bring to the boil. Boil 1 minute, drain and remove the outer shells. Return to the saucepan and cook in boiling, salted water until tender.
The brown coating of the chestnuts will come off during boiling. Chop the chestnuts

Pickled Beetroot

Boiled Cauliflower

8 Servings

2 hard-boiled egg yolks
1 teaspoon dried parsley flakes
2 tablespoons soured cream
¼ teaspoon white pepper
1 head cauliflower
1 teaspoon salt
Black pepper

Cook the cauliflower in plenty of boiling, salted water for about 15 minutes. Halve the tomatoes and sprinkle with basil and herb salt. Flake the tomatoes in a preheated 425°F/220°C/gas mark 7 oven for 10 minutes.
Let the spinach defrost and cook briefly over a gentle heat.
Combine the cauliflower and tomatoes and serve the sauce separately.

Creamed Celery with Pecan Nuts

4 to 6 servings

2 lbs/900 grams celery, cut diagonally into
   ½-inch/1-cm pieces
1 tin cream of celery soup
1 teaspoon salt
6 oz/170 grams pecan halves
Buttered breadcrumbs

Place the celery in a greased casserole. Add the undiluted soup and sprinkle with salt. Sprinkle with pecan nuts. Cover all with buttered breadcrumbs. Cook in the oven at 400°F/200°C/gas mark 6 for 20 minutes.

Chick Pea Ratatouille

4 servings

1 or 2 garlic cloves (optional)
1 onion
1 green pepper
1 oz/30 grams butter
2 tins chopped tomatoes
Juice of half a lemon
1 teaspoon herb salt
Black pepper
1 tin chick peas
6 fl oz/170 ml soured cream
1 bunch parsley, finely chopped

Peel and finely chop the garlic and onion. Shred the pepper.
In a heavy saucepan, fry the onion and garlic in butter until soft but not browned. Add the pepper, tomatoes and lemon juice. Season with herb salt and black pepper. Simmer to reduce liquid for 7 or 8 minutes. Mix in the chick peas and bring to the boil.
Serve sprinkled with parsley and a spoonful of soured cream. Black bread goes well with this dish.

Confetti Corn

6 servings

6 ears corn
2 oz/60 grams butter
2 oz/60 grams sweet pepper, chopped
2 oz/60 grams red sweet pepper, chopped
1 tablespoon fresh parsley, finely chopped

Remove the husks and fibres from the corn. Cook in boiling water 8 to 10 minutes, until tender. Drain. Cool until easily handled and cut the kernels from the cobs.
Melt the butter in a saucepan and add the peppers and parsley. Cook over a low heat, stirring constantly, until the peppers are tender. Stir in the corn and heat through.

Corn Fritters

4 to 6 servings

1 lb/450 grams tinned corn, drained
1 egg
½ teaspoon salt
2½ fl oz/75 ml milk
4 oz/115 grams flour
2 teaspoons baking powder
2 teaspoons butter, melted
½ teaspoon sugar
Deep fat for frying

While the corn is draining, mix the egg, salt, milk, flour, baking powder, melted butter and sugar. Stir with a long-handled, wooden spoon. Add the drained corn. Allow the mixture to sit 5 minutes. Drop by teaspoonfuls into hot fat. Cook until puffy and golden brown. Drain on kitchen towel. Transfer to a warmed dish.

Sauerkraut

Alabama Style Corn

Quantity varies

Fresh ears of corn
Water
Salt Butter, softened
Dill
Parsley
Chives
Leek
Tarragon

Rinse the corn and remove the husks. Save the best pieces of husk. Rinse the corn and husks again. Place the husks in the bottom of a shallow pan. Save a few husks to cover the corn. Add the corn. Cover with husks and boil in lightly salted water for 10 to 12 minutes. Serve with herb butter and salt.

To make the herb butter: season soft butter with dill, parsley, chives, leek, tarragon or spices of your choice.

Corn Casserole with Ham and Cheese

3 or 4 servings

6 ears of corn (cut the corn off the cob)
3 or 4 slices ham
12 fl oz/350 ml milk
3 eggs
12 oz–1 lb/345–450 grams mature cheese, grated
Pinch of nutmeg

Place the corn and ham in a greased ovenproof dish.

Beat together eggs and milk. Add cheese and nutmeg. Pour this mixture over the corn and ham. Bake at 400°F/200°C/gas mark 6 for 25 minutes.

Fresh Corn Pudding

6 servings

1 lb/450 grams fresh sweetcorn, cut from the cob
2 teaspoons sugar
1½ teaspoons salt
Pinch pepper
3 eggs, lightly beaten
1 oz/30 grams butter
1 pint/½ l milk

Combine the corn, sugar, salt and pepper in a bowl. Add the eggs and mix well.

Place the butter and milk in a saucepan. Heat until the butter is melted, then stir into the corn mixture. Turn into a greased 2 pint/1¼ l casserole. Place the casserole in a pan of hot water. Bake in a preheated 350°F/180°C/gas mark 4 oven for 1 hour or until a knife inserted in the centre comes out clean. Garnish with fresh parsley.

Cucumbers in Dill

6 to 8 servings

4 cucumbers, peeled and thinly sliced
½ pint/¼ l boiling water
8 fl oz/220 ml soured cream
2½ fl oz/75 ml lemon juice
3 tablespoons dill, finely chopped
1½ teaspoons salt
Pinch pepper
1 teaspoon sugar

Pour boiling water over the cucumbers. Let them stand 5 minutes; drain. Plunge into iced water, then drain.

Mix the remaining ingredients together. Pour them over the cucumbers, tossing until well mixed. Chill 30 minutes before serving.

Cucumbers in Soured Cream

4 servings

4 cucumbers
½ pint/¼ l soured cream with chives
1 small lettuce, trimmed and cleaned
1 tablespoon parsley

Wash cucumbers thoroughly. Slice into small wedges.

Combine soured cream and cucumbers; mix to coat cucumbers.

Arrange lettuce leaves in salad bowls. Pour the cucumber mixture on the lettuce beds. Garnish with parsley.

Dill Pickles

6 pints

4½ lb/2 kilos small green cucumbers
Dill sprigs
Several bay leaves
2 tablespoons yellow mustard seeds
1 piece horseradish, cut into small cubes

pickle juice
1½ pints/850 ml water
1½ tablespoons white vinegar
1½ lb/700 grams sugar
2½ oz/75 grams fine salt

Brush the cucumbers well in warm water and cut them into thick slices. In jars alternate the cucumber slices with sprigs of dill, bay leaves, mustard seeds and horseradish cubes.

Bring all the pickle juice ingredients to the boil. Pour the juice over the cucumbers. Let the mixture become cold. Seal the jars and store in a cold place. After 2 weeks their flavour will have developed.

Anchovy Stuffed Aubergine

4 servings

1 medium-large aubergine
1 small onion, finely chopped
½ oz/15 grams butter
4 oz/115 grams tinned skinless anchovies
1 rounded teaspoon flour
½ pint/¼ l double cream or soured cream
1 oz/30 grams finely chopped parsley
About 3 oz/85 grams finely grated cheese,
   preferably mature Gruyère

Divide the aubergine lengthwise. Dig out the flesh from the skin, and finely chop it. inside

Sauté the onion in the butter until soft but not brown. Drain and mash the anchovies. Add to the onion.

Save the anchovy liquid. Whip it together with the flour. Add to the anchovy mixture. Let it simmer a few minutes. Add the cream and let it simmer until it thickens. Blend in the aubergine and parsley. Remove from the heat.

Fill the aubergine skins with the mixture. Place them on an ovenproof plate. Sprinkle the grated cheese over the aubergines. Cook in 400°F/200°C/gas mark 6 oven for 30 to 35 minutes or until the top has browned. Let the dish cool before serving as an opening course, preferably with beer.

If this dish is served warm, it is rather glutinous. When served cooled or cold, it is delicious.

Baked Maize

6 servings

1 pint/½ l milk
1 pint/½ l water
8 oz/225 grams quick-cooking maize meal or
   hominy grits
1 teaspoon salt
2 eggs
8 oz/225 grams mature Cheddar cheese, grated
1 oz/30 grams butter

Mix the milk, water, maize and salt in a heavy saucepan and simmer until thick, about 5 minutes. Stir occasionally.

Beat the eggs and add a little of the maize mixture to warm them. Then add the eggs to the saucepan. Mix in the cheese. Turn into a well-greased, 2- pint/1¼-litre ovenproof dish. Dot with butter. Cook in a preheated 350°F/180°C/gas mark 4 oven for 35–45 minutes, or until lightly brown on top.

Creole Lentils

4 servings

4 oz/115 grams dried lentils
½ oz/15 grams butter
1 green pepper, finely chopped
1 small onion, finely chopped
8 oz/225 grams tomatoes, chopped
½ teaspoon salt
Pinch pepper
Pinch filé powder
1 lb/450 grams cooked whole-grain rice

Cover the lentils with water and soak them overnight. Drain, cover with fresh water and simmer for 50 minutes or until tender.

Melt the butter in a pan and sauté the green pepper and onion until limp. Add the tomatoes, salt, pepper and filé powder, if desired. Drain the lentils and add to the pan, simmer until heated through. Serve hot over cooked rice.

Fried Okra

4 to 6 servings

1 lb/450 grams fresh young okra
Salt and pepper to taste
4 to 8 oz/115 to 225 grams cornmeal
Fat for deep frying

Wash the okra and cut it into 1-inch/2½-cm pieces. Liberally sprinkle the pieces with salt and pepper.

Put the cornmeal into a brown paper bag. Shake the okra in the bag until each piece is coated. Fry in deep fat (375°F/190°C) until golden brown and crisp. Drain on kitchen towel.

Cauliflower with Green Sauce

Fried Aubergine

6 to 8 servings

1 aubergine, peeled and thinly sliced
Salt
1 egg, beaten
Pepper
Breadcrumbs
Oil

Generously salt each aubergine slice. Place the slices in a pile and top with a weighted plate. Drain for ½ hour.

Dip the aubergine in egg mixed with milk and pepper, then in breadcrumbs. Fry quickly in hot oil until golden brown.

Stuffed Aubergine

6 servings

3 small aubergines (about 2 lb/900 grams)
1 lb/450 grams lean minced lamb or beef
1 lb/450 grams tinned, stewed tomatoes
½ pint/¼ l tomato juice
½ teaspoon dried mint or marjoram
¼ teaspoon ground cinnamon
¼ teaspoon ground nutmeg
Salt and pepper, to taste
6 teaspoons seasoned breadcrumbs
6 teaspoons sharp Parmesan cheese, grated
1 tablespoon lemon juice

Cut the aubergines in half lengthways. Scoop out the centres and reserve the scooped out aubergine pulp. Dice the pulp. Spread the meat in a shallow layer in a nonstick pan. Brown it with no fat added. Break it into chunks and turn it, to brown evenly. Drain and discard any melted fat.

Add the diced aubergine pulp to the meat mixture. Stir in the tomatoes, juice, mint, cinnamon, nutmeg, salt and pepper. Simmer, uncovered, 15 to 20 minutes, until most of the liquid has evaporated.

Spoon the meat mixture into the aubergine shells and sprinkle it with breadcrumbs, Parmesan cheese and lemon juice. Arrange the stuffed aubergine halves on a shallow baking tray. Cook, uncovered, at 375°F/190°C/gas mark 5 for about 20 to 25 minutes, until the aubergine is tender.

Glazed Onions

6 servings

1½ oz/45 grams butter
2 oz/60 grams sugar
24 small white onions, peeled
¼ pint/140 ml chicken broth

Melt the butter in a large pan and add the sugar,

then the onions. Sauté, stirring, until golden brown. Add the broth, cover and cook down until syrupy and the onions are done. Baste frequently.

Onion Pie

6 to 8 servings

Frozen shortcrust pastry for a 9-inch/22-cm flan
1½ oz/45 grams lard or shortening
1 clove garlic, mashed to a pulp with 1 teaspoon salt
2 lb/900 grams onions, peeled and sliced
3 eggs
½ teaspoon freshly ground black pepper
8 to 12 black olives, pitted and halved
4 to 6 anchovies (optional)

Prepare the pastry according to package directions. Let it stand at room temperature to dry after you fit it into the flan dish.

Heat the shortening in a large pan. When hot, add the garlic. Add the onions at once. Stir with a large spoon. Reduce the heat to low after 2 to 3 minutes and continue cooking, stirring frequently. Do not let the onions brown, but be sure at least half of them are golden in colour and that all are fully cooked, translucent and limp.

When onions are cooked, remove from heat.

Beat the eggs with a fork. Brush the surface of the pastry generously with beaten egg. Place the pie shell in a preheated 375°F/190°C/gas mark 5 oven. Stir black pepper into the onions. After the pie shell has cooked 2 to 3 minutes, remove it from the oven, spoon the onions into the shell and pour the remaining beaten egg over the onions. Bake 12 to 15 minutes. Remove from the oven, distribute olives evenly over the pie, and if you use anchovies, chop them in small pieces and sprinkle them on top. Return to the oven for a minute or 2, cool and serve as a first course for dinner or as a main course for lunch.

Honey and Orange Glazed Parsnips

6 servings

3 cups parsnips, diagonally sliced
3/4 cup boiling water
½ teaspoon salt
2 teaspoons butter
1 tablespoon honey
¼ cup orange juice
1 teaspoon orange peel, grated

Place the parsnips in a saucepan with water and salt and cook until tender, about 10 minutes. Drain and combine the remaining ingredients and heat. Add the parsnips.

Chick Pea Ratatouille

Peanut Loaf

8 servings

10 oz/285 grams crunchy peanut butter
12 oz/345 grams cooked lima beans
2 oz/60 grams onion, finely chopped
½ teaspoon basil
1 teaspoon salt
¼ teaspoon pepper
5 oz/140 grams soft breadcrumbs
12 oz/345 grams Cheddar cheese, grated
15 fl oz/425 ml milk
2 tablespoons parsley, chopped
4 eggs, well beaten
15 fl oz/425 ml well seasoned tomato sauce

Combine all the ingredients except the tomato sauce, mixing well. Spoon the mixture into a greased 9 × 5 × 3-inch/22 × 12 × 8-cm loaf tin. Cook in a 350°F/180°C/gas mark 4 oven for 40 to 45 minutes. Serve hot with tomato sauce.

Peas and Cucumbers

4 servings

1 medium sized cucumber
2 lb/900 grams fresh green peas, shelled
2½ fl oz/75 ml water

½ small head lettuce, shredded
1 oz/30 grams butter or margarine
1 teaspoon sugar
½ teaspoon salt
Pinch pepper
2½ fl oz/75 ml soured cream or plain yoghurt
1 teaspoon lemon juice
Paprika

Cut the unpeeled cucumber lengthwise into quarters, then crosswise into 1-inch/2½-cm pieces. Bring the cucumber pieces, peas and water to the boiling. Reduce the heat. Cover and simmer until the peas are tender, about 10 minutes. Drain. Stir in the lettuce, butter, sugar, salt and pepper and heat until the lettuce is hot. Mix the soured cream and lemon juice. Toss or serve with vegetables. Sprinkle with paprika.

Creamed Peas and Corn

6 servings

10 oz/285 grams frozen peas
10 oz/285 grams frozen corn
1 oz/30 grams butter
1 oz/30 grams flour
½ pint/¼ l milk
½ teaspoon salt
¼ teaspoon white pepper

Cook the peas and corn as directed on the packets. While the vegetables are cooking, melt the butter in a saucepan. Add the flour and cook 2 minutes, stirring constantly. Add the milk, salt and pepper. Cook until thick, then remove from the heat.

Drain the cooked vegetables. Add the sauce and mix well. Serve immediately.

Corn Alabama Style

Black-Eyed Peas Supreme

8 servings

2 lb/900 grams tinned black-eyed peas, drained
1 onion, sliced into thin rings
¼ pint/140 ml olive oil
2½ fl oz/75 ml wine vinegar
1 medium sized clove garlic, crushed
1 tablespoon Worcester sauce
1 teaspoon salt
Pepper to taste

Place the peas and onion in an ovenproof bowl. Combine the oil, vinegar and seasonings in a small pan and bring to the boil. Immediately pour the mixture over the peas and onions and stir gently. Refrigerate several hours or overnight.

New Peas

6 to 8 servings

2 lb/900 grams peas, shelled
2 teaspoons sugar
2 teaspoons salt
6 pea pods
1 small green onion with top, chopped
Water

1 oz/30 grams butter
½ teaspoon pepper
½ pint/¼ l single cream

Place the peas in a saucepan with the sugar, salt, pea pods, onion and enough water to cover. Cook for 10 to 15 minutes, or until the water has almost evaporated and the peas are tender. Add the butter and heat until melted. Add the pepper and cream and heat.

Mangetout

4 servings

1 lb/450 grams mangetout
12 oz/345 grams slice of cooked ham
1 teaspoon sugar
1 very small onion
Salt
1 oz/30 grams butter, melted

Prepare the mangetout. Bring the ham to the boil in unsalted water. Add the mangetout, sugar and onion. Cook about 20 minutes, until the mangetout are tender. Drain. Salt to taste and coat with melted butter.

Corn Casserole with Ham and Cheese

Spicy Peppers

4 servings

2 cloves garlic, crushed
2 tablespoons olive oil
4 red peppers (or 2 red and 2 green), seeded,
    deveined and cut into thin strips
2 tablespoons red wine vinegar
Salt

In a large pan, cook the garlic for 3 minutes in olive oil until golden.

Turn the heat up to high and add the peppers. Toss for 5 minutes until the peppers are hot and still crisp. Turn off the heat. Deglaze the pan with red wine vinegar. Taste and season with salt if desired.

Salt Pickles

About 6 pints

20 firm, green cucumbers
2 onions, peeled and sliced
20 whole allspice, crushed
Dill sprigs
Blackcurrant leaves
A piece of horseradish cut into small pieces

pickling liquid
8 pints/4½ l water
2 cups coarse salt
4 fl oz/110 ml white wine vinegar

Brush the cucumbers extremely well in warm water. In jars, alternate the cucumbers with the onions, allspice, dill, currant and horseradish.

Boil together the water, salt and vinegar. Let cool. Pour the pickling liquid over the cucumbers, seal and store in a cold place. The pickles are ready to eat after 2 to 3 weeks.

Potatoes and Apples

6 servings

4 medium sized potatoes
2 medium sized cooking apples
Juice of 1 lemon
1½ oz/45 grams butter
1 small onion, thinly sliced
¼ teaspoon salt
¼ teaspoon cinnamon
Pinch cloves
3 slices bread, toasted and cubed
2 to 3 eggs
¼ pint/140 ml milk
¼ pint/140 ml single cream
½ teaspoon sugar

Put the potatoes in boiling, salted water. Cover and reduce the heat to simmer. Cook 8 to 10 minutes or until tender. Drain. Refrigerate overnight or until chilled .

Peel the potatoes, then grate them coarsely. Peel and core the apples. Slice them thinly and toss with lemon juice.

Melt the butter in a large pan. Add the potatoes, apples, onion, salt, cinnamon and cloves. Cook 5 minutes. Add the bread cubes to the potato mixture. Lightly beat the eggs, milk, cream and sugar and pour them over the potato-bread mixture. Toss lightly.

Transfer the mixture to a buttered 12 × 8-inch/ 30 × 20-cm baking dish. Bake at 375°F/190°C/gas mark 5 for 10 to 15 minutes, or until the top is browned and crisp.

Stuffed Peppers

6 servings

6 large green peppers, halved lengthwise and
    seeded
2½ teaspoons salt
1 lb/450 grams minced beef
1 medium sized onion, chopped
1 medium sized carrot, peeled and grated
1 lb/450 grams cooked brown rice
½ to 1 teaspoon dried oregano, crushed
15 oz/425 grams tinned tomato sauce

Cover the peppers with boiling water and add ¼ teaspoon of salt and boil 5 minutes, then drain. Place them in a single layer in a 13½ × 9 × 2-inch/ 34 × 22 × 5-cm baking dish.

In a 10-inch/25-cm pan over moderate hat, cook the beef and onion, crumbling with a fork, until the meat loses its red colour. Stir in the carrot, rice, 1½ teaspoons of salt, oregano and ½ of the tomato sauce. Fill the peppers with the mixture. Spread the remaining tomato sauce over the meat mixture. Cook in a preheated 350°F/180°C/gas mark 4 oven, basting every 15 minutes with pan juices, until the peppers are tender and the meat mixture is hot—about 45 minutes.

Potato Balls

4 servings

4 firm large potatoes, peeled
Water
Butter

Scoop round balls out of the potatoes with the help of a melon baller (see the picture). Take out these balls as close to each other as possible. The easiest way to do this is to cut and scoop at the same time with the melon baller when going down into the potato.

Boil the potato balls for several minutes in water and then fry them in butter until they are golden brown.

Leftovers from the potatoes can be made into mashed potatoes.

Dill Pickles

Roast Potatoes

8 servings

12 medium sized potatoes, peeled and cut in half
    lengthwise
1 lb/450 grams beef suet, chopped
Salt and pepper to taste

Place the potatoes in a pan of salted water and boil
8 minutes. Drain. Melt the beef suet in a shallow,
ovenproof dish. Add the potatoes and cook in a
325°F/163°C/gas mark 3 oven about 1 hour, or until
tender, turning occasionally. Season with salt and
pepper.

Potatoes in Buttermilk

4 servings

1 oz/30 grams butter or margarine
1 lb/450 grams potatoes, peeled and chopped
½ teaspoon salt
Pinch coarsely ground pepper
½ pint/¼ l thick buttermilk

Melt the butter in a saucepan. Cook the potatoes
until browned. Add salt, pepper and buttermilk and
cook over low heat until the potatoes are tender and
the liquid thickened. Sprinkle with paprika.

New Potatoes with Cottage Cheese Sauce

6 to 8 servings

2 to 3 lb/900–1350 grams small new potatoes
Salt

cottage cheese sauce
¼ pint/140 ml plain yoghurt
12 oz/345 grams cottage cheese, creamed in
    blender
1 onion, finely chopped
4 hard-boiled eggs
1 tablespoon lemon juice
Salt and pepper to taste
3 tablespoons chopped chives or spring onions,
    thinly sliced

Scrub the potatoes with a soft brush but do not
peel. Boil in salted water 20 to 30 minutes, until
tender.

Stir the yoghurt into the cottage cheese and add
the onion. Strain the egg yolks through a sieve, chop
the egg whites. Add to the cottage cheese mixture.
Season with lemon juice, salt and pepper. Stir in the
chives. Serve the sauce with the potatoes.

Baked Potatoes with Crab Stuffing

4 to 6 servings

4 medium large baking potatoes, baked
4 oz/115 grams butter
2½ fl oz/75 double cream
1 tablespoon onion, finely grated
8 oz/225 grams mature Cheddar cheese, grated
8 oz/225 grams flaked crabmeat, picked over
4 oz/115 grams mushrooms, sliced and sautéed
Pinch pepper
1 teaspoon salt

As soon as the potatoes are cooked, cut them in half lengthwise and scoop out the pulp, taking care not to tear the skins. Mash the potatoes thoroughly (or put through a blender). Heat the butter and cream over very low heat until the butter melts. Beat the butter cream mixture into the potatoes. Stir in the grated onion, 2/3 of the cheese, crabmeat and mushrooms and season with salt and pepper. Pile the mixture into the potato shells and sprinkle with the remaining cheese. Cook in a 350°F/180°C/gas mark 4 oven until the cheese melts and the potatoes are very hot, about 20 minutes. Brown the potatoes under the grill for a few seconds.

Anchovy Stuffed Aubergine

Hash Browns

6 servings

1½ lb/700 grams potatoes, cooked and cubed
2 oz/60 grams onion, finely chopped
2 oz/60 grams parsley, finely chopped
1½ oz/45 grams flour
1½ teaspoons salt
½ teaspoon pepper
2½ fl oz/75 ml single cream
1½ oz/45 grams bacon fat

Mix the potatoes, onion, parsley, flour, salt and pepper together. Add the cream and stir.

Heat 2 tablespoons of the fat in a heavy pan. Spread the potatoes on the bottom of the pan, packing them down with a spatula. Cook over medium heat, shaking the pan constantly, until the bottom is brown and crusty, 10 to 15 minutes. Place on a hot dish, browned side up. Wipe the pan with a kitchen towel.

Heat the remaining fat in the pan. Slide the potatoes back into the pan, browned side up. Cook 5 to 10 minutes more, shaking constantly and firming edges with a spatula. Turn on to a hot serving dish and cut into wedges.

Potato Cakes

4 serving

3 large potatoes, grated
½ small onion, grated
2 eggs. lightly beaten
1 oz/30 grams flour
1 teaspoon salt
Pinch pepper
Oil for frying

Press the liquid from the potatoes and mix with the onion, eggs, flour and seasonings. Heat about ¼ inch/½ cm of oil in a frying pan. Form the potato mixture into 8 cakes and fry in hot oil until crisp and brown on both sides. Drain on kitchen towel. Serve topped with poached eggs and hot muffins.

Home Fried Potatoes

4 to 6 servings

6 tablespoons oil
3 lb/1¼ kilo potatoes, peeled and cubed
1 onion, cut in quarters
Onion salt
Garlic salt
Paprika

Heat the oil in a heavy frying pan and add the potatoes and onion. Sprinkle with onion salt and garlic salt to taste. Then sprinkle with paprika. Fry for about 5 minutes, then lower the heat and simmer for about 10 minutes, or until the potatoes are soft.

Oven Fried Potatoes

5 servings

4 medium sized potatoes, peeled and sliced ½ inch/1 cm thick
1½ oz/45 grams fat, melted
1 teaspoon salt
½ teaspoon pepper
½ teaspoon paprika

Brush the potato slices with melted fat. Preheat the oven to 425°F/220°C/gas mark 7 and bake the potatoes, basting frequently with the fat, until they are tender and brown on both sides. Season.

Potato Pie

4 servings

5 potatoes, chopped
4 oz/115 grams margarine
1 teaspoon salt
½ teaspoon pepper
1 lb/450 grams onions, diced
12 oz/345 grams green peppers, chopped
5 tomatoes, or the equivalent in tomato sauce or crushed tomatoes
2½ fl oz/75 ml honey
2 bay leaves
¼ teaspoon powdered cloves
Grated cheese
Oregano
Tarragon (optional)

Steam the potatoes and mash with the margarine, a dash of salt and pepper. Press into an oiled pan.

Sauté the onions and peppers for about 5 minutes. Then add the tomatoes, honey, salt, pepper, bay leaves and cloves. Cook until the mixture resembles a sauce, but still retains a bit of its crispness. Pour it over the potatoes and bake about 30 minutes at 375°F/190°C/gas mark 5. Sprinkle with grated cheese, oregano and tarragon if desired.

Potato Twists

10 servings

8 oz/225 grams hot mashed potatoes
½ oz/15 grams lard, melted
1 oz/30 grams butter, melted
1 teaspoon salt
1½ oz/45 grams sugar
½ pint/¼ l scalded milk
1 egg, lightly beaten
1 oz/30 grams dried yeast dissolved in ¼ pint/140 ml potato water
1½ lb/700 grams flour (approximately), sifted

Mix the mashed potatoes, lard, butter, salt and sugar in a large mixing bowl. Add lukewarm scalded milk and let stand 5 minutes. Add the egg and the yeast in potato water. Gradually stir in the flour. Cover tightly and set aside in a warm place to rise, about 1 hour.

Turn the dough out on a floured board and knead vigorously, adding more flour to stiffen if needed. Return the dough to a greased bowl and let it rise again. Turn it out and knead some more, chopping through the dough with a knife. Return one third of the dough to the bowl and divide the refining dough into 2 parts. Roll one of these parts into 3 long strips. Pinch the strips together at the ends and plait them to form a loaf. Repeat with the remaining part. Place the loaves in 3½ × 7½-inch/9 × 19-cm loaf tins. Brush the tops with a little milk. Repeat the process with the dough in the bowl, separating it to make 2 smaller plaits. Place the small plaits on top of the large plaits, then brush with melted butter. Let them rise until the loaves have doubled in size.

Bake in a 450°F/230°C/gas mark 8 oven for a few minutes, until loaves have begun to brown. Lower the heat and bake 45–50 minutes.

Potatoes with Ham

6 servings

1 small slice ham, cut into small pieces
6 or 8 potatoes, thinly sliced
1 oz/30 grams flour
2 oz/60 grams butter
Onion salt
15 fl oz/425 ml milk
1 teaspoon parsley, finely chopped
Breadcrumbs

Cover the bottom of a greased baking dish with the ham. Place a layer of potatoes over the ham. Sprinkle with flour, dot with butter and season with onion salt and pepper and pour in milk to cover. Add another layer of ham and potatoes. Sprinkle again with flour and seasonings, then add milk. Add more layers of potatoes, if needed, to three-quarters fill the dish. The milk should just cover the potatoes.

Sprinkle the parsley and breadcrumbs over the top. Dot with butter. Place the baking dish in a large pan with a little water in the bottom. Bake in a 350°F/180°C/gas mark 4 oven until the potatoes are tender.

Stuffed Baked Potatoes

6 servings

6 large jacket potatoes
8 oz/225 grams cream cheese
¼ pint/140 ml mayonnaise or soured cream
1 teaspoon prepared mustard
¼ pint/140 ml cream
1½ teaspoons salt
¼ teaspoon white pepper
2 oz/60 grams parsley, finely chopped
2 tablespoons chives

Scrub the potatoes clean and wrap each in foil. Bake in a preheated 400°F/200°C/gas mark 6 oven for 1¼-1½ hours, until fork-tender.

While the potatoes are baking, combine the cream cheese, mayonnaise, mustard, cream, salt and pepper in a small mixing bowl. Beat at medium speed with a hand mixer until smooth.

Unwrap the baked potatoes and cut off the tops of each lengthwise, about ½-inch/¼-cm thick. Carefully scoop out the potatoes, leaving the skins intact. Place the potato pulp in a large mixing bowl and mash it with a potato masher.

Add the cream cheese mixture to the mashed potatoes and whip with an electric mixer until smooth and well mixed. Spoon it back into the potato skins. Sprinkle parsley and chives on top. Arrange the stuffed potatoes on a baking sheet. Heat in a 350°F/180°C/gas mark 4 oven for 15 minutes.

New Potatoes Vinaigrette

4 servings

10 to 12 hot or warm boiled new potatoes, about 6 oz/170 grams
1 small bunch chives
2 onions, thinly sliced

vinaigrette dressing
2½ fl oz/75 ml vinegar
2½ fl oz/75 ml water
4 fl oz/110 ml oil, preferably olive oil
¼ teaspoon salt
½ teaspoon black pepper

Cut the potatoes into slices. Do not peel. The skins are thin and add a decorative touch. Place the potato slices in a bowl. Snip the chives into the bowl. Place onions on top of the potatoes.

Combine the dressing ingredients. Whisk or beat with a fork until smooth. Pour the dressing over the potatoes. Refrigerate for several hours before serving.

Creamed Spinach

4 servings

¼ pint/140 ml water
¼ teaspoon salt
10 oz/285 grams frozen chopped spinach
1 oz/30 grams butter or margarine
1 oz/30 grams flour
Pinch garlic salt
White pepper to taste
8 fl oz/220 ml single cream
Pinch ground nutmeg
Hard-boiled egg slices to garnish

Bring water and salt to the boil in a medium sized saucepan. Add the spinach and re-boil. Break up the frozen spinach with a fork and cover. Reduce the heat to low and cook 4 minutes. Drain well and keep warm.

Melt the butter in a small saucepan. Add the flour, garlic salt and pepper. Stir well. Cook until bubbly. Add the cream and stir well. Cook over a low heat until thickened. Season with nutmeg. Combine with spinach and mix thoroughly. Garnish with hard-boiled egg slices.

Winter Marrow with Sliced Apples

6 servings

3 fresh winter marrows
Salt to taste
2 or 3 fresh cooking apples
Butter
6 oz/170 grams brown sugar
Nutmeg to taste

Cut each marrow in half and remove the seeds. Place, cut side down, in a shallow, greased baking dish. Add ¼ pint/140 ml boiling water. Cover. Bake in a preheated 350°F/180°C/gas mark 4 oven for 10 minutes. Remove from the oven. Take off the cover, turn the marrow cut side up and sprinkle with salt.

Peel and core the apples and cut them into wedges. Fill the marrows with apples. Dot them generously with butter. Sprinkle each marrow half with 1 oz/30 grams of brown sugar, then with a little nutmeg. Pour ¼ pint/140 ml of boiling water into the baking dish. Bake 30 minutes or until the marrow and apples are tender.

Herb and Spinach Timbales

6 servings

1¼ pints/700 ml milk, scalded
1 oz/30 grams butter or margarine
1¼ lb/565 grams frozen chopped spinach, thawed and well drained
3 eggs, beaten
¼ teaspoon dried tarragon leaves, crushed
¼ teaspoon onion salt
¼ teaspoon salt
Pinch pepper

Combine the hot milk and butter in a bowl, stirring until the butter is melted. Stir in the spinach, eggs, tarragon, onion salt, salt and pepper. Mix well. Spoon into 6 greased, glass ramekins. Set them in a 13 × 9 × 2-inch/33 × 22 × 5-cm baking tin. Place on the oven rack. Pour very hot water into the tin to a depth of 1 inch/2½ cm. Bake in a 350°F/180°C/gas mark 4 oven for 30 minutes or until a knife inserted in the centre comes out clean. Loosen the edges with a spatula and turn out onto a serving dish. Serve immediately.

Potato Balls

New Potatoes Vinaigrette

Marrow Casserole

6 servings

1 small yellow onion
1 oz/30 grams bacon fat
4 medium yellow marrows
Salt and pepper
2 large eggs
4 fl oz/110 ml cream
1 oz/30 grams soft breadcrumbs

Sauté the onion in the bacon fat. Wash the marrow carefully and cut it in chunks. Place them in a well greased ovenproof casserole. Season with salt and pepper.

Beat the eggs with the cream and pour them over the casserole. Sprinkle with the breadcrumbs and bake in a preheated 350°F/180°C/gas mark 4 oven, until the marrow is tender, about 30 minutes.

Sautéed Marrow

6 servings

3 tablespoons olive or salad oil
12 oz/345 grams courgette, diced
12 oz/345 grams yellow marrow, diced
4 oz/115 grams onion, chopped
1 clove garlic, crushed

8 oz/225 grams tomatoes, diced
1 tablespoon Worcester sauce
1 tablespoon tomato paste
1 tablespoon salt

In a large pan, heat the oil. Add the marrow, courgette, onion and garlic. Sauté 3 minutes, stirring carefully. Combine and add the remaining ingredients. Cover and simmer 8 to 10 minutes, until the vegetables are crisp and tender, stirring occasionally.

Courgette with Stilton

6 servings

3 courgettes
6 oz/170 grams Stilton cheese
1 small cream cheese
4 oz/115 grams radishes, finely chopped

Rinse and dry the courgettes. Divide them in half lengthways. Spoon out the flesh and chop it.

Coarsely grate the cheese. Stir until soft, together with the cream cheese. Add the courgette flesh and the radishes. Divide the cheese mixture among the courgette halves. Do not serve them too chilled. Accompany with hard rolls.

Curried Spinach and Yoghurt

4 to 6 servings

2 tablespoon oil
½ medium sized onion, thinly sliced
2 cloves garlic, finely chopped
2 lb/900 grams fresh spinach, washed, trimmed,
    and coarsely chopped
15 fl oz/425 ml plain yoghurt
1½ teaspoons curry powder
Salt and pepper
1 teaspoon dried mint

Heat the oil in a large pan and sauté the onions and garlic over a medium heat until well softened. Add the spinach and cook until soft. Then blend the yoghurt with the curry powder and combine with the spinach. When the mixture is heated add salt and pepper to taste and sprinkle with dried mint.

Winter Marrow with Maple Syrup

4 servings

2 large winter marrow
Olive oil
2 oz/60 grams butter
4 tablespoons maple syrup
Salt
Freshly ground pepper

Preheat oven to 350°F/180°C/ gas mark 4. Rub the marrow skins with olive oil, to keep them crisp and maintain their shape. Place the squash in the centre of the oven on a sheet of foil and cook for 60–75 minutes, depending on the size of the marrow.

When cooked, remove the marrows from the oven and cut in half. Scoop out the seeds and fibres. Remove the flesh and mash with a fork, blending in the butter, maple syrup, salt and pepper. Place equal amounts of the mixture in each of the 4 halves of skin, fluffing up the mixture. Put them back in the oven and reheat for about 5 minutes. Serve hot.

Sweet Potatoes, Apples and Sausage

6 servings

2 lb/900 grams cooking apples, unpeeled and
    thinly sliced
2 lb/900 grams sweet potatoes, uncooked and
    thinly sliced
2 teaspoons onion, very finely chopped
2 teaspoons salt
¼ pint/140 ml maple syrup
¼ pint/140 ml apple juice
2 oz/60 grams butter, melted
1 lb/450 grams pork sausage meat
1½ oz/45 grams dry breadcrumbs

Place first a layer of apple, then a layer of sweet potato slices in a greased, 4-pint/2¼-litre catsserole.

Sprinkle each layer with onion and salt. Mix the syrup, apple juice and butter together and pour the sauce over the apples and potatoes. Cover and bake in a 350°F/180°C/gas mark 4 oven for 1 hour.

While the potatoes are cooking, crumble the sausage into a pan and brown. Drain the sausage and combine with breadcrumbs. After the potatoes have cooked, uncover the casserole and spread with the sausage mixture. Bake uncovered for 20 minutes more.

Sweet Potato Balls

4 to 6 servings

½ teaspoon salt
Dash pepper
1 lb/450 grams sweet potatoes, mashed
4 marshmallows
1 cup breadcrumbs
1 egg, beaten
2 tablespoons water
Fat for deep frying

Mix the salt and pepper with the sweet potatoes and roll into 8 balls. Put 1 marshmallow into the centre of each ball then roll it in the crumbs.

Combine the egg and water. Dip the balls into this mixture. Roll again in crumbs. Fry in heated, deep fat for about 4 minutes, until golden brown and crispy. Drain.

Sweet Potato and Banana Casserole

6 servings

4 medium sized sweet potatoes
2 oz/60 grams butter
1½ teaspoons salt
4 bananas, sliced
3½ oz/100 grams brown sugar
8 fl oz/220 ml orange juice

Cook the sweet potatoes in boiling water until tender but still firm. Cool. Peel and slice them ½-inch/¼-cm thick. Place in a buttered casserole in alternate layers of potatoes, dotted with butter and sprinkled with salt, and bananas sprinkled with brown sugar. End the top layer with bananas dotted with butter. Add the orange juice. Bake in a 350°F/180°C/gas mark 4 oven for about 30 minutes or until the top is browned.

Sweet Potato Chips

4 servings

2 medium or large sweet potatoes, peeled
Vegetable oil
3 tablespoons raspberry vinegar
Salt to taste

Wash the potatoes and cut them into very thin strings. Pat them dry on kitchen towel. Heat oil to 260–275°F/125–135°C. Drop in half of the potatoes and cook for 5 minutes. Drain well on kitchen towel. Repeat with the remaining potatoes. (This may be done an hour or 2 in advance.)

Reheat the oil to 375°F/190°C and fry the potatoes in batches for 30 seconds to 1 minute, or until they are lightly browned. Drain, sprinkle with vinegar and salt very lightly.

Sweet Potatoes with Maple Syrup

4 servings

¼ pint/140 ml maple syrup
2 oz/60 grams butter or margarine
1 lb/450 grams sweet potatoes, cooked and
    sliced, or 1 lb/450 grams tinned sweet
    potatoes, drained

Place the syrup and butter in a saucepan. Bring to the boil and cook until thickened.

Add the sweet potatoes and cook over a low heat until the potatoes are hot and glazed.

Sweet Potato Pudding with Raisins and Nuts

8 servings

4 oz/115 grams butter
1 lb/900 grams sweet potatoes, grated
4 oz/115 grams sugar
½ teaspoon cloves
1 teaspoon cinnamon
½ pint/¼ l milk
4 oz/115 grams dark cane syrup
4 oz/115 grams nuts, chopped
1 teaspoon allspice
8 oz/225 grams raisins
3 eggs, beaten

Melt the butter in a heavy iron pan in the oven. In a bowl, mix all the ingredients together, adding the eggs last. Pour the mixture into the hot pan of butter and mix well. Bake in a 350°F/180°C/gas mark 4 oven for 45 minutes, stirring twice.

Courgette with Stilton

Spicy Sweet Potato Pie

6 to 8 servings

12 oz/345 grams sweet potatoes, cooked and
  mashed
4 oz/115 grams sugar
1 teaspoon cinnamon
1 teaspoon allspice
½ teaspoon salt
3 eggs, well beaten
½ pint/¼ l milk
1 oz/30 grams butter, melted
1 9-inch/22-cm unbaked pie shell

Combine the mashed sweet potatoes, sugar, cinnamon, allspice, and salt. Add the eggs.

Mix the milk and butter and stir into the potato mixture.

The mixture will be fairly liquid. Pour it into an unbaked pastry shell. Bake at 350°F/180°C/gas mark 4 for 40 to 45 minutes.

Sweet Potato Puff

2 to 4 servings

1 lb/450 grams sweet potatoes, mashed
1 oz/30 grams butter or margarine
Salt and pepper to taste
2½ fl oz/75 ml milk or cream
1 egg, separated

Combine the mashed potatoes, melted butter, seasonings and milk. Add a beaten egg yolk and beat until light and fluffy. Fold in a stiffly beaten egg white. Place in a greased casserole and cook in a 350°F/180°C/gs mark 4 oven for 30 minutes, or until puffy and browned. If desired, 2 oz/60 grams of walnuts may be added.

Stuffed Tomato with Dill

4 servings

4 medium sized tomatoes
1 oz/30 grams butter, melted
½ teaspoon salt
¼ teaspoon white pepper
½ teaspoon dried dill
¼ pint/140 ml water
8 oz/225 grams frozen peas

Slice the tops off the tomatoes and carefully spoon out the centres.

Melt the butter. Add salt, white pepper and dill. Brush the insides of the tomatoes with this mixture. Bake in a preheated 400°F/200°C/gas mark 6 oven 15 minutes or until tender.

While the tomatoes are baking, bring ¼ pint/140 ml of water rapidly to the boil. Add the peas and cook 8 to 10 minutes, until tender. Fill the tomato halves with hot peas. Serve immediately.

Corn Stuffed Tomatoes

10 servings

10 medium sized tomatoes
2 lbs/900 grams cooked corn or tinned and
  drained whole kernel corn
1 teaspoon salt
¼ teaspoon pepper
2 oz/60 grams butter or margarine, melted

Slice off the tops of the tomatoes, then scoop out the pulp. Mix the pulp with the corn, salt, pepper and butter.

Stuff the tomatoes with the mixture. Place in a greased ovenproof dish and cook in a preheated 375°F/190°C/gas mark 5 oven about 20 minutes.

Country Style Tomatoes

4 servings

2 rashers bacon, cooked and crumbled
1 small onion, sliced into rings
1 lb/450 grams tinned tomatoes
¼ teaspoon celery seeds
Salt and pepper to taste

Cook the onion rings in bacon fat until tender, but not brown. Add the tomatoes, celery seeds, salt and pepper. Cook until the tomatoes are heated through. Sprinkle the bacon on top.

Stuffed Tomatoes with Lentils

4 servings

1 oz/30 grams butter or margarine
3 oz/85 grams onion, chopped 3 tablespoons
  spring onion tops, chopped
4 large tomatoes
½ teaspoon dried parsley
Dash dried leaf thyme
Dash cayenne pepper
2 oz/60 grams plus 1½ oz/45 grams soft fresh
  breadcrumbs

In a pan over medium heat, melt 1 tablespoon of butter or margarine. Add the onion and spring onion and cook until tender.

Meanwhile, cut a thin slice off the top of each tomato. Scoop out the pulp to make a shell. Chop the pulp coarsely and add it to the onion in the pan. Stir in the parsley, thyme and pepper. Simmer 10 minutes, until the liquid has cooked off. Stir in 2 oz/60 grams of breadcrumbs. Spoon the mixture into the tomato shells.

In a small bowl, mix the remaining butter and breadcrumbs together. Sprinkle onto the filled tomatoes. Cook on a baking tray in a 350°F/180°C/gas mark 4 oven for 25 to 30 minutes.

Assorted Vegetable Fritters

6 to 8 servings

6 oz/170 grams flour
1 teaspoon salt
2 tablespoons oil
1 egg
½ pint/¼ l water
1 courgette, sliced
1 aubergine, sliced
Cauliflower florets
1 tablespoon sweetcorn

In a bowl, combine the flour and salt. Add the oil, egg and cold water. Mix until thick. If the batter does not adhere to the vegetables, add more water. Dip the vegetables into the batter 1 slice or piece at a time. For the corn: stir in just enough to hold the corn together. Deep-fry in hot oil until brown. Keep warm in a low oven until ready to serve.

Courgette and Cottage Cheese Casserole

6 servings

3 medium sized courgettes, sliced
2 oz/60 grams onion, chopped
2 tablespoons vegetable oil
1 lb/450 grams cottage cheese
1 teaspoon basil
2½ oz/75 grams Parmesan cheese

Saute the courgettes and onion in oil.
Whip the cottage cheese with basil in a blender. Place alternating layers of courgette and cheese in a 3 pint/1½ l casserole. Sprinkle with grated Parmesan cheese. Bake, uncovered, in a preheated 350°F/180°C/ gas mark 4 oven for 25 to 30 minutes.

Fried Courgette

4 to 6 servings

3 to 4 medium sized courgettes, sliced into rounds
1 egg
1 tablespoon milk
1½ oz/45 grams flour
1 teaspoon salt
1 teaspoon garlic salt
Deep fat for frying

Wash the courgettes. Slice it into rounds about ½-inch/¼-cm thick. Set aside.
Combine the egg, milk, flour, salt and garlic salt in a bowl. Mix well to form a batter. Dip each courgette slice in the batter. Fry in deep fat until crisp and golden brown. Drain on kitchen towel.

Mixed Vegetables

4 servings

8 oz/225 grams mushrooms
About 12 oz/345 grams small carrots, trimmed and scraped
½ oz/15 grams butter
8 oz/225 grams, chopped
2½ fl oz/75 ml water
Salt to taste
Freshly ground pepper to taste
2½ fl oz/75 ml double cream
1 tablespoon parsley, finely chopped

If the mushrooms are small, leave them whole. If they are large, cut them lengthwise in half. Cut the carrots into thin, ¼-inch/½-cm rounds.
Heat the butter in a saucepan and add the mushrooms, shaking the pan and tossing them so that they cook evenly, about 2 minutes. Add the carrots, celery, salt and pepper and cover tightly. Cook 8 to 10 minutes.
Add the cream and reduce over a high heat, about 2 minutes. Sprinkle with chopped parsley and serve hot.

Oven Baked Vegetables

Spanish Vegetables

Spring Vegetable Bake

6 servings

6 carrots, cut in strips
3 small courgettes, cut in ¼-inch/½-cm diagonal
   slices
8 oz/225 grams cherry tomatoes
4 oz/115 grams herb-seasoned croutons
1 oz/30 grams cornflour
15 fl oz/425 ml milk
2 oz/60 grams butter or magarine
1 teaspoon salt
¼ teaspoon pepper
1 teaspoon dried basil leaves

Cook the carrots in boiling, salted water about 5 minutes or until tender but still crisp. Drain. In a 2 pint/1¼ l casserole toss the vegetables and croutons.

In a saucepan stir the cornflour and milk together until smooth, add the butter, salt and pepper. Bring to a boil over a medium heat, stirring constantly, and boil 1 minute. Pour over the vegetables. Sprinkle with basil. Bake in a 350°F/180°C/gas mark 4 oven 25 minutes, or until the vegetables are tender.

Oven Baked Vegetables

4 servings

1 lb/450 grams carrots
1 lb/450 grams beetroots
10 oz/285 grams parsnips
4 oz/115 grams celery stalks
3 tablespoons oil
½ teaspoon salt

Peel the carrots, beetroots, parsnips and celery. Cut them into ¼-inch/½ cm wide strips. Place the vegetables in a casserole. Pour the oil over them and sprinkle with a little salt. Bake in a preheated 425°F/220°C/gas mark 7 oven for 25 to 30 minutes, until cooked. Turn them over several times while baking.

Spanish Vegetables

4 servings

6 oz/170 grams split peas, plus water (1 teaspoon
   salt to 1 pint/½ l water)
1 small aubergine (about 10 oz/285 grams) or the
   same amount of marrow
1 green pepper
1 red pepper
2 onions
½ oz/15 grams margarine
12 fl oz/350 ml chicken or beef broth
2 cloves garlic, crushed
1 teaspoon salt
1 teaspoon thyme
Pinch of ground saffron (optional)
4 hard-boiled eggs, halved
Granary bread

Soak the split peas in salted water 10 to 12 hours. Pour off the water and boil in new lightly salted water 1 to 1½ hours. Drain.

Slice the aubergine or marrow. Halve the peppers, take out the seeds and membranes and cut them into strips.

Peel the onions and chop into large pieces. Sauté the onion in a little margarine. Add the aubergine or marrow and the peppers. Add the broth, garlic, salt, thyme and saffron. Boil the vegetables approximately 15 minutes until they become soft. Add more water if necessary. Stir in the split peas. Season to taste. Serve with the hard-boiled egg halves and bread.

Pasta, Rice and Stuffings

Apple Stuffing

Quantity varies

4 slices bread, diced
6 oz/170 grams butter
1 tablespoon lemon juice
1 teaspoon salt
8 oz/225 grams cooking apples, chopped
1 teaspoon mint, chopped

Mix the bread, butter, lemon juice, moistening with a little water if needed. Add the salt, apples and mint. Do not pack too tightly.

Bread Stuffing

Quantity varies

2½ oz/75 grams butter or margarine
3 tablespoons onion, chopped
1 lb/450 grams dry breadcrumbs
1 teaspoon salt
¼ teaspoon pepper
Sage to taste
Hot chicken broth or water

Melt the butter in a saucepan and cook the onion until it is soft but not brown. Add the breadcrumbs and seasonings. Mix in the remaining butter and enough broth to moisten the stuffing.

Oyster Stuffing

Quantity varies

Liquid from 2 pints/1¼ l oysters
1 loaf stale bread, crumbled
8 oz/225 grams melted butter
1 teaspoon salt
¼ teaspoon pepper
1 egg, beaten
2½ fl oz/75 ml milk (optional)
2 pints/1¼ l oysters

Heat the oyster liquid and skim it. Pour the liquid over the bread. Add butter, seasonings and the egg. If the stuffing is too dry, pour in a little milk. Add the oysters carefully and do not break them.

Apple Rice

227

Pecan Stuffing

Quantity varies

8 oz/225 grams wild rice
1½ pints/850 ml chicken stock
1 carrot, quartered
2 bay leaves
Salt
1 large onion, chopped
4 oz/115 grams butter or margarine
2 lb/900 grams mushrooms, sliced
4 sticks celery, sliced
1 oz/30 grams parsley, chopped
2 teaspoons sage
½ pint/¼ l chicken stock
8 slices wholemeal bread, cubed
1 lb/450 grams pecan nuts, halved or chopped

Cook the wild rice in 1½ pints/850 ml chicken stock with the carrot, bay leaves and a pinch of salt for 40 minutes. Remove the carrot quarters and bay leaves. Sauté the onion in butter with the mushrooms and celery, until soft. Add the parsley, sage and the remaining chicken stock to the mushroom mixture and simmer 8 to 10 minutes. Toss with wholemeal bread, pecan nuts and cooked rice.

Season with salt and pepper to taste. For a moister dressing add more chicken stock as desired. Use as stuffing or bake in a casserole at 325°F/163°C/gas mark 3 for about 30 minutes.

Rice Dressing

Quantity varies

1 oz/30 grams flour
2 tablespoons vegetable oil
8 oz/225 grams onion, chopped
8 oz/225 grams celery, chopped
4 oz/115 grams green pepper, chopped
2 cloves garlic, crushed
8 oz/225 grams lean minced beef
8 oz/225 grams pork
8 oz/225 grams chicken giblets, chopped
2 teaspoons salt
¼ teaspoon black pepper
¼ teaspoon red pepper
½ pint/¼ l chicken broth
1½ lb/700 grams hot cooked rice
8 oz/225 grams spring onion tops, sliced

Brown the flour in oil until it is a deep red brown, stirring constantly to prevent burning. Add onions, celery, green pepper and garlic. Cook until the vegetables are tender. Stir in beef, pork, giblets and seasonings. Continue cooking until the meat loses its colour. Blend in the broth. Cover and simmer 25 minutes. Stir in the onion tops. Cook 5 minutes longer.

Wild Rice Stuffing

Quantity varies

2 lb/900 grams cooked wild rice
1 turkey liver, optional
12 oz/345 grams pecan nuts, coarsely chopped
4 oz/115 grams butter
8 oz/225 grams onion, finely chopped
8 oz/225 grams celery, finely chopped
4 oz/115 grams mushrooms, cut into ½-inch/1-cm cubes
Salt to taste
Freshly ground pepper to taste

Prepare the wild rice and set it aside. Finely chop the liver and set it side. Toast the chopped pecan nuts lightly in a frying pan.

Heat the butter in a heavy frying pan and add the onion and celery. Cook, stirring, until soft. Add the mushrooms and chopped liver. Add salt and pepper. Cook, stirring, about 5 minutes. Add the wild rice and pecan nuts and blend thoroughly. Let cool.

Striped Rice

Bread and Chestnut Dressing

Quantity varies

6 oz/170 grams fresh chestnuts
2 oz/60 grams margarine or butter
2 oz/60 grams onions, diced
7 slices bread, diced
1 egg, beaten
Pinch white pepper
¼ teaspoon celery seed
½ teaspoon sage
¼ teaspoon salt
12–16 fl oz/350–450 ml chicken or turkey stock
Margarine or butter (for greasing casserole dish)

Score the chestnuts with a cross. Cover with water and simmer about 15 minutes. Drain and peel the chestnuts while warm. Chop in ¼-inch/½-cm pieces.

Melt the margarine or butter. Sauté the onions and chestnuts until the onions are tender. Combine the diced bread, egg and seasonings. Add the onions and chestnuts and mix until the chestnuts are evenly distributed.

Add the stock slowly until the bread mixture is evenly moistened. Mix thoroughly and place in a greased casserole dish to a depth of 2 inches/5 cms. Bake uncovered at 375°F/190°C/gas mark 5 for 35 to 40 minutes.

Sage and Onion Stuffing

Quantity varies

1 lb/450 grams pork sausage meat
1 large onion, chopped
2 oz/60 grams butter
6 slices white bread
1 teaspoon dried sage
1 teaspoon mixed dried herbs
2 heaped teaspoons parsley, chopped
1 egg
Salt and pepper

Moisten the bread and squeeze dry. Beat the egg and mix together all the stuffing ingredients in a large bowl until well blended.

Leave to stand for about 10 minutes before using to stuff poultry.

Apple Rice

4 servings

2½ fl oz/75 ml round-grained rice
8 to 16 fl oz/220 to 440 ml water
½ teaspoon salt
3 cooking apples
2 tablespoons sugar
4 fl oz/110 ml whipped cream (can be omitted if the rice is to be eaten warm)
1 oz/30 grams roasted sliced almonds

Rice Pilaf

Boil the rice in the water, into which the salt has been added, for about 10 minutes.

Peel the apples, if desired, and carefully remove all of the core. Cut the apples into small cubes. Stir the fruit into the rice together with the sugar. Boil for 5 minutes, then let stand for 5 minutes. Let the rice cool.

Whip the cream and stir it into the apple rice. Add the roasted almonds or sprinkle them on top of the rice. Serve with cinnamon or ginger, or with milk if the rice is warm.

Rice and Peanut Bake

4 servings

8 oz/225 grams peanut butter
Water
1 medium sized onion
1 teaspoon sage
1 teaspoon salt
1 lb/450 grams cooked rice

Mix the peanut butter with water until it is the consistency of thick cream. Add the remaining ingredients and mix well. Bake at 350°F/180°C/gas mark 4 for 45 minutes to 1 hour, or until firm.

Green Chillies and Rice Frittata

4 servings

4 oz/110 grams onions, finely chopped
½ oz/15 grams butter or margarine
8 eggs
¼ pint/140 ml milk
1 teaspoon salt
1 teaspoon Worcester sauce
4 to 5 drops tabasco sauce (optional)
1 lb/450 grams cooked rice
4 oz/115 grams tinned chopped green chillies,
    undrained
1 medium sized tomato, chopped
4 oz/115 grams Cheddar cheese, grated

In a 10-inch/25-cm pan, cook the onion in butter until tender. Beat the eggs with milk and seasonings. Stir in the rice, chillies and tomato. Pour the rice mixture into a pan. Reduce the heat to medium low. Cover. Cook until the top is almost set, 12 to 15 minutes. Sprinkle with cheese. Cover the pan, then remove it from the heat and let stand about 10 minutes.

Savoury Chicken Rice with Oranges

6 servings

1 lb/450 grams mushrooms, diced
8 oz/225 grams onions, chopped
6 oz/170 grams green sweet pepper, finely
    chopped
8 oz/225 grams celery, finely chopped
1 large carrot, grated
6 tablespoons olive oil
1½ lb/700 grams cooked chicken, diced
½ cucumber, peeled and diced
10 oz/285 grams tinned tomato purée
Salt and pepper to taste
2 pints/1¼ l chicken stock
10 oz/285 grams long grain rice
Orange slices

Sauté the mushrooms, onion, green pepper, celery and carrot in 4 tablespoons olive oil in a large saucepan until tender, stirring frequently. Add the chicken, cucumber, tomato purée, salt and pepper and 8 fl oz/220 ml chicken stock, stirring to combine. Cover and simmer for 5 minutes, stirring occasionally.

Sauté the rice in a frying pan in the remaining olive oil until golden, stirring constantly. Add rice to the tomato mixture. Stir in the remaining chicken stock

Vegetable and Pasta Gratin

Pasta with Ham

and cover. Cook for about 30 minutes or until the rice is tender and the liquid absorbed, stirring frequently. Turn into a serving bowl. Garnish the edge with fresh orange slices.

Rice with Mushrooms

6 servings

10 oz/285 grams tinned beef consommé
8 oz/225 grams rice
8 oz/225 grams fresh mushrooms
1 tablespoon lemon juice
2 oz/60 grams butter
2 oz/60 grams onion, chopped
1 oz/30 grams fresh parsley, chopped

Combine the consommé and 1 pint/½ litre of water in a 3-pint/½-litre saucepan and bring to the boil. Add the rice and stir well. Reduce the heat and cover. Simmer for about 15 minutes or until the rice is tender and all the liquid is absorbed.

Meanwhile, wash the mushrooms briefly under cold water and wipe them dry. Thinly slice the mushrooms, then toss with the lemon juice. Melt the butter in a small saucepan, then add the mushrooms and onions and sauté for 5 minutes.

Add the mushroom mixture and the parsley to the hot rice and toss well.

Rice and Peas

6 to 8 servings

1 tablespoon olive oil
1 oz/30 grams butter
2 oz/60 grams onion, finely chopped
1 rasher bacon, diced
1 lb/450 grams fresh green peas
8 oz/225 grams long grain rice
1 pint/½ l chicken stock
Salt and freshly ground pepper to taste
1 tablespoon Parmesan cheese, grated

Heat the oil and butter in a heavy pan, then add the onion and bacon and cook over low heat for 3 minutes, stirring constantly. Add the peas and cook, stirring for 5 minutes. Add the rice and stir until coated with the oil mixture. Stir in the chicken stock, salt and pepper and cover.

Cook over low heat, stirring occasionally, for 15 to 20 minutes or until the rice is tender and all the liquid is absorbed.

Add the cheese just before serving and toss to mix well.

Pasta with Mushroom Sauce

Add the rice to the pan and pour in the water. Increase the heat to high and bring the liquid to the boil. Cover the pan, reduce the heat to low and simmer, stirring occasionally for 20 to 25 minutes or until the rice is tender and all the water has been absorbed.

Remove the pan from the heat and transfer the mixture to a warmed serving dish. Arrange the onion rings on top and serve.

Striped Rice with Minced Meat

4 servings

12 oz/345 grams rice
1 stock cube
1 onion
Butter
1 lb/450 grams minced beef
1 tin crushed tomatoes
Salt
Pepper
1 red pepper
1 green pepper
1 tin strained tomatoes
Vegetable broth

Boil the rice according to the directions on the packet. Use a stock cube instead of salt when preparing the rice.

Chop the onion and brown it in a little butter. Stir in the minced meat with a fork so that it crumbles while browning. Add the crushed tomatoes and allow to boil for about 20 minutes. Season with salt and pepper.

Chop each of the peppers separately. Preheat oven to 450°F/230°C/gas mark 8. Alternate the rice and the minced meat in an ovenproof dish. Place the green and red chopped peppers on top. Dot with a little butter and bake in the oven for 15 minutes.

Make the sauce using strained tomatoes from a tin or fresh tomatoes which are first boiled and then strained. Stir a small amount of vegetable broth into the tomatoes and season with salt and pepper.

Rice with Fruit and Nuts

4 to 6 servings

2½ fl oz/75 ml corn oil
6 oz/170 grams dried apricots, soaked overnight, drained and chopped
3 oz/85 grams dried prunes, soaked overnight, drained and chopped
4 oz/115 grams seedless raisins, soaked in cold water for 30 minutes and drained
2 carrots, scraped and thinly sliced
2 large bananas, thinly sliced
4 oz/115 grams walnuts, chopped
2 tablespoons pine nuts
1 tablespoon clear honey
10 oz/285 grams long grain rice, washed, soaked in cold water for 30 minutes and drained
1 pint/½ l water
1 small onion, sliced and ringed

In a large saucepan, heat the oil over moderate heat. When the oil is hot, add the apricots, prunes, raisins, carrots and orange juice. Cook, stirring occasionally, for 5 minutes. Reduce the heat to low and add the bananas, walnuts, pine nuts and honey and stir well to blend.

Pasta with Cold Sauce

Rice Pilaf

4 servings

10 oz/285 grams long grained rice
4 whole cloves
1 piece of cinnamon, about 2 inches/5 cm long
1 onion, sliced
8 cardamom seeds
2 bay leaves
30 almonds
3 oz/85 grams raisins

Boil the rice with water and salt according to the directions on the packet. Add the cloves, cinnamon, onion, cardamom and bay leaves while the rice is cooking. Boil as long as the directions on the packet specify.

Scald and peel the almonds. Cut them in half lengthwise.

Remove the bay leaves and the piece of cinnamon from the prepared rice and mix in the almonds and raisins.

Sausage Rice

14 servings

1½ lb/700 grams uncooked rice
1 lb/450 grams sausage meat 8 oz/225 grams celery, chopped
2 medium sized onions, chopped
1 green pepper, diced
1 egg, beaten
Salt and pepper to taste

Boil the rice and set it aside in a colander.

Use a large pan to cook the sausage meat thoroughly. Then sauté the celery, onion and green peppers in some of the sausage fat. When the vegetables are very lightly browned, add the rice. Stir well about 3 minutes. Remove to a large bowl. Add the egg and seasonings and mix well.

Put the rice in well greased casseroles for serving or freezing. Reheat in oven until rice is hot.

Epicurean Wild Rice

6 servings

2½ oz/75 grams butter
2 oz/60 grams fresh parsley, finely chopped
4 oz/115 grams spring onions, chopped
8 oz/225 grams celery, diagonally sliced
10 oz/285 grams wild rice
1 tin chicken consommé
12 fl oz/350 ml boiling water
1 teaspoon salt
½ teaspoon dried marjoram
¼ pint/140 ml sherry

Melt the butter in a large saucepan, then add the parsley, onions and celery and sauté until soft but not brown. Add the rice, consommé, water, salt and marjoram and cover. Bake in a preheated 350°F/180°C/gas mark 4 oven for about 45 minutes or until the rice is tender, stirring occasionally and adding boiling water if needed.

Remove the cover and stir in the sherry. Bake for about 5 minutes longer or until the sherry is absorbed.

Green Ribbon Pasta with Tomato

8 servings

12 oz/345 grams green fettucine
¼ pint/140 ml olive oil
2 lb/900 grams tomatoes, chopped, skinned and seeded
1 teaspoon salt
Pinch freshly ground black pepper
1 teaspoon basil

Cook the pasta according to the packet directions. Prepare the sauce while the pasta is cooking. Heat the oil in a pan until sizzling, then stir in the tomatoes and seasonings. Cook for about 5 minutes or until the tomatoes are tender, stirring occasionally with a wooden spoon.

Drain the pasta and arrange in a serving dish, then spoon the sauce over the pasta. Serve immediately with freshly grated Parmesan cheese.

Pasta Kugel

10 servings

1 lb/450 grams wide flat pasta
4 oz/115 grams butter
4 eggs
1½ lb/700 grams apple sauce
1 pint/½ l soured cream
1 lb/450 grams cottage cheese
4 oz/115 grams raisins (optional)
8 oz/225 grams sugar
1 oz/30 grams brown sugar
1 tablespoon cinnamon

Boil and drain the pasta. In a large bowl, add the butter, eggs, apple sauce, soured cream, cottage cheese and raisins. Mix well and fold in the sugar. Place the mixture in a greased 9 × 13-inch/22/33-cm casserole. Sprinkle the top with brown sugar and cinnamon, mixed together. Bake in a 350°F/180°C/gas mark 4 oven for 40 to 60 minutes.

Vegetable and Pasta Gratin

4 to 6 servings

2 onions
2 green peppers
1 lb/450 grams aubergine or marrow
5 or 6 tomatoes
2 tablespoons melted margarine or oil
2 cloves garlic, crushed
2 to 3 tablespoons chilli sauce or tomato paste
1 teaspoon salt
1 to 2 teaspoons thyme or oregano
7 to 8 oz/200 to 225 grams pasta
6 to 10 oz/170 to 285 grams cheese, coarsely
  grated

Slice the onions.

Remove seeds and membranes from the peppers and dice.

Slice the aubergine or marrow.

Dip the tomatoes in hot water. Peel off the skins. Cut the tomatoes into pieces.

Heat margarine or oil in a large pot. Sauté the onion. It should not become brown, only a golden yellow. Add the vegetables. Stir, and season with garlic, chilli sauce, salt and thyme or oregano. Cover

Pasta with Mediterranean Sauce

and simmer over low heat for 10 to 15 minutes. Uncover and simmer 15 minutes, until the mixture thickens. Should it become too thick, thin with water.

Meanwhile boil the noodles according to the packet directions.

Grease a baking dish. Place half of the pasta in the bottom of the dish. Cover with the vegetable mixture. End with the pasta and a large amount of grated cheese on top. Bake in a preheated 425°F/220°C/gas mark 7 oven for about 10 minutes.

This is ideal for freezing.

Stilton Pasta

4 servings

4 oz/115 grams pasta, cooked
8 oz/225 grams Stilton cheese, crumbled
½ pint/¼ l soured cream
1 egg, lightly beaten
½ teaspoon salt
Dash pepper
2 oz/60 grams butter, melted

Toss the cooked pasta with the rest of the ingredients. Place in a well buttered 3-pint/1½-litre casserole. Bake in a preheated 350°F/180°C/gas mark 4 oven for about 1 hour or until bubbling and set.

Pasta with Ham

About 4 servings

7 oz/200 grams smoked ham
7 oz/200 grams tinned whole or sliced
  mushrooms
1 leek
Butter or margarine
6 oz/170 grams soured cream
1 tablespoon French mustard
Salt
Pepper
A little milk, if necessary
8 oz/225 grams pasta of your choice

Cut the ham into strips. Drain the mushrooms. Shred the leek. Sauté the ham, mushrooms and leek in a little butter. Add the cream and mustard. Blend well. Heat mixture and season with salt and pepper. Add a little milk if the sauce becomes too thick.

Cook the pasta according to packet directions. Serve ham sauce over the pasta.

Pasta with Mushroom Sauce

4 servings

8 oz /225 grams tagliatelle
14 oz/400 grams tinned chopped tomatoes
1 tin cream of mushroom soup, concentrated
2 tablespoons tomato purée
Salt
Black pepper
2 tablespoons finely chopped parsley
1 tablespoon finely chopped dill
Crumbled tarragon
½–1 oz/30–60 grams plain flour
4 fl oz/110 ml water, milk or cream
4 thin slices of lemon
8 oz/225 grams fresh mushrooms
Parsley for garnish

Bring water for the pasta to the boil. Cook pasta according to packet instructions.

Pour the chopped tomatoes, undiluted soup and tomato purée into a saucepan. Season with salt and pepper. Add parsley, dill and tarragon. Mix well. Bring to the boil.

Blend the flour and liquid and add to the sauce. Bring to the boil, stirring all the time. (If the sauce is thick enough, omit the extra thickening.) Add the lemon slices. Simmer the sauce for 5 minutes.

Meanwhile clean the mushrooms and brown them well in a little butter.

Serve the tagliatelle topped with the sauce and mushrooms and sprinkled with a little parsley. Accompany with grated cheese and a green salad.

Pasta with Salmon Sauce

Fettucine with Peaches

4 servings

8 oz fettucine
6 pints/3½ l boiling water
1 tablespoon salt
1 tablespoon oil
2 firm ripe fresh peaches
4 oz/115 grams ham, cut into julienne strips
  (optional)
Butter
¼ pint/140 ml double or single cream
1 egg yolk
4 oz/115 grams Cheddar cheese, grated
1 tablespoon parsley, finely chopped
Nutmeg

Cook the fettucine in boiling water with salt and oil until tender but firm, about 9 minutes. Dip the peaches in boiling water a few seconds and slip off the skins.

Cut the fruit in wedges. Sauté the ham in butter 1 minute. Add the peaches. Add the cream, lightly beaten with an egg yolk. Heat gently and stir in the cheese. Drain the fettucine well. Sprinkle with parsley, add the peach mixture and toss gently. Serve lightly sprinkled with nutmeg, if desired.

Pasta with Ham and Peas

Courgettes and Fettucine with Garlic-Basil Sauce

4 to 6 servings

2 medium sized courgettes, cut into
   1½-inch/3½-cm julienne strips
2½ fl oz/75 ml olive oil
½ oz/15 grams butter
3 large cloves garlic, crushed
3 tablespoons fresh basil, chopped
12 oz/345 grams fettucine
4 oz/115 grams Parmesan cheese, grated
Salt

Steam the courgettes for 3 minutes and set aside. Combine the oil, butter, garlic and basil in a small saucepan and simmer gently, covered, for 15 minutes (garlic should not be allowed to brown).

Cook the fettucine in boiling, salted water until just tender. Drain and toss with the courgettes, garlic-basil sauce and cheese. Salt to taste.

Pasta with Cold Sauce

4 to 6 servings

10 oz/285 grams tagliatelle
2 tablespoons chopped parsley
½ oz/15 grams grated Parmesan cheese
1 clove garlic
6 fl oz/170 ml olive oil
1 tablespoon dried basil
3 tablespoons finely chopped blanched almonds
Salt
Pepper

Boil the pasta according to the directions on the packet.

Grind the parsley, cheese and garlic in a mortar with a little olive oil. Add basil, almonds, salt and pepper. Add remaining olive oil in a fine, thin trickle.

Serve the cold sauce with pasta, preferably prepared "al dente," so that the elasticity is retained.

Pasta with Luxurious Sauce

4 to 6 servings

10 oz/285 grams pasta, preferably both yellow
   and green
Water

Pasta with Smart Sauce

Salt
1 oz/30 grams butter
1 jar black caviar
1 jar red caviar
½ pint/¼ l soured cream

Boil the pasta as usual in salted water. Let drain in a colander. Pour back into the pot and stir with a dab of butter until the butter melts. Serve with the soured cream and the black and red caviar. A fresh salad goes well with this dish.

Pasta with Mediterranean Sauce

4 to 6 servings

10 oz/285 grams pasta
1 large red onion, chopped
1 green pepper, cubed
1 small aubergine, sliced
Olive oil for frying
2 cloves garlic, crushed
Salt
Black pepper
2 teaspoons thyme
½ teaspoon curry
1 teaspoon cayenne pepper
1 tin crushed tomatoes
10 oz to 1 lb/285 to 450 grams shelled prawns

Boil the pasta in the usual manner.
Brown the onion, green pepper and aubergine separately, in olive oil, then place in a pot. Add the crushed garlic, salt and pepper. Add the thyme, curry and a few grains of the cayenne pepper. Pour in the tomatoes. Let the sauce simmer until it thickens, about 15 minutes.
Warm the prawns in the sauce.
Sprinkle with a little parsley if desired. Serve with the pasta.

Pasta with Salmon Sauce

4 to 6 servings

10 oz/285 grams tagliatelle, farfalle or another
    variety of spaghetti
2 tablespoons white wine
1½ to 2 tablespoons lemon juice
½ pint/¼ l double cream
3 tablespoons finely chopped dill
Salt
Pepper
3½ oz/100 grams gravadlax, cut in thin strips

Boil the pasta according to the directions of the packet.
Warm the wine and the lemon juice in a pot. Let it evaporate a little. Add the cream. Let simmer, while stirring constantly, over low heat for about 10 minutes, until the sauce thickens and becomes very

Spaghetti with Prawns

creamy. Season with dill and perhaps a few more drops of the lemon juice, plus the salt and pepper.
Pour the sauce over the pasta or serve separately along with the salmon strips.

Pasta with Smart Sauce

4 to 6 servings

10 oz/285 grams spaghetti (or another variety of
    pasta)
12 fl oz/350 ml double cream
3–4 oz/85–115 grams Stilton cheese, crumbled
4–6 oz/115–170 grams Parmesan cheese, grated
About 15 walnuts, divided into smaller pieces

Boil the pasta in salted water according to the directions on the packet.
Warm the cream together with the Stilton and Parmesan cheeses in a pot over low heat. Stir the sauce slowly until it thickens. Pour it over the pasta. Garnish with the walnuts.

Pasta with Ham and Peas

4 to 6 servings

10 oz/285 grams shell macaroni
Butter
4 oz/115 grams smoked ham, finely cubed
1 large clove garlic, crushed
6 oz/170 grams fresh mushrooms, sliced
5 oz/140 grams green peas
2 to 3 tablespoons white wine
4 fl oz/110 ml single cream
1½ to 2 oz/45 to 60 grams grated Parmesan
    cheese
Parsley, finely chopped
Black pepper

Boil the pasta according to the directions on the packet.

Melt a little butter. Add the ham cubes, crushed garlic and mushrooms. Add the peas and the wine. Let simmer.

Pour the cream and add a dab of butter into the pasta. Mix well. Stir in the ham mixture, then the cheese. Sprinkle with parsley. Turn the pepper mill several times over the dish.

Pasta with Vegetable Sauce

4 servings

1 leek (or 1 large onion)
2 peppers
1 clove garlic (optional)
1oz/30 grams butter
1 piece of cucumber, about 7 oz/200 grams
5 or 6 tomatoes
½ teaspoon salt
¼ teaspoon black pepper
1 small bay leaf
1 small tin anchovies
About 15 black olives
8 to 12 oz/225 to 345 grams spaghetti

Rinse and slice the leek, or peel and chop the onion. Take out the seeds and membrane and slice the peppers. Sauté the leek or onion, the peppers and the crushed garlic clove for a few minutes in butter.

Cut the cucumber into cubes. You may wish to peel the tomatoes by dipping them in boiling water and pulling off the skins. Cut the tomatoes into pieces. Add the cucumber and then the tomatoes to the peppers. Simmer the mixture for a few minutes, uncovered. Then add the salt, pepper and bay leaf. Cover and simmer over low heat about 15 minutes.

Drain the anchovies. Cut them into pieces. Add them to the vegetable mixture. Simmer for a few minutes. Season to taste. Add the olives.

Spaghetti with Spinach

Cook the spaghetti according to packet instructions. Serve the sauce with the spaghetti, a green salad and grated cheese.

Spaghetti with Tuna Fish Sauce

4 servings

7 oz/200 grams tinned tuna fish in brine
1 onion, peeled and chopped
1 clove garlic, crushed
Butter or margarine
8 fl oz/220 ml cream
1 tablespoon lemon juice
2 to 3 tablespoons snipped dill
Salt
Pepper
12 oz/345 grams spaghetti

Drain the tuna fish. Sauté the onion and garlic in butter in a frying pan. Pour in the cream and add the pieces of tuna fish. Carefully warm and season with lemon, dill, salt and pepper.

Boil the spaghetti according to packet directions. Serve the sauce with the newly boiled spaghetti.

Spaghetti with Spinach and Mussels

4 servings

6 pints/3½ l water
1½ tablespoons salt
6 oz/170 grams frozen spinach
8 oz/225 grams tinned mussels in water
8 to 12 oz/225 to 345 grams spaghetti
Parmesan cheese
1 clove garlic, crushed
Black pepper

Put the water and salt in a pot and bring to the boil. Place the spinach block and the liquid from the tinned mussels in a pan and allow the spinach to melt slowly, about 10 minutes. Meanwhile, chop three quarters of the mussels, reserving the rest for garnish.

When the water boils, cook the spaghetti. Mix the chopped mussels with the spinach and cheese, garlic, salt and pepper. Bring the sauce to the boil.

Drain the spaghetti and serve with the sauce, garnished with the whole mussels. Serve more cheese separately.

Spaghetti with Prawns

4 servings

4 tablespoons shallots, finely chopped
1 clove garlic, crushed
Butter or margarine
12 fl oz/350 ml double cream
About 1 tablespoon chilli sauce
2 oz/60 grams snipped parsley
Salt
Pepper
1 to 1½ lb/450 to 700 grams prawns with shells
12 oz/345 grams spaghetti

Sauté the onion and the garlic in the butter until they become soft and glossy but not brown. Stir in the cream, chilli sauce and parsley. Add the shelled prawns and warm up the sauce. Season with salt and pepper.

Boil the spaghetti according to packet directions. Serve the sauce with the freshly made spaghetti.

Pasta with Vegetable Sauce

Lasagne

Spaghetti Bourgignon

4 servings

½ onion
1 small piece celeriac (optional)
½ oz/15 grams margarine
10 oz/285 grams minced meat
3 rashers of bacon
4 oz/115 grams mushrooms
Pinch black pepper
1 tablespoon tomato paste
½ oz/15 grams flour
4 fl oz/110 ml red wine plus 1 cup water
½ to 1 teaspoon salt
8 to 12 oz/225 to 345 grams spaghetti

Chop the onion and celeriac finely. Sauté both ingredients in margarine until they become glossy. Increase the heat and add the ground meat. Stir with a fork so that it crumbles and becomes brown.

Cut the bacon into pieces and add to the meat. Continue to brown. Also add the mushrooms.

Mix in the pepper, tomato paste and the flour. Add the wine and water and let the sauce simmer for several minutes. Dilute with more water if the mixture becomes too dry. Season to taste with salt.

Serve with spaghetti or your favourite pasta.

Lasagne

4 servings

9 leaves lasagne pasta
2 onions, peeled and chopped
12 oz/345 grams minced meat
14 oz/400 grams tinned chopped tomatoes
1 tablespoon tomato paste
1 stock cube
½ teaspoon salt
¼ teaspoon white or black pepper
About 1 teaspoon crushed oregano or basil

cheese sauce
1½ oz/45 grams butter or margarine
2½ oz/75 grams flour
1½ pints/850 ml milk
½ to 1 teaspoon salt
Black pepper
Ground nutmeg
10 oz/285 grams grated cheese

Boil the pasta leaves.

Make the meat sauce. Brown the onions and meat in a frying pan, while stirring, so that it becomes a crumbled mixture. Add the tomatoes, tomato paste, stock cube and salt and pepper. Cover and simmer for 20 to 30 minutes. Season with oregano or basil towards the end of the simmering time.

Make the cheese sauce. Melt the butter and stir in the flour. Add the milk and bring to the boil while stirring constantly. Let the sauce boil for 3 to 5 minutes. Stir in the cheese and season with salt, pepper and the ground nutmeg.

Alternate the lasagne with the meat sauce and cheese sauce in a greased, ovenproof dish. Start and finish with the cheese sauce. Three layers of the pasta are usually about right. Finally sprinkle plenty of grated cheese on top.

Bake for 15 to 20 minutes at 425°F/220°C/gas mark 7 if the dish has just been prepared and the sauces are still warm. Bake it for 30 to 40 minutes at 400°F/200°C/gas mark 6 if the lasagne is cold.

Spaghetti Bourgignon

Spaghetti with Tuna Fish Sauce

Breads, Pancakes, and Waffles

Apple Bread

Makes 1 loaf

1 oz/30 grams butter
6 oz/170 grams sugar
1 teaspoon cinnamon
1 apple, peeled and thinly sliced
A few raisins
¼ oz/8 grams active dry yeast
8 fl oz/220 ml warm water
1 teaspoon salt
9 oz/255 grams plain strong flour, sifted
1 egg
1 oz/30 grams shortening

Melt the butter in a 9 × 9-inch/22 × 22-cm baking tin. Mix 4 oz/115 grams of the sugar with the cinnamon in a small bowl. Sprinkle this mixture on the melted butter. Arrange the apple slices in rows on the sugar mixture in the tin. Sprinkle with a few raisins.

Stir the water and yeast together in a large bowl. Add the remaining sugar, salt and 4 oz/115 grams of flour. Beat for 2 minutes or until a dropping consistency is obtained. Add the egg, shortening and remaining flour and beat until smooth.

Drop the dough a small spoonful at a time over the apples and raisins in the tin. Cover and leave to rise for 50–60 minutes or until double in size. Bake at 375°F/190°C/gas mark 5 for 30–35 minutes or until brown. Immediately remove the bread from the tin by turning out onto a serving plate.

Beer Herb Bread

Makes 2 loaves

¼ oz/8 grams dry yeast
¼ pint/140 ml lukewarm water
½ pint/¼ l pale ale, lukewarm
2 oz/60 grams sugar
1 tablespoon salt
1 oz/30 grams butter, melted
2 eggs, lightly beaten
1 teaspoon sage
2 teaspoons thyme
3 teaspoons savory
1 small onion, grated
1½ lb/700 grams plain strong flour

Sprinkle the yeast over the water and stir until dissolved. Add the beer, sugar, salt and melted butter to the yeast mixture. Add the eggs, herbs, grated onion and 1 lb/450 grams of the flour and beat until smooth. Add enough of the remaining flour until the mixture becomes difficult to beat.

Turn the dough out onto a lightly floured board and begin kneading, adding enough flour so that the dough does not stick to your hands or the board. Knead until the dough is smooth and elastic. Place the dough in a lightly oiled bowl, cover it with a damp cloth and leave to rise in a warm place until doubled in bulk—about 1½ hours.

Punch the dough down and leave to stand for 10 to 15 minutes. Divide the dough into 2 pieces and shape each into a round loaf. Place each in a round pie dish, cover and leave to rise again until doubled in size. Bake the loaves in a preheated oven at 400°F/200°C/gas mark 6 for 35 minutes. Remove the loaves immediately from the pie dishes and leave to cool on wire racks.

Serve the bread slightly warm.

Swedish Overnight Bread

Apricot Nut Bread

Makes 1 loaf

½ pint/¼ l boiling water
8 oz/225 grams dried apricots, chopped
12 oz/345 grams unsifted plain strong flour
1 tablespoon baking powder
½ teaspoon salt
2½oz/75 grams butter or margarine
8 oz/225 grams sugar
2 eggs
8 oz/225 grams golden syrup
8 oz./225 grams nuts, chopped

Grease and lightly flour a 9×5×3-inch/ 22×13×8-cm loaf tin. Pour water over the apricots and let stand 15 minutes. Stir the flour, baking powder and salt together.

In a large bowl mix the butter, sugar, eggs and syrup until smooth and well blended. Mix in the apricot mixture and nuts. Gradually mix in the dry ingredients. Pour the mixture into the tin and bake in an oven at 350°F/180°C/gas mark 4 for about 1¼ hours or until a baking needle inserted in the centre of the loaf comes out clean. Cool in the tin for 10 minutes. Remove and cool on a rack.

Batter Bread

Makes 2 loaves

½ pint/¼ l milk
3 oz/85 grams sugar
2 teaspoons salt
1 oz/30 grams butter
½ pint/¼ l warm water
½ oz/15 grams dry yeast
18 oz/500 grams plain strong flour

Heat the milk, sugar, salt and butter on a low heat until the butter has melted and the sugar and salt dissolved. Do not boil. Set aside to cool slightly.

Add the yeast to the warm water and stir until dissolved. Add the cooled mixture. Gradually add the flour. Stir until well blended. Cover with a tea towel. Store in a warm place to rise, for about 40 minutes.

Stir the batter and beat vigorously a few times. Divide into 2 parts and place each in a well greased, round casserole. Bake at 375°F/190°C/gas mark 5 for 30 to 45 minutes, until crusty on top. Cool on a rack.

Banana Bread

Makes 1 loaf

7 oz/200 grams unsifted plain flour
1 tablespoon baking powder
½ teaspoon salt
6 oz/170 grams sugar

8 oz/225 grams shortening
2 eggs
8 oz/225 grams bananas, mashed
4 oz/115 grams walnuts, chopped (optional)

Grease a 9×5-inch/22×13-cm tin.

Mix the flour, baking powder and salt thoroughly. Beat the sugar, shortening and eggs together until light and fluffy. Mix in the bananas. Add the dry ingredients and stir just until smooth. Pour into the prepared tin and bake in a preheated 350°F/180°C/ gas mark 4 oven until firmly set when lightly touched in the centre, 50–60 minutes. (Bread may crack across the top). Remove from the tin after 10 minutes. Cool on a rack.

Black Bread

Makes 2 loaves

1 lb/450 grams brown wholemeal flour
1 lb/450 grams stoneground white flour
½ oz/15 grams active dry yeast
¼ pint/140 ml warm water
2 oz/60 grams unsweetened cocoa
2 tablespoons caraway seeds
2 teaspoons salt
2 teaspoons instant coffee
12 oz/345 grams honey
2½ fl oz/75 ml vinegar
2 oz/60 grams butter

Combine the flours in a large bowl and set aside 12 oz/345 grams. Sprinkle the yeast over the warm water and stir until blended. Set aside. In a large bowl stir the reserved flour mixture, cocoa, caraway seeds, salt and instant coffee together.

Heat 1 pint/½ l water, honey, vinegar and butter in a saucepan, until just warm. The butter does not need to be completely melted. Blend well with the cocoa mixture. Add the yeast and stir until thoroughly combined. Stir in enough additional flour, 4 oz/115 grams at a time, until, the dough no longer clings to the sides of the bowl.

Turn out onto a lightly floured surface. Cover and leave for 10 minutes. Knead until smooth and elastic, about 15 minutes. Place in a greased bowl. Turn over and cover. Leave to rise in a warm place for about 1 hour, or until doubled in size. Punch down and turn onto a lightly floured surface. Divide in half. Shape each half into a smooth ball. Place each ball in the centre of a greased, 8-inch/20-cm round cake tin. Cover and leave to rise in a warm place for about 1 hour, or until doubled in size.

Bake at 350°F/180°C/gas mark 4 for 45 to 50 minutes, or until the loaves sound hollow when tapped lightly. Remove from the tins and put on wire racks.

Bilberry Nut Bread

Makes 1 loaf

2 oz/60 grams butter
8 oz/225 grams sugar
2 eggs
12 oz/345 grams stoneground flour, sifted
4 teaspoons baking powder
1 teaspoon salt
½ pint/¼ l milk
8 oz/225 grams fresh bilberries
4 oz/115 grams pecan nuts, chopped

Cream the butter in a mixing bowl. Gradually add the sugar and beat until light and fluffy. Beat in the eggs, one at a time. Sift the flour, baking powder and salt together. Reserve 2 to 3 tablespoons of the flour mixture.

Add the remaining mixture to the creamed mixture alternately with the milk, beginning and ending with the dry ingredients. Toss the reserved flour with the berries and nuts and stir into the batter. Turn into a buttered 9 × 5 × 3-inch/22 × 13 × 7-cm loaf tin. Bake in a preheated oven at 350°F/180°C/gas mark 4 for 60 to 70 minutes.

Rye Bread, Lager Buns, Breakfast Rolls and in front, Lager Bread, Scalded Rye Loaf & Old Fashioned Christmas Bread

Lager Bread

Makes 4 large loaves

1 oz/30 grams compressed fresh yeast
3½ oz/100 grams butter or margarine
2 pint/¼ l lager or stout
4 fl oz/110 ml golden syrup
1 tablespoon salt
1½ tablespoons ground ginger
1 tablespoon ground bitter orange peel
1 tablespoon aniseed and fennel (mixed)
6 oz/170 grams raisins (optional)
About 3 lb/1350 grams wholemeal flour, sifted

Crumble the yeast into a bowl. Melt the butter in a saucepan and pour in the beer and the syrup. Heat the liquid to 100°F/38°C and dissolve the yeast in a small amount of it. Add the rest of the liquid, the spices, the raisins and most of the flour. Work into a dough and leave to rise for 30 to 45 minutes.

Knead the dough on a baking board until smooth and elastic (10 to 15 minutes) and shape into loaves or buns. Place on a greased baking sheet and let the dough rise, covered, for 20 to 30 minutes. Bake loaves at 400°F/200°C/gas mark 6 for 30 to 40 minutes. (Bake buns at 425°F/220°C/gas mark 7).

Brioche Bread

Makes 2 loaves

½ oz/15 grams dry yeast
2½ fl oz/75 ml lukewarm water
¼ pint/140 ml lukewarm milk
2 tablespoons sugar
1½ teaspoons salt
18 oz/500 grams plain strong flour, sifted
8 oz/225 grams butter, cut into small pieces and
   softened
4 eggs
1 additional egg yolk

glaze
1 egg yolk
1 tablespoon milk

Combine the lukewarm water and yeast. Stir to dissolve. Add the milk, sugar and salt. With an electric mixer, beat in half of the flour and the butter until well mixed. Add the eggs and egg yolk alternately with the remaining flour and continue to beat until the dough is smooth and no longer sticky.

Place the dough in a buttered bowl and cover with a damp towel. Let it rise until doubled in size, about 3 hours. Punch the dough down and form into 2 loaves. Place them in buttered loaf tins and leave to rise until they reach the top of the tins.

Combine the egg yolk and milk for the glaze and brush the tops of the loaves with this mixture. Bake in a preheated oven at 400°F/200°C/gas mark 6 for 15 minutes. Reduce the heat to 350°F/180°C/gas mark 4 and bake for another 30 minutes. Cool the loaves in the tins for 15 minutes before turning out onto a wire rack.

Boston Brown Bread

Makes 1 loaf

2 oz/60 grams stoneground flour
2 oz/60 grams rye flour
2 oz/60 grams wholemeal flour
1 teaspoon bicarbonate of soda
½ teaspoon salt
8 fl oz/220 ml milk
1½ oz/45 grams butter, melted
6 oz/170 grams molasses
4 oz/115 grams currants

Mix the dry ingredients together in a large bowl. Mix the milk, butter, molasses and currants together in a separate bowl. Add the milk mixture to the dry ingredients and mix well.

Pour the dough into a buttered 2-pint/1½-litre mould that can be fitted into a double boiler. Steam for 1½-2 hours or until a baking needle, inserted in the centre, comes out cleanly.

Rough Baking Tin Bread

Cheddar Cheese Bread

Makes 2 loaves

¼ pint/140 ml warm water
½ oz/15 grams dry yeast
2 tablespoons sugar
½ pint/¼ l scalded milk, or ¼ pint/140 ml
   evaporated milk and ¼ pint/140 ml hot water
1 oz/30 grams shortening
2 teaspoons salt
1¼ lb/565 grams stoneground, unblended flour,
   divided
1 lb/450 grams mature Cheddar cheese, grated
Melted butter

Dissolve the yeast and 1 teaspoon of sugar in water in a small bowl. Leave to stand for 5 to 10 minutes, or until the mixture expands and becomes bubbly. Set aside.

Combine the shortening, remaining sugar and salt with milk in a large bowl. Stir until the shortening melts.

Stir in 4 oz/115 grams of flour. Add the cheese and then the reserved yeast mixture. Gradually stir in enough of the remaining flour to make a stiff dough.

Turn out onto a lightly floured board. Knead for 8 to 10 minutes or until smooth and elastic. Dust the board and dough with more flour if necessary to prevent sticking.

Shape into a ball. Place in a large, greased bowl. Turn the ball to grease it all over. Cover and let stand to rise in a warm, draught free place for 1 hour or until doubled in size.

Punch down the dough and turn out on a lightly floured board. Cover and let rise for 10 minutes. Cut the dough in half and shape into 2 loaves. Grease two 9 × 5 × 3-inch/22 × 13 × 8-cm loaf tins.

Place the dough in the tins. Cover and let rise in a warm, draught free place for 30 minutes or until the dough has risen to the rim of the tins.

Bake at 375°F/190°C/gas mark 5 for 35 minutes or until the crust is brown and the top sounds hollow when tapped. Remove from the tins and cool on racks. Brush the tops lightly with melted butter.

Breakfast Rolls

Makes about 30 rolls

1 oz/30 grams fresh yeast
1¼ pints/650 ml lukewarm water
2 tablespoons oil
2 teaspoons salt
1½ lb/700 grams strong, plain flour
Egg white

Crumble the yeast into a bowl. Add the water and stir so that the yeast dissolves. Add the oil, salt and most of the flour. Knead for 10 minutes or until smooth and elastic. Cover and let rise for about 40 minutes.

Knead the dough and shape into rolls. Cover and let rise on a greased baking sheet for 40 to 50 minutes.

Brush with a lightly beaten egg white and cook at 475°F/245°C/gas mark 9 for about 10 minutes.

Rye Bread

Makes 4 loaves or 25 rolls

¼ oz/8 grams compressed yeast
1 pint/½ l lukewarm water
About 1 tablespoon salt
9 oz/255 grams rye flour, sifted
9 oz/255 grams strong, plain flour
Coarse rye flour

Dissolve the yeast in the water. Add the salt, sifted rye flour and most of the plain flour. Make into a workable dough and let rise, covered, for 30 minutes.

Knead the dough and work in coarse rye flour. Form into about 25 rolls or 4 French bread sticks. Place on a greased baking sheet and cover. Let rise for 40 to 50 minutes in a slightly cool place. French bread should be slashed with a knife immediately after being shaped. Bake the rolls or bread at 475°F/245°C/gas mark 9 for 12 to 15 minutes.

Old Fashioned Christmas Bread

Makes 4 loaves

the first day
2 pints/1¼ l boiling water
2½ lb/1150 grams rye flour, sifted
¼ oz/8 grams compressed yeast dissolved in a little lukewarm water

the next day
1.7 oz/50 grams yeast dissolved in a little lukewarm water
6 oz/170 grams golden syrup
1 tablespoon salt
3 oz/85 grams butter, melted
1¼ lb/565 grams rye flour, sifted

The first day, pour the boiling water over the flour and work into an even, firm dough. Cover with a tea towel and leave to cool. Add the dissolved yeast, cover well and let the dough rise overnight.

The next day, add the dissolved yeast, syrup, salt, melted and cooled butter and the flour. Work into a firm dough. Knead well and let rise for 30 to 60 minutes.

Shape the dough into loaves with no cracks in them. Place on a greased baking sheet and cover. Leave to rise until almost doubled in size. Prick the loaves with a fork before they have finished rising. Bake at 425°F/220°C/gas mark 7 for about 15 minutes. Lower the heat to between 350 and 400°F/180 and 200°C/gas marks 4 and 6 and bake for another 30 minutes. Brush the loaves with syrup and let them cool, well wrapped in cloths.

Cherry Nut Bread

Makes 1 loaf

2 oz/60 grams shortening
8 oz/225 grams sugar
1 teaspoon salt
2 eggs
6 oz/170 grams plain flour
1½ teaspoons baking powder
8 oz/225 grams tinned, stoned cherries
4 oz/115 grams pecan nuts, chopped

Combine the shortening, sugar, salt and eggs in a medium sized mixing bowl. Beat well and set it aside. Combine the flour and baking powder and mix well. Drain the cherries, reserving the liquid. Add the flour mixture to the egg mixture alternately with the reserved cherry liquid, mixing after each addition. Stir in the cherries and pecan nuts.

Spoon the mixture into a floured, greased 9 × 5 × 3-inch/22 × 13 × 8-cm loaf tin. Bake at 350°F/180°C/gas mark 4 for 1 hour. Cool in the tin for 10 minutes. Remove to a rack and cool completely.

Scalded Rye Bread

Makes 1 round loaf

1½ pints/850 ml water
½ teaspoon salt
9 oz/255 grams coarse rye flour
¼ oz/8 grams compressed yeast
2 teaspoons ground fennel
4 oz/115 grams golden syrup
17 oz/475 grams flour

Bring the water to the boil and add the salt and vinegar. Pour the boiling mixture over the coarse rye flour. Work the dough, cover and let stand at room temperature overnight.

Crumble the yeast and dissolve it in several tablespoons of lukewarm water. Add the yeast to the dough together with the fennel, syrup and most of the flour. Make into a workable dough, cover and let rise for 30 to 40 minutes.

Knead the dough with a little more flour and shape into a smooth, round loaf. Place on a greased baking sheet. Prick with a fork and let rise under a damp tea towel for about 45 minutes.

Bake at 400°F/200°C/gas mark 6 for about 20 minutes. Lower the heat to 350°F/180°C/gas mark 4 and bake for a further 30 to 40 minutes. Let the loaf cool, well wrapped in cloths.

Cinnamon Bread

Makes 2 loaves

½ pint/¼ l milk, scalded
2 oz/60 grams shortening
8 oz/225 grams sugar
2 teaspoons salt
½ oz/15 grams active dry yeast
¼ pint/140 ml warm water
1½ lb/700 grams strong, plain flour
2 eggs, lightly beaten
1 tablespoon ground cinnamon
½ oz/15 grams soft butter

Mix the milk, shortening, 4 oz/115 grams of the sugar and salt together in a bowl. Cool to lukewarm. Sprinkle the yeast on warm water in a large bowl and stir until it is dissolved. Stir in half the flour, eggs and the milk mixture. Beat for 2 minutes with an electric mixer at medium speed, scraping the bowl occasionally. Stir in enough additional flour with your hands to make a soft dough that leaves the sides of the bowl. Turn out onto a lightly floured board and knead until smooth—about 10 minutes.

Place the dough in a lightly greased bowl and turn it, to grease all over. Cover and let rise in a warm place until it has doubled in size—about 1½ hours. Punch it down, cover and leave it to rise again until almost doubled—about 30 minutes. Turn onto the board and divide it in half. Make a ball out of each

half. Cover and let rest for 10 minutes.

Roll each half into a 12 × 7-inch/30 × 18-cm rectangle. Combine the remaining sugar and cinnamon, reserving a tablespoon of this mixture for topping. Sprinkle the dough rectangles evenly with the sugar-cinnamon mixture, then sprinkle 1 teaspoon of cold water over each rectangle. Smooth with a spatula. Roll as for Swiss roll, starting at the narrow end. Seal the long edge and tuck under the ends. Place, sealed edge down, in 2 greased 9 × 5 × 3-inch/22 × 13 × 8-cm loaf tins. Cover and let rise until almost double in size—45 to 60 minutes.

Brush the tops of the loaves with soft butter and sprinkle with the reserved sugar-cinnamon mixture. Bake in a 375°F/190°C/gas mark 5 oven for 35 to 40 minutes. If necessary, cover the tops of the loaves with foil for the last 15 minutes of baking to prevent excessive browning. Remove the bread from the tins and cool on wire racks.

Cornbread

6 servings

4 oz/115 grams stoneground flour
4 oz/115 grams plain, strong flour
1 tablespoon baking powder
½ teaspoon salt
2–4 oz/60–115 grams sugar (optional)
1 egg
½ pint/¼ l milk
2½ fl oz/75 ml fat or oil, melted

Mix the flours, baking powder, salt and sugar. Set aside.

Beat the egg. Add the milk and fat. Add to the flour mixture, stir just enough to mix. Fill a greased tin half full.

Bake at 425°F/220°C/gas mark 7 for 20 to 25 minutes, until lightly browned.

Rough Baking Tin Bread

12 pieces

3½, ¼ oz/8 grams cakes compressed yeast
1¼ pints/850 ml water
2 teaspoons salt
1¼ lb/565 grams coarse bread flour made from wheat and rye
Margarine

Crumble the yeast in a bowl. Warm the water to 100°F/38°C and dissolve the yeast in a little of the water. Then add the rest of the water. Add the salt and all the flour and work the dough, which should be rather loose. Let the dough rise for 1 hour.

Knead the dough in the bowl and let it rise for another hour in the bowl.

Grease a baking tin, about 12 × 16 inches/30 × 40 cm, with margarine. Pour the dough into the tin and flatten it with a floured hand. Cut the dough into 12 pieces. Cover with a cloth. Place the baking tin on top of the stove and preheat the oven to 450°F/230°C/gas mark 8.

When the oven has become warm, bake the bread on the bottom shelf of the oven for 15 minutes. Then decrease the heat to 250°F/120°C/gas mark ¼ and let the bread bake for 60 more minutes. Wrap the bread in a cloth. Eat it while it is still warm (it may also be heated up).

Cranberry Nut Bread

Makes 1 loaf

8 oz/225 grams strong, plain flour
8 oz/225 grams sugar
1½ teaspoons baking powder
½ teaspoon salt
2 oz/60 grams shortening
8 fl oz/220 ml orange juice
1 tablespoon orange rind, grated
1 egg, well beaten
4 oz/115 grams nuts, chopped
½–1 lb/225–450 grams cranberries, chopped and sprinkled with sugar

Light Dinner Bread

Sift the flour with all the dry ingredients; cut in the shortening. Combine the orange juice and grated rind with the egg. Pour the mixture over the dry ingredients. Mix with enough to dampen. Fold in the chopped nuts and cranberries.

Bake at 350°F/180°C/gas mark 4 for 1 hour in a loaf tin.

Dark Date Nut Bread

Makes 1 loaf

¼ pint/140 ml boiling water
4 oz/115 grams mixed sultanas and raisins
4 oz/115 grams dates, chopped
1 oz/30 grams butter
Scant 1 teaspoon baking soda
3 oz/85 grams plus 1 oz/30 grams strong, brown flour, sifted
4 oz/115 grams sugar
¼ teaspoon salt
1 egg
½ teaspoon vanilla essence
2 oz/60 grams nuts, chopped

Pour boiling water over the raisins, dates, butter and baking soda. Let stand. Mix the flour, sugar and salt. Add the fruit mixture, including the water and the remaining ingredients. Beat well.

Pour the mixture into a greased and floured 1-lb/450-gram loaf tin. Bake 60–70 minutes, until done.

Dilly Bread

Makes 1 loaf

¼ oz/8 grams dry yeast
2½ fl oz/75 ml warm water
8 oz/225 grams cottage cheese, room temperature
2 oz/60 grams sugar
1 tablespoon dried onion
½ oz/15 grams butter
2 teaspoons dill
1 teaspoon salt
¼ teaspoon bicarbonate of soda
1 unbeaten egg
9 oz/255 grams strong, plain flour

Soften the yeast in warm water. Add the lukewarm cottage cheese, sugar, onion, butter, dill, salt, bicarbonate of soda and egg. Stir well. Add the flour to form a stiff dough. Finish kneading the bread. When the dough is well kneaded, cover; let it rise in a warm place at least 60 minutes.

Beat down the dough; place in a greased 3 pint/1½ l round casserole. Allow it to rise 40 minutes more. Bake at 350°F/180°C/gas mark 4 45 minutes. Turn out the bread onto a rack. While still hot, brush the top with melted butter and sprinkle with salt.

Light Dinner Bread (Food Processor Method)

Makes 1 loaf

1 lb/450 grams flour
1 teaspoon salt
1½ teaspoons ground caraway
1 oz/30 grams margarine
18 fl oz/500 ml milk
½ oz/15 grams dry yeast

Place the flour, salt and caraway in your food processor. Melt the margarine in a pan. Add the milk and heat to 100°F/38°C. Dissolve the yeast in the liquid mixture.

Using the plastic mixing attachment, start the food processor. Pour in the liquid mixture through the feeder funnel. Run the machine for 20 to 30 seconds. Take off the top and let the dough rise, covered with a cloth, for about 30 minutes.

Work the dough on a floured board. Shape it into an oval loaf and place it on a buttered baking sheet. Cut slits in the top of the bread with a sharp knife. Let the bread rise, covered, for about 30 minutes. Meanwhile, preheat the oven to 400°F/200°C/gas mark 6.

Bake in the lower part of the oven for 30 to 35 minutes. Let the bread cool under a cloth.

The dough can also be rolled out into 24 rolls. Bake them in the middle of the oven at 425°F/220°C/gas mark 7 for about 10 minutes.

Easy Bread

Makes 2 loaves

1 oz/30 grams fresh yeast
2 oz/60 grams margarine or butter
2 pints/1¼ l milk
1 tablespoon salt
1 tablespoon ground caraway (optional)
11 oz/315 grams stoneground wholemeal flour
1 lb/450 grams plain strong white flour

Preheat oven to 400°F/200°C/gas mark 6. Grease and dust with wholemeal flour 2 3-pint/1½-litre loaf tins.

Crumble yeast in a large bowl. Melt the margarine and add the milk. Heat until lukewarm (100°F/38°C). Pour the mixture over the yeast and stir in the salt, caraway (if desired) and all the flour. Work together into a loose dough.

Place the dough in the loaf tins. Sprinkle with a little wholemeal flour. Let rise for 25 to 30 minutes.

Bake for 35 to 40 minutes at 400°F/200°C/gas mark 6. Turn out onto a rack and let cool under a cloth.

Caraway Seed Rolls

Makes 36 rolls

1¼ oz/38 grams fresh yeast
2 oz/60 grams margarine or butter
14 fl oz/400 ml water
2 teaspoons salt
½ teaspoon ground aniseed or caraway (optional)
1½ lb/700 grams flour
Sufficient flour for rolling out the dough

Grease 2 baking sheets.

Crumble the yeast into a large bowl. Melt the margarine and add the water. Heat until lukewarm (100°F/38°C). Pour the mixture over the yeast and stir. Add the salt, aniseed or caraway and 1½ lb/700 grams of the flour. Vigorously work the dough. Add and work in more of the flour. The dough should be rather firm. Let the dough stand in the bowl for at least 10 minutes, preferably let the dough rise under a cloth for at least 30 minutes.

Turn the dough out onto a floured board and work again until smooth. Divide the dough into 2 parts. Form each part into a long roll about 20 inches/50 cm long. Divide each of these into smaller pieces with a knife. Dip one of the cut edges in flour. Place the rolls on the baking sheets. The rolls can be made even more attractive by cutting 5 slits in each piece. Let rise 30 to 40 minutes. Preheat oven to 450°F/245°C/gas mark 9.

Bake in the middle of the oven for about 6 minutes. The rolls taste best when served warm and fresh from the oven.

Square Decorated Country Bread

Makes 1 round loaf

1 oz/30 grams fresh yeast
1 pint/½ water, at 100°F/38°C
2 tablespoons oil
2 teaspoons salt
20–22 oz/600 grams stoneground flour

Grease and dust a 9-inch/23-cm round cake tin.

Crumble the yeast into a large bowl. Add the warm water and the oil. Stir so that the yeast dissolves. Add the salt and 1¼ lb/565 grams of the flour. Work the dough vigorously. Add 2 oz/60 grams more flour and work the dough again. It should be rather loose. Sprinkle a little flour over the dough and let it rise under a cloth for about 30 minutes.

Work the dough again in the bowl until it is smooth. Pour or dab it into the prepared pan. Even out the surface with a floured hand. Preheat oven to 475°F/245°C/gas mark 9. Let dough rise for 30 minutes.

Decorate the bread using a sharp knife just before baking (see illustration p. 253). Brush the surface with water. Bake on the bottom shelf for 10 minutes at 475°F/245°C/gas mark 9. Decrease heat to 400°F/200°C/gas mark 6 and bake for another 30 minutes. If the bread starts to get too dark, place the baking sheet on the highest shelf of the oven, toward the end of the baking time.

Turn out the bread and let it cool on a rack under a cloth.

Honey Spice Bread

Makes 2 loaves

½ oz/15 grams dry yeast
2½ fl oz/75 ml oz lukewarm water
1 egg
8 oz/225 grams honey
1 tablespoon ground coriander
½ teaspoon ground cinnamon
¼ teaspoon ground cloves
1½ teaspoons salt
½ pint/¼ l lukewarm milk
3 oz/85 grams butter, melted
1–1¼ lb/450–565 grams flour

Sprinkle the yeast over the lukewarm water, stirring until dissolved.

Combine the egg, honey, spices and salt in a large bowl and beat with a whisk until well mixed. Add the yeast mixture, milk and 2 oz/60 grams melted butter and beat again. Stir in the flour, 2 oz/60 grams at a time, until the dough can be gathered into a soft ball. Blend in the remaining flour with your fingers.

Turn the dough out onto a lightly floured surface and knead until it is smooth and elastic. Do not add any additional flour. The dough should be rather soft. To prevent sticking, rub your hands occasionally with some of the remaining melted butter.

Form the dough into a ball and place in a lightly oiled bowl, turning to cover all surfaces. Place a damp towel over the bowl and let the dough rise until doubled in bulk.

When dough has risen, punch it down a few times and knead again for a few minutes. You may divide the dough in half and shape into two loaves or form the dough into a round and place in a 6-pint/3½-litre buttered casserole. Let the dough rise in the tins or in the casserole until it almost reaches the top.

Bake in a preheated 300°F/150°C/gas mark 2 oven for 1 hour for the tin loaves or 1 hour 10 minutes for the round, until the top is crusty and golden brown. Cool on a wire rack.

Easy Bread, Rolls, Square Decorated Country Bread & a Selection of American Muffins

Fruit Loaf

Makes 1 loaf

1 lb/450 grams mixed dried fruit, finely chopped
6 oz/170 grams flour, sifted
3 teaspoons baking powder
½ teaspoon salt
6 oz/170 grams sugar
6 oz/170 grams butter
2 eggs, beaten
1 tablespoon milk
¼ teaspoon almond essence

Soak the dried fruit in enough boiling water to cover for 10 minutes, then drain well. Sift the flour, baking powder, salt and sugar together into a mixing bowl. Cut in the butter with a pastry blender until the mixture is the consistency of fine breadcrumbs. Stir in the dried fruit until evenly distributed. Add the eggs, milk and almond extract and beat thoroughly. The mixture will be very stiff.

Spread the mixture in a well greased loaf tin. Bake in a preheated 350°F/180°C/gas mark 4 oven for 1 hour or until the bread is done. Cool slightly, then remove from the tin. Serve warm with butter.

Gingerbread

Makes 16 to 20 squares

12 oz/345 grams flour
¼ teaspoon salt
2 tablespoons ground ginger
2 teaspoons mixed spice
2 teaspoons ground cinnamon
4 oz/115 grams brown sugar
4 tablespoons milk
8 oz/225 grams golden syrup
2 tablespoons treacle
4 oz/115 grams butter or margarine
3 eggs
2 teaspoons bicarbonate of soda

Grease and line a 10 × 7 × 2½-inch/25 × 18 × 7-cm baking tin. Sift the flour, salt and spices together. Add the sugar.

Put 3 tablespoons of milk into a small pan with the syrup and butter or margarine and melt over low heat. Add the beaten egg and stir all into the flour mixture. Beat well.

Dissolve the soda in the remaining 1 tablespoon of warm milk and beat into the mixture.

Spread evenly in the prepared tin and bake in a preheated 375°F/190°C/gas mark 5 oven about 50 minutes. Cool in the tin and cut into squares.

Treacle Pumpkin Bread

Makes 1 loaf

2½ oz/75 grams shortening
8 oz/225 grams sugar
2 eggs
8 oz/225 grams treacle
8 oz/225 grams pumpkin, mashed
8 oz/225 grams flour
¼ teaspoon baking powder
1 teaspoon bicarbonate of soda
½ teaspoon salt
2 teaspoons mixed spice
8 oz/225 grams walnuts, coarsely chopped

Cream the shortening and stir in the sugar and eggs. Stir in the treacle and pumpkin. Stir in the remaining ingredients and beat well.

Bake in a greased loaf tin for 1 hour or more at 350°F/180°C/gas mark 4. Turn out and cool on a rack. Slice thinly and spread with butter or cream cheese.

Onion Bread

Makes 2 loaves

½ pint/¼ l milk, scalded
3 oz/85 grams sugar
1 tablespoon salt
1½ tablespoons vegetable oil
3, ¼-oz/8-gram packets dry yeast
8 fl oz/220 ml warm water
4 oz/115 grams onion, finely chopped
1½ lb/700 grams flour

Pour the milk into a large mixing bowl. Add the sugar, salt and oil and mix until the sugar is dissolved. Cool until lukewarm. Dissolve the yeast in the warm water, then stir into the milk mixture. Add the onion and 1 lb/450 grams of the flour and mix until blended. Add enough of the remaining flour, a small amount at a time, to make a stiff dough. Knead well. Cover and let rise for 45 minutes.

Punch the dough down, then place it in 2 greased loaf tins. Let it rise until doubled in bulk. Bake in a preheated 350°F/180°C/gas mark 4 oven for 1 hour, or until the bread sounds hollow when tapped with your fingers. Remove from the tins and place on wire racks to cool.

Orange Bread

Makes 1 loaf

12 oz/345 grams flour
3 tablespoons baking powder
5 oz/140 grams sugar
1 teaspoon salt
12 fl oz/350 ml milk
1 oz/30 grams butter, melted
1 egg, beaten
Peel of 1 orange, finely chopped

Sift the dry ingredients into a mixing bowl. Add the milk, butter and egg. Mix with a wooden spoon. Add the orange peel. Place the mixture in a greased 9×5×2-inch/22×13×5-cm loaf tin. Let rise 15 minutes.

Bake the bread in a 350°F/180°C/gas mark 4 oven 50 minutes.

Honey Tea Bread

Makes 1 loaf

½ pint/¼ l milk
1 lb/450 grams honey
2 oz/60 grams butter, cut into small pieces
2 eggs, lightly beaten
5 oz/140 grams wholemeal flour
5 oz/140 grams strong, plain white flour
1 teaspoon salt
3 teaspoons baking powder
4 oz/115 grams walnuts

Place the milk and honey in a heavy saucepan and heat, stirring until well blended. Add the butter to the milk mixture and stir until the butter is dissolved. Beat in the eggs. Stir in the flours, salt and baking powder. Fold in the nuts.

Pour the mixture into a well buttered and floured loaf tin. Bake in a preheated 325°F/163°C/gas mark 3 oven 1 hour to 1 hour 20 minutes, or until a baking needle comes out clean. Cool 15 minutes before removing from the tin. Cool further before slicing.

Lemon Bread

Makes 1 loaf

2½ oz/75 grams butter, melted
10 oz/285 grams sugar
2 eggs
¼ teaspoon almond essence
6 oz/170 grams strong, plain flour, sifted
1 teaspoon baking powder
1 teaspoon salt
¼ pint/140 ml milk
1 tablespoon lemon peel, grated
4 oz/115 grams nuts, chopped
3 tablespoons fresh lemon juice

Mix the butter and 8 oz/225 grams of sugar together and beat in the eggs, 1 at a time. Add the almond extract. Sift the dry ingredients together and add them to the egg mixture alternately with the milk. Stir until just mixed. Fold in the lemon peel and nuts.

Turn the mixture into a greased, 8½×4½×2½-inch/22×13×8×-cm loaf tin. Bake at 350°F/180°C/gas mark 4 about 70 minutes, or until the loaf is done in the centre.

Mix the lemon juice and remaining sugar. Immediately spoon the glaze over the hot loaf. Cool 10 minutes. Remove the bread from the tin and cool on a rack. Do not cut for 24 hours.

Potato Bread

Parmesan Bread

Makes 1 round loaf

¼ oz/8 grams dry yeast
2½ fl oz/75 ml lukewarm water
8 oz/225 grams plain flour, sifted
1 oz/30 grams sugar
½ teaspoon salt
2½ oz/75 grams butter
1 egg, lightly beaten
2½ fl oz/75 ml lukewarm milk
4 oz/115 grams Parmesan cheese, grated
2 tablespoons parsley, chopped

Sprinkle the yeast over the water, stirring until dissolved. Sift the dry ingredients into a mixing bowl. With a pastry blender, cut the butter into the flour mixture until it resembles breadcrumbs. Add the egg, yeast mixture and milk and beat the mixture well. Stir in the cheese and parsley.

Turn into an oiled, 8-inch/22-cm round cake tin, cover with a damp cloth and let rise until doubled in bulk. Dot the loaf with butter and bake in a preheated 375°F/190°C/gas mark 5 oven for 20 to 25 minutes. Let the bread cool a little, then cut into pie-shaped wedges.

Fine Baking Tin Bread

Glazed Orange and Raisin Bread

Makes 2 loaves

½ pint/¼ l milk, scalded
1½ teaspoons salt
4 oz/115 grams sugar
4 oz/115 grams butter or shortening, softened
½ oz/15 grams active dry yeast
2½ fl oz/75 ml warm water
1¼–1½ lb/700 grams flour, sifted
2 eggs
1 teaspoon orange peel, grated
1 teaspoon ground ginger
12 oz/345 grams raisins

orange-nut glaze
4 oz/115 grams icing sugar, sifted
1 oz/30 grams butter, softened
4 oz/115 grams walnuts, finely chopped
2–4 tablespoons orange juice

Pour the milk over the salt, sugar and butter in a large bowl. Mix well and cool to lukewarm.

Sprinkle the yeast on warm water, stirring until dissolved. Add the yeast mixture and about ½ the flour to the milk mixture. Beat 2 minutes with an electric mixer at medium speed, scraping the bowl occasionally.

Beat in the eggs, orange peel, ginger, raisins and 2 oz/60 grams of flour. Then mix in enough remaining flour, a little at a time, first with a spoon and then with your hands, to make a soft dough that leaves the sides of the bowl.

Turn the dough onto a lightly floured board. Knead just until smooth. Roll it into a ball and place in a lightly greased bowl, turning the ball over to grease its top. Cover and let rise in a warm place until doubled in bulk, 1–1½ hours. Punch it down and let it rest 15 minutes. Divide the dough in half. Shape each half into a loaf and place in 2 greased 9 × 5 × 3-inch/22 × 13 × 8-cm loaf tins. Make 3 diagonal, ¼-inch/½-cm deep slashes across the top of each loaf. Cover and let rise in a warm place only until doubled, about 1 hour.

Bake in a 375°F/190°C/gas mark 5 oven 40 to 50 minutes. Cover with a sheet of aluminium foil after the first 20 minutes of baking if the loaves are browning too fast. Remove the loaves from the tins and place on wire racks.

Blend all the ingredients for the orange-nut glaze together until the glaze is of spreading consistency. Spread the glaze on top of the warm loaves, then leave to cool.

Swedish Overnight Bread

Makes 4 loaves

14 oz/400 grams bran
3¼/2 l pints water
1 oz/30 grams fresh yeast
2 to 2½ tablespoons salt
2 tablespoons oil
3 lb/1350 grams flour

Bring the bran to the boil in 1 pint/½ litre water and then let it carefully simmer for 10 minutes. Pour into a bowl and add the remaining cold water. Let stand until cold.

Grease 4 bread tins.

Crumble the yeast into the dough liquid, add the salt and oil and work in the flour. Pour the dough out onto a board and knead well. Divide the dough into 4 parts and make loaves of each. Place in the refrigerator, covered with a cloth, and allow to stand until the next morning.

Preheat the oven to 400°F/200°C/gas mark 6 and place the baking tins directly from the refrigerator into the warm oven for 45 minutes. Bake in 2 batches, allowing 2 of the tins to remain in the refrigerator while the other 2 are in the oven.

Cool the loaves on a rack, covered with a tea towel.

Potato Bread

Makes 2 loaves

8 medium large potatoes
1 teaspoon salt
1¼/700 ml pints skimmed milk
2 tablespoons oil
3, ¼ oz/8 grams cakes compressed yeast
1½ lb/700 grams unbleached flour
4 oz/115 grams coarse rye flour
1 tablespoon ground fennel

Peel the potatoes, boil them until soft and mash them with the salt, a small amount of the milk and the oil. Add the rest of the milk, warm to finger temperature (100°F/38°C). Stir the yeast into a small amount of the mixture and pour into the dough.

Add most of the unbleached flour, the rye flour, plus the fennel and knead into a workable dough. Let rise until doubled in size (about 45 minutes), covered under a cloth.

Knead the dough on a board and divide it into 2 parts. Form each part into 2 round rolls. Let rise until double in size, about 40 minutes. Cut a diamond pattern on the top of the loaves, using a sharp knife. Bake at 400°F/200°C/gas mark 6 for about 40 minutes. Test with a baking needle.

Pumpkin Bread

Makes 2 loaves

1 lb/450 grams flour, unsifted
1½ lb/700 grams sugar
2 teaspoons baking soda
1½ teaspoons salt
1 teaspoon baking powder
1 teaspoon cinnamon
1 teaspoon nutmeg
½ teaspoon cloves
¼ teaspoon ginger
1 lb/450 grams cooked pumpkin
½ pint/¼ l oil
4 eggs
8 fl oz/220 ml water

Grease 2, 9 × 5 × 3-inch/22 × 13 × 8-cm loaf tins. Mix the dry ingredients thoroughly in a large bowl. Beat the pumpkin, oil, eggs and water together. Add the dry ingredients. Stir just until the dry ingredients are moistened. Do not over mix.

Pour half of the mixture into each loaf tin. Bake at 350°F/180°C/gas mark 4 for 1–1¼ hours, or until a baking needle inserted in the centre of the loaf comes out clean. Cool on a rack. Remove the bread from the tins after 10 minutes.

Fine Baking Tin Bread

Makes 4 loaves

4 oz/115 grams fresh yeast
3½ oz/100 grams butter or margarine
2 pints/1¼ l water
½ pint/¼ l lager
4 teaspoons salt
2 tablespoons golden syrup
4¼ lb/2 kilos wholemeal flour

Crumble the yeast into a large bowl. Melt the butter and pour in the water and the beer. Dissolve the yeast in a little of the lukewarm liquid mixture. Add the rest of the liquid, plus the salt, syrup and most of the flour. Make into a workable dough.

Place the entire dough in a greased baking tin, about 12 × 16 inches/30 × 40 cm and flatten it with a floured hand. Prick the surface with a fork. Let the dough rise, covered with a damp cloth, for about 1 hour.

Bake at 475°F/245°C/gas mark 9 for about 15 minutes, until the bread has become a golden brown. Decrease the heat to 400°F/200°C/gas mark 6 and bake for another 30 minutes.

Cut the bread into 4 loaves when it has become cold.

Pumpernickel Bread

Makes 3 round loaves

2¼ lb/1150 grams plain, strong white flour
12 oz/345 grams rye flour
2 tablespoons salt
8 oz/225 grams all-bran cereal
6 oz/170 grams stoneground flour
½ oz/15 grams dry yeast
1½ pints/2 l water
4 oz/115 grams treacle
2 squares cooking chocolate
½ oz/15 grams butter
1 lb/450 grams mashed potatoes, at room
   temperature
1 tablespoon caraway seeds

Combine the flours. Place 8 oz/225 grams of the flour mixture, the salt, cereal and dry yeast in a bowl. Combine the water, treacle, chocolate and butter in a saucepan and heat over low heat until the chocolate and butter melt. Gradually add the liquids to the flour mixture and beat 2 minutes with an electric mixer at medium speed. Add the potatoes and another 4 oz/115 grams of the flour mixture, or enough to make a thick batter. Beat at high speed for 2 minutes. Stir in additional flour and the caraway seeds. When the dough begins to pull away from the sides of the bowl, turn it out onto a floured board. Cover and let rest 15 minutes.

Knead, using more flour as necessary, until the dough is smooth and elastic, about 15 minutes. Place in an oiled bowl. Cover with a damp towel and set in a warm place to rise until doubled in bulk. Punch the dough down with your fist a few times. Cover and let rise again about 45 minutes.

Punch the dough down and turn out onto the board. Divide it into 3 equal pieces and shape each into a round ball. Oil 3 8×9-inch/19×22-cm cake tins and place the dough in these. Cover and let rise until doubles in bulk. Bake in a preheated 350°F/180°C/gas mark 4 oven for about 50 minutes. Immediately remove from the tins and cool the loaves on wire racks.

Fancy Saffron Breads

Quantity varies according to shape

3, ¼ oz/8 grams packets compressed yeast
7 oz/200 grams butter or margarine
1 pint/½ l milk
½ teaspoon saffron
6 oz/170 grams sugar
½ teaspoon salt
About 1½ lb/700 grams flour
Egg
Decorate with: raisins, chopped almonds etc

Crumble the yeast into a bowl. Melt the butter in a pan, pour in the milk and heat until lukewarm (100°F/38°C). Dissolve the yeast in a little of the liquid. Then add the rest of the liquid, in which finely ground saffron has been mixed. Add the sugar, salt, egg and most of the flour. Make into a workable dough and let rise in a draught free spot, covered, for about 40 minutes.

Knead the dough on a slab and make into various shapes (see illustration p. 259).

Small Breads are placed on a greased baking sheet. Cover and let rise until about doubles in size. Brush with a beaten egg and bake at 475°F/245°C/gas mark 9.

Large Breads and Tea Cakes such as braided cakes are baked at 400–425°F/200–220°C/gas marks 6–7.

Baking Tip: Mixing the saffron with a little brandy is an old-fashioned trick for getting the most flavour out of the spice. Grind the saffron in a mortar with a sugar cube. Then stir it into a little brandy or milk.

Hard Rye Bread Wafers

Fancy Saffron Breads

Courgette Bread

Makes 2 loaves

3 eggs, beaten until frothy
1 lb/450 grams sugar
½ pint/¼ l oil
1 tablespoon vanilla essence
1 lb/450 grams courgette, coarsely grated
8 oz/225 grams nuts, chopped
8 oz/225 grams flour (white or wholemeal)
1 tablespoon cinnamon
2 teaspoons bicarbonate of soda
2 teaspoons salt
¼ teaspoon baking powder
8 oz/225 grams raisins

Beat the eggs until frothy. Gradually beat the sugar, oil and vanilla into the eggs until thick and creamy. Stir in the remaining ingredients.

Pour into 2 greased and floured, 8 × 3 × 4-inch/ 22 × 13 × 8-cm loaf tins. Bake at 350°F/180°C/gas mark 4 for 1 hour. The bread keeps for a long time and becomes more moist with age.

Tea Breads

Makes 16 individual breads

8 fl oz/220 ml milk
¼ oz/8 grams compressed yeast
1 egg
1 oz/30 grams sugar
½ teaspoon salt
About 8 oz/225 grams flour
2½ oz/75 grams butter
Egg
Poppy seeds

Heat the milk so that it is lukewarm (100°F/38°C). Dissolve the yeast in the milk. Add the egg, sugar, salt and flour and knead well. Let stand and rise in a warm place for about 20 minutes.

Preheat oven to 400°F/200°C/gas mark 6.

Punch down the dough and knead again. Roll it out into a rectangle about 10 × 16 inches/25 × 40 cms inches. Slice the butter with a cheese wire and lay the slices out over half the dough. Fold the other half over the buttered half. Roll the dough and fold it together into 3 layers. Roll again and fold it again in the same way. Repeat 1 or 2 more times.

Finally, roll out the dough so that it is about 12 × 30 inches/30 × 75 cms and fold it lengthwise into 3 layers. Cut the dough into 2-inch/5-cm wide pieces and let it rise on a baking sheet for about 15 minutes. Brush with the egg and sprinkle with poppy seeds. Bake for about 15 minutes at 400°F/200°C/gas mark 6.

Hard Rye Bread Wafers

Makes about 25 slices of bread

¼ oz/8 grams compressed yeast
1 pint/½ l water at 100°F/38°C
12 oz/345 grams coarse rye flour
8 oz/225 grams strong, plain flour
2½ teaspoons salt
1 teaspoon sugar for the rising process
2 teaspoons caraway

Crumble the yeast into a large bowl and dissolve it in the 100°F/38°C water. Add the remaining ingredients and work together into a smooth dough. Sprinkle with a little flour, cover with a cloth and let rise for about 30 minutes.

Knead the dough and roll it out so that it is very, very thin. Cut out large round "pancakes" with the help of a plate that is about 7 inches/16 cms in diameter. Prick the dough with a fork, place the rounds on a baking sheet, spread a cloth over them and let rise for about 20 minutes.

Preheat the oven to 400°F/200°C/gas mark 6 while the dough is rising. Bake for 5 minutes. Turn the slices over and bake for another 5 minutes.

South Carolina Spoon Bread

Makes 1 loaf

1 pint/½ l milk
1 oz/30 grams stoneground flour
1½ oz/45 grams butter
1 teaspoon salt
3 eggs, separated

Heat the milk in a double boiler, stir in the flour and cook slowly until thick and smooth. Remove from the heat and add the butter and salt. Let the mixture cool while you beat the egg whites stiff.

Beat the egg yolks and add to the flour mixture, then fold in egg whites and bake for 30 minutes in a buttered tin in a 325–375°F/163–190°C/gas marks 3–5 oven.

Spice Bread

Makes 2 loaves

1 oz/30 grams dry yeast
2½ fl oz/75 ml lukewarm water
¼ teaspoon sugar
1 pint/½ l milk, scalded

2½ oz/75 grams butter
2 oz/60 grams brown sugar
4 oz/115 grams honey
2 teaspoons salt
4 fl oz/110 ml orange juice
1 egg lightly beaten
1 tablespoon cumin
1 lb/450 grams wholemeal flour
14 oz/400 grams strong, plain flour
1 oz/30 grams softened butter
2 tablespoons honey

Sprinkle the yeast over the warm water. Add the sugar and stir to dissolve. Add the butter, brown sugar, honey, salt and orange juice to the scalded milk. Cool the mixture to lukewarm. Add the yeast mixture, the egg, cumin and the wholemeal flour; beat until smooth. Add enough of the white flour to produce a stiff dough. When the dough begins to pull away from the sides of the bowl, turn it onto a floured board and begin kneading, using as much white flour as is necessary to prevent sticking. Knead until the dough is smooth and elastic.

Place the dough in an oiled bowl, cover it with a damp cloth and allow it to rise until doubled in bulk.

Tea Breads

Punch the dough down again, shape it into a ball and divide it in half. Place each half in a buttered loaf tin, cover and let the loaves rise until doubled in bulk. Bake the loaves in a preheated 425°F/220°C/gas mark 7 oven for 10 minutes. Reduce the heat to 350°F/180°C/gas mark 4 and continue baking for 25 to 30 minutes or until the loaves are done.

Let the loaves cool in the tins on a wire rack for 5 minutes. Combine the remaining butter and honey. Turn the loaves out of the tins and brush the tops with this mixture. Allow the bread to cool further on the racks.

Pan Bread

Makes 1 loaf

8 oz/225 grams strong, plain flour
4 teaspoons baking powder
2 teaspoons salt
12 fl oz/345 ml milk
1 oz/30 grams butter

Mix the dry ingredients in a bowl. Add the milk and blend with a wooden spoon. It will have a biscuit-like spongy texture.

Heat the butter in a medium sized pan. Keep the heat low. Spread the butter around evenly. Pour in the mixture. Cook 15 minutes or until the underside is golden brown. Lift with a large spatula; turn to cook the other side 15 minutes.

Turn the bread out onto a round plate. Serve at once.

Walnut Bread

Makes 3 small loaves

1 pint/¼ l water
2 tablespoons oil
9 oz/255 grams yeast
2 teaspoons salt
2½ oz/75 grams wheat bran
13 oz/375 grams strong, plain flour
11 oz/315 grams light rye flour
4 oz/115 grams walnuts, chopped into large
   pieces

Warm the water and the oil to 100°F/38°C. Dissolve the yeast in a little of the liquid, then add the rest of the liquid. Blend in the salt, wheat bran, flours and nuts. Pour in the liquid and make into a workable dough; let the dough rise under a cloth for about 45 minutes.

Knead the dough and shape it into three small loaves or two larger loaves. Slash the top with a sharp knife, brush with water and sprinkle with a little of the rye flour. Let rise until doubled in bulk.

Bake in the oven at 400°F/200°C/gas mark 6 for 30 to 40 minutes. Test with a baking needle to make sure the bread is done.

Stoneground Bread in a Baking Tin

Makes 15 pieces

11 oz stoneground flour
6 oz/170 grams plain flour
1 teaspoon salt
2 teaspoons ground bitter orange peel
1 oz/30 grams margarine
18 fl oz/500 ml water
4 oz/115 grams golden syrup
¼ oz/8 grams compressed yeast
Brush with 1 egg

Place the flour, salt and the bitter orange peel in your food processor. Melt the margarine in a pan and pour in the water and syrup. Heat to 100°F/38°C. Dissolve the yeast in the liquid mixture.

Using the plastic mixer attachment, start the machine; pour in the liquid through the feeder funnel. Knead the dough quickly 20 to 30 seconds. Take off the lid and let the dough rise under a cloth for 30 minutes. Preheat the oven to 425°F/220°C/gas mark 7.

Turn the dough out onto a baking board and work it lightly. Flatten the dough into a greased baking tin. Cut the dough into 15 pieces with a floured pastry cutter or knife. Cover and let the bread rise for about 30 minutes.

Brush the bread with the beaten egg. Bake in the middle of the oven for about 15 minutes. Break the bread into pieces when it has cooled.

Hush Puppies

Makes 24

2 oz/60 grams flour
2 teaspoons baking powder
½ teaspoon salt
6 oz/170 grams stoneground flour
1 small onion, finely chopped
2½ fl oz/75 ml oz milk
1 egg, beaten
Deep fat for frying

Put the dry ingredients into a large bowl in the order listed. Add the onion, then the milk and egg. Stir until all the ingredients are well blended.

Heat the fat to 375°F/190°C/ in a deep pan. Drop the batter by teaspoonfuls into the hot fat; fry until golden brown all over. Remove; drain the hush puppies on kitchen towel. Keep warm until ready to serve.

To vary the hush puppies, use the above recipe, substituting 4 oz/115 grams chopped apple or 4 oz/115 grams cooked sweetcorn in place of the onion.

Fried Mush

Makes 1 loaf

3 pints/1½ l boiling water
2 oz/60 grams stoneground flour
¼ pint/140 ml water
1 teaspoon salt
1 egg yolk
2 tablespoons milk
4 oz/115 grams crumbs
Butter or bacon fat
Maple syrup

Place boiling water in the top of a double boiler, combine the flour, water and salt and add the mixture to the boiling water a little at a time, stirring. Cook over high heat for 5 minutes, cover and steam for 15 minutes longer. Pour into a greased bread tin. Cool, then cut into ¼-inch/½-cm slices.

Combine the egg yolk and milk. Dip the slices into the egg yolk mixture, then in the crumbs. Let stand a few minutes, then fry in butter or bacon fat in a hot pan. Turn carefully, fry the other side. Serve with maple syrup.

Country Rounds

Makes 20

8 oz/225 grams flour
4 teaspoons baking powder
8 oz/225 grams unsalted butter
Pinch salt
Milk

Grease a large mixing bowl. Sift the flour, baking powder and salt into a bowl; add cold butter cut into pieces. With a pastry blender, work the dough until crumbly. Add just enough cold milk to hold the dough together; form a ball and press onto a floured surface, patting down until about ½-inch/1-cm thick.

Flour a pastry cutter. Cut the dough into rounds and place 2 inches apart on a greased baking sheet. Chill for 1 hour.

Preheat the oven to 450°F/230°C/gas mark 8. Prick the tops of the rounds with the tines of a fork. Bake for 10–12 minutes.

Cottage Cheesies

Makes 24

8 oz/225 grams flour
1 teaspoon baking powder
¼ teaspoon bicarbonate of soda
Pinch salt
2 teaspoons sugar
1 oz/30 grams butter
4 oz/115 grams cottage cheese

1 large egg
2 tablespoons milk

In a medium bowl, stir the flour, baking powder, soda, salt and sugar together; cut in the butter. In a small bowl, with an electric beater at high speed, beat the cheese until it is as smooth as ricotta, at least 2 minutes; add the egg and milk; beat until blended. Add the cheese mixture to the flour mixture and stir with a fork until flour mixture is moistened and rather sticky.

Turn the dough, by level tablespoons, into buttered bun tins. Bake in a preheated 450°F/230°C/gas mark 8 oven until a baking needle inserted in the centre comes out clean, about 15 minutes. Serve hot.

Popovers

Makes 8 large popovers

4 oz/115 grams flour
¼ teaspoon salt
2 eggs, beaten
½ pint/¼ l milk
½ oz/15 grams shortening, melted

Stoneground Bread made in a Baking Tin

Walnut Bread

Sift the flour and salt together. Mix the eggs, milk, and shortening; add gradually to the flour. Beat until smooth, with a whisk or electric mixer, about 1 minute. Fill greased bun tins, nearly full.

Bake 20 minutes in a preheated 450°F/230°C/gas mark 8 oven. Reduce the heat to 350°F/180°C/gas mark bake 15 minutes, until the popovers are firm.

Sweet Cream Rounds

Makes 36

1 lb/450 grams flour, sifted
1 teaspoon salt
2 tablespoons baking powder
15 fl oz/425 ml double cream
4 tablespoons water (optional)

Sift the flour, salt and baking powder together. Stir in the double cream with a fork, just until all the flour is moistened; add water if necessary to get the proper consistency.

Knead on a lightly floured surface, about 10 times. Roll 1-inch/2½-cm thick and cut with a small floured cutter. Bake on an ungreased baking sheet in a 450°F/230°C/gas mark 8 oven 12 minutes, or until golden brown.

Jam Topped Slices

Makes about 60 slices

6 oz/170 grams flour
2 oz/60 grams sugar
7 oz/200 grams margarine or butter, at room temperature
2½ oz/75 grams jam
3 oz/85 grams icing sugar
½ tablespoon water

Preheat oven to 400°F/200°C/gas mark 6.

Place the flour and sugar in your food processor. Divide the margarine or butter into 6 to 8 pieces and add to the flour and sugar. Using the plastic mixer attachment, start the machine and let the mixture blend for 20 to 30 seconds. Let the dough stand in a cold place for about an hour.

Roll the dough out into 4, flat, long bun shapes and place them on a baking sheet lined with grease-proof paper. Make a depression down the middle of each. Fill with jam. Bake in the middle of the oven for about 10 minutes. Leave to cool on the baking sheet.

Mix the icing sugar and water together. Brush it over the buns and cut them into slanted slices.

Cinnamon Nut Rolls

Makes 36 rolls

¼ oz/8 grams active dry yeast
½ pint/¼ l milk, scalded and cooled to warm
    (110 to 115°F)
3 oz/85 grams shortening
3 oz/85 grams butter or margarine
6 oz/170 grams sugar
1 teaspoon salt
2 egg yolks or 1 egg, beaten
12 oz/345 grams plain flour, sifted
Melted butter or margarine
4 oz/115 grams brown sugar
2 teaspoons ground cinnamon
1 lb/450 grams golden syrup
8 oz/225 grams brown sugar
2 oz/60 grams butter
12 oz/345 grams pecan nuts

Sprinkle the yeast on warm milk, stirring until dissolved. Cream the shortening and 1 oz/30 grams of the butter and add 2 oz/60 grams of sugar and salt. Beat until light and fluffy. Add the egg yolks, yeast and enough flour to make a soft dough that leaves the sides of the bowl. Turn out onto a lightly floured cloth or board; knead until smooth and elastic.

Place in a greased bowl; turn the greased side of the dough up. Cover; let it rise until doubled in bulk. divide the dough in half; roll into 2 18×9-inch/ 44×22-cm rectangles, about ¼-inch/½-cm thick. Brush with melted butter.

Mix the remaining sugar, 4 oz/115 grams of brown sugar and cinnamon together; sprinkle each piece of dough with half of the sugar mixture. Roll like a swiss roll, cut into 1-inch/2½-cm slices.

Mix the syrup, 8 oz/225 grams of brown sugar and 2 oz/60 grams butter together; heat slowly or in top of a double boiler. Place 1 tablespoon of syrup and 4 to 5 pecan nuts, rounded side down, in greased bun tins. Drop the dough slices, cut side down, in syrup; cover and let rise until doubled in bulk.

Bake in a 400°F/200°C/gas mark 6 oven 12 to 15 minutes. Remove from the oven at once. Turn the rolls, pecan side up, onto a large tray. Let the tins stay on top of the rolls a minute, so the syrup drains onto them.

Milkies

Makes 24

2 teaspoons white vinegar
8 fl oz/220 ml milk
7 oz/200 grams flour, sifted
2 teaspoons baking powder
½ teaspoon bicarbonate of soda
1 teaspoon salt
2½ oz/75 grams butter

Melted butter

"Sour" the pasteurized milk by mixing it with the vinegar and letting it stand at room temperature for 10 or 15 minutes until it looks curdled.

Sift the dry ingredients together. Cut in the 2½ oz/ 75 grams butter. Add the soured milk all at once and stir quickly with a fork until a soft dough forms.

Turn onto a floured board and knead the dough gently and quickly for 30 seconds. Roll the dough lightly ½ inch/1 cm thick. Cut with a floured, 1½- inch/ 4-cm pastry cutter. Prick the tops with a fork and brush with melted butter. Bake on an ungreased baking sheet in a preheated 425°F/220°C/gas mark 7 oven 12–15 minutes.

Parker House Rolls

Makes 36 rolls

½ pint/¼ l milk, scalded
1 oz/30 grams shortening
2 oz/60 grams sugar
1 teaspoon salt
¼ oz/8 grams fresh yeast
2½ fl oz/75 ml oz lukewarm water
1 egg, well beaten
14 oz/400 grams flour

Combine the milk, shortening, sugar and salt. Cool until lukewarm. Add yeast softened in lukewarm water, then add the egg. Gradually stir in the flour to form a soft dough. Beat vigorously. Cover and let it rise in a warm place (82°F/28°C) until doubled in bulk, about 2 hours.

Turn out onto a lightly floured surface. Roll the dough ¼ inch/½ cm thick. Cut with a biscuit cutter. Brush with melted butter. Make a crease across each. Fold so the top half slightly overlaps. Press the edges together at the crease. Place close together on a lightly greased baking tin. Bake at 400°F/200°C/gas mark 6 about 15 minutes. Serve hot.

Refrigerator Rolls

Makes 36 rolls

½ oz/15 grams active dried yeast
18 fl oz/500 ml warm water
4 oz/115 grams sugar
1 tablespoon salt
1½ lb/700 grams plain flour
1 egg
2 oz/60 grams soft shortening, butter or
    margarine

Sprinkle the yeast over warm water, stirring until dissolved. Stir in the sugar, salt and ½ the flour with an electric mixer on medium speed for 2 minutes, or by hand until the mixture is smooth. Beat in the egg and shortening and mix in the remaining flour with your hands or a spoon until the dough is easy to handle. Shape the dough into a ball and place it in a lightly greased bowl, turn the greased side of the dough up. Cover tightly with aluminium foil, or place the bowl in a plastic bag.

Put the dough in the refrigerator and let rise at least 2 hours, or until doubled in bulk. Punch down the dough and shape into individual rolls. Brush the tops with melted butter; cover and let rise in a warm place until nearly doubled, about 1½ hours. Bake in a 400°F/200°C/gas mark 6 oven 12 to 15 minutes.

The dough may be kept up to 5 days in the refrigerator with 45°F/6°C or lower temperature. Punch down the dough everyday until you use it.

Plain Muffins

Makes 12 muffins

4 oz/115 grams stoneground flour
4 oz/115 grams flour
1 teaspoon salt
2½ teaspoons baking powder
½ pint/¼ l milk
2 eggs, well beaten
1 oz/30 grams shortening, melted

Place the dry ingredients in a large mixing bowl. Combine the milk and eggs in a smaller bowl and add to the dry ingredients. Stir in the shortening until all ingredients are well blended. Drop by spoonfuls into 2-inch/5-cm paper baking cases, filling them about ½ full. Bake at 400°F/200°C/gas mark 6 about 20 minutes.

Serve the muffins with hot butter and your favourite jam or jelly, or break the muffins in half, cover with syrup and eat with a fork.

Cottage Cheese Muffins

Makes 12 to 15 muffins

1 lb/450 grams cottage cheese
2 tablespoons soured cream
2 oz/60 grams sugar
4 eggs
4 oz/115 grams packet biscuit mix
1 teaspoon vanilla essence

Beat all the ingredients except the eggs until smooth, either in a blender or a food processor. Add the eggs one at a time and continue beating until smooth.

Pour the mixture into paper baking cases until they are ½ full. Bake at 350°F/180°C/gas mark 4 for 45–50 minutes.

Bilberry Muffins

Makes 12 muffins

4 oz/115 grams butter
8 oz/225 grams plus 2 teaspoons sugar
2 eggs
8 oz/225 grams flour
2 teaspoons baking powder
½ teaspoon salt
¼ pint/140 ml milk
1 lb/450 grams fresh or frozen bilberries
1 teaspoon vanilla essence

On the low speed of an electric mixer, cream the butter and 4 oz/115 grams of the sugar until fluffy. Add the eggs, one at a time, and mix until blended. Sift the flour, baking powder and salt together. Mix the dry ingredients with the butter mixture alternately with the milk. Add the bilberries and vanilla essence.

Pile the mixture high in paper baking cases and sprinkle with the remaining 2 teaspoons of sugar. Bake at 375°F/190°C/gas mark 5 for 30 minutes.

Jam Topped Slices

French Buns

Makes 32 buns

2½ oz/75 grams margarine or butter
1 pint/½ l milk
½ oz/15 grams compressed yeast
2 teaspoons salt
1½ lb/700 grams plain flour

Melt the butter in a pan. Add the milk and allow the mixture to become finger temperature (100°F/38°C). Mix the yeast in a small amount of the milk mixture and then pour over the rest of the milk. Add most of the flour and the salt. Work into a smooth dough and let rise in a draught free place for about 40 minutes.

Knead the dough on a board. Divide the dough into 4 parts. Roll each dough piece out into a long roll and cut each roll into 8 pieces. Dip the pieces in the rest of the flour. Place them on a greased baking sheet. Let rise for about 30 minutes.

Bake in a hot oven, 425°F/220°C/gas mark 7 to 450°F/230°C/gas mark 8, for about 8 to 10 minutes. Serve with marmalade or jam.

Almond Muffins

Makes about 12 muffins

2 boiled, cold potatoes
2½ oz/75 grams almonds
2½ oz/75 grams soft butter or margarine
5 oz/140 grams sugar
2 eggs
Grated peel of ½ lemon
2½ oz/75 grams flour
1½ teaspoons baking powder

Grate the potatoes. Grind the almonds (they do not need to be scalded and peeled). Mix the butter and sugar together until light. Add the eggs, one at a time, and beat vigorously. Carefully stir in the potatoes, the almonds, the lemon peel and the flour which has been mixed with the baking powder.

Fill paper baking cases until about ½ full and bake at 400°F/200°C/gas mark 6 until they feel dry, about 15 minutes.

You can also brush melted cooking chocolate on top of the muffins and place a piece of almond in the chocolate. Do this shortly before serving.

Pecan Wholemeal Muffins

Makes 12 muffins

4 oz/115 grams flour
3 teaspoons baking powder
4 oz/115 grams sugar
1 teaspoon salt
4 oz/115 grams wholemeal flour
8 oz/225 grams pecan nuts, chopped

2 oz/60 grams butter, melted
½ pint/¼ l milk
2 eggs

Mix the flour, baking powder, sugar and salt together in a medium sized bowl. Stir in the wholemeal flour and nuts. Add the butter, milk and eggs to the dry ingredients and blend until thoroughly moistened. Spoon the mixture into paper baking cases. Bake at 375°F/190°C/gas mark 5 for 15 to 18 minutes.

Drop Doughnuts

Makes 36 doughnuts

2 oz/60 grams soft butter
8 oz/225 grams sugar
2 egg yolks, beaten
1 whole egg, beaten
1 lb/450 grams flour
2 teaspoons baking powder
¼ teaspoon nutmeg
½ teaspoon bicarbonate of soda
8 fl oz/220 ml buttermilk
Caster sugar

Cream the butter and sugar. Stir in the egg yolks and whole egg and blend. In a separate bowl, sift all the dry ingredients together except caster sugar. Add to the creamed mixture, alternating with buttermilk. Stir to mix all ingredients.

Cook by dropping spoonfuls of dough into 375°F/190°C/gas mark 5 deep fat. Fry a few at a time, to keep the fat temperature constant. Turn to brown on all sides. Drain on kitchen towel and sprinkle with caster sugar.

Cranberry Muffins

Makes 10 muffins

7 oz/200 grams flour
5 oz/140 grams sugar
2½ teaspoons baking powder
1 teaspoon salt
1 egg, well beaten
4 fl oz/110 ml milk
3 oz/85 grams melted shortening
8 oz/225 grams cranberries, chopped
3 oz/85 grams sugar

Mix the flour with 2 oz/60 grams of the sugar, the baking powder and salt. Combine the egg and milk and add all at once to the flour mixture. Add the shortening and stir only until the dry ingredients are dampened. (Mixture will be lumpy.)

Sprinkle the cranberries with the remaining sugar and stir in. Spoon into paper baking cases, filling each about ½ full. Bake at 400°F/200°C/gas mark 6 for 25 to 30 minutes, or until done.

Lemon Muffins

Makes about 15 muffins

2 eggs
3 oz/85 grams sugar
4 fl oz/110 ml single cream
2 oz/60 grams melted butter or margarine, cooled
Grated peel and juice of ½ lemon
5 oz/140 grams flour
1½ teaspoons baking powder

Beat the eggs and sugar together until light. Add the cream, the cooled, melted butter and the peel and juice of the lemon. Mix the flour with the baking powder and add it to the other ingredients.

Spoon the mixture into paper muffin cups. Fill them about ½ full, since they rise during baking. Bake at 400°F/200°C/gas mark 6 to 425°F/220°C/gas mark 7 for about 10 minutes. When serving the muffins, icing sugar may be sprinkled on top.

American Muffins are now very popular—here are some classic variations:

Raisin Muffins with Cardamom: Instead of lemon, use 6 oz/170 grams raisins and ½ teaspoon ground cardamom, which is mixed with the flour before it is added to the mixture.

Apple Muffins: 2 peeled, grated apples are mixed in instead of the lemon.

Chocolate Muffins: 4 oz/115 grams dark cooking chocolate is used instead of the lemon.

Orange Muffins with Wholemeal Flour: Instead of the lemon, use the grated peel of 1 orange. Substitute half the cream with orange juice and half the flour with wholemeal flour. For an added touch, ice the muffins with icing sugar mixed with a little orange juice and sprinkle candied orange peel on top.

Sweet Milk Doughnuts

Makes 48 doughnuts

18 oz/500 grams flour, sifted
3½ teaspoons baking powder
1 teaspoon salt
½ teaspoon ground nutmeg
¼ teaspoon ground cinnamon
3 eggs, beaten
1 teaspoon vanilla essence
6 oz/170 grams sugar
1½ oz/45 grams soft butter or margarine
4 fl oz/110 ml milk
Fat for frying

Sift the dry ingredients together. Beat the eggs, vanilla and sugar. Mix in the butter. Add the milk and sifted dry ingredients alternately. Mix into a soft dough.

Turn the dough onto a lightly floured board. Knead lightly for 30 seconds, then roll out ½-inch/1-

cm thick. Cut with a floured doughnut cutter. Remove the trimmings.

Lift each doughnut on a spatula and carefully place into deep, hot fat (375°F/190°C/). Put as many into the fat at a time as can be turned easily. Cook until browned and drain on kitchen towel.

Flannel Cakes

Makes 35 to 40 cakes

½ pint/¼ l milk, scalded
1 oz/30 grams butter
½ pint/¼ l cold milk
2 egg yolks, beaten
¼ oz/8 grams fresh yeast, dissolved in lukewarm water
½ teaspoon salt
1 lb/450 grams flour
2 egg whites, beaten

Melt the butter in the scalded milk, then add the cold milk. Add the egg yolks and the yeast in lukewarm water. Sift the salt with the flour and add enough to the milk mixture to make a stiff batter. Let it rise, covered, in a warm place overnight.

In the morning, add the egg whites. If additional flour is needed, add and set the bowl aside to rise a second time. Fry on a hot flat griddle until browned.

Apple Griddlecakes

Makes 30 small cakes

8 oz/225 grams plain flour, sifted
5 teaspoons baking powder
2 teaspoons salt
3 oz/85 grams sugar
1 teaspoon ground cinnamon
1 pint/½ l milk
3 oz/85 grams melted shortening or salad oil
2 eggs, beaten
8 oz/225 grams unpeeled apples, finely chopped

Sift the dry ingredients together. Add the milk, shortening and flour mixture to the eggs and beat until smooth. Fold in the apples.

Heat a lightly greased or heavy frying pan slowly until moderately hot. Test the temperature by sprinkling a few drops of water on it—if they splutter the temperature is right.

Pour on about 2½ fl oz/75 ml of mixture for each cake. Cook until the top is bubbly and edges dry, turn and brown on the other side.

Bilberry and Soured Cream Pancakes

Makes 12 pancakes

4 oz/115 grams plain flour, sifted
3 teaspoons baking powder
¼ teaspoon salt
1 oz/30 grams sugar

1 egg
½ pint/¼ l milk
2½ fl oz/75 ml soured cream
1 oz/30 grams butter, melted
4 oz/115 grams bilberries

Sift the dry ingredients together. Beat the egg, milk and cream together. Pour the milk mixture over the dry ingredients and blend with a rotary beater until just smooth. Stir in the butter. Fold in the berries.

Pour 2 tablespoons onto a hot griddle for each pancake. Brown on 1 side until golden. Turn and brown on the other side. If the pancakes brown too fast, lower the heat. Serve them hot with butter and maple syrup.

Raspberry and Soured Cream Waffles

Makes 4 waffles

8 oz/225 grams fresh raspberries
1 pint/½ l sweetened whipped cream
8 fl oz/220 ml strong black coffee
8 fl oz/220 ml milk
½ pint/¼ l soured cream
1 egg
2½ fl oz/75 ml vegetable oil
15 fl oz/425 ml pancake batter

Fold the raspberries into the whipped cream and chill.

Combine the coffee, milk, soured cream, egg and oil in a bowl. Blend well. Add the pancake mixture and beat with an electric mixer until smooth. Pour onto a hot waffle iron and cook until the steaming stops. Repeat with the remaining batter. Serve immediately with the whipped cream mixture.

4 oz/115 grams of raspberry jam can be substituted for fresh raspberries, if desired.

Stuffed Pancakes

Makes 12 6-inch/15-cm pancakes

2 eggs
4 oz/115 grams flour
1 pint/½ l milk
¼ teaspoon salt
½ oz/15 grams margarine

filling
8 oz/225 grams fresh mushrooms
12 oz/60 grams smoked ham
1 leek
1 oz/30 grams parsley, finely chopped
12 fl oz/350 ml soured cream
½ teaspoon salt
1 teaspoon French mustard
4 oz/115 grams freshly grated cheese

Make a smooth pancake batter by beating together the eggs, flour and 8 fl oz/220 ml of the milk. Then add the rest of the milk and the salt.

Make the pancakes, allowing 3 pancakes per person. As the pancakes are done, place one on top of the other. Preheat oven to 475°F/245°C/gas mark 9.

Rinse and slice the mushrooms. Cut the ham into small, fine cubes and the leek into thin slices and chop the parsley. Mix together the soured cream and mustard. Blend carefully as cream will become thin if stirred too vigorously. Fill the pancakes with the chopped ingredients and the soured cream, roll them up and place them on an ovenproof plate.

Cover with the grated cheese and bake on the top shelf of a 475°F/245°C/gas mark 9 oven for 10 to 12 minutes. The pancakes can be made several hours in advance.

Seven Kinds of American Muffin

Pecan Waffles

Makes 5 to 6 waffles

6 oz/170 grams flour
1½ oz/45 grams sugar
2½ teaspoons baking powder
½ teaspoon salt
3 eggs, separated, whites beaten stiff
15 fl oz/425 ml milk
2½ oz/75 grams butter, melted
2 oz/60 grams pecan nuts, chopped

Beat the egg yolks until thick and combine with the milk and butter. Add the dry ingredients. When the batter is well mixed, gently add the pecan nuts. Fold in the egg whites. Cook in a hot waffle iron. Serve with golden syrup.

Baked French Toast

Makes 12 pieces

6 oz/170 grams cornflake crumbs
2 eggs
8 fl oz/220 ml milk
½ teaspoon vanilla essence
6 slices bread, cut into halves diagonally
2 oz/60 grams margarine or butter, melted
Maple syrup or honey

Measure the cornflake crumbs into a shallow dish. Set aside.

In a second shallow dish, beat the eggs until foamy. Stir in the milk and vanilla. Dip the bread into the egg mixture, turning once and allowing time for both sides to take up the liquid. Coat evenly with the crumbs. Place in a single layer on a well greased baking sheet. Drizzle with melted margarine.

Bake in a 450°F/230°C/gas mark 8 oven about 10 minutes or until lightly browned. Serve with warm maple syrup or honey.

Stuffed Pancakes

Desserts

Apple Cobbler

6 to 8 servings

2 lb/900 grams peeled, sliced cooking apples
11 oz/315 grams sugar
Large pinch cinnamon
½ teaspoon almond essence (optional)
1 oz/30 grams butter
6 oz/170 grams sifted flour
2 teaspoons baking powder
½ teaspoon salt
2 oz/60 grams butter
1 egg, beaten
8 fl oz/220 ml milk

Place the apples in a 3-pint/1½-litre casserole. Sprinkle with 8 oz/225 grams sugar, cinnamon and almond essence. Dot with 1 oz/30 grams of butter.

Sift the flour, baking powder, sugar and salt into a mixing bowl. Cut in 2 oz/60 grams/60 grams butter until mixture forms a crumble.

Combine the egg and milk. Pour into dry ingredients. Stir just enough to combine and spoon over apples in baking dish.

Bake in a 425°F/220°C/gas mark 7 oven about 30 minutes, until browned. Serve with fresh cream, soured cream or ice cream as desired.

Apple Compote

4 servings

About 2–2½ lb/900–1125 grams apples
14 fl oz/400 ml water
5 oz/140 grams sugar
Juice from ½ lemon

Peel the apples and cut into wedges. Remove the cores. Place the apples in water immediately after they have been peeled so that they do not turn brown. Bring the water to the boil. Add the sugar and lemon juice. Simmer the apples until just soft.

Remove the apples. Place them in a bowl. Let the syrup boil for several more minutes. Pour the syrup over the compote and let it become cold. Serve the compote cold.

Baked Nut Apples

271

Baked Apple with Almond Hat

Baked Apple with Almond Hat

4 servings

pastry
8 oz/225 grams flour
1 oz/30 grams sugar
5 oz/140 grams margarine
1 egg
1 tablespoon cold water

filling
4 tasty small apples
3 oz/85 grams almond paste

when serving
1 pint/½ l ice cream
8 fl oz/220 grams whipped cream

Quickly cut and knead together all the pastry ingredients or spin in a food processor. Refrigerate.

Peel and core the apples.

Press the apple-corer into the almond paste to make an almond paste core with which to fill the apples. Roll out a bit of the almond paste and cut out 4 little rounds for the hats.

Divide the pastry into 4. Roll out each on grease-

Apple Compote

Baked Nut Apples

6 servings

6 apples
2 oz/60 grams butter or margarine
1½-2 oz/45–60 grams chopped nuts
2 oz/60 grams sugar

Core the apples. Cut off a piece of the core and place it back in the bottom. This is so the filling does not run out easily. Place the apples in a greased, ovenproof dish.

Mix the butter, nuts and sugar together. Fill the holes in the apples with the mixture. Bake at 425°F/220°C/gas mark 7 until the apples are soft, about 20 minutes.

Serve with lightly whipped cream, custard or ice cream.

Variation: To make Port Wine Apples, beat together 1½-2 oz/45–60 grams finely chopped marzipan and 2 oz/60 grams butter or margarine. Fill the holes from the apple cores with this mixture. Drip 2 to 3 tablespoons syrup over apples. Pour 2½ fl oz/75 ml port into the bottom of the dish. Bake the apples as described above. While baking, baste the apples several times with the port syrup.

Serve the apples hot with ice cold, lightly whipped cream or with ice cream that has been stirred until it is soft.

proof paper, with a flour-coated rolling pin. Cut the pastry around a plate. Put the apples in the middle of the 4 pastry rounds. Turn them upside down so that the pastry hangs down around the apples. Press the hats on the tops.

The preceding can be prepared in advance.

Bake the apples at 400°F/200°C/gas mark 6 on the lowest shelf. The almond paste can be protected with aluminium foil during the first 25 minutes of baking.

Whip the cream. Cut the ice cream into cubes. Mix together and serve.

Apple Puff Pastries

10 pastries

18 oz/500 grams frozen puff pastry
5 oz/140 grams sugar
1 to 2 teaspoons cinnamon
2 lb/900 grams frozen apple slices, or 4 to 6 apples, depending on size
1 egg, beaten
Greaseproof paper for 2 baking sheets

Take the puff pastry out of the freezer and defrost at least 15 minutes.

Mix together the sugar and cinnamon. Sprinkle ½ tablespoon of the mixture evenly over each piece of puff pastry. Press in the mixture when the pieces are rolled out into about 4-inch/10-cm long rectangles. Turn over the rectangles so that the sugar-cinnamon mixture is on the bottom. Place the apple slices (close together) in two rows across, with a slight space between the two rows, on half of the rectangle. Sprinkle ½ tablespoon sugar and cinnamon mixture on each. Brush with the beaten egg along the edges and between the two apple rows. Fold half of the pastry over the apple covered half. Cut between the rows of apples. Press the edges together with a fork. Two pastries are made from each rectangle. Place them on baking sheets that have been covered with greaseproof paper. They can stand until it is time to bake them.

Brush with egg. Bake in the centre of a preheated 400°F/200°C/gas mark 6 oven for 15 to 20 minutes.

These taste best when fresh, but they can be reheated.

Silver Apples

4 servings

4 ripe cooking apples
½ lemon
8 fl oz/220 ml apricot purée
4 tablespoons water
2 oz/60 grams sugar
A few drops vanilla essence
4 drops bitter almond oil
4 pieces aluminium foil

Peel the apples. Rub them with the lemon so the fruit will not discolour.

Boil the apricot purée together with the water and sugar until thickened. Add the vanilla essence and the bitter almond oil.

Shape the pieces of aluminium foil into deep bowls. Place one apple in each and divide the sauce over the apples. Fold and close the aluminium bowls well. Bake in a 425°F/220°C/gas mark 7 oven for about 25 minutes.

Serve with vanilla ice cream, if desired.

Variation: Pears can be baked in the same way.

Tosca Apples

4 servings

4 medium apples or 6 to 8 small apples
2 pints/1¼ l water
3–6 oz/85–170 grams sugar
Shreds of lemon peel

tosca batter
3½ oz/100 grams margarine
4 oz/115 grams sugar
1 oz/30 grams flour
2 tablespoons milk
3 oz/85 grams sliced almonds

If the apples are soft they do not need to be boiled first. Peel, core and halve them. Otherwise, boil the apples in a syrup made from the water, sugar and shreds of lemon peel.

Place the apples in batches in the syrup and let them simmer until partially soft, 5 to 10 minutes. Remove the apple halves with a draining spoon. Melt the margarine for the tosca. Stir in the sugar, flour and milk. Let the batter come just to a simmering point but do not let it boil. Mix in the almonds.

Place the apples close together on a baking sheet. Divide the tosca on the tops. Bake at 425°F/220°C/gas mark 7 for 10 to 15 minutes, until the tosca has become an attractive, golden brown.

Serve the apples warm with cold whipped cream, preferably flavoured with a dash of rum and finely grated lemon peel.

Silver Apples

Apple Surprise

2 or 3 servings

3 cooking apples
2½ oz/75 grams raisins
12 fl oz/350°F/180°C/gas mark 4 ml soured cream or yoghurt, chilled
3 to 4 tablespoons frozen orange juice, partially thawed
2 tablespoons roasted oatmeal flakes
Brown sugar

Peel and finely grate the apples. Mix the grated apples and the raisins with the chilled soured cream. Quickly fold in the partially thawed orange juice (it should be slightly icy) with the soured cream mixture. Spoon into tall glasses. Sprinkle with roasted oatmeal flakes and brown sugar. Serve immediately.

Fried Bananas

4 to 6 servings

1 oz/30 grams flour
1 teaspoon cinnamon
6 bananas, sliced lengthwise
About 2 oz/60 grams shortening

Mix the flour and cinnamon together. Thoroughly coat each piece of banana with the mixture. If bananas are very long, you may prefer to quarter them.

Heat the shortening in a medium sized frying pan. Brown the floured bananas. Slowly turn them once. Remove them to a heated serving dish. Sprinkle with sugar.

Rum Bananas

4 servings

4 firm ripe bananas
2 oz/60 grams butter
2 oz/60 grams brown sugar
Lemon juice
¼ pint/140 ml rum

Peel the bananas and cut them into halves lengthwise.

Melt the butter in an ovenproof casserole and add the banana halves. Sprinkle with the sugar and bake in a preheated 450°F/245°C/gas mark 8 oven about 10 minutes, until the bananas are thoroughly hot and the sugar is melted. Sprinkle with lemon juice and baste. Return to the oven for 2 minutes.

Warm the rum and pour it over the bananas. Flambé and serve immediately.

Cherry Cobbler

8 servings

4 oz/115 grams butter or margarine
6 oz/170 grams sugar
1 egg, beaten
4 fl oz/110 ml milk
8 oz/225 grams flour
2 teaspoons baking powder
½ teaspoon salt
2 tins cherry pie filling

Cream butter and sugar. Add egg and mix well. Blend in milk.

Combine the dry ingredients and add to the butter mixture. Spread half the mixture in a greased 8-inch/20-cm diameter deep pie dish. Cover with 1½ tins of pie filling. Spread with remaining mixture. Top with remaining filling. Bake in a 375°F/190°C/gas mark 5 oven 30 minutes or until done. Serve warm with single, or whipped double cream, or with vanilla ice cream.

Tosca Apples

Cranberry Apple Crisp

6 to 8 servings

5 or 6 medium apples, peeled, cored and sliced
1 lb/450 grams whole fresh or frozen cranberries
2 tablespoons honey
4 oz/115 grams butter or margarine
8 oz/225 grams rolled oats
2 oz/60 grams wholemeal flour
6 oz/170 grams brown sugar
4 oz/115 grams chopped nuts
½ teaspoon vanilla essence

Combine the apple slices and cranberries. Drizzle with honey and toss lightly to coat.

With pastry blender cut the butter into the oats, flour and brown sugar. Mix until crumbly. Stir in the nuts and vanilla essence.

Place the apples and cranberries in a greased 12 × 8-inch/30 × 20-cm baking dish. Top with the oat mixture. Bake at 350°F/180°C/gas mark 4 about 50 minutes or until browned and bubbly.

Serve warm, with whipped cream if desired.

Berry-Filled Melon

Floating Grapes

4 servings

1½ lb/700 grams large green grapes
8 fl oz/220 ml water
4 oz/115 grams sugar
1 tablespoon aromatic honey
Grated peel of ½ lemon
8 fl oz/220 ml brandy
4 fl oz/110 ml Cointreau or similar orange liqueur

Prepare this dessert at least 24 hours in advance.

Cut the grapes in half and remove the seeds, using a little pointed knife. Divide the grapes among 4 tall glasses.

Boil a syrup of water and sugar. Let cool. Add honey, lemon peel, brandy and liqueur. Stir and pour over the grapes in the glasses so that they are almost totally covered. Place the glasses in the refrigerator until it is time to serve them the following day.

Serve with chilled, whipped cream and slivers of almonds.

Fresh Blackberry Cobbler

6 servings

4 oz/115 grams sugar
½ oz/15 grams cornflour
2 lb/900 grams blackberries
1 teaspoon lemon juice
4 oz/115 grams flour
1 oz/30 grams sugar
1½ teaspoons baking powder
½ teaspoon salt
1½ oz/45 grams shortening
¼ pint/140 ml milk

Blend 4 oz/115 sugar and the cornflour in a medium saucepan. Stir in the blackberries and lemon juice. Cook, stirring constantly, until mixture thickens and boils. Boil and stir 1 minute. Pour into ungreased 4-pint/2¼- litre casserole and place in oven while preparing topping.

Measure flour, remaining sugar, baking powder and salt in bowl. Add shortening and milk. Mix until dough forms a ball. Drop dough by 6 spoonfuls onto hot fruit. Bake, uncovered, in a preheated 400°F/200°C/gas mark 6 oven 25 to 30 minutes or until done. Serve warm.

Apple Surprise

Melon and Mixed Berries

1 serving

½ small honeydew melon
3 to 4 tablespoons red berries, for example wild
    strawberries and currants (preferably 2 kinds)
1 teaspoon sugar
Several drops Calvados

Cut the melon in half and fill with the berries. Sprinkle the sugar on top. Moisten with a few drops of Calvados.

Melon Basket with Fruit Salad

Quantity varies

1 watermelon
Mixed fresh fruit
Nuts (optional)
Port

Make a melon basket by cutting out a watermelon (see illustration). Spoon out the flesh, removing as many of the seeds as possible. Cut the flesh into cubes.

Make a fruit salad with fresh fruit, for example; oranges, apples, pears, pineapple, kiwi fruit, bananas, strawberries, mango etc. Even nuts can be added.

Dash a little port over the salad before serving. Serve with ice cream.

Fruit with Honeydew Sauce

Quantity varies

1 honeydew melon
Strawberries
Pears
Bananas
Ice cream (optional)

Cut a lid off the melon. Dig out all the seeds, then the flesh, with a spoon. Press the flesh through a fine strainer and use the liquid for the melon sauce. Use the melon shell as a bowl from which to serve the fruit salad or ice cream.

Fill the melon shell with strawberries, pears and bananas. Serve with the melon sauce.

Variation: Spoon ice cream into the melon boat. Pour the melon sauce over the ice cream.

Fruit with Honeydew Sauce   *Floating Grapes*

Orange Compôte with Cream

4 to 6 servings

6 oranges
Juice from 3 oranges
2½ fl oz/75 ml Tia Maria
Sugar
½–1 oz/15–30 grams cornflour
Water
Double cream or soured cream

Peel the six oranges with a knife so that all the white membranes are removed. Break into segments. Place them in a bowl. Pour the juice from three of the oranges into a pan. Pour in the Tia Maria and a little sugar, if necessary.

Mix the cornflour with a little water.

Bring the orange juice to the boil. Thicken with a little cornflour until the juice has the right consistency. Adjust the flavour, if desired, with a little more liqueur. Mix with the orange segments.

Serve the compote warm or cold with the cream.

Orange Compôte with Cream

Mango Purée

1 serving

1 well ripened mango
2 tablespoons cottage cheese

Peel the mango and take out the flesh with a small sharp knife. Mix the fruit and cottage cheese into a smooth purée. Use an electric blender or press it through a sieve.

Ice Cream Filled Oranges

4 servings

4 oranges
Vanilla ice cream
2 to 3 tablespoons frozen orange juice
2 egg whites
2 oz/60 grams sugar
Several drops of rum, brandy or orange liqueur

Cut a lid off the oranges. Spoon out the fruit. (Save the juice to drink.)

Beat the ice cream until soft. Flavour with the frozen orange juice. Fill the orange skins with the ice cream. Place in the freezer for several hours so that the ice cream becomes frozen again.

Beat the egg whites until stiff. Stir in the sugar and liqueur. Top the oranges with the meringue. Bake for about 4 minutes in a very hot oven until the meringue has become golden brown. Serve immediately.

Orange Parfait

4 to 8 servings

4 oranges
4 egg yolks
6 oz/170 grams sugar
12 fl oz/350 ml double cream
2 to 3 egg whites

Cut a lid off the oranges, or cut them in half. Dig out the flesh with a teaspoon and strain it, keeping the juice.

Beat the egg yolks until light and fluffy with 4 oz/ 115 grams of the sugar. Whip the cream until firm then fold it into the egg yolk mixture together with about 4 fl oz/110 ml of the orange juice.

Fill the oranges and freeze them.

When it is time to serve, make the meringue "hats." Preheat the oven to 475°F/245°C/gas mark 9. Remove the oranges from the freezer about 40 minutes in advance so that they are not completely frozen.

Beat the egg whites in a clean bowl with a clean beater. Add 1 oz/30 grams sugar per egg white and continue to beat until the whites become stiff peaks.

Pipe the meringue with a forcing bag or spoon it into the oranges and place them in the middle of the oven for 1 to 2 minutes, until the meringue has become golden brown.

Melon Basket with Fruit Salad

Sorbet Filled Pears in Caramel Sauce

Baked Ginger Peaches

6 servings

1½ lb/700 grams tinned peach halves
2 oz/60 grams brown sugar
2 teaspoons diced preserved ginger
1 oz/30 grams butter

Put the peaches, cut side up, into a shallow baking dish. Add peach syrup. Sprinkle with sugar and ginger. Dot with butter. Bake in a 350°F/180°C/gas mark 4 oven until brown, 15 to 20 minutes.

Fresh Peach Crisp

6 servings

8 or 9 fresh peaches
4 oz/115 grams flour
½ teaspoon cinnamon
8 oz/225 grams sugar
4 oz/115 grams soft butter
Single cream

Peel and slice the peaches. Place in a lightly buttered 8-inch/20-cm square baking dish.

Orange Parfait

Sift together the flour, cinnamon and sugar in a bowl. Cut in the butter with a pastry blender or 2 knives until the mixture resembles coarse breadcrumbs. Sprinkle mixture evenly over peaches. Bake 45 to 50 minutes in a 375°F/190°C/gas mark 5 oven or until the topping is golden brown. Serve warm with cream, if desired.

Baked Pears

6 servings

6 medium pears
6 whole cloves
15 fl oz/425 ml wine
6 oz/170 grams sugar
8 fl oz/220 ml water

Pierce each pear tail with a clove. Place unpeeled pears in a deep casserole.

Combine the remaining ingredients and pour over the pears. Cover and bake at 400°F/200°C/gas mark 6 for about 30 minutes or until done. Baste occasionally.

Ice Cream Filled Oranges

Sorbet Filled Pears in Caramel Sauce

4 servings

1¼–1½ pints/700–850 ml water
5 oz/140 grams sugar
2 or 3 thin slices of lemon
4 ripe pears (not too soft)
15 fl oz/425 ml unsweetened whipped cream
4–8 fl oz/110–220 ml orange sorbet

caramel sauce
8 fl oz/220 ml double cream or 4 fl oz/110 ml
    double cream plus 4 fl oz/110 ml soured
    cream
2½ oz/75 grams sugar
3 tablespoons syrup
1½ teaspoons cocoa (unsweetened)
½ teaspoon vanilla essence

Make a syrup by boiling the water with the sugar and lemon slices.

Peel the pears. Remove the core with a corer so that a hole is left down the middle of the fruit. Drip a little lemon juice over the pears. Place the pears in the boiling syrup and cover. Boil the fruit until done.

Pears on Almond Crusts with Caramel Sauce

Cooking time can vary between 5 to 15 minutes, depending on how ripe the pears are and the kind used. Test with a needle or toothpick. The pears should still be slightly firm without being hard on the inside. Put the pears and syrup in the refrigerator and leave to cool.

Make the caramel sauce while the pears are cooling. Mix all the sauce ingredients together in a pan. Bring to the boil, beating constantly. Boil for 3 to 4 minutes. Cool the sauce, continuing to beat, by setting the pot in a pan of cold water.

When it is time to serve the pears, whip the cream. Divide it between 4 individual dessert bowls. Set a pear on each mound of cream.

Stir the sorbet until soft. Place it in a heavy forcing bag. Press the sorbet out into the hole of the pears so that they are well filled. Spoon the caramel sauce over the pears and around the cream. Serve immediately. Serve any remaining sauce in a separate dish. A white port goes well with this dessert.

Ice Cream Filled Pineapple

4 servings

2 small pineapples, divided lengthwise
2 tablespoons Grand Marnier or other liqueur
14 fl oz/400 ml vanilla ice cream
8 fl oz/220 ml whipping cream
8 to 10 crushed walnuts

Spoon out the pineapple flesh. Cut it into cubes, Place the cubes in the pineapple shell. Drip Grand Marnier over the cubes. Fill with vanilla ice cream. Garnish with whipped cream and walnuts.

Pineapple Dessert

8 servings

5 or 6 egg yolks
5 oz/140 grams sugar
4 oranges
Ice cream, thawed
1 pineapple
Chocolate shavings

Beat the egg yolks and sugar until fluffy.

Carve out the orange flesh with a knife. Add the orange meat and juices to the egg mixture. Fold in thawed ice cream. Stir until smooth. Pour the mixture into a ring mould. Freeze for 8 to 10 hours.

Turn the dessert out onto a serving tray. Garnish with peeled and sliced fresh pineapple. Decorate with chocolate shavings. Cover the hole with the top of the pineapple.

Ice Cream Filled Pineapple

Combine the water, sugar and cinnamon. Bring to the boil. Simmer the pears in the syrup until they have become soft. Let them thoroughly cool in the syrup.

Mix the almond crust ingredients together. Spread the mixture into thin rounds on a greased and floured baking sheet, so that they are about 6 inches/ 15 cms in diameter. When using greaseproof paper, draw rings on the paper and fill these rings. Bake in a hot 425°F/220°C/gas mark 7 oven until the crusts are brown but not burned. While they are still warm, carefully loosen them from the baking sheet, using a sharp knife. Shape them into bowls by placing them over a bowl, or similar shaped object, to cool.

Boil all the caramel sauce ingredients together. Do not boil too long or the sauce will be too thick when it cools. Beat until it becomes cold.

Place a little vanilla ice cream on each almond crust. Push a pear down into each ice cream and pour a little sauce over them. Pour the rest of the sauce into a serving dish and serve separately.

Strawberries with Rum and Lime Cream

8 servings

2 lb/900 grams fresh strawberries
5 tablespoons undiluted lime squash
5 tablespoons rum
5 oz/140 grams sugar
8 oz/220 grams double cream, whipped
2 oz/60 grams sugar
2 tablespoons rum

Wash, hull and slice the strawberries.

Mix the lime squash with 5 tablespoons rum and 5 oz/140 grams sugar. Pour over the strawberries. Mix gently. Cover and marinate in a refrigerator 3 to 4 hours.

Whip the cream with 2 oz/60 grams sugar and 2 tablespoons rum until thick and creamy but not stiff. Serve the strawberries and cream separately.

Strawberry Bowl

6 to 8 servings

1½ lb/700 grams strawberries, sliced, sweetened to taste
2 oz/60 grams melted butter or margarine
1 packet sponge fingers
2 oz/60 grams sugar mixed with 1½ teaspoons ground cinnamon
4 oz/115 grams pecan nuts, chopped
½ pint/¼ l whipping cream, whipped, sweetened with 2 oz/60 grams sugar

Chill strawberries about ½ hour.

Pears on Almond Crusts with Caramel Sauce

4 servings

4 pears
Lemon
1 pint/½ l water
10 oz/285 grams sugar
¼ teaspoon vanilla essence
1 stick of cinnamon

almond crusts
1 egg
2 egg whites
5 oz/140 grams sugar
5 oz/140 grams grated almonds
2 oz/60 grams melted butter
1 oz/30 grams flour

caramel sauce
4 fl oz/110 ml cream
2½ oz/75 grams sugar
1 tablespoon syrup
1 teaspoon cocoa
¼ teaspoon vanilla essence

Peel the pears. Rub them with lemon.

Meanwhile, brush a baking sheet with melted butter. Halve each sponge finger lengthways. Lightly brush both sides with butter. Dip both sides into the sugar and cinnamon mixture. Press the pecan nuts into the sponge.

Line a large serving bowl with the fingers. Spoon half of the strawberries over them. Spoon whipped cream over the strawberries. Spoon remaining strawberries over cream and top with any remaining sponge fingers. Serve immediately.

Strawberry Snow

6 servings

1½ lb/700 grams fresh strawberries
Sugar to taste
4 egg whites
8 fl oz/220 ml whipping cream

Sprinkle the strawberries with sugar to taste and crush the berries. Keep 6 whole strawberries for decoration.

Beat the egg whites until stiff. Beat the whipping cream until stiff.

Flambéed Fruit

Meringue Twist with Fresh Berries

Gently mix together the berries, whipped cream and stiff egg whites. Spoon this into dessert bowls. Put 1 whole strawberry on top of each serving.

Flambéed Fruit

6 to 8 servings

14 oz/400 grams tinned peach halves
14 oz/400 grams tinned apricot halves
14 oz/400 grams tinned cherries
10 oz/285 grams tinned kiwi fruit
6 oz/170 grams redcurrant jelly
8 fl oz/225 grams brandy

Drain the fruits well, using a sieve. Save the juices for making a fruit cup or something similar. Cut the peach and apricot halves in half.

Melt the jelly in a chafing pan over low heat. Do not let it boil. Add all the fruit. Cover and heat until the fruit is piping hot.

Place the chafing dish over a flame on the table.

Carefully heat the brandy and pour it over the fruit. Flambé and stir gently. Have a pan nearby to smother the flame should it become too high. Serve the flambéed fruit immediately.

Meringue Twist with Fresh Berries

12 servings

12 fl oz/350 ml whipping cream
Approximately 12 small meringues (bought or
    homemade)
Blackberries
Raspberries

Whip the cream. Alternate the whipped cream, meringues and berries in a dish. Serve immediately.

Fruit and Mint Cup

6 servings

8 oz/225 grams banana slices
1 tablespoon lemon juice
8 oz/225 grams fresh strawberries, halved
4 oz/115 grams seedless grapes, whole
6 oz/170 grams pineapple chunks, drained
¼ pint/140 ml mint syrup
Few sprigs of mint leaves

Coat banana slices with lemon juice.
Lightly mix fruits in a large bowl. Pour syrup over
fruits. Chill about 30 minutes. Garnish with mint
leaves and serve immediately.

Bread and Almond Pudding

4 to 6 servings

3 oz/85 grams raisins
About 4 fl oz/110 ml inexpensive white wine
    (preferably sweet)
6 oz/170 grams almonds
2 eggs
5 oz/140 grams sugar
8 fl oz/220 ml milk
8 fl oz/220 ml double cream
About 1 slice white bread, crust removed, cut
    into cubes
1½ teaspoons cinnamon
1 teaspoon nutmeg

Soak the raisins for about 30 minutes in the wine.
If the raisins are dry, warm the mixture slightly. Strain
off the wine (save this for another recipe).
Scald, peel, dry and grind the almonds.
Beat the eggs and sugar together until white and
light. Add the milk, cream and remaining ingredients.
Blend well. Pour into a greased round dish or into
individual dishes. Stir with a fork so the raisins do
not sink to the bottom. Bake in a pan of water in a
350°F/180°C/gas mark 4 oven for about 25 minutes
or until the pudding has become firm and has a
golden brown crust on the top.
Serve hot or warm with chilled whipped cream,
grated orange peel and a dash of orange liqueur.

Bread and Almond Pudding

Cloud Pudding

4 to 6 servings

caramel
6 oz/170 grams sugar
2 tablespoons boiling water

for "cloud"
6 egg whites
5 oz/140 grams sugar

decoration
1 lb/450 grams redcurrants or other berries
8 fl oz/220 ml whipping cream

To prepare the caramel: place the sugar in a clean,
dry frying pan and let it melt over low heat while
stirring. When the sugar has melted and is light
brown, add the water. Stir and pour the caramel mixture into a 3-pint/1½-litre ring mould. Twist and
scoop up the mixture with a spoon so the mould is
covered with caramel all the way up to the edge.
Preheat oven to 400°F/200°C/gas mark 6. Place a
roasting tin filled with water on the bottom rack of
the oven.
To prepare the "cloud": whip the egg whites and
sugar into a stiff foam in a clean bowl with a dry,
clean beater.

Fill the mould with the foam. Place it in the water-filled tin in the oven at 400°F/200°C/gas mark 6 for 10 minutes. Decrease the oven temperature to 250°F/120°C/gas mark ¼ and let it bake for another 2 hours. Take out the mould. Loosen around the inner and outer edges with a knife. Turn out onto a plate. Pour the caramel sauce over the mould. Decorate with berries and whipped cream

This can be served immediately, or after it has cooled. It can be made in advance and kept on a plate until serving time.

Traditional Noodle Pudding

7 servings

2½ oz/75 grams butter
1¼ lb/565 grams peeled cooking apples cut into ½-inch/1-cm slices
7 oz/200 grams /200 grams sugar
2½ oz/75 grams dark brown sugar
2 teaspoons ground cinnamon
2 tablespoons finely chopped walnuts
1¼ lb/565 grams drained, cooked flat pasta
¼ pint/140 ml soured cream
10 oz/285 grams creamed cottage cheese, sieved
½ teaspoon salt
2 eggs, well beaten

Melt 1½ oz/45 grams butter in a heavy saucepan. Add sliced apples. Sprinkle with 3 oz/85 grams sugar. Stir until apples are completely coated with butter. Cover and cook over low heat about 8 minutes.

Mix brown sugar, ½ teaspoon cinnamon and nuts well. Spread the mixture evenly over the bottom of a well-greased 8 × 8 × 2-inch/20 × 20 × 5-cm tin.

Add 1 oz/30 grams butter to the noodles and toss until well coated. Add soured cream, cottage cheese, salt, eggs, cooked apples and their liquid and 2 oz/60 grams sugar which has been mixed with 1 teaspoon cinnamon. Blend well. Put the noodle mixture over brown sugar layer in the tin. Bake in a moderate 325°F/163°C/gas mark 3 oven for 50 minutes or until done. Immediately sprinkle a mixture of 2 oz/60 grams sugar and ½ teaspoon cinnamon over top. Serve at once.

Cloud Pudding

Chocolate Creams

Plum Pudding

4 puddings

12 oz/345 grams dried currants
1 lb/450 grams seedless raisins
1 lb/450 grams sultanas
6 oz/170 grams finely chopped candied mixed
    fruit peel
6 oz/170 grams finely chopped glacé cherries
8 oz/225 grams blanched flaked almonds
1 medium sized cooking apple, peeled, quartered,
    cored and coarsely chopped
1 small carrot, scraped and coarsely chopped
2 tablespoons finely grated orange peel
2 teaspoons finely grated lemon peel
8 oz/225 grams finely chopped beef suet
8 oz/225 grams flour
1 lb/450 grams fresh soft crumbs, made from
    wholemeal bread, ground in a blender or
    shredded with a fork
8 oz/225 grams dark brown sugar
1 teaspoon ground mixed spice
1 teaspoon salt
6 eggs
½ pint/¼ l brandy
4 fl oz/110 ml fresh orange juice
2½ fl oz/75 ml fresh lemon juice
¼ pint/140 ml brandy, to flambé (optional)

In a large, deep bowl combine the currants, seedless raisins, sultanas, candied fruit peel, cherries, almonds, apple, carrot, orange and lemon peel and beef suet, tossing them about with a spoon or your hands until well mixed. Stir in the flour, breadcrumbs, brown sugar, spice and salt.

In a separate bowl beat the eggs until frothy. Stir in ½ pint/¼ litre brandy and orange and lemon juice. Pour this mixture over the fruit mixture. Knead vigorously with both hands, then beat with a wooden spoon until all ingredients are blended. Place a damp tea towel over the bowl and refrigerate for at least 12 hours.

Spoon the mixture into 4 separate 2-pint/1¼-litre pudding basins, filling them to within 2 inches/5 cms of their tops. Cover each basin with a strip of buttered foil, turning the edges down and pressing the foil tightly around the sides to secure it. Place a damp cloth over each basin and tie it in place around the sides with a long piece of string. Bring 2 opposite corners of the cloth up to the top and knot them in the centre of the basin, then bring up the remaining 2 corners and knot them similarly. Place the basins in a large pan and pour in enough boiling water to come about three quarters of the way up their sides.

Raspberry Cream Baskets

Bring the water to the boil over a high heat and cover the pan tightly. Reduce the heat to its lowest point and steam the puddings for 8 hours. As the water in the pan boils away, replenish it with additional boiling water.

When the puddings are done, remove them from the water and let them cool to room temperature. Then remove the cloths and foil and re-cover the basins tightly with fresh foil. Refrigerate the puddings for at least 3 weeks before serving. Plum puddings can be kept up to a year in the refrigerator or other cool place.

To serve: place the basin in a pan and pour in enough boiling water to come about three quarters of the way up the sides of the basin. Bring to the boil over a high heat. Cover the pan. Reduce the heat to low and steam for 2 hours. Run a knife around the inside edges of the basin and place an inverted serving plate over it. Grasping the basin and plate firmly together, turn them over. The pudding should slide out.

To flambé the pudding: before you serve it, warm ¼ pint/140 ml of brandy in a small saucepan over low heat and flambé over the pudding.

Chocolate Creams

30 large or 50 small creams

7 oz/200 grams icing sugar
5 oz/140 grams cocoa
2½ oz/75 grams butter
4 fl oz/110 ml double cream
1½ tablespoons brandy
7–9 oz/200–255 grams dark cooking chocolate

Sift the icing sugar and cocoa together into a bowl. Crumble the soft butter into the mixture. Add the cream and brandy. Mix well, using an electric beater. In the beginning the mixture will seem impossibly dry, but after a while it will turn into a smooth dough. Refrigerate for several hours. Roll the chocolate into balls and refrigerate again.

Melt the cooking chocolate over a barely simmering double boiler. Roll the balls in the chocolate, using 2 forks. Place the balls on greaseproof paper and let the chocolate harden. This process has even better results if the balls are placed in a net while the chocolate is hardening.

Instead of using cooking chocolate the balls can be coated with cocoa.

Note: It is best to make these creams a week before eating. The proportions given in the recipe are important, so it is best not to double the recipe. Instead, make one batch at a time.

Pasha

Raspberry Cream Baskets

About 10 baskets

1 egg
2 oz/60 grams sugar
1 oz/30 grams flour
½ oz/15 grams/15 grams melted butter or margarine

filling
Whipped cream
Raspberries

Beat together the egg and sugar. Stir in the flour and butter. On a well greased baking sheet, spread the mixture into thin, round biscuits with ample space between them. Bake in a 400°F/200°C/gas mark 6 oven for about 4 minutes. Loosen them immediately from the baking sheet. Shape them into baskets, using a cup or glass—or form them into cones by rolling them up. The biscuits harden quickly, so do not make too many at a time. If the biscuits become hard before you have shaped them, just place them back in the oven for a few minutes.

Whip the cream and stir in a small amount of raspberries. Fill the bowls. Garnish with a raspberry. Serve immediately.

Unfilled baskets can be stored in a dry place.

Baked Custard

6 servings

1½ pints/850 ml milk
4 eggs
2½ oz/75 grams sugar
¼ teaspoon salt
1 teaspoon vanilla essence
Nutmeg or cinnamon (optional)

Heat milk until hot but not boiling.

Beat eggs in a large bowl. Add sugar and salt. Add milk slowly, stirring all the time. Mix in vanilla. Pour into a baking tin. Sprinkle with nutmeg or cinnamon. Bake at 300°F/150°C/gas mark 2 about 1 hour, until a knife stuck in the centre comes out clean.

Baked Caramel Custard

6 servings

6 oz/170 grams sugar
2 large eggs or 4 yolks
2½ oz/75 grams sugar
¼ teaspoon salt
½ teaspoon vanilla essence
1 pint/½ l milk, scalded

Butterscotch Ice Cream with Blackberry Liqueur

Melt 6 oz/170 grams sugar in a small saucepan, stirring constantly until pale brown. Divide the caramelized sugar among 6 ramekins. Turn these so the caramel will coat the sides. Let the sugar harden.

Meanwhile, mix eggs, 2½ oz/75 grams sugar, salt and vanilla. Add milk gradually. Strain into the prepared ramekins. Place them in a baking tin of hot water.

Bake in a 350°F/180°C/gas mark 4 oven 30 to 35 minutes or until a knife comes out clean. Remove from hot water immediately. Serve chilled and turned out.

Little Chocolate Pots

6 servings

15 fl oz/425 ml milk
1 pint/½ l chocolate chips
2 eggs
2 oz/60 grams sugar
Pinch of salt

Pour the milk into a heavy saucepan and bring to the boil.

Combine remaining ingredients in a blender or food-processor. Pour in the hot milk and blend at low speed 1 minute or until smooth. Pour into 6 small moulds. Chill at least 2 hours before serving. Garnish, if desired, with piped whipped cream, dusted with chopped nuts.

Butterscotch Ice Cream with Blackberry Liqueur

5 servings

2 oz/60 grams sugar
4 fl oz/110 ml hot water
8 fl oz/220 ml double cream
1 pint/½ l vanilla ice cream
Crème de mure or similar liqueur

Melt the sugar in a dry, clean frying pan. Remove the pan from the heat when the sugar has melted. Add the hot water. Beat and stir over heat until the sugar melts again. Then boil into a rich, thick sauce. Cool.

Beat the cream. Stir the cooled butterscotch sauce into the cream. Refrigerate the cream while cutting the ice cream into cubes.

Quickly, partially mix the ice cream and cream together. Place it in a ring mould or in individual glasses. Freeze for at least ½ hour or more.

Dip the mould into hot water before turning the ice cream out onto a serving plate. Serve with crème de mure.

Tropical Cup

Elderberry Parfait

Pasha

12 to 15 servings

2 lb/900 grams cottage cheese
8 oz/225 grams plus 1 oz/30 grams butter, room
   temperature
5 oz/140 grams icing sugar
3 egg yolks, beaten lightly
8 fl oz/220 ml double cream or soured cream
2½ oz/75 grams raisins or currants
2½ oz/75 grams red and green candied peel
2 oz/60 grams candied orange peel
2 oz/60 grams coarsely chopped walnuts or
   almonds

Mix the cottage cheese with the butter in a food processor, or strain it several times through a fine strainer, until the mixture becomes very smooth. Mix this with the sugar, egg yolks and cream. Add the raisins, candied and preserved peel and the nuts. The mixture should now be of a dropping consistency.

Cover the inside of a large funnel with a thin, damp cloth and fill it with the mixture. Add more of the mixture as the liquid slowly drains off. Fold the cloth over the mixture and place a saucer upside down on top. Place a weight on the saucer. Place the funnel over a bowl that can collect the liquid that drains off.

Refrigerate the pasha for at least 24 hours, preferably longer. Turn it upside down, decorate it and serve it as dessert.

Tropical Cup

1 serving

8 to 10 strawberries
1½ oz/45 grams sugar
1 peeled mango, cut in half
Butter for frying
Several drops of brandy (or several drops of
   lemon juice)
2 to 3 tablespoons vanilla ice cream

Mix well the strawberries and sugar in a blender, or press through a sieve.

Fry the mango slowly over low heat in a little butter in a frying pan. Sprinkle with a little brandy and flambé. Place the mango in a boat shaped dessert bowl. Put vanilla ice cream on top and pour the strawberry sauce over all.

Elderberry Parfait

8 servings

1¼ pint/700 ml whipping cream
4 egg yolks
2½ oz/75 grams sugar
4 fl oz/110 ml elderberry juice

Whip the cream until it is very thick.

Beat the egg yolks and sugar together until light and airy. Add to the cream. Fold in the elderberry juice. Pour the mixture into a dish and place in the freezer for at least 3 to 4 hours. Serve with whipped cream.

Melon à la Mode

4 servings

2 canteloupe melons
8 tablespoons nougat ice cream
4 tablespoons brandy

Wash the melons, cut them in half and remove the seeds. Put the melon halves on serving plates. Just before serving, place 2 spoonfuls of the ice cream in each melon half and pour a tablespoon of brandy on top.

Peach Ice Cream

About 2½ pints/1½ litres

1 envelope unflavoured gelatine
½ pint/¼ l cold water
1 tin sweetened condensed milk
1 pint single cream
2 teaspoons vanilla essence
8 oz/225 grams mashed peaches

In a small saucepan soften the gelatine in 2½ fl oz/75 ml water. Heat and stir until dissolved. Stir in remaining water. Add condensed milk, vanilla and peaches. Refrigerate for at least 3 hours.

Pour into freezer container and freeze according to manufacturer's directions. Transfer to the refrigerator about 2 hours before serving.

Melon à la Mode

Rum and Raisin Ice Cream

16 servings (4 pints)

½ pint/¼ l milk
1½ pint/850 ml double cream
6 egg yolks
8 oz/225 grams granulated sugar
1 teaspoon vanilla essence
1 teaspoon cornflour
14 oz/400 grams raisins
8 fl oz/220 ml water
2½ fl oz/75 grams rum
1 pint/½ l double cream
2 oz/60 grams granulated sugar

Pour the milk and ½ pint/¼ litre of cream into the top of a double boiler.

Beat together the egg yolks, sugar, vanilla and cornflour. Add to the double boiler and cook over simmering water, stirring constantly, until the mixture thickens. Remove from heat and cool.

Heat raisins and water to boiling. Remove from heat, cool and drain. Discard water. Add raisins and rum to cooled custard. Chill for several hours.

Whip 1 pint/½ litre double cream until soft peaks form. Beat in 2 tablespoons sugar. Fold whipped cream into custard and place mixture in a tightly covered freezer container. Place in the freezer for 2 hours.

Remove ice cream from the freezer container and stir thoroughly to break up frozen pieces and redistribute raisins. Return mixture to container and freeze until firm.

Ice Cream and Peaches with Almond Sauce

4 servings

ice cream
14 fl oz/400 ml whipping cream
2 egg yolks
5 oz/140 grams icing sugar
Small amount of orange liqueur (optional)
Peeled fresh or tinned peaches, whole or sliced in half

almond sauce
6 oz/170 grams extra finely ground almonds
Slightly more than ½ tablespoon grated orange peel
2 egg yolks
8 fl oz/220 ml double cream
1½ oz/45 grams icing sugar

Ice Cream and Peaches with Almond Sauce

Beat the whipping cream for the ice cream into stiff peaks.

Whip the egg yolks and sugar together until white and fluffy. Carefully fold the whipped cream into the egg and sugar mixture. Flavour with orange liqueur, if desired. Freeze the mixture overnight. Stir the mixture once during the beginning of the freezing process.

Blend the almonds with the orange peel.

Mix the egg yolks with the cream and sugar, preferably in a stainless steel pan. Add the almond mixture. Bring the sauce to a slow boil, stirring constantly. Watch the pan carefully until the sauce thickens. Cool sauce until warm. Serve warm with the ice cream and peaches.

Strawberry Frappé with Almond Crisps

8 servings

1 block strawberry ice cream
2 lb/900 grams fresh strawberries
4 fl oz/110 ml milk
1 block vanilla ice cream
2 kiwi fruits
8 strawberries as garnish

almond crisps
4 oz/115 grams sliced almonds
2 oz/60 grams flour
4 oz/115 grams sugar
4½ oz 125 grams melted butter
2 tablespoons double cream

Prepare immediately before serving.

Remove strawberry ice cream from the freezer and divide it into pieces.

Mix the strawberries in several batches, in a blender or food processor, together with the strawberry ice cream and a little milk. Pour into large coupe glasses or into small bowls. Place a ball of vanilla ice cream in the middle of the glass. Place a slice of kiwi fruit on top of the ice cream ball. Top with a strawberry. Serve with almond crisps.

To make almond crisps: mix all the listed ingredients together. Drop the mixture onto a greased baking sheet, using a dessert spoon. Leave ample space between the spoonfuls. Bake the biscuits in a preheated 400°F/200°C/gas mark 6 oven for about 10 minutes, until they have become golden brown. Let them cool before carefully removing them from the baking sheet with a thin spatula. Place on a flat surface until cold.

Strawberry Frappé

Royal Dessert

Coffee Ice

6 servings

1 pint/½ l water
8 oz/225 grams sugar
2 pints/1¼ l espresso coffee (fresh or made from
   instant according to package directions)
¼ pint/140 ml whipping cream
½ teaspoon vanilla essence
2 oz/60 grams sugar
Chopped pistachio nuts (optional)

Combine the water and sugar in a small, heavy saucepan. Bring to the boil over a moderate heat, stirring until the sugar is dissolved. Reduce heat to low. Cook, stirring occasionally, 3 to 4 minutes, until the mixture is syrupy. Combine with coffee, mixing well, then cool. Place in freezer trays. Freeze for 3 hours. Stir several times the first hour, until firm ice is formed.

Whip the cream, vanilla and sugar until stiff.

Empty the coffee ice into a blender or food processor and whirl briefly to break up ice crystals. Serve in chilled sorbet glasses, top with whipped cream. Sprinkle with chopped pistachio nuts.

Wine Sorbet

6 servings

1 small bottle of white wine
2½ oz/75 grams sugar
2 egg whites

Mix the wine and sugar until the sugar has dissolved. Pour the mixture into a wide bowl. Place it in the freezer. Stir occasionally until it has started to freeze.

Beat the egg whites until stiff. Fold them into the mixture. Freeze again.

Thirty to 60 minutes before serving, beat the sorbet with an electric beater. Return to the freezer. Serve in sorbet glasses.

Royal Dessert

4 servings

8 medium meringues
8 scoops vanilla ice cream
8 fl oz/220 ml chocolate sauce
8 fl oz/220 ml whipping cream
Grated cooking chocolate

Mint Sorbet

Alternate the meringues and ice cream in a tall glass. Pour the chocolate sauce over them. Top with whipped cream and the grated cooking chocolate. Serve with bananas or fresh berries, if desired.

Peach Sorbet

About 12 servings

12 oz/345 grams sieved tinned peaches
¼ pint/140 ml lemon juice
12 oz/345 grams sugar
2 teaspoons plain gelatine
2½ fl oz/75 ml cold water
¼ pint/140 ml boiling water
1 pint/½ l whipping cream
2 egg yolks, beaten
2 egg whites, beaten

Mix together the peaches, lemon juice and sugar.

Dissolve the gelatine in cold water and let stand for 5 minutes. Stir in the boiling water. When dissolved, add to the first mixture and freeze slightly. Remove from freezer and beat. Add 1 pint/½ litre whipped cream, egg yolks and egg whites. Mix thoroughly and return to freezing tray. Freeze until firm.

Lemon Sorbet

4 servings

3 lemons
3 oz/85 grams icing sugar
½ pint/¼ l water
2 egg whites
Strawberries for garnish

Peel the lemons with a knife, completely removing the pith. Halve the lemons and remove the pips. Mix the lemons in a blender or food processor until they become smooth. Add the icing sugar and water. Freeze the sorbet slightly. Beat the mixture several times while it is freezing.

Beat the egg whites into dry, stiff peaks. Mix them into the half-frozen sorbet. Continue to freeze.

When it is time to serve the sorbet, beat it until smooth, then spoon it into glasses or a bowl. Garnish with strawberries. Eat immediately with small biscuits.

Mint Sorbet

2 servings

8 fl oz/220 ml water
2 oz/60 grams sugar
The juice of ½ lemon
2 tablespoons white wine
2 to 3 tablespoons crème de menthe
1 egg white
1 oz/30 grams icing sugar

Combine the water, sugar, lemon juice, wine and the liqueur in a stainless steel bowl. Stir well, until the sugar is dissolved. Freeze the sorbet 2 to 3 hours, or until half frozen.

Beat the egg white until stiff. Add the icing sugar and beat until the meringue is stiff. Stir into the half frozen sorbet and return to the freezer 2 to 3 hours.

Spoon the sorbet into tall glasses and serve immediately.

Apple Filled Crêpes

4 servings

4 cooking apples
½ lemon
1 lb/450 grams frozen sliced strawberries in sugar
2½ fl oz/75 ml water
8 crepes, newly made or warmed up in the oven
2–3 oz/60–85 grams skinned, thinly sliced, roasted almonds

sauce
2½ fl oz/75 ml concentrated apple juice
2½ fl oz/75 ml water
½ oz/15 grams potato flour

Crêpes with Fresh Berries

Lemon Sorbet

1 to 2 tablespoons double cream or soured cream

If desired, peel the apples. Core them. Divide each apple into 8 to 10 wedges.

Peel the lemon with a potato peeler so that just the yellow is removed.

Place the apples in a pan. Squeeze the lemon juice over them. Add the strawberries. Simmer the fruit over a low heat for about 5 minutes, until the apples feel soft.

Finely chop the lemon peel. Add it to the fruit mixture.

Prepare the sauce. Beat together the juice, water and potato flour. Simmer the mixture until it becomes a clear, thick sauce. Stir in the cream.

Fill the crepes with the fruit mixture and roll them up.

Serve the crepes from a serving dish, garnished with the sauce and sprinkled with the roasted almonds.

This dish can be prepared in advance and then warmed up in the oven. The crepes, however, will not remain crisp.

Crêpes with Fresh Berries

About 40 crepes

3 eggs
3–4 oz/85–115 grams flour
1 pint/¼ l milk (can be mixed with a small
    amount of cream)
½ teaspoon salt
3 oz/85 grams melted butter or margarine
Oil
Fresh berries

Beat the eggs, flour and a little of the milk together into a smooth batter. Add the rest of the milk, the salt and melted butter.

Pour several drops of oil in a small (5 to 6 inches/ 13 to 16 cm) frying pan or crepe pan and heat it so that it almost starts to smoke. Remove the pan from the heat and dry it with kitchen towel. Pour in the batter so that it just covers the bottom of the pan. Cook the crepes until light brown on both sides. If you the make the crepes in advance, store them in aluminium foil.

Serve them hot or cold with berries or jam.

Gooseberry Soufflé

4 servings

½ pint/¼ l gooseberry pureé
4 eggs
¼ pint/140 ml double cream
½ oz/15 grams gelatine
2 oz/60 grams caster sugar
Water
Food colouring

to decorate
8 fl oz/220 ml double cream, whipped
Roasted almonds, finely chopped

Mix the pureé, egg yolks and sugar and whisk this mixture over the heat until slightly thickened. Remove from heat and whisk until bowl has cooled.

Whip the cream lightly and stir into the above mixture. Soak the gelatine in water and dissolve over the heat. Add it to the mixture with any colouring, if desired.

Whisk the egg whites until very stiff and fold into the mixture. Spoon into a soufflé dish.

Decorate with whipped cream and the almonds.

Apple Filled Crêpes

Soufflé Filled Crêpes with Raspberry Sauce

Almond Soufflé with Cognac Sauce

4 servings

1½ oz/45 grams butter
1 oz/30 grams flour
8 fl oz/220 ml milk
Pinch salt
6 oz/170 grams sugar
1 teaspoon almond essence
1 drop bitter almond oil (optional)
4 egg yolks
6 oz/170 grams scalded, skinned and finely
    chopped almonds, roasted
6 egg whites
12 whole almonds, scalded and skinned

cognac sauce
4 egg yolks
4 teaspoons sugar
4 tablespoons cognac
4 tablespoons double cream, warmed

Heat the butter and flour together in a pan. Dilute, beating constantly, with the milk, a few drops at a time. Add the salt, sugar, almond essence and bitter almond oil. Remove from the heat. Let cool a few minutes, while beating. Add the egg yolks, one at a time. Beat constantly. Blend in the roasted chopped almonds.

Grease well a large, high soufflé dish or 4 large individual dishes.

Beat the egg whites until very dry and very stiff. Fold them carefully into the almond mixture. Pour the mixture into the dish or dishes until slightly more than half full. Divide the whole almonds on top. Bake in a 350°F/180°C/gas mark 4 oven on the lowest shelf for 30 to 35 minutes or until the soufflé has set and the surface has become slightly brown. Serve immediately with the cognac sauce served in a separate bowl.

Make the cognac sauce by beating the egg yolks and sugar together. Then beat over boiling water until the mixture thickens. Beat in the cognac and warmed cream. Just before the sauce is to be served. Beat for several more minutes over heat.

Almond Soufflé with Cognac Sauce

Fruit in Cream

6 servings

2 apples
2 oranges
2 bananas
4 oz/115 grams sugar
½ pint/¼ l whipping cream
2 oz/60 grams chopped almonds

Peel all the fruits and cut them in slices or pieces. Sprinkle the sugar over the fruit. Let it stand for 10 minutes.

Whip the cream until stiff and fold it into the fruit. Sprinkle the chopped nuts over the top and serve.

Orange Soufflé

4 servings

3 large oranges
About 12 fl oz/350 ml double cream
2½ oz/75 grams sugar
4 large eggs, separated

Grate the rind off the oranges and store the rind in an airtight container or cling film. Squeeze the

juice out of the oranges. Strain and carefully simmer the juice over low heat until it becomes a thick juice. Stir occasionally, going all the way down to the bottom of the pan.

Simmer the cream in a pan over low heat, while stirring until it is almost thick. Remove from the heat. Immediately stir in the sugar. Let the cream mixture cool. Stir in the yolks, one at a time, then add the thickened orange juice and grated orange rind.

Grease 4 small soufflé moulds. Each mould should hold about 16 fl oz/450 ml. Use your fingertips to grease. Go all the way up over the edge. Be generous with the amount of butter used. Sugar the butter.

Whip the egg whites until they are as dry as possible, then beat for another few minutes. Mix quarter of the whipped egg whites with the orange juice mixture until well blended. Fold in the rest of the egg whites with great care.

Divide the mixture among the soufflé dishes. Place them in a preheated 350°F/180°C/gas mark 4 oven on the bottom shelf for about 25 minutes. During the final minutes, the soufflé should stop rising. Remove from the oven. Serve immediately, preferably with Madeira wine.

Frozen Chocolate Soufflé

Apricot Soufflé

Soufflé Filled Crepes with Raspberry Sauce

12 crepes

crepe batter
6 oz/170 grams flour
½ pint/¼ l milk
2 eggs
1 oz/30 grams sugar
¼ teaspoon salt

soufflé mixture
4 egg yolks
2½ oz/75 grams sugar
1 oz/30 grams flour
½ pint/¼ l milk
4 fl oz/110 ml Grand Marnier
4 egg whites
Icing sugar

raspberry sauce
8 oz/225 grams frozen raspberries
8 oz/225 grams frozen blackberries
Icing sugar

Mix together the crepe batter ingredients. Pour several drops of oil in a small frying pan. Heat it so that it almost starts to smoke. Remove the pan from the heat and dry it with paper. Pour in the batter so that it just covers the bottom of the pan. It should be like a very thin pancake. Fry the crepes until light brown. Twelve crepes can be made with this batter. If you make the crepes in advance, store them in aluminium foil.

To make the soufflé mixture: beat the egg yolks and sugar together for about a minute. Stir in the flour.

Heat up the milk—it should not be allowed to boil—and pour it slowly into the egg mixture, beating constantly. Bring to the boil, lower the heat and simmer for about 2 minutes. Beat constantly. Remove the pan from the heat and add the liqueur.

Beat the egg whites until stiff. If you have any extra egg whites, add them also.

When the egg yolk mixture has cooled, fold in the egg whites very carefully.

Place the crepes on a greased baking sheet or large ovenproof plate. Place 3 to 4 tablespoons of the soufflé mixture on half of the crepes. Fold the other half loosely over the mixture. Place in a preheated 425°F/220°C/gas mark 7 oven for about 7 to 10 minutes, until the crepes have risen and have become browned. Sprinkle the icing sugar over the crepes, using a sieve. Serve immediately.

To make the sauce: mash the raspberries in a blender until they become a smooth sauce. Pass through a sieve. Add sugar if necessary. Cover half

Liqueur Soufflé

the plate with the sauce. Decorate with the blackberries.

Sweet sherry, port or dessert wine can be served with this dessert.

Frozen Chocolate Soufflé

4 servings

½ vanilla pod
3 oz/85 grams icing sugar
3 egg yolks
3–4 oz/85–115 grams cooking chocolate
2 teaspoons instant coffee
2½ fl oz/75 ml creme de cacao or similar liqueur
12 fl oz/350 ml whipping cream

Cut the ½ vanilla pod lengthwise into 4 pieces. Scrape out the flesh and place in the top of a non-aluminium double-boiler. Also add the rest of the pod and the sugar and egg yolks. Place the pan over simmering water. Beat vigorously until the mixture becomes creamy but is still light and fluffy. Remove the pan from the double boiler. Beat until the mixture is completely cold.

Melt the chocolate. Add it to the egg mixture, together with the instant coffee and liqueur. Chill the mixture thoroughly.

Beat the cream until stiff. Stir the chocolate mixture and cream together.

Tape pieces of greaseproof paper onto individual soufflé dishes so that they stick up 1 inch/2½ cms over the edges. Fill the dishes with the chocolate mixture to the top of the paper edges. Place in the freezer, but do not allow the dessert to freeze completely. The inner part should still be unfrozen, which gives the dessert the character of a soufflé. It takes about 3 to 4 hours for small dishes and longer if you use a large soufflé dish.

Just before serving, remove the paper edging. Decorate with small rolls of chocolate, or sift a little cocoa on top.

Apricot Soufflé

4 servings

1 packet dried apricots
4 oz/115 grams scalded almonds
6–10 oz/170–285 grams sugar

4 egg whites
Butter for greasing the pan

Thoroughly rinse the apricots. Place them to soak in water. Then boil the apricots in water until they become soft.

Finely chop the almonds. Strain the apricots. Mix them with the sugar and almonds.

Beat the egg whites into stiff peaks. Fold half of the whites into the apricot purée. Fold in the rest of the egg whites with a few large, deep turns of a spoon. Pour the batter into a generously greased soufflé mould and bake in a 400°F/200°C/gas mark 6 oven for about 30 minutes.

Remove the soufflé from the oven. Garnish it with a few extra chopped almonds. Serve immediately, preferably with softly whipped cream that has been flavoured with brandy.

If you pour the mixture into individual soufflé dishes, baking time should be decreased to about 20 minutes.

Yoghurt Mousse with Berry Sauce

4 servings

2 envelopes unflavoured gelatine
¼ pint/140 ml water
1 pint/½ l yoghurt
8 fl oz/220 ml double cream or soured cream
2 egg yolks
2–3 oz/60–85 grams sugar
2 teaspoons vanilla sugar
2 egg whites
Strained raspberries or whole fresh berries
   (strawberries, currants or raspberries) for
   garnish

Put gelatine granules in water for about 5 minutes.

Beat together the yoghurt, cream and egg yolks. Sweeten with the sugar and vanilla sugar.

Melt the gelatine over low heat, then pour in a thin stream into the yoghurt mixture. Stir.

Beat the egg whites into stiff peaks. Fold into the yoghurt mixture. Pour into a round mould or a round cake tin. Place the mousse in the refrigerator for about 3 hours.

When the mousse is to be served, dip the pan in hot water, then turn it upside down. Pour strained raspberries over the mousse, or garnish it with fresh berries.

Orange Soufflé

Liqueur Soufflé

6 servings

1½ oz/45 grams flour
8 fl oz/220 ml milk
½ oz/15 grams butter
2 oz/170 ml sugar
4 fl oz/110 ml orange liqueur
3 egg yolks
2½ oz/75 grams crumbled madeira cake
10 egg whites
2 teaspoons cornflour
Butter and sugar for a 4-pint/2¼-litre soufflé dish
Icing sugar to sprinkle over the soufflé

Prepare the soufflé mixture as follows: measure the flour into a non-aluminium pan. Add the milk a little at a time, whisking constantly so that it does not become lumpy. Let the mixture come to the boil, beating constantly. Leave to boil for 2 to 3 minutes. Beat vigorously the entire time. Add the butter, sugar and half of the liqueur. Mix well. Remove the pan from the heat. Place it on a damp cloth so that it stands in place. Add the egg yolks one at a time while the batter is still hot. Beat vigorously the entire time.

Let the cake crumbs swell in the remaining liqueur.

Beat the egg whites into very dry, stiff peaks. Mix in the cornflour.

Grease the soufflé dish well. Sprinkle it with sugar.

Lighten the mixture by folding in quarter of the egg whites. Carefully fold in the rest of the egg whites and the cake crumbs. Mix well with a wooden spoon, but do not stir unnecessarily or the whites will sink together. Fill the dish and place it on the lowest oven shelf. Bake in a preheated 425°F/220°C/gas mark 7 oven for 25 minutes without opening the oven door. Sprinkle icing sugar over the soufflé, using a sieve. Serve immediately.

Frozen Chocolate Mousse with Orange Cream

8 servings

15 fl oz/425 ml whipping cream
1 tin frozen orange juice
1 packet sponge fingers

chocolate mousse
8 oz/225 grams dessert chocolate
6 egg yolks
6 egg whites

Frozen Chocolate Mousse with Orange Cream

Prepare the mousse first. Slowly melt the chocolate over low heat or over a double boiler. Stir the egg yolks, one at a time, into the warm, liquid chocolate. Let the mixture totally cool before folding in the egg whites, which have been beaten into stiff peaks.

Whip the cream into firm peaks. Beat in the thawed orange juice.

Place the sponge fingers standing up, tightly together, around a high, round tin. Alternate spooning in the chocolate mousse and the orange cream in layers. Start with the chocolate mousse. Place the tin in the freezer for at least 12 hours. Decorate with orange slices or wedges, which can be dipped into melted chocolate for added effect.

Pies and Tarts

Apple Flan with Creamy Filling

Makes 1 12-inch/30-cm pie

pastry

7 oz/200 grams flour
7 oz/200 grams butter or margarine
2 oz/60 grams sugar
2 tablespoons water

filling

4 to 6 fresh apples, peeled and sliced
2 oz/60 grams sugar
½ teaspoon cinnamon, or 2 to 3 tablespoons
    Cointreau or Grand Marnier
12 fl oz/350 ml double cream
2 oz/60 grams sugar
3 egg yolks

Work together the flour, butter and sugar. Add the water and knead quickly together into a dough. Refrigerate for ½ hour. Grease a 12-inch/30-cm round flan dish with about 1 tablespoon margarine. Divide the dough into 2 parts. Roll out each part between 2 sheets of cling film into half moons, as large as half the dish. Pull off the plastic from one of the sides. Turn the pastry upside down onto the dish and pull off the plastic from the other side. Place the other half of the pastry so that it overlaps in the middle. With your hand, flatten the pastry up over the sides of the dish. Refrigerate for 15 minutes.

Preheat oven to 425°F/220°C/gas mark 7. Cover the edge of the dish with aluminium foil so that the pastry edge does not slip down while baking. Prick the pie shell with a fork. Bake for 10 minutes.

Fill the flan case with the apple slices. Sprinkle with the sugar and cinnamon. Leave out the cinnamon if liqueur is to be used instead in the egg mixture.

Lightly whip the cream. Sweeten it with sugar and mix it with the egg yolks and perhaps 2 to 3 tablespoons liqueur. Pour the mixture over the apples and bake in the middle of the oven for 25 minutes.

Almond Pie

307

Apple Pie

Almond Pie

Makes 1 10-inch/25-cm pie

pastry
3½ oz/100 grams butter, at room temperature
4 oz/115 grams marzipan, finely chopped
3½ oz/100 grams flour
1 teaspoon salt
1 egg

filling
8 oz/225 grams marzipan, finely chopped
Juice of 1 lemon
4 oz/115 grams almonds
4 egg whites

Chop the butter, marzipan, flour and salt together. Mix in the egg so that the mixture becomes a workable dough. Refrigerate for about an hour.

Mix the marzipan for the filling with the lemon juice and place to one side for the time being.

Preheat the oven to 350°F/180°C/gas mark 4. Roll out the dough, using a little flour, and cover the bottom and sides of a springform pie tin. The tin should have a diameter of about 10 inches/25 cms. Prick the pastry with a fork and bake it in the middle of the oven for about 10 minutes.

Scald and peel the almonds, then cut them in half. Beat the egg whites into dry, stiff peaks. Fold the marzipan into the egg whites and spread the marzipan mixture into the pie case. Cover with the almond halves.

Bake the pie in the middle of the oven for another 20 minutes. Remove from the oven and allow to cool before carefully removing the detachable sides of the tin. Place the pie on a serving plate.

Apple Pie

Makes 1 9-inch/22-cm pie

pastry
8 oz/225 grams butter or margarine
8 oz/225 grams flour
4 fl oz/110 ml water
1 egg, beaten

filling
2 lb/900 grams cooking apples
2½-5 oz/75–140 grams sugar
2 to 3 teaspoons cinnamon

Crumble the butter into the flour. Add the water. Quickly work into a dough. Refrigerate.

Roll out the dough thinly. Cover an iron pot (or an ovenproof dish with high edges) with the dough. Save some of the dough for the top crust.

Peel and cut the apples into thin wedges. Alternate them in the pot with the sugar and cinnamon. Cover with pastry top. Pinch the edges well together. Brush with the beaten egg. Prick small air holes in the dough. Bake on the bottom of the oven at 350°F/180°C/gas mark 4 for about 1 hour.

Serve the pie warm with cream or ice cream.

Crisp Top Apple Pie

6 servings

4 to 5 apples
A little sugar on the apples if they are cookers (optional)
2½ oz/75 grams instant ginger cake mix
1½-2½ oz/45–75 grams cold butter

Peel and cut the apples into thin wedges. Place in a greased, ovenproof dish. Sprinkle the cake mix (that is, dry, without adding any water or eggs) over the dish. Cover the dish with thin slices of butter. Use cold butter and, preferably, a wire cutter.

Bake at 425°F/220°C/gas mark 7 until the pie is golden brown, 20 to 25 minutes. Serve the pie warm with cream or ice cream.

Angel Pie

Makes 1 9-inch/22-cm pie

3 egg whites
Pinch cream of tartar
8 oz/225 grams sugar
25 digestive biscuits, crushed
4–8 oz/115–225 grams walnuts, chopped
4 oz/115 grams plain chocolate
3 tablespoons hot water
1 teaspoon vanilla essence
½ pint/¼ l double cream, whipped
Chocolate shavings for decoration

With an electric mixer, beat the egg whites and cream of tartar until soft peaks form. Beating on high speed, add sugar gradually until the meringue forms stiff peaks. Fold in the crushed crackers and nuts.

Turn into a lightly greased 9-inch/22-cm flan dish. With a spatula, push the meringue up the sides of the dish, forming a pie shell shape. Bake at 325°F/163°C/gas mark 3 about 40 minutes, until lightly browned. Remove and cool on a wire rack.

Meanwhile, melt the chocolate in the top of a double boiler. Add the water to the chocolate and blend.

Cool until thickened. Stir in vanilla. Fold the chocolate into whipped cream until the colour is solid. Spoon into the cooled meringue shell and chill 2 hours before serving. Decorate with chocolate shavings.

Puff Pastry Tartlets with Apples

Quantity varies

Frozen puff pastry
Cooking apples
1 egg yolk
1 lemon
Apricot sauce (apricot jam stirred with a little water)

Line small tart tins with rolled out puff pastry dough and place them in the freezer.

Peel the apples, remove the cores and cut them into thin slices. Arrange the slices in the tins. Drip a little lemon juice on top. Brush the edges with the egg, mixed with a little water. Bake in a 425°F/220°C/gas mark 7 oven for 15 to 20 minutes.

Heat the apricot jam with a little water and brush the apple slices to give an attractive surface. Serve warm with whipped cream

Apple Flan with Creamy Filling

French Apple Pie

Makes 1 10-inch/25-cm pie

pastry
9 oz/255 grams flour
9 oz/255 grams margarine
4 tablespoons cream

filling
3½ oz/100 grams marzipan
1 egg
3 apples
3 oz/85 grams sugar

glaze
3 to 4 tablespoons apricot or pineapple purée
2 tablespoons raisins

Cut the pastry ingredients together. Form into a ball without kneading. Cover and refrigerate for about 40 minutes. Roll the dough out on a baking sheet into a thin, 10-inch/25 cm square. Trim the edges evenly and roll them into a ½-inch/1-cm rim. Mix the marzipan smoothly with the egg and spread this over the pastry. Bake at 425°F/220°C/gas mark 7 for 10 minutes.

Peel and core the apples and cut them into thin slices. Place the slices, overlapping, on the baked pastry square. Sprinkle with a little sugar. Bake for another 15 minutes at 400°F/200°C/gas mark 6.

Warm the raisins in a little water and drain. Take the pie out of the oven. Brush with the apricot purée and sprinkle with the raisins.

Banana Cream Pie

Makes 1 9-inch/22-cm pie

1 cooked flan case
4 oz/115 grams sugar
¼ teaspoon salt
1½ oz/45 grams flour
14 fl oz/400 ml milk
8 fl oz/220 ml water
3 egg yolks, beaten
8 oz/225 grams bananas, thinly sliced

meringue
3 egg whites
2½ oz/75 grams sugar
½ teaspoon baking powder

Combine the sugar, salt, flour, milk and water over low heat. When hot, add a small amount to the egg yolks. Mix. Pour the egg yolks back into the mixture and cook 3 to 4 minutes. Add the bananas. Pour into the flan case.

To make the meringue: beat egg whites until almost stiff. Add sugar gradually, beating continuously. Add baking powder and beat until glossy. Top the pie with the meringue.

Fresh Apricot Pie

Makes 1 9-inch/22-cm pie

8 oz/225 grams frozen shortcrust pastry
5 oz/140 grams sugar
½ pint/¼ l pineapple juice
18 fresh apricots, stoned and halved
2 teaspoons cornflour
½ teaspoons salt
1 oz/30 grams margarine
½ teaspoon vanilla essence

Line a 9-inch/22-cm pie dish with half the thawed dough. Combine the sugar and pineapple juice and boil 1 minute. Simmer the apricots, a few at a time, in the syrup, until just tender. Lift the apricots carefully from their juice and arrange in the pie case.

Mix the cornflour with a little cold water and add to the juice and cook until thickened. Add salt, margarine and vanilla and pour over the apricots. Cover with a lattice pastry top. Bake in a 450°F/230°C/gas mark 8 oven for 10 minutes. Reduce heat to 350°F/180°C/gas mark 4 and bake about 20 minutes longer.

Blueberry Custard Cream Pie

Makes 1 10-inch/25-cm pie

pastry
3½ oz/100 grams butter or margarine
1½ oz/45 grams icing sugar
4 oz/115 grams flour

filling
1 packet instant blancmange
4 fl oz/110 ml double cream, whipped
2 envelopes plain gelatine
10 oz/285 grams blueberries
8 fl oz/220 ml currant juice or blueberry juice

Mix all the ingredients for the pastry together and leave to stand in a cool place. Line a lightly buttered cake tin—with detachable bottom—with the pastry. Fasten a strip of aluminium foil around the edge so that the pastry does not slide down during baking. Bake at 400°F/200°C/gas mark 6 for about 20 minutes.

Make the blancmange according to directions on the packet. Soak 1 tablespoon of the gelatine in a little water, then stir them into the warm pudding and mix so that it melts. When the blancmange has cooled, add the whipped cream.

Take the pastry case out of the tin and fill it with the blancmange. Place blueberries on top. Dissolve the remaining gelatine and blend with the juice. Pour this over the berries when it starts to harden.

Serve with a dab of whipped cream.

Blackberry Pie

Makes 1 8-inch/19-cm pie

8 oz/225 grams frozen shortcrust
1½ lb/700 grams blackberries
8 oz/225 grams sugar
2 tablespoons orange juice
1 oz/30 grams flour
Pinch nutmeg
½ oz/15 grams butter

Line an 8-inch/19-cm pie dish with pastry and chill.

Cook the berries and sugar over low heat, stirring. Bring to a slow boil, then simmer 3 minutes. Cool. Add the orange juice.

Sprinkle a little flour over the pastry base and pour in the berries, sprinkle with flour and nutmeg and dot with butter. Put on the top crust, seal the edges with a little milk and crimp them. Cut air holes in the centre of the pastry. Bake at 450°F/230°C/gas mark 8 for 10 minutes. Lower the heat to 350°F/180°C/gas mark 4 and bake for another ½ hour, or until the pastry is lightly browned. Serve with cream.

Crisp Top Apple Pie

Whisky Pie

Makes 1 10-inch/25-cm pie

pie base
2 oz/60 grams butter
2 oz/60 grams cooking chocolate
2 eggs
¼ teaspoon salt
8 oz/225 grams sugar
½ teaspoon vanilla essence
3 oz/85 grams flour
4 oz/115 grams walnuts, chopped

filling and topping
5 egg yolks
8 oz/225 grams sugar
1¼-oz/38-gram envelope plain gelatine
2½ fl oz/75 ml cold water
¼ pint/140 ml whisky
1½ pints/850 ml whipping cream
Grated chocolate curls or shavings

To make the pie base, melt the butter and chocolate in the top of a double boiler over hot water. Cool the mixture. In a bowl, beat the eggs and salt until light and foamy. Add sugar and vanilla gradually and continue beating until well creamed. Stir the cooled chocolate mixture into the egg mixture and then fold in the flour. Gently stir in the nuts. turn into an ungreased 10-inch/25-cm flan dish, lining the bottom. Bake in a 350°F/180°C/gas mark 4 oven 25 minutes or until a knitting needle inserted in the centre comes out clean. Cool.

To make the filling, beat the egg yolks until thick and lemon-coloured. Slowly beat in 6 oz/170 grams of sugar. Soften the gelatine in cold water and add to it one third of the whisky. Heat the gelatine mixture in a double boiler over boiling water until the gelatine dissolves. Pour into the yolk mixture and stir briskly. Stir in the remaining whisky. Whip ½ pint/¼ litre of the cream and fold into the yolk mixture. Pour the filling over the cooled pie base and refrigerate at least 4 hours.

To make the topping: whip the remaining cream, gradually adding the remaining sugar. Top with whipped cream and garnish with chocolate curls or shavings.

Pennsylvania Cheese Pie

Makes 1 9-inch/22-cm pie

8 oz/225 grams frozen shortcrust pastry
2 teaspoons cornflour
5 oz/140 grams sugar
8 oz/225 grams cottage cheese, sieved
2 eggs, separated
2 tablespoons milk
Pinch salt
1 tablespoon lemon rind, grated

Mix the cornflour and sugar. Add cottage cheese, egg yolks, milk, salt and lemon rind and blend well. Fold in stiffly beaten egg whites and pour into the unbaked pastry case.

Bake in a 450°F/230°C/gas mark 8 oven for 10 minutes. Reduce the temperature to 325°F/163°C/gas mark 3 and continue baking 25 to 30 minutes.

Super Chocolate Pie

Makes 1 9-inch/22-cm pie

flan case
3 egg whites
Salt
¼ teaspoon cream of tartar
5 oz/140 grams sugar, sifted
½ teaspoon vanilla essence
2½ oz/75 grams walnuts or pecan nuts, finely chopped

chocolate cream filling
5 oz/140 grams plain chocolate
½ pint/¼ l double cream
2½ fl oz/75 ml hot milk
1 teaspoon vanilla essence
Salt

cream topping
8 fl oz/220 ml double cream
1 oz/30 grams icing sugar
Grated chocolate curls or shavings

Base: beat egg whites, salt and cream of tartar until soft peaks form. Beat in sugar, gradually, until very stiff, then beat in the vanilla.

Butter the bottom and sides of a 9-inch/22-cm pyrex flan dish. Spread meringue over the bottom and sides as high as possible. Sprinkle nuts over the bottom. Bake in a preheated 275°F/135°C/gas mark ½ oven for 1 hour. If after 10 minutes the sides start to sag, gently push them back into place. Allow to cool in the oven 30 minutes. Remove and cool completely.

Melt the chocolate in the top of a double boiler. Add milk, vanilla and salt. Stir until smooth. Cool.

Whip the cream until stiff and fold into the cooled chocolate. Spread the filling in the cooled flan. Refrigerate for 4 hours.

To serve, whip the cream with icing sugar and spread over the pie. Decorate with chocolate.

Puff Pastry Tartlets can be filled with Apples (below left) or other Fruits

Cherry Pie

Makes 1 9-inch/22-cm pie

pastry
8 oz/225 grams flour
2–3 oz/60–85 grams sugar (optional)
5 oz/140 grams butter or margarine
2 tablespoons water or cream

filling
About 1 lb/450 grams stoned cherries
2–3 oz/60–85 grams sugar

Mix the flour and sugar together and place in a pile on a baking board. Slice the butter and place on top. Chop the butter and flour together using a long knife until the mixture is crumbly. Pour the water or cream on the top and quickly work into a dough. Refrigerate for ½ hour. Roll out two thirds of the dough and cover a 9-inch/22-cm pie dish on both the bottom and sides. Pile the cherries and sugar alternately in the pastry base.

Make strips from the dough and make a lattice pattern on top of the cherries. Bake at 425°F/220°C/gas mark 7 for about 30 minutes, until the surface has become golden brown.

Serve warm or cold, with whipped cream, if desired.

Chocolate Pecan Pie

Makes 1 9-inch/22-cm pie

8 oz/225 grams frozen shortcrust pastry
1 oz/30 grams margarine
2 oz/60 grams cooking chocolate
2 eggs
1 lb/450 grams golden syrup
8 oz/225 grams sugar
1 teaspoon vanilla essence
Pinch salt
8 oz/225 grams pecan nuts

In a small saucepan over low heat, melt the margarine and chocolate and cool. In a small bowl, beat the eggs lightly with an electric mixer. Mix in the syrup, sugar, margarine, chocolate, vanilla and salt. Stir in the pecan nuts. Pour the filling into the unbaked pastry shell.

Bake in a 400°F/200°C/gas mark 6 oven for 15 minutes. Reduce heat to 350°F/180°C/gas mark 4 and bake 30 to 35 minutes longer (filling should be slightly less set in the centre than around the edge). Cool. Serve with whipped cream topping, if desired.

Blueberry Cream Pie

Fruit Flan

Makes 1 9-inch/22-cm flan

4 oz/115 grams butter or margarine
2 oz/60 grams sugar
1 egg
8 oz/225 grams flour

filling
8 fl oz/220 ml soured cream
1 oz/30 grams icing sugar
½ to 1 tablespoon vanilla essence
About 3 peeled and sliced kiwi, or similar fruit

Beat the butter and sugar together until smooth. Add the egg and the flour. Refrigerate the dough for at least 1 hour.

Roll or flatten out the dough and line a greased 9-inch/22-cm flan dish with the dough. Prick well. Bake at 350°F/180°C/gas mark 4 for about 20 minutes.

Blend the cream and the icing sugar together and flavour with the vanilla essence. Spread a thin layer of the filling over the bottom of the cooled pastry shell and place sliced kiwi fruit on top. Serve the rest of the cream filling separately.

Rainbow Ice Cream Pie

Makes 1 9-inch/22-cm pie

sauce
4 oz/115 grams mixed candied fruits, chopped
2 oz/60 grams pecan nuts, chopped
8 oz/225 grams golden syrup
2 oz/60 grams sugar
2½ fl oz/75 ml orange juice
½ teaspoon rum flavouring

crumb pastry
3 oz/85 grams biscuit crumbs
1½ oz/45 grams butter, melted
11 to 12 digestive biscuits.

filling
1 pint/½ l chocolate ice cream
1 pint/½ l vanilla ice cream
1 pint/½ l strawberry ice cream

Combine the fruits, pecan nuts, syrup, sugar and orange juice in a saucepan. Bring to the boil and simmer for one minute. Remove from the heat and stir in rum flavouring. Set aside and chill.

Combine the biscuit crumbs and butter; mix well. Press the mixture evenly over the bottom of a buttered 9-inch/22-cm flan dish. Stand whole biscuits upright around the edge. Chill.

Spoon chocolate ice cream into the biscuit base and drizzle with ¼ of the sauce. Repeat, using a layer of vanilla ice cream, then sauce, then a layer of strawberry ice cream and more sauce. Freeze until serving time. Serve the remaining sauce separately.

Fruit Flan

Lemon Chiffon Pie

Makes 1 8-inch/19-cm pie

1 cooked pastry case
1 envelope unflavoured gelatine
2½ fl oz/75 ml cold water
8 oz/225 grams sugar
¼ pint/140 ml lemon juice
½ teaspoon salt
4 egg yolks, beaten
1 teaspoon lemon rind, grated
4 egg whites
¼ pint/140 ml double cream, whipped

Soften the gelatine in cold water. Add 4 oz/115 grams of the sugar, lemon juice and salt to the beaten egg yolks in the top of a double boiler; cook over boiling water until thick. Add the lemon rind and softened gelatine. Stir until the gelatine is dissolved. Cool.

Beat the egg whites until stiff. Gradually beat in the sugar until the mixture is smooth and glossy. Fold the egg whites into the gelatine mixture. Pour into the pie shell. Chill until firm. Just before serving, garnish with whipped cream.

Kiwi Tarts

10 to 12 servings

rich shortcrust pastry
6–8 oz/170–225 grams flour
2 oz/60 grams sugar
½ teaspoon salt
1 egg
Few drops vanilla essence
6 oz/170 grams butter, at room temperature
1 tablespoon grated almonds (optional)

filling
4 eggs
½ pint/¼ l whipping cream
2½ oz/75 grams sugar
1 tablespoon Kirsch
10 kiwi fruits

Mix the flour, sugar and salt together. Form an indentation in the middle and place the egg, vanilla and butter in the hole. Mix the dough together with your finger tips until it becomes smooth. Refrigerate, preferably in a plastic bag.

Line tart tins with the shortcrust dough. Prick the dough. Bake the pastry for about 10 minutes at 400°F/200°C/gas mark 6 for 20 minutes. Sprinkle a little extra sugar on the top and place under the grill so that they become slightly browned without the pastry becoming burned.

You can use almost any kind of fruit or berry in this recipe: plums, cherries, pineapples, peaches and wild strawberries.

Cranberry Pie

Makes 1 9-inch/22-cm pie

1 uncooked pastry case
1 lb/450 grams cranberries
8 oz/225 grams sugar
½ pint/¼ l water
½ oz/15 grams cornflour
1 teaspoon butter, softened

Wash and pick over the cranberries. Cook the sugar and water for 2 minutes; add the cranberries and cook for 5 minutes.

Mix the cornflour and the softened butter and add enough of the hot cranberry liquid to make a smooth paste. Stir this mixture into the simmering cranberries. Cook 3 minutes, stirring constantly.

Pour the cranberry mixture into the unbaked pie case. Cross with a lattice top. Bake 10 to 15 minutes in a preheated 450°F/230°C/gas mark 8 oven. Reduce the heat to 350°F/180°C/gas mark 4 and bake 25 to 30 minutes longer.

Strawberry Flan

Makes 1 7-inch/18-cm flan

French flan pastry
4 oz/115 grams plain flour
2 oz/60 grams butter
2 oz/60 grams caster sugar
2 egg yolks
2 drops of vanilla essence

filling
½-1 lb/225–450 grams strawberries
8 oz/225 grams redcurrant jelly

Prepare the pastry as for Kiwi Tarts, roll out and line the flan tin. Bake in oven preset at 375°F/190°C/gas mark 5 oven for 12 to 15 minutes.

Hull the strawberries. Prepare a redcurrant glaze by heating jelly with a little warm water.

When the flan case is cool, fill with the strawberries and brush with the hot glaze. Allow it to set before serving.

Mango or Apricot Pie

Makes 1 9-inch/22-cm pie

8 digestive biscuits
4½ oz/130 grams butter, melted
2 oz/60 grams brown sugar
4 teaspoons ginger
8 fl oz/220 ml cream
8 fl oz/220 ml soured cream
2 oz/60 grams sugar
1 drop mint oil or 2½ oz/75 grams chopped mint (optional)
3 fresh mangos or 1½-2 lb/700–900 grams tinned apricots
Juice and grated peel of 1 lemon
2 envelopes unflavoured gelatine
Kiwi fruit, for garnish

Crush the biscuits and mix them with melted butter, brown sugar and ginger. Cover a 9-inch/22-cm pie tin—with detachable bottom—with the mixture. Push down with a spoon to cover the tin. Refrigerate.

Whip the cream and mix it with soured cream and sugar. (Flavour with mint oil or chopped mint, if you wish.) Place in pie tin.

Strain or purée the mangos or apricots and mix with the lemon juice and peel. Place the gelatine in water, then dissolve it over low heat in its own liquid. Add the gelatine to the fruit mixture. Cool, stirring frequently.

Cover the cream mixture with the fruit mixture when it has thickened somewhat and garnish with kiwi fruit.

Cherry Pie

Mango or Apricot Pie

Spoon into the flan case and chill until firm. Spread with additional whipped cream. Sprinkle additional grated lime peel around the edge of the pie.

Old Time Lemon Pie

Makes 1 8-inch/19-cm pie

8-inch/19-cm flan case, baked (see index)
8 oz/225 grams sugar
12 fl oz/350 ml water
½ oz/15 grams butter
1 oz/30 grams cornflour
3 tablespoons cold water
3 eggs, separated
2 tablespoons milk
6 tablespoons lemon juice
1 teaspoon lemon peel, grated
6 oz/170 grams sugar
1 teaspoon lemon juice

Combine the sugar, water and butter in a saucepan and heat until the sugar dissolves. Blend the cornflour with cold water, add to the hot mixture and cook slowly until clear, about 8 minutes.

In a bowl, beat the egg yolks with milk, slowly stir into the cornflour mixture. Cook 2 minutes, stirring constantly. Remove from the heat. Add 6 tablespoons lemon juice and the lemon peel and let the mixture cool. Pour into a cooled, baked flan case.

Beat the egg whites until stiff but not dry, adding the 6 oz/170 grams of sugar gradually. Add 1 teaspoon of lemon juice towards the end of the beating. Spread the meringue over the cooled filling, sealing to the edges of the pastry to avoid shrinking. Brown in a 350°F/180°C/gas mark 4 oven for 12 to 15 minutes.

Maple Syrup Pie

Makes 1 9-inch/22-cm pie

9-inch/22-cm flan case, cooked (see index)
1 lb/450 grams plus 1 tablespoon maple syrup
½ pint/¼ l hot water
1 teaspoon butter
1 oz/30 grams cornflour
Pinch salt
2 eggs, separated

Combine 1 lb/450 grams of syrup, hot water cornflour and butter. Bring to the boil. Mix the cornflour, salt and enough cold water to make a thin paste. Add the egg yolks to the paste and beat well.

Add the hot syrup mixture gradually and return to the heat. Cook until thickened, stirring constantly. Cool slightly.

Pour the mixture into a cooked flan case. Beat the egg whites until stiff, slowly adding tablespoon of syrup. Pile on the pie and brown until golden in a 400°F/200°C/gas mark 6 oven. Add chopped nuts if desired.

Key Lime Pie

Makes 1 9-inch/22-cm pie

9-inch/22-cm flan case, baked (see index)
1 tablespoon plain gelatine
8 oz/225 grams sugar
¼ teaspoon salt
4 eggs, separated
¼ pint/140 ml lime juice
2½ fl oz/75 ml water
1 teaspoon lime peel, grated
Green food colouring
½ pint/¼ l whipping cream, whipped

Mix the gelatine, 4 oz/115 grams sugar and salt in a saucepan.

Beat the egg yolks, lime juice and water together. Stir into the gelatine mixture. Cool over medium heat, stirring constantly, until the mixture just comes to the boil. Remove from the heat and stir in the grated peel. Add enough colouring for a pale green colour. Chill, stirring occasionally, until thickened.

Beat the egg whites until soft peaks form. Add the remaining sugar gradually. Beat until stiff peaks form. Fold the gelatine mixture into the egg whites; fold in the whipped cream.

Mincemeat and Pecan Pie

Makes 1 9-inch/22-cm pie

Pastry for 9-inch/22-cm flan (see index)
9 oz/255 grams mincemeat
8 oz/225 grams golden syrup
2 oz/60 grams margarine
3 eggs, lightly beaten
4 oz/115 grams pecan nuts, coarsely chopped
1 tablespoon orange rind, grated
2½ fl oz/75 ml sherry

In a medium saucepan, stir the mincemeat, syrup and margarine together. Stirring constantly, bring to the boil over medium heat. Remove from the heat. Gradually mix in the eggs. Add pecan nuts and orange rind. Pour into the unbaked pastry case.

Bake in a 350°F/180°C/gas mark 4 oven 40 to 50 minutes or until a knife inserted near the centre comes out clean. Pour sherry over the filling. Cool.

Montgomery Pie

Makes 2 8-inch/19-cm pies

Pastry for 2 8-inch/19-cm flans (see index)
Juice and grated rind of 1 lemon
1 egg, lightly beaten
8 oz/225 grams sugar
½ pint/¼ l water
8 oz/225 grams treacle
1 pint/½ l milk
10 oz/285 grams flour
2 teaspoons baking powder

Mix the lemon juice and rind, egg, sugar, water and treacle together. Pour into the flan cases.

Mix the milk, flour and baking powder together. Spoon this mixture over the lemon and treacle mixture in the flans. Do not stir. Bake 30 minutes in a 375°F/190°C/gas mark 5 oven.

Lemon Meringue Pie

Makes 1 9-inch/22-cm pie

9-inch/22-cm flan case, baked (see index)
3½ oz/100 grams cornflour
10 oz/285 grams sugar
¼ teaspoon salt
15 fl oz/425 ml hot water
3 egg yolks, beaten
¼ pint/140 ml lemon juice
1 teaspoon lemon rind, grated
1 oz/30 grams butter or margarine

meringue
3 egg whites
1 tablespoon lemon juice
6 oz/170 grams sugar

Mix the cornflour, sugar and salt in a saucepan. Stir in hot water gradually and bring to the boil over direct heat. Cook for 8 to 10 minutes over medium heat, stirring constantly until thick and clear. Remove from the heat. Stir several spoonfuls of this hot mixture into the beaten egg yolks. Mix well. Pour egg yolks back into the saucepan. Bring to the boil, then reduce heat and cook slowly for 4 to 5 minutes, stirring constantly. Remove from the heat and gradually add lemon juice, rind and butter. Cool thoroughly, then pour into the cooled baked flan case.

Top with meringue. Put the egg whites (at room temperature) in a deep, medium sized bowl. Add lemon juice. Beat until the whites stand in soft peaks. Add 6 oz/170 grams of sugar gradually, beating well after each addition. Beat until the egg whites stand in firm, glossy peaks. Spread over the cooled filling, starting at the edges and working toward the centre of the pie, attaching the meringue securely to the edges of the crust. Bake at 350°F/180°C/gas mark 4 for 15 to 20 minutes. Cool but do not refrigerate before serving.

Oatmeal Pie with Nectar Mousse

Oatmeal Pie with Nectar Mousse

Makes 1 10-inch/25-cm pie

pastry
10 oz/285 grams oatmeal
3 oz/85 grams flour
2 oz/60 grams sugar
5½ oz/155 grams margarine

filling
2 envelopes gelatine
2½ fl oz/75 ml concentrated fruit juice
8 fl oz/220 ml cold water
8 fl oz/220 ml double cream
About teaspoon vanilla essence
1 lb/450 grams fresh or frozen blackcurrants

Cut and knead the pastry ingredients together. Press out the dough onto the bottom and sides of a flan ring with a detachable bottom. Bake the pastry for 20 minutes at 350°F/180°C/gas mark 4 on the oven's lowest shelf.

Dissolve the gelatine in a little water, then melt the gelatine in the juice over low heat. Add the cold water. Stir occasionally until the mixture starts to thicken. Whip the cream and add it to the gelatine

Cranberry Glazed Pear Pie

mixture, which has thickened. Sweeten with vanilla and pour this mousse into the cooled pie shell.

Pile blackcurrants on the top.

Spicy Peach Pie

Makes 1 8-inch/19-cm pie

Pastry for 8-inch/19-cm flan (see index), with ¼ teaspoon nutmeg, cinnamon and allspice added to the flour
1½-2 lb/700–900 grams tinned cling peach slices
4 oz/115 grams sugar
¼ teaspoon nutmeg
1 oz/30 grams cornflour
¼ teaspoon salt
1 teaspoon orange rind, grated
1 tablespoon lemon juice
1 oz/30 grams butter or margarine

Grease an 8-inch/19-cm round pie dish. Arrange the peaches and syrup in the dish. Blend the sugar, nutmeg, cornflour, salt and orange rind together. Sprinkle over the peaches. Sprinkle the lemon juice over the pie. Dot with bits of butter or margarine.

Roll out the pastry to ½ inch/1 cm larger than the baking dish. Cut slits to let the steam escape and place over the peaches. Press the overhanging pastry firmly against the edge of the dish. Flute the edges. Bake 25 to 30 minutes in a preheated 425°F/220°C/gas mark 7 oven.

Cranberry Glazed Pear Pie

Makes 1 9-inch/22-cm pie

pastry
6 oz/170 grams butter
6 oz/170 grams flour
2 tablespoons water

filling
5 oz/140 grams marzipan, coarsely grated
2 to 3 ripe pears
1½ teaspoons lemon juice

glaze
9 oz/255 grams cranberry jelly

topping
8–12 fl oz/220–350 ml whipped cream, flavoured with a little vanilla essence

Mix together the pastry ingredients in a bowl. Let stand in a cool place for about hour. Flatten out the dough in a 9-inch/22-cm pie dish with a detachable bottom. Make sure that the dough has an even thickness across the bottom of the dish and that it also covers the sides of the dish. Prick the bottom with a fork.

Preheat the oven to 425°F/220°C/gas mark 7 and

bake the pie crust for 10 minutes. Divide the marzipan over the pie crust. Core and cut the pears in thin slices and place them in the pie crust in an attractive design. Moisten the pear slices with the lemon juice.

Place the pie on a shelf in the middle of the oven and bake for 10 to 12 minutes. Melt the jelly and pour it over the pie after it has been baked and is still warm.

When the pie has cooled, place it on a board or a plate. Serve it with whipped cream.

Crunchy Pear Pie

Makes 1 9-inch/22-cm pie

1 uncooked pastry case (see index)
2 oz/60 grams sugar
1 oz/30 grams cornflour
Pinch salt
½ teaspoon ginger
15 fl oz/425 ml juice drained from canned pears
1 teaspoon lemon rind, grated
1 tablespoon lemon juice
1 lb/450 grams pear halves, drained
4 oz/115 grams flour, sifted
4 oz/115 grams brown sugar, firmly packed
4 oz/115 grams butter or margarine
4 oz/115 grams nuts, chopped

Combine the sugar, cornflour, salt and ¼ teaspoon of ginger in a saucepan. Blend in the pear juice. Cook over medium heat, stirring constantly, until the mixture thickens and comes to the boil. Remove from the heat. Add lemon rind and lemon juice. Cut the pear halves in half lengthwise. Arrange in the unbaked pastry case. Pour thickened syrup over the pears.

Blend the flour, brown sugar, butter and remaining sugar with a pastry blender until the mixture looks like coarse crumbs. Stir in nuts. Sprinkle on top of the pears. Bake in a 425°F/220°C/gas mark 7 oven 20 to 25 minutes.

Pecan Pie

Makes 1 9-inch/22-cm pie

1 uncooked pastry case
5 eggs
6 oz/170 grams sugar
1 lb/450 grams treacle
12 oz/345 grams pecan nuts, chopped or halved
½ teaspoon salt
2 teaspoons vanilla essence
Whipped cream

Beat the eggs lightly in a large bowl. Add sugar, treacle, nuts, salt and vanilla. Mix until nicely blended. Pour into the uncooked pie shell. Bake at 325°F/

163°C/gas mark 3 for 50 minutes. When cool, garnish with whipped cream; serve at once.

Strawberry Tart with Vanilla Cream Custard

Makes 1 9-inch/22-cm pie

1 uncooked pastry case (see index)
Strawberries
1 packet instant strawberry blancmange
Apricot jam
Chopped pistachio nuts

Line a pie dish with the pastry, then cover the pastry with greaseproof paper and pour in dried beans or peas to bake blind.

Bake the crust at 400°F/200°C/gas mark 6 until golden brown, about 10 minutes. Cover the bottom with blancmange, made according to packet directions, and place sliced strawberries on top. Brush with the apricot jam, which has been mixed with a little water, and sprinkle with chopped pistachio nuts.

This recipe may be made using all different kinds of berries: blackberries, raspberries and wild strawberries. Serve warm with ice cream or whipped cream.

Pie with Pineapple Mousse

Rhubarb Pie

Makes 1 9-inch/22-cm pie

10 oz/285 grams frozen shortcrust pastry
2 lb/900 grams unpeeled young rhubarb stalks, diced
1 oz/30 grams flour
10 oz-1 lb/285–450 grams sugar
1 teaspoon orange rind, grated
½ oz/15 grams butter

Line a 9-inch/22-cm pie dish with pastry.

Combine the remaining ingredients in a bowl and toss well. Turn into the pastry case. Dot with 1 oz/30 grams of butter. Cover the pie with a well pricked pastry top or a lattice. Bake in a 450°F/230°C/gas mark 8 oven for 10 minutes. Reduce the heat to 350°F/180°C/gas mark 4 and bake for a further 35 to 40 minutes, until golden brown.

Treacle Tart

Makes 1 9-inch/22-cm pie

1 uncooked pastry case

crumb mixture
4 oz/115 grams butter
6 oz/170 grams flour
4 oz/115 grams light brown sugar

liquid mixture
1 lb/450 grams treacle
1 egg, beaten
8 fl oz/220 ml boiling water
Scant 1 teaspoon bicarbonate of soda

Mix the crumb mixture together with your hands. Mix the liquid mixture together. Pour it into the uncooked pastry case. Sprinkle the crumb mixture on top of the liquid mixture. Bake at 400°F/200°C/gas mark 6 for 15 minutes. Reduce the heat to 350°F/180°C/gas mark 4. Bake approximately 30 minutes more, or until the mixture is set.

Pie with Pineapple Mousse

Makes 1 9-inch/22-cm pie

pastry
5 oz/140 grams flour
2 oz/60 grams sugar
3½ oz/100 grams margarine or butter
2½ oz/75 grams cottage cheese

mousse
18 oz/500 grams tinned pineapple slices in their own juice
2 envelopes gelatine
3 eggs, separated
2 oz/60 grams sugar
8 fl oz/220 ml whipping cream
3½ oz/100 grams cooking chocolate

Measure the flour and sugar into a bowl. Crumble the margarine into the mixture. Add the cottage cheese and make into a workable dough. (You can also place all the ingredients in a food processor and mix into a dough.) Refrigerate 1 hour.

Pour the juice from the pineapple (about 8 fl oz/220 ml) into a pan. Add the gelatine and let it soak in the juice for about 5 minutes, until soft. Then melt the gelatine in the juice over low heat.

Separate the egg yolks and whites. Beat the yolks together with the sugar. Beat the egg whites into stiff peaks. Whip the cream. Cut the pineapple slices into pieces and save 3 to 4 slices for decoration.

Mix the egg yolk mixture, whipped cream and pieces of pineapple together. Add the juice in an even trickle while stirring constantly. Mix well. Fold in the egg whites. Refrigerate this mousse for about 1 hour so that it becomes partially firm.

Preheat the oven to 400°F/200°C/gas mark 6. Press the dough into a pie dish or ovenproof dish. Prick well. Bake the pastry for about 20 minutes in the oven. Meanwhile, melt about 3 oz/85 grams of the cooking chocolate over very low heat.

Remove the pastry from the oven. Spread the chocolate in the pastry case. Leave to cool.

When the mousse has become partially firm, spread it over the chocolate in the pie. Place the dessert back in the refrigerator to become totally firm.

Decorate with slices of pineapple and chopped chocolate.

Summer Pie

Makes 1 9-inch/22-cm pie

3 oz/85 grams flour
6 oz/170 grams oatmeal
2½ oz/75 grams sugar
1 teaspoon baking powder
3½ oz/100 grams butter or margarine

filling
Fresh berries: for example, blackberries and raspberries

Mix all the dry ingredients together in a bowl. Work in the butter until the mixture is crumbly. Place half of the dough in a greased and floured, 9-inch/22-cm round pie tin with detachable sides. Flatten the crumbs slightly and press them up towards the sides.

Sprinkle a layer of berries over the crumbs and then cover with the rest of the crumbs. Bake at 400°F/200°C/gas mark 6 for 20 to 25 minutes.

Serve the pie warm with partially thawed vanilla ice cream or lightly whipped cream.

Strawberry Heart

Strawberry Heart

4 to 6 servings

pastry
6 oz/170 grams flour
2 oz/60 grams sugar
5 oz/140 grams margarine

almond paste
2 oz/60 grams marzipan
1 egg yolk
1 tablespoons water

meringue
1 egg white
2 oz/60 grams sugar
1–2 lb/450–900 grams strawberries
A little wine (optional)

Cut and knead the pastry ingredients together into a dough. Roll it out directly onto greaseproof paper with a floured rolling pin. Cut out a plate-sized circle, a large heart or an oval. Remove any excess dough.

Grate and mix the marzipan with the egg yolk and ½ tablespoon of the water. Put it into a forcing bag and pipe a border along the outer edge of the crust.

Press out the rest of the almond paste into a cup and stir in 1 tablespoon of water so that the paste becomes thinner in consistency. Spread this out inside the paste border.

Whip the egg white until stiff, first without and then with the sugar. Use the forcing bag again—it does not have to be washed between uses—and press out a row of little peaks along the marzipan line.

Bake the pie at 350°F/180°C/gas mark 4 for 20 minutes on the lowest shelf of the oven.

Fill the cooled pie with whole or halved strawberries, which can also be made glossy with a little wine (estimate 1 tablespoon gelatine per 2½ fl oz/75 ml liquid).

Biscuit Crumb Pastry Case

Makes 1 8-inch/19-cm pie case
8 oz/225 grams biscuit crumbs, e.g. shortbread
6 tablespoons unblanched almonds, ground
5 tablespoons single cream
5 oz/140 grams butter, melted
¼ teaspoon cinnamon

Crush the crumbs by hand or in a food processor. Mix the crumbs well with the butter. Press firmly into the bottom and sides of a flan dish. Chill.

Shortcrust Pastry Case

Makes 1 9-inch/22-cm pastry case
8 oz/225 grams flour, sifted
½ teaspoon salt
5 oz/140 grams plus ½ oz/15 grams shortening
2 to 2½ tablespoons cold water

Place the flour and salt in a mixing bowl. Cut in the shortening with a pastry blender or 2 knives until the mixture is the consistency of coarse crumbs. Sprinkle on the cold water, a little bit at a time, tossing the mixture lightly and stirring with a fork. The dough should not be sticky and should be just moist enough to hold together when pressed gently with a fork.

Shape 1 smooth ball of dough and roll out a little larger than a 9-inch/22-cm pie dish. For a cooked shell, prick the bottom and sides with a fork. Bake at 450°F/230°C/gas mark 8 for about 10 minutes.

Yoghurt Pastry

Makes 1 9-inch/22-cm pie case
8 oz/225 grams flour, sifted
½ teaspoon salt
4 oz/115 grams hydrogenated shortening
3 to 4 tablespoons yoghurt

Stir the flour and salt together. Cut in the shortening until the pieces are the size of very coarse crumbs. Sprinkle yoghurt over this mixture and stir lightly with a fork until the dough can be formed into a ball. Let rest about 10 minutes.

Roll out on a piece of floured greaseproof paper until the pastry is 1½ inches/4 cms larger than the inverted pie dish. Ease the dough into the dish without stretching. Trim ½ inch/1 cm beyond the edge of the dish and fold under to make a double thickness of dough around the rim. Flute the edge.

For a cooked pie case, prick the bottom and sides with a fork. Bake at 450°F/230°C/gas mark 8 on top shelf of oven for about 10 minutes.

Digestive Biscuit Pastry Case

Makes 1 9-inch/22-cm pie case
16 to 18 digestive biscuits, crumbled
2 oz/60 grams sugar
2 oz/60 grams butter or margarine, softened
¼ teaspoon ground nutmeg or cinnamon
 (optional)

Combine the biscuit crumbs, sugar, butter and nutmeg and blend until crumbly. Reserve 1½ oz/45 grams of crumbs to sprinkle on top of the pie, if desired. Press the remaining crumbs evenly on the bottom and sides of a 9-inch/22-cm pie dish, making a small rim.

Bake in a 375°F/190°C/gas mark 5 oven for 8 minutes, or until the edges are lightly browned. Cool, then fill as the recipe directs.

For an unbaked pastry case, use the same ingredients as for the baked case. Do not make a rim on the pie shell. Chill for about 1 hour, or until set, before filling.

Rich Shortcrust Pastry

Makes 1 9-inch/22-cm pastry case

8 oz/225 grams flour, sifted
4 oz/115 grams sugar
6 oz/170 grams butter and lard, mixed
1 egg

Combine all the ingredients. Form into a ball and chill. Roll out lightly on a floured board. Line a 9-inch/22-cm pie dish with the pastry and chill again.

For pies with strips on top, reserve a third of the dough and add to it 1 teaspoon of baking powder and 2 tablespoons of milk. Mix again and roll out. Cut in strips and place on top of the pie, all in one direction. These strips may not be crossed because they puff up. Use for fruit and berry pies.

Shortcrust Pie Pastry

Makes 1 9-inch/22-cm pie

10 oz/285 grams flour, sifted
1 teaspoon salt
5 oz/140 grams shortening or 5 oz/140 grams
    lard
4 to 5 tablespoons cold water

Place the flour and salt in a mixing bowl. Cut in the shortening with a pastry blender or 2 knives until the mixture is the consistency of coarse crumbs.

Sprinkle on the cold water, 1 tablespoon at a time, tossing the mixture lightly and stirring with a fork. Add water each time to the driest part of the mixture. The dough should not be sticky and should be just moist enough to hold together when pressed gently with a fork.

Shape the dough into a smooth ball with your hands. Roll it to be a little larger than a 9-inch/22-cm pie dish.

Meringue Shell

Makes 1 9-inch/22-cm pie shell

3 egg whites (at room temperature)
¼ teaspoon cream of tartar
Pinch salt
6 oz/170 grams sugar

Mix the egg whites, cream of tartar and salt together. Beat until frothy. (Do not under beat.) Gradually add the sugar and beat until stiff peaks form. The meringue should be shiny and moist, with all the sugar dissolved.

Spread over the bottom and sides of a well greased 9-inch/22-cm pie dish. Bake in a 275°F/135°C/gas mark ½ oven for 1½ hours. Turn off the oven and leave meringue in the oven with a closed door for 1 hour. Finish cooling the meringue in the dish away from draughts. Spoon in the filling and chill.

Baked meringue shells almost always crack and fall in, in the centre.

Summer Pie

Cakes, Gâteaux and Biscuits

Almond Mousse Layer Cake

Makes 6 to 8 portions

cake
6 oz/170 grams almonds
2½ oz/75 grams sugar
3 egg whites

mocha cream icing
5 oz/140 grams cooking chocolate
8 fl oz/220 ml double cream
1 oz/30 grams icing sugar
2 tablespoons strong coffee, or 3 or 5 drops
   peppermint oil, or 2 tablespoons rum
2 egg yolks

garnish
Chocolate or roasted slivered almonds

Grind the unskinned almonds. Mix them with the sugar.

Beat the egg whites until stiff. Carefully fold in the almonds and sugar. Spread the mixture into 2 rounds about 3 inches/8 cms in diameter, on a baking sheet that has been covered with greaseproof paper. Bake in the centre of a preheated 350°F/180°C/gas mark 4 oven until they feel dry and are light brown in colour, about 15 minutes. Let them cool. Loosen them from the paper with a sharp knife.

Break the chocolate into pieces. Place in a bowl. Cover with foil. Place the bowl over a pan of boiling water. Remove the pan from the heat and let the chocolate melt slowly.

Whip the cream, but not too stiffly. Add the sugar, flavouring, egg yolks and 2 tablespoons of the cream to the chocolate. Beat vigorously. Let cool. Mix in the rest of the cream.

Forgotten Meringue Cake

Sandwich the layers together with slightly more than half of the chocolate mixture between the layers. Spread the rest of this on top. Refrigerate the cake for at least 2 hours before serving.

Garnish with chocolate almonds or chocolate curls.

Almond Mousse Layer Cake

327

Saffron Advent Cake

Makes 10 portions

8 oz/225 grams plain flour
3 teaspoons baking powder
6 oz/170 grams sugar
3½ oz/100 grams butter or margarine
4 fl oz/110 ml milk
1 egg
¼ teaspoon saffron, ground
Butter and breadcrumbs or flour for preparing
 the tin
3 or 4 apples, thinly sliced
A little sugar and several knobs of butter

Blend the flour, baking powder and sugar. Crumble the butter into the mixture until it is grainy.

Beat together the milk, egg and saffron. Pour into the flour mixture. Quickly work together into a dough. Place the dough in a greased shallow cake tin preferably with a detachable edge (springform) which has been dusted with breadcrumbs or flour. Stick thin slices of apples close together into the dough. Sprinkle with a little sugar. Place several dabs of butter on top. Bake in a 425°F/220°C/gas mark 7 oven for 25 to 30 minutes.

Alexander Cake

Makes 8 to 10 portions

cake
2 oz/60 grams almonds
5 egg whites
6 oz/170 grams sugar

custard cream
5 egg yolks
12 fl oz/350 ml double cream
6 oz/170 grams sugar
1 teaspoon cornflour
2 teaspoons rum

garnish
Toasted sliced almonds

Grind the almonds.

Beat the egg whites into stiff peaks. Fold in the almonds and sugar. Spread the mixture into 2 heart shaped layers on a greased baking sheet. Bake in a 350°F/180°C/gas mark 4 oven for about 15 minutes.

Mix the egg yolks, cream, sugar and cornflour together in a thick bottomed pan or in a double boiler. Let the custard cream simmer slowly, stirring constantly, for 10 to 15 minutes, until it becomes thick.

Saffron Advent Cake and Orange-Nut Ring

Stir in the rum. Cool. Spread part of the custard cream over one of the cake layers. Place the second layer on top. Spread the rest of the custard cream over one of the cake layers. Place the second layer on top. Spread the rest of the custard cream over the second layer. Garnish with almonds.

Angel Food Cake

Makes 12 servings

2 oz/60 grams plain flour
4 oz/115 grams plus 1 oz/30 grams sugar
2½ fl oz/75 ml egg whites
Pinch salt
½ teaspoon cream of tartar
½ teaspoon vanilla essence

Use a 6-inch/15-cm cake tin, not greased. Sift the flour and sugar separately 3 times, then sift the flour with ¼ of the sugar.

Put the egg whites and salt in a large, clean, dry bowl and beat until frothy. Sprinkle on the cream of tartar and continue beating until the white stands up in peaks. Avoid overbeating, or the white will lose its glossiness. Lightly beat in the remaining sugar and flavourings. Then, using a tablespoon, fold in the sifted flour-sugar mixture carefully and gradually.

Pour into a ring mould and gently cut through the mixture with a knife to release air bubbles. Bake for 40–45 minutes in a 290°F/145°C/gas mark 1½ oven increasing the heat to 335°F/170°C/gas mark 3½ for the last 10–15 minutes. Allow the cake to stand in the inverted pan for 30 minutes, then turn out onto a cooling rack.

Almond Apple Cake

Makes 4 portions

6 medium apples
2½ oz/75 grams almonds
5 oz/140 grams margarine or butter
2½ oz/75 grams sugar
2 eggs
3 oz/85 grams breadcrumbs

Grease an ovenproof dish.

Coarsely grate the apples, with peel, and place the gratings in the bottom of the dish.

Grind the almonds.

Beat the margarine and sugar until light. Add the eggs, almonds and breadcrumbs. Mix. Spread the mixture over the apples. Bake in a preheated 400°F/200°C/gas mark 6 oven for about 30 minutes.

Serve with custard or cream.

Alexander Cake

Almond Shortcrust Cake

Makes 8 to 12 portions

shortcrust pastry

1 egg
5 oz/140 grams butter or margarine
2½ oz/75 grams sugar
8 oz/225 grams self-raising flour

filling

7 oz/200 grams almonds
3½ oz/100 grams butter or margarine
5 oz/140 grams sugar
2 eggs
Few drops vanilla essence
¼ teaspoon ground cardamom
¼ teaspoon baking powder

Make the pastry. Beat the egg. Save a tablespoon for brushing the pastry. Work all the ingredients of the pastry together into a dough. Refrigerate for about an hour.

Roll out about two thirds of the dough. Line a greased tin with detachable edge, about 9 inches/22 cms in diameter, with the dough. The dough should go 1 inch/2½ cms up the sides of the tin. To make the filling, grind the almonds (the skins do not need to be removed). Beat the butter and sugar together until light. Add the eggs, one at a time. Beat vigorously.

Mix the almonds with the vanilla, cardamom and baking powder. Add to the egg mixture. Spread out in the tin. Bake in a 350°F/180°C/gas mark 4 oven for about 20 minutes.

Roll out the rest of the dough. Cut out strips and place them crisscross over one another on the partially baked cake. Finally place a border of dough around the edge of the cake. Brush with egg. Bake for 25 minutes. Let the cake cool before removing the detachable edge.

Apple Cake

Makes 10 portions

½ oz/15 grams margarine and 1 oz/30 grams
    breadcrumbs or flour for preparing the cake tin
6 oz/170 grams self-raising flour
6 oz/170 grams sugar
2 oz/60 grams margarine

Almond Shortcrust Cake

Almond Apple Cake

Apple Cake

8 fl oz/220 ml milk
2–3 apples, sliced
1 teaspoon cinnamon and 1½ oz/45 grams sugar, mixed together

Grease a 9-inch/22-cm round cake tin. Dust it with breadcrumbs or flour.

Mix together the flour and sugar.

Finely chop the margarine into the flour mixture. Crumble it with your fingertips. For those with a food processor, use the metal knife attachment. Add the milk. Quickly mix together into a batter. Pour the batter into the greased tin. Press the apple slices down into the cake. Make a decorative sun ray pattern. Sprinkle the cinnamon and sugar mixture over the cake. Bake in a preheated 350°F/180°C/gas mark 4 oven for 40 to 45 minutes.

Turn the cake out of the tin and tip it right side up again onto the plate from which it is to be served.

French Apple Cake

Makes about 10 portions

4 oz/115 grams butter
4 oz/115 grams sugar
About 6 oz/170 grams ground almonds
Juice and grated peel of ½ lemon
2 egg yolks
3 egg whites, beaten until stiff
Apple compote made from 6 to 8 apples, or 1 pint/½ l apple sauce
12 fl oz/350 ml whipped cream, flavoured with sugar and vanilla or sherry

Allow the butter to soften and then beat it with the sugar until it becomes airy and light in colour. Add the ground almonds, grated lemon peel and lemon juice. Add the egg yolks, one at a time and finally fold in the beaten egg whites.

Pour apple compote or apple sauce into a greased tin. Cover with the mixture. Bake at 400°F/200°C/gas mark 6 for 20 minutes. (This may be prepared a day in advance. Cover with aluminium foil and warm when it is time to serve the cake. It tastes best when served warm.) Serve with cream that has been lightly whipped.

sugar. Place several knobs of butter here and there on the cake. Bake in a 425 to 450°F/220 to 230°C/gas marks 7 to 8 oven for about 20 minutes. Cut the cake into pieces when serving.

Quick Puff Pastry Apple Cake

Makes 4 portions

8 oz/225 grams puff pastry, frozen
1 apple
2 oz/60 grams marzipan
1½ oz/45 grams sugar
1 tablespoon cinnamon
1 egg

Thaw the puff pastry. Roll it out on a floured board. Make it round or rectangular, depending on your serving plate. Place on a baking sheet.

Grate the apple and marzipan. Sprinkle them over the pastry. Sprinkle with the sugar and cinnamon.

Beat the egg. Brush it around the pastry edges. Bake in a 425°F/220°C/gas mark 7 oven for about 20 minutes.

Serve with ice cream, or with whipped cream sweetened with a little vanilla and sugar.

Quick Apple Cake

Quick Apple Cake

Makes 6 to 8 portions

10 oz/285 grams plain flour
3 teaspoons baking powder
10 oz/285 grams sugar
5 oz/140 grams butter or margarine
12 fl oz/350 ml coffee cream
About 6 apples
Grated peel from 1 orange and 1 lemon
A little squeezed juice (optional)
Sugar
Knobs of butter

Mix the flour, baking powder and sugar together in a bowl. Crumble the butter into the mixture so that it resembles small pebbles. Add the cream and work quickly into a dough. Spread the dough into a baking tin that has been covered with buttered greaseproof paper. The dough should measure about 9 × 13 inches/22 × 32 cms.

Core the apples. Cut the apples into thin wedges. Place the wedges close together on top of the dough. Sprinkle with the peel from the orange and lemon. Squeeze several drops of orange or lemon juice over the top of the cake. Sprinkle with a small amount of

Cakes, Gâteaux and Biscuits

Quick Puff Pastry Apple Cake

Berry Roll

Makes about 8 portions

3 eggs
5 oz/140 grams sugar
3 oz/85 grams plain flour
1 teaspoon baking powder

filling
6 oz/170 grams jam or fresh berries

Beat the eggs and sugar together until light and airy. Carefully fold in the flour, which has first been blended with the baking powder. Spread the batter in a 12 × 15-inch/30 × 38-cm baking tin that has been lined with greaseproof paper. Bake in a 425°F/220°C/ gas mark 7 to 450°F/230°C/gas mark 8 oven for about 5 minutes. Turn the cake out onto sugared grease-proof paper. Peel away the paper on which the cake was baked. (Brush the paper with cold water if it does not loosen easily). Spread the filling on the warm cake. Roll it up from the long side.

Variation: Place ice cream on a cake slice and top with berries.

French Apple Cake

Bilberry Cake

Makes 8 to 10 portions

6 oz/170 grams self-raising flour, sifted
8 oz/225 grams sugar
Dash salt
4 oz/115 grams butter, softened
2 lb/900 grams bilberries
1 tablespoon lemon juice
6 oz/170 grams quick cooking tapioca
¼ teaspoon salt
Pinch cinnamon

Combine the flour, 4 oz/115 grams of sugar, dash salt and butter. Mix with a pastry blender or fork until the crumbs are formed. Measure 6 oz/170 grams and set aside.

Press the remaining crumbs over the bottom and up the sides of a 9-inch/22-cm springform tin.

Combine the berries, lemon juice, remaining sugar, tapioca, salt and cinnamon. Let stand 15 minutes. Spoon the berry mixture into the crumb lined tin. Bake at 425°F/220°C/gas mark 7 for 20 minutes. Then sprinkle with the reserved crumbs. Bake 20 to 25 minutes longer, or until the crumbs are golden brown. Serve warm or cold with whipped cream.

Berry Roll

American Cheesecake

Makes about 8 portions

8 oz/225 grams plain biscuits (e.g. digestives)
1 teaspoon cinnamon
3½ oz/100 grams melted butter

filling
18 oz/500 grams cream cheese
6 oz/170 grams sugar
3 eggs
½ teaspoon vanilla essence

top layer
About 12 fl oz/350 ml soured cream

Finely crush the biscuits. Mix them with the cinnamon and butter. Press the crumb mixture onto the bottom and partially up the sides of a tin with a detachable bottom. The tin should be at least 9 inches/22 cms in diameter, preferably even larger. Bake in a preheated 350°F/180°C/gas mark 4 oven for 5 minutes.

Beat the cream cheese until creamy. Add the eggs, sugar and vanilla sugar. Pour the mixture into the tin and bake for 45 minutes.

Spread the cream over the cake. Place in the oven for 5 minutes.

Let the cake cool. Serve it chilled. The cake can be stored in the refrigerator for several days as long as it is covered well. It can also be frozen.

Serve well chilled. If desired, decorate with berries, fruit or jam.

Crisp Cheesecake

Makes 10 portions

6 oz/170 grams butter
6 oz/170 grams self-raising flour
3 oz/85 grams grated Parmesan cheese
4 tablespoons double cream

decoration
2–3 oz/85 grams scalded, peeled almonds, cut in half
1 egg

filling
5 egg yolks
8 fl oz/220 ml double cream
5 oz/140 grams butter
4–6 oz/115–170 grams finely grated mature cheese
Pinch cayenne pepper

garnish
Green and black grapes

Chop together the butter, flour and the Parmesan cheese, either by hand with a chopping knife or in a food processor, using the metal knife attachment. Add the cream. Make a dough. Divide the dough into 2 parts. Make each part into a round, thick cake. Cover them with cling film and refrigerate for an hour or more.

Scald the almonds. Peel and cut them in half.

Separate the egg yolks from the whites for the filling. (The egg whites are not needed in this recipe.) Place the egg yolks in a saucepan. Beat them together with the cream. Let thicken over a double boiler. Stir occasionally with a wooden fork. The yolks should not be allowed to boil. Remove from the heat and stir in the butter in pieces. Let each piece of butter totally mix with the egg yolks before adding the next piece. Finally add the cheese and cayenne pepper. Let cool.

Remove the dough from the refrigerator. Roll out the dough into plate size round layers. Roll out between pieces of cling film. Pull away the cling film from the top. Place a plate over the dough and even off the edges. Turn the dough upside down onto greaseproof paper. Remove the other piece of cling film. Brush the layers with a beaten egg. Decorate one with almonds. Bake in a preheated 400°F/200°C/gas mark 6 oven for 10 minutes. Let cool on the paper.

Place the round without the almonds on a serving plate. It can be moved with the help of the bottom part of a round tin with a detachable bottom. Spread the cheese filling over it. Place the almond layer on top.

The cake should be made several hours in advance. Garnish it with the grapes.

The layers can be frozen separately. If the cake is put together before it is frozen, it will become soft when thawing and will lose its crispness.

Mint Chocolate Cake

Makes about 8 portions

2½ oz/75 grams cooking chocolate
2½ oz/75 grams butter or margarine
6 oz/170 grams sugar
¼ teaspoon vanilla essence
2 eggs
4 oz/115 grams self-raising flour
4 fl oz/110 ml cream

mint filling
2½ oz/75 grams sugar
4 fl oz/110 ml strong coffee
3 egg yolks

2½ oz/75 grams unsalted butter, room temperature
2 oz/60 grams melted light cooking chocolate
2 to 3 drops peppermint oil

Break the cooking chocolate into smaller pieces. Melt in a double boiler.

Mix the butter, sugar and vanilla until airy. Add the eggs, one at a time. Beat the mixture until smooth. Blend in the chocolate.

Add the flour and the cream to the mixture. Pour the mixture into a well greased and floured 4-lb/1800-gram tin. Bake in a 350°F/180°C/gas mark 4 oven about 50 minutes. Test with a baking needle.

To make the mint filling, boil the sugar and coffee together until syrupy.

Beat the egg yolks lightly. Add the sugar and coffee mixture in a thin trickle, stirring constantly and vigorously. Let cool. Add the butter in pieces continuing to beat vigorously. Flavour with the melted chocolate and peppermint oil

Divide the cake into 3 layers. Spread the mint filling between the layers.

Serve the cake with cold whipped cream.

American Cheesecake

Walnut Cheesecake

Makes about 8 portions

4 oz/115 grams walnuts
8 oz/225 grams blue cheese
6 oz/170 grams butter
About 4 oz/115 grams firm whipped cream
 cheese
8 fl oz/220 ml double cream

garnish
Green and black grapes
Chives

Remove several of the more decorative walnuts for the garnish. Finely chop or grind the rest of the walnuts. Add them to the blue cheese and 3½ oz/100 grams of the butter. Make into a soft mixture.

Warm the whipped cheese in the cream and mix in the rest of the butter. Remove from the heat as soon as the cheese has melted. Spread half of the cheese mixture, about ½ inch/1 cm thick, over the bottom of a small springform tin. (Place cut grease-proof paper on the bottom of this.) Cover with the soft blue cheese mixture. Even the top with a small, warmed spatula. Decorate with the reserved walnuts. Refrigerate for at least 24 hours.

Remove the edge and bottom of the tin when the cake is cold. Take the cake out of the refrigerator and serve it at room temperature. Garnish with grapes. Make division lines on the cake with chives.

This cake tastes best when it is two days old and not served too cold.

Sticky Chocolate Cake

Makes 8 to 12 portions

10 oz/285 grams sugar
¼ teaspoon salt
4 tablespoons cocoa
3 oz/85 grams self-raising flour
2 eggs
3½ oz/100 grams melted, cooled butter
½ teaspoon vanilla essence
Butter and breadcrumbs or flour for preparing
 the tin
4–6 oz/115–170 grams sliced almonds

Mix all the dry ingredients together. Mix in the eggs, butter and vanilla.

Grease a 9-inch/22-cm round cake tin, preferably a springform. Sprinkle it with breadcrumbs or flour. Spread the mixture in the tin. Sprinkle with the sliced almonds. Bake in the bottom of a preheated 325°F/163°C/gas mark 3 oven for about 35 minutes. The cake should be sticky on the inside.

Serve with whipped cream and berries or fruit.

Crisp Cheesecake

Chocolate Cake

Makes about 10 portions

2 eggs
6 oz/170 grams sugar
4 tablespoons cocoa
4 oz/115 grams self-raising flour
3 oz/85 grams melted butter or margarine
¼ teaspoon salt

mocha cream filling
2 oz/60 grams butter
6 oz/170 grams icing sugar
2 tablespoons strong coffee

topping
8 fl oz/220 ml whipping cream
Slivered cooking chocolate
Marzipan fruits for decoration (optional)

Mix the eggs and sugar together, but do not beat. Add the cocoa, flour, butter and salt. Stir until no longer lumpy. Pour into a greased springform cake tin that has been sprinkled with breadcrumbs. Bake in a 350°F/180°C/gas mark 4 oven for about 25 minutes. The cake should not be entirely dry.

To make the cream filling, stir the butter, icing

sugar and coffee into a smooth cream. It should have a strong coffee flavour.

Spread the cream filling over the cold cake, which has not been removed from the bottom of the cake tin. Spread the whipped cream on top and sprinkle with the slivered cooking chocolate. Garnish with marzipan fruits. Serve cold.

Minute Chocolate Cake

Makes 8 to 10 portions

3 oz/85 grams chocolate pudding mix
Double cream
1 teaspoon instant coffee
1 to 2 tablespoons cocoa
1 meringue cake layer (not too thin)
4 fl oz/110 ml whipped cream
Cocoa
Thin slices of chocolate

Mix the chocolate pudding powder according to the packet directions, but substitute half the milk with double cream. Add the instant coffee and cocoa to create a fuller taste. Adjust the flavouring. Immediately spread the pudding icing over the meringue

cake. Spread a layer of whipped cream on top of this. Sift cocoa on top. Press the chocolate slices into the whipped cream. Refrigerate the cake before serving.

Vanilla Slices

Makes 10 to 12 portions

6–8 oz/170–225 grams butter or margarine
4 eggs
1 lb/450 grams sugar
1 lb/450 grams self-raising flour
¼ teaspoon vanilla essence
Grated peel of 2 well rinsed lemons
4 oz/115 grams flaked almonds

Melt the butter. Let it cool.

Quickly mix the egg, sugar, flour, vanilla and lemon peel with the butter. Stir just until the ingredients are mixed together, but no longer. Spread out in a baking tin 12 × 16 inches/30 × 40 cms that has been covered with a buttered sheet of greaseproof paper. Sprinkle with the almonds. Bake in a 400°F/200°C/gas mark 6 oven for about 25 minutes. Cut the cake into bite sized pieces.

Walnut Cheesecake

Vanilla Slices, Marzipan Cake with Chocolate , Coconut Squares and Apple Squares

French Chocolate Cake

Makes about 10 portions

7 oz/200 grams plain chocolate
6 oz/170 grams butter or margarine
4 eggs
6 oz/170 grams sugar
8 oz/225 grams self-raising flour
2½ oz/75 grams hazel nuts, coarsely chopped

Grease a springform tin with detachable bottom that has a diameter of about 9 inches/22 cms. Preheat the oven to 425°F/220°C/gas mark 7.

Melt the cooking chocolate and butter in a thick bottomed pan over low heat. Beat the eggs and sugar until light and airy. Carefully stir the cooled chocolate mixture into the egg mixture.

Blend the flour and nuts together and fold carefully into the mixture. It is important to fold it in gently.

Pour the mixture into the tin and bake in the oven for about 15 minutes. The cake should not become firm. The uncooked mixture tastes like a delicious filling.

You may garnish the cooled cake with a little bit of grated chocolate and a ring of whipped cream.

Cinnamon Cake

Makes about 8 portions

3½ oz/100 grams butter or margarine
6 oz/170 grams sugar
3 large eggs
6 oz/170 grams self-raising flour
½ teaspoon vanilla essence
8 fl oz/220 ml soured cream
Butter
Breadcrumbs or flour

filling
Almost 2 oz/60 grams sugar
1 teaspoon cinnamon

Beat the butter and sugar together until light and fluffy. Add the eggs, one at a time, beating constantly.

Stir the vanilla into the cream. Alternate adding the flour and the cream to the mixture. Pour half of the mixture into a 4-lb/1800-gram greased baking tin that

Chocolate Cake

French Chocolate Cake

has been dusted with breadcrumbs or flour. Sprinkle with about half of the sugar and cinnamon mixed together. Spread the rest on top. Sprinkle with the rest of the sugar and cinnamon. Bake the cake in a 350°F/180°C/gas mark 4 oven for about 1 hour. Cover the cake with aluminium foil if it should start to get too dark while baking.

Old Fashioned Honeycake

Makes 8 portions

5 oz/140 grams butter
1½ lb/700 grams honey
3 eggs
12 oz/345 grams self-raising flour, sifted
1 teaspoon cinnamon
1 teaspoon powdered cloves
½ teaspoon salt
1 lb/450 grams raisins, chopped
¼ pint/140 ml milk

Cream the butter and add the honey. Beat the eggs and add, mixing well. Sift the flour, cinnamon, cloves and salt together. Add the chopped raisins. Add the flour alternately with the milk to the creamed mix-

ture. Pour into a loaf tin and bake in a 350°F/180°C/gas mark 4 oven for 1½ hours.

Hazelnut Cake

Makes 8 portions

6 oz/170 grams hazelnuts, skinned
5 bitter almonds
6 oz/170 grams self-raising flour
3 oz/85 grams butter or margarine
8 fl oz/220 ml coffee cream
2 eggs
6 oz/170 grams sugar
Butter and breadcrumbs or flour for preparing the tin

Grind the hazelnuts with the bitter almonds. Mix with the flour and the baking powder.

Melt the margarine in a pan. Pour in the cream.

Beat the eggs and sugar together until fluffy and light. Add the flour and butter cream mixtures. Pour the mixture into a well greased 4-lb/1800-gram baking tin that has also been dusted with breadcrumbs or flour. Bake in a 350°F/180°C/gas mark 4 oven for about 55 minutes. Test with a baking needle.

Mint Chocolate Cake

Old Fashioned Gingerbread Cake

Makes 12 to 14 portions

5 oz/140 grams butter or margarine
3 eggs
10 oz/285 grams sugar
1 tablespoon ginger
1 tablespoon cinnamon
1 tablespoon ground cloves
6 oz/170 grams cranberry jam
4 fl oz/110 ml soured cream
8 oz/225 grams plain flour
1 teaspoon bicarbonate of soda
Butter and breadcrumbs or flour for preparing
   the tin

Melt the butter.
Beat the eggs and sugar together until light and airy. Stir in the cooled butter, spices, jam, cream and the flour that first has been blended with the bicarbonate of soda. Pour into a 2 lb/900-gram greased loaf tin that has been dusted with breadcrumbs or flour. Bake in a 350°F/180°C/gas mark 4 oven for about 1 hour or until the cake feels dry.

Minute Chocolate Cake

Apricot Cream of Wheat Cake

Makes 4 servings

7 oz/200 grams dried apricots
12 fl oz/350 ml water
2 oz/60 grams sugar
½ oz/15 grams potato flour

cake layers
2 eggs
2½ oz/75 grams cream of wheat
½ oz/15 grams butter or margarine

topping
Icing sugar

Place the rinsed fruit in a saucepan with ½ pint/¼ litre of water. Let stand for 30 minutes.
Simmer the apricots over low heat for about 10 minutes. Add the sugar. Simmer for a few more minutes or until the apricots feel soft.
Prepare the cake layers. Mix the potato flour with 2½ fl oz/75 ml water. Add to the fruit, stirring constantly. Bring to the boil.
Beat the eggs and sugar together. Stir in the cream

of wheat. Cook a third of the cake batter in a greased frying pan about 4 minutes on each side. Repeat with the remaining batter, so that you have 3 cake layers. When the layers have cooled, make them into a cake with the warm, stewed apricots in between the layers. Sprinkle icing sugar over the cake, using a sieve, just before serving the cake.

Marzipan Cake with Chocolate

Makes about 8 portions

10 oz/285 grams marzipan
3½ oz/100 grams butter or margarine
3 eggs
3 oz/85 grams self-raising flour
3½ oz/100 grams plain chocolate, melted
Skinned almonds

Finely grate the marzipan on a grater. Mix it with the butter. Beat until light. Add the eggs, one at a time. Mix in the flour. Spread into a small baking tin, about 8 × 12 inches/20 × 30 cms, which has been lined with a buttered sheet of greaseproof paper. Bake in a 400°F/200°C/gas mark 6 oven for 8 to 10 minutes. Cool on rack. Spread melted chocolate over the cake. Garnish with skinned almonds, whole or

chopped. Cut the cake into pieces before the chocolate has totally hardened.

Variation: Cover the entire surface with thin apple slices and bake as above. Exclude the chocolate.

Forgotten Meringue Cake

Makes 8 to 10 portions

5 egg whites
6 oz/170 grams sugar
½ teaspoon baking powder

filling
Ice cream
Strawberries

Beat the egg whites until stiff. Add the sugar and baking powder, beating continuously. Pour the mixture into a greased ring mould. Smooth the top slightly. Heat the oven to 450°F/230°C/gas mark 8. When the oven has reached the desired temperature, turn it off. Then place the meringue in the oven. Let it stay there for about 9 hours or overnight.

Garnish with ice cream and strawberries in the middle. You can use other kinds of berries, fresh or frozen, depending on the season.

Apricot Cream of Wheat Cake

Ice Cream Cake

Makes 8 to 10 portions

1 layer nut cake (bought, or made)
Butter and breadcrumbs or flour for preparing
    the tin
1 meringue layer (bought, or made from 2 egg
    whites and 4 oz/115 grams sugar)

filling
1 pint/½ l vanilla ice cream

decoration
8 fl oz/220 ml whipped cream
Roasted hazelnuts

To make the meringue layer, beat the egg whites
into stiff, firm peaks. Fold in the sugar. Bake on a
well greased, floured baking sheet in a 250°F/120°C/
gas mark ¼ oven until the layer feels dry and light.

Cut the ice cream into slices. Cover the nut cake
layer with these. Place the meringue layer on top.

Whip the cream. Spread it over the meringue.
Sprinkle roasted nuts on top. Freeze the cake for
about 1 hour. It can also be served immediately.

Ice Cream Cake with Chocolate Icing

Makes about 6 portions

2 pint/1¼ l vanilla ice cream
4–6 oz/115–170 grams chopped walnuts
2 to 3 tablespoons white rum (optional)
4¼ oz/130 grams cooking chocolate

decoration
Roasted almonds or pistachio nuts
Crystallised violets or silver balls

Stir the ice cream until soft. Add the walnuts. Add
the rum.

Quickly pour the mixture into a springform tin.
Place in the freezer to harden.

Melt the cooking chocolate over a double boiler.
When the ice cream has hardened, release the
spring on the edge and remove the side of the tin.
Brush the sides and the top with a carelessly applied
first layer of chocolate. Place the ice cream back in
the freezer on the tin base. Let it freeze again for ½
to 1 hour. Take out of the freezer. Brush again with
the chocolate. None of the ice cream should show
through after this brushing. If it does, patch up the
spots with more of the chocolate. Spread out the rest
of the chocolate with a spatula. Sprinkle with the decoration before the chocolate hardens. Place again in
the freezer.

Remove the ice cream from the freezer shortly
before it is to be served, but do not detach it from
the bottom of the dish.

Ice Cream Cake

Variations: The ice cream is also tasty when about
½ tablespoon instant coffee is added. The ice cream
cake shown in the picture has been made from dou-
bling this recipe.

Custard Layer Cake

Makes about 10 portions

3 cake layers

topping
8 oz/225 grams marzipan
2 small egg whites
About 1 lb/450 grams fresh berries; for example,
    strawberries, raspberries, etc.
Jelly (strawberry, raspberry, etc.)

filling
½ packet custard, made up
About 6 oz/170 grams fruit jam; for example,
    strawberry, raspberry, etc.

Make the topping first. Grate the marzipan. Mix it smoothly with the egg whites. Press the mixture through a forcing bag in a crisscross decoration, with a round edge around the crisscross, onto one of the cake layers. Bake in a 350°F/180°C/gas mark 4 oven for about 10 minutes or until the marzipan is golden brown. Let stand until cold.

Place the other two cake layers together with a layer of jam between them. Spread a layer of cold custard on the second cake layer. Place the cake layer with the marzipan on top.

Decorate the cake by placing fresh berries in the marzipan squares. Pour a little melted jelly over the berries.

Refrigerate the cake so that the cake layers soak up the juices of the fruit.

Variation: Instead of using jam, mash fresh berries and mix them with a little sugar.

Mocha Cream Cake

Makes about 8 portions

cake layers
2 eggs
5 oz/140 grams sugar
3 oz/85 grams plain flour
1 oz/30 grams potato flour
1 teaspoon baking powder
2 tablespoons warm water
Butter and breadcrumbs or flour for preparing the tin

meringue layer
2 small egg whites
2½ oz/75 grams sugar

mocha cream filling
4 oz/115 grams butter
8 oz/225 grams icing sugar
1 small egg
2 to 3 tablespoons very strong instant coffee

nougat
5 oz/140 grams sugar

To make the cake layers: beat the eggs and sugar together until very light.

Mix the flour, potato flour and baking powder together. Sift them into the mixture. Carefully stir in the warm water. Pour the mixture into a well greased 7-inch/18-cm round cake tin that has been dusted with breadcrumbs or flour. Bake in a 300 to 350°F/ 150 to 180°C/gas marks 1 to 4 oven for about 25 to 30 minutes.

To make the meringue layer: beat the egg whites into firm, stiff peaks. Fold in the sugar. On a greased and floured baking sheet spread out the mixture,

Hazelnut Cake

slightly smaller in diameter than the cake. Bake in a 250°F/120°C/gas mark ¼ oven for about 15 minutes. Lower the temperature slightly and bake until the cake feels dry and light.

To make the mocha cream filling: stir the butter until soft. Beat in sugar and egg. (If you use an electric beater, you can add all the ingredients at the same time.) Flavour with the strong coffee. Beat vigorously.

To make the nougat: melt the sugar in a frying pan. Stir until it becomes a smooth, light brown mass. Pour out onto a baking sheet that has been greased with cooking oil. When the nougat is cold, crush it into pieces, using a mortar.

Divide the cake into 2 layers. Put the 2 cake layers and the meringue layer together with the mocha cream filling in between. Spread the cream filling around the top and sides of the cake. Sprinkle nougat over the cake. Decorate with the rest of the mocha cream filling and the nougat.

Macaroon Cake

Makes 6 portions

1 lb/450 grams marzipan
2 eggs

chocolate cream filling
14 fl oz/400 ml whipping cream
1½ oz/45 grams icing sugar
1½ oz/45 grams cocoa
3 tablespoons strong, cold coffee

decoration
Roasted sliced almonds
Silver balls (optional)

Finely grate the marzipan. Mix it with the eggs. Stir until smooth. Spread out into 4 thin, round layers, about 7 inches/18 cm in diameter, on buttered greaseproof paper that has been sprinkled with flour. Bake in a 400°F/200°C/gas mark 6 oven for 8 to 10 minutes or until the layers have become golden brown. Let them cool on a flat surface.

To make the filling, whip the cream. Stir in the icing sugar, cocoa and coffee, which both have first been sifted. Adjust the flavouring.

Jam and Custard Filled Cake

Place the cake layers together with the filling in between and on top. Sprinkle with the almonds and edible silver balls.

Refrigerate the cake overnight or for several hours before it is to be served.

Special Birthday Cake

Makes 10 to 12 portions

3½ oz/100 grams butter or margarine
4 or 5 plain biscuits, finely chopped (e.g. digestives)
4 oz/115 grams milk chocolate
1¼ lb/565 grams self-raising flour
2 lb/900 grams sugar
12 fl oz/350 ml soured milk
4 eggs
2½ oz/75 grams candied orange peel
4 oz/115 grams coarsely chopped walnuts
4 oz/115 grams milk chocolate, chopped
Icing sugar
1 orange, thinly chopped

Melt the butter in a saucepan. Add the crumbled biscuits. Allow to cool.

Melt the chocolate with 2 tablespoons water in a saucepan. Stir until smooth.

In a large bowl mix the flour, sugar, milk, melted chocolate, eggs and candied peel. Mix until smooth and creamy. Add the walnuts and the chopped chocolate to the biscuit mixture. Pour the cake mixture into a round, large, well greased cake tin. Pour the biscuit mixture over it. It sinks to the bottom. Bake in a preheated 350°F/180°C/gas mark 4 oven for 45 to 55 minutes. Top with icing sugar and thinly sliced oranges.

Mocha Parfait Cake

Makes 6 to 8 portions

14 fl oz/400 ml double cream
4 egg yolks
3 oz/85 grams sifted icing sugar
1 teaspoon vanilla essence
4 tablespoons instant coffee

decoration
3½ oz/100 grams cooking chocolate
1 tablespoon instant coffee granules

Whip and refrigerate the cream.

Beat the egg yolks with the icing sugar and vanilla in a round bottomed bowl over a double boiler. The water in the double boiler should not be allowed to boil. Beat until airy and white. Remove from the heat. Place in a pan of cold water. Add the instant coffee. Beat until the mixture becomes cold. Fold into the whipped cream. Pour into a tin that holds at least 2 pints/1¼ litres. Freeze for at least 4 hours. Remove

Ice Cream Cake with Chocolate Icing

the parfait from the freezer 1 hour before it is to be served.

Melt the cooking chocolate over a double boiler. Add the instant coffee. Spread the chocolate in a thin layer on aluminium foil (the shiny side). Let it cool. It can be refrigerated.

Wrinkle up the foil so that the chocolate breaks into small pieces. Remove the pieces. Sprinkle them over or around the parfait cake.

Mocha Cake

makes 8 to 10 portions

cake
About 10 oz/285 grams marzipan
2 egg whites from large eggs, lightly beaten

coffee cream filling
About 18 fl oz/500 ml double cream
Instant coffee, dissolved in a very small amount of warm water

decoration
Peeled, thinly slivered almonds
1 tablespoon instant coffee, dissolved in ½ tablespoon warm water

4 oz/115 grams marzipan
A little whipped cream
Chocolate beans

Finely grate the marzipan, using a grater. Beat it smoothly with the egg whites. Spread the mixture out into 3 thin rounds, about 8 inches/20 cm in diameter, on greased and floured greaseproof paper. Bake in a 400°F/200°C/gas mark 6 oven for about 10 minutes. Let them cool so that they remain flat.

Whip the cream into peaks. Add the instant coffee that has been dissolved in a little warm water. It should be very concentrated.

Place the cakes together with the mocha whipped cream between the layers, on top and on the sides. Press almonds around the edge.

Mix the coffee with the marzipan. Roll it out on greaseproof paper into a thin round the same size as the cake layers. Place it on top of the cake and garnish with a little mocha cream and the chocolate beans around the edge.

The cake will stay fresh for 2 days, protected by the marzipan. It tastes best when it has been refrigerated several hours or overnight before serving.

Macaroon Cake

which has been sprinkled with breadcrumbs. Bake in a preheated 350°F/180°C/gas mark 4 oven for about 40 minutes or until the cake feels dry. Let the cake cool before removing it from the tin.

To make the icing, beat together in a saucepan the egg yolks, sugar, cream and potato flour. Let it come to the boil and become a custard. Remove from the heat. Beat until cool.

Beat the butter until soft and smooth. Beat it into the custard a little at a time.

To make the nougat, melt the sugar in a frying pan. Stir in the almonds. Pour the mixture onto an oiled baking sheet. Let it cool. Finely chop the nougat.

Divide the cake into 2 layers. Spread the icing between the layers and around the entire cake. Sprinkle the nougat over the entire cake and press into the icing so that it does not fall off. Refrigerate cake several hours before serving.

Variation: Moisten the cake with a little rum and water before applying the icing. The icing can also be flavoured with rum.

Special Birthday Cake

Nougat Ring

Makes about 8 portions

cake
2 eggs
6 oz/170 grams sugar
2½ fl oz/75 ml warm water
3 oz/85 grams self-raising flour
Breadcrumbs

egg custard icing
2 egg yolks
2½ oz/75 grams sugar
8 fl oz/220 ml coffee cream
1 teaspoon potato flour
8 oz/225 grams butter

nougat
6 oz/170 grams sugar
2½ oz/75 grams chopped almonds

Beat the eggs and sugar together until very light. Add the warm water. Sift in the flour. Pour the mixture into a well greased 10-inch/25-cm ring mould

Orange and Chocolate Mousse Cake

Makes 12 to 14 portions

cake layers
Butter and breadcrumbs or flour
4 eggs
5 oz/140 grams sugar
2½ oz/75 grams plain flour
2½ oz/75 grams potato flour
2 teaspoons baking powder

orange chocolate filling
18 fl oz/500 grams whipped cream
7 oz/200 grams tinned frozen orange juice
5 eggs, separated
7 oz/200 grams cooking chocolate
2 envelopes gelatine

decoration
4 oz/115 grams cooking chocolate
1 orange
2 oz/60 grams flaked almonds

Grease a 10-inch/25-cm cake tin. Sprinkle it with breadcrumbs or dust with flour.

Beat the eggs and sugar together until light and fluffy.

Blend the other ingredients together. Add them to the egg and sugar mixture. Stir until well mixed. Pour into the prepared cake tin. Bake in a preheated 400°F/200°C/gas mark 6 oven on the lowest shelf for 30 to 35 minutes. Test with a baking needle to make sure the cake is done. If the baking needle comes out dry, remove the cake from the oven. Let the cake stand for a few minutes before turning it out onto a rack to cool. Let it cool under the cake tin. Cut the cold cake into three layers.

To make the filling, beat the cream until it starts to stand in peaks. Add the thawed orange juice. Beat for a few minutes so that the juice and the whipped cream become well blended. Refrigerate.

Separate the egg yolks and the whites.

Melt the chocolate over a double boiler. Add the egg yolks, one at a time, stirring constantly. Place the gelatine in cold water. Let it soak.

Beat the egg whites into stiff, dry peaks. Squeeze out the gelatine. Stir it into the warm chocolate mixture. Carefully fold the chocolate into the egg whites. Blend well.

Put the cake together in the following order: cake, orange cream, cake, chocolate cream and cake. Finish with a pretty layer of orange cream around and on top of the cake. To prepare the decoration, melt the chocolate over a double boiler. Peel the orange. Cut the orange into thin slices. Dip half of each orange slice in the chocolate. Let it harden on a piece of greaseproof paper.

Roast the almonds in the oven or in a frying pan.

Mocha Cake

Press them into the sides of the cake. Place the orange slices on top of the cake.

This cake can be prepared a day ahead and kept refrigerated. It is best not to freeze it.

Orange Nut Ring

Makes 10 portions

6 oz/170 grams soft butter or margarine
3 eggs
8 oz/225 grams sugar
Grated peel of 1 large or 2 smaller oranges
2–3 oz/60–85 grams chopped nuts
6 oz/170 grams flour
Breadcrumbs

Beat the butter. Beat the eggs and sugar together until light and airy. Beat the mixture into the butter. Carefully stir in the orange peel, nuts and flour. Pour into a greased ring mould that has been sprinkled with breadcrumbs. Bake in a 350°F/180°C/gas mark 4 oven until the cake feels dry, 30 to 40 minutes.

The flavour of this cake is enhanced if it is moistened with a sugar syrup (icing sugar flavoured with squeezed orange juice and even a little orange liqueur or brandy). Prick the cake all over and spoon the liquid over the cake.

Serve the cake with berries and lightly whipped cream.

Mocha Cream Cake

Nut Roll Cake

Makes about 8 portions

5 oz/140 grams hazelnuts
1 oz/30 grams potato flour
6 oz/170 grams sugar
2 teaspoons baking powder
3 eggs

butter cream filling
3½ oz/100 grams butter or margarine
5 oz/75 grams icing sugar
1 egg
½ teaspoon vanilla essence

Attach the metal knife to your food processor. Finely chop the nuts in the machine. Add the potato flour, sugar, baking powder and eggs. Quickly mix for 20 to 30 seconds. Spread out on a baking sheet or in a 12×16-inch/30×40-cm baking tin that has been covered with greaseproof paper. Bake in the centre of a preheated 450°F/230°C/gas mark 8 oven for about 5 minutes. Sprinkle a little sugar over the cake. Turn it over onto a sheet of aluminium foil. Pull off the paper on which the cake was baked. Let the cake cool, covered with a cloth.

Meanwhile, make the filling. Keep the metal knife attachment on the food processor. Divide the butter or margarine into 4 to 6 pieces. Place them and the other filling ingredients in the food processor. Start the machine and quickly mix together the ingredients to a smooth icing. Spread the butter cream filling on the cake. Roll as for Swiss roll.

Orange Cake

Makes about 12 portions

cake
Butter
Breadcrumbs or flour
4 eggs
6 oz/170 grams sugar
3 oz/85 grams flour
3 oz/85 grams potato flour
1 teaspoon baking powder
Juice and peel from 1 orange

orange curd
3 oranges
8 oz/225 grams sugar
3½ oz/100 grams butter
2 eggs, beaten

garnish
4 oz/115 grams flaked almonds
3 oranges

filling
Orange curd
12 fl oz/350 ml double cream, whipped

jelly
2 envelopes gelatine
8 fl oz/220 ml freshly squeezed and strained
   orange juice
2 oz/60 grams sugar

Grease a 9-inch/22-cm round springform cake tin. Sprinkle with breadcrumbs.

Beat the eggs and sugar until white and airy.

Sift the flours with the baking powder. Add to the egg and sugar mixture. Add the juice and peel. Pour into the cake tin and bake in a preheated 350°F/180°C/gas mark 4 oven for about 30 minutes. It is important not to take the cake out too early, as it will easily collapse. Take it out of the cake tin. Let it cool.

To make the orange curd, grate the peel of three oranges. Press the juice out of two of them. Place the peels, juice, sugar and butter in a bowl over boiling water. Heat until the butter has melted. Mix in the eggs. Beat until the mixture is thick and airy. It is best to make the orange curd a day before the cake is to be made.

Roast the almonds. Peel the oranges so that even the outer membrane is removed. Slice the oranges.

Mix the orange curd with the whipped double cream.

Divide the cake into three layers. Spread the orange curd between the layers, on top and around the sides of the cake. Press the almonds around the sides of the cake. Cover the top of the cake with the sliced oranges. Cover with cling film. Refrigerate.

Moisten the gelatine in 2½ fl oz/75 ml cold water for 5 minutes.

Heat 2½ fl oz/75 ml orange juice. Melt it in the hot juice, stirring constantly. Mix in the sugar. Remove from the heat. Beat the mixture into the remaining ice cold juice. Refrigerate the mixture.

Lightly grease the same cake tin used in making the cake layers. Cut out a piece of greaseproof paper the same size as the bottom of the cake tin. Press it into the greased tin. Place the cake tin in the freezer for 5 minutes so that it becomes really cold. Pour the liquid gelatine onto the paper in the cake tin. Freeze immediately. After 15 minutes the gelatine should be hard and frozen. Take it out of the cake tin. Place it with the paper side up on top of the cake's orange slices. Pull the paper carefully away from the gelatine. Keep the cake refrigerated until it is to be served.

Plum Cake

Makes 8 portions

4 oz/115 grams granulated sugar
4 oz/115 grams shortening
2 eggs
2½ fl oz/75 ml milk
4 oz/115 grams self-raising flour
4 oz/115 grams wholemeal flour
Dash salt
1 teaspoon vanilla essence
12 oz/345 grams fresh purple plum halves
4 oz/115 grams pecan nuts, chopped
½ teaspoon cinnamon

Cream the granulated sugar and shortening until smooth. Add the eggs. Beat until blended. Add the milk alternately with the combined flours and salt and blend. Stir in the vanilla. Pour the mixture into a greased and floured 9-inch/22- cm square cake tin. Top with plum halves.

Combine the pecan nuts, brown sugar and cinnamon. Sprinkle over the plum halves. Bake in a 350°F/180°C/gas mark 4 oven 30 minutes or until done.

Nougat Ring

Brandy Sponge

Makes about 8 portions

6 oz/170 grams butter or margarine
6 oz/170 grams self-raising flour
3 eggs
6 oz/170 grams sugar
2 tablespoons brandy
Butter and breadcrumbs or flour for preparing
    the tin

Beat the butter and flour together until very light and fluffy.

In another bowl, beat the eggs and sugar together until light and airy. Add the egg mixture to the butter mixture. Add only a little at a time, and beat constantly. Add the brandy, one tablespoon at a time. Pour into a well greased 9- inch/22-cm baking tin that has been dusted with breadcrumbs or flour. Bake in a 350°F/180°C/gas mark 4 oven for about 40 minutes.

Soured Cream Pound Cake

Makes 12 to 16 portions

10 oz/285 grams butter, at room temperature
1½ lb/700 grams sugar
6 large eggs, at room temperature
½ pint/¼ l soured cream
12 oz/345 grams self-raising flour
Pinch salt
1 teaspoon flavouring (either vanilla, lemon or
    half vanilla/half almond)
2 tablespoons brandy (optional)
Icing sugar

Cream the butter by hand or with an electric mixer until it reaches the consistency of whipped cream. Slowly dribble in the sugar a tablespoon at a time and beat well. Add the eggs one at a time, beating well after each addition. Stir in the soured cream.

Put the measured flour into a sifter with salt and sift 3 times. Add the flour 2 oz/60 grams at a time to the creamed mixture, blending well with the mixer set at lowest speed. Add flavouring and brandy, to taste. Beat again to combine thoroughly.

Pour into a greased 10-inch/25-cm ring mould and bake in a 325°F/163°C/gas mark 3 oven for 1 to 1½ hours, until the cake is done. Cool 15 minutes in the tin on a cake rack before turning out on a rack to cool completely. Sprinkle with icing sugar. This cake may be served with fresh strawberries and whipped cream.

Mocha Parfait Cake

Quick Sacher Cake

Makes 8 to 10 portions

5 oz/140 grams cooking chocolate
5 oz/140 grams butter
6 oz/170 grams sugar
4 eggs, separated
4 oz/115 grams self-raising flour
Butter and breadcrumbs or flour for preparing
    the tin

garnish
2½ oz/75 grams apricot jam
3½ oz/100 grams cooking chocolate
1 oz/30 grams butter
Whipped cream to taste

Melt the chocolate in the top of a double boiler.

Beat the butter and sugar until light. Add the egg yolks. Stir in the chocolate and the flour.

Beat the egg whites until stiff. Fold them into the mixture. Pour into a greased tin that has also been dusted with breadcrumbs or flour. Bake for about 30 minutes in a 350°F/180°C/gas mark 4 oven. Let the cake cool.

Spread the jam over the entire cake.

Melt the chocolate. Add the butter. Spread this mixture over the cake.

Serve cold with plenty of whipped cream.

Lightly Frozen Cake

Makes 6 to 8 portions

2 meringue cake layers, bought or homemade
8–12 fl oz/225–345 grams whipped cream

meringue layers
3 or 4 egg whites
5 oz/140 grams sugar

chocolate sauce
2½ fl oz/75 ml double cream
1½ oz/45 grams cooking chocolate, broken into pieces

To make the meringue layers, beat the egg whites in a clean bowl with a dry, clean beater until they form stiff, dry peaks. Continue to beat for a few more minutes. Sprinkle with the sugar. Fold the sugar into the egg whites with a couple of deep strokes with a spoon.

Draw 2 circles on a piece of baking paper. Spread the meringue on the paper within these circles. Bake in a 300°F/150°C/gas mark 1 oven for about 45 minutes. The meringue is done when it separates from the paper.

Make the chocolate sauce by placing the double cream and the chocolate into a saucepan. Heat and stir until the chocolate melts and the sauce is smooth.

To put the cake together, alternate meringue cake layers, chocolate sauce and whipped cream. Place the cake in the freezer for an hour or until time to serve it. If it is in the freezer longer than an hour, thaw before serving.

Swedish Coffee Cake Ring

Makes 2 rings

¼ oz/8 grams compressed yeast
3½ oz/100 grams butter
8 fl oz/220 ml milk
2½ oz/75 grams sugar
½ teaspoon cardamom
¼ teaspoon salt
About 12 oz/345 grams flour

filling
2½ oz/75 grams butter
2 oz/60 grams sugar

decoration
1 egg, beaten
Whole almonds

Crumble the yeast into a large mixing bowl.

Melt the butter in a saucepan. Add the milk. Warm to finger temperature (100°F/38°C). Pour over the yeast so that the yeast dissolves. Add the sugar, cardamom, salt and flour. Work the dough until it becomes smooth and shiny. Cover, and let rise for about 30 minutes.

Knead the dough. Divide it in half. Roll out each half into a rectangle.

Make the filling by mixing the butter and sugar until mixture is soft and smooth. Spread the filling over the dough, but not all the way to the edges. Roll up the dough. Pinch the edges tightly together. Form into a ring. Place on a greased baking sheet with the rolled edge facing down.

Brush the ends with a beaten egg. Fasten them together well. Let this rise under a cloth until it is very airy, 30 to 40 minutes.

Brush with egg. Place the almonds on top. Bake in a 400°F/200°C/gas mark 6 oven for about 20 minutes.

Nut Roll Cake

Spice Cake

Makes 16 portions

14 oz/400 grams seedless raisins
1 lb/450 grams sugar
4 oz/115 grams shortening
1½ pints/850 ml water
½ teaspoon salt
1¼ lb/1150 grams self-raising flour, sifted
3 teaspoons cinnamon
1 teaspoon cloves
1 teaspoon allspice

Place the raisins, sugar, shortening, water and salt in a saucepan and cook about 5 minutes, stirring. Cool. Add the flour and spices and mix well.

Bake in 2 small, or 1 large, greased and floured loaf tins in a 350°F/180°C/gas mark 4 oven for 45–60 minutes.

Cherry and Marzipan Cake

Makes 8 to 12 portions

8 oz/225 grams marzipan
3 tablespoons cherry liqueur or juice
3 egg yolks
½ oz/15 grams potato flour
½ teaspoon baking powder
Butter and breadcrumbs or flour for preparing
   the tin
3 egg whites

filling
3½ oz/100 grams soft butter
2½ oz/75 grams icing sugar
2 egg yolks
1½ tablespoons cherry liqueur or juice
1 small tin pears

decoration
9 oz/255 grams cooking chocolate
Small marzipan balls

Coarsely grate the marzipan. Mix it well with the liqueur or juice. Beat in the egg yolks, one at a time. Mix in the flour, which has first been blended with the baking powder.

Grease a 9-inch/22-cm round cake tin with detachable bottom. Sprinkle it with breadcrumbs.

Beat the egg whites into dry, stiff peaks. Carefully fold them into the mixture. Pour into the cake tin. Bake in a preheated 350°F/180°C/gas mark 4 oven for 30 to 40 minutes. Test the cake with a baking needle to make sure it is done. Let the cake cool before removing the edge of the cake tin. Carefully separate the bottom of the tin from the cake.

Beat the butter and icing sugar together until light and airy. Add the egg yolks, one at a time. Add the juice, a little at a time.

When the cake has cooled, divide it into 2 layers. Spread the filling over 1 of the layers. Cover it with a layer of ¼-inch/½-cm thick pear slices. Place the other cake layer on top.

Ice the cake with melted chocolate. (Save a little chocolate for grating on top). It is easiest to spread the chocolate with a flat plastic spatula. Decorate with marzipan balls.

Summer Marzipan Cake with Strawberries

Makes 8 to 10 portions

10 oz/285 grams marzipan
3 eggs
Grated peel of 1 orange
Butter and breadcrumbs or flour for preparing
   the tin

topping
Whipped cream
Sliced and whole strawberries

Coarsely grate the marzipan. Mix it with the eggs and orange peel. Beat it into a smooth mixture. Pour into a well greased 8-inch/20-cm cake tin that has been coated with breadcrumbs. Bake in a 350°F/180°C/gas mark 4 oven for 35 to 40 minutes. Let cool.

Place a layer of sliced strawberries on the cold cake, then a layer of whipped cream. Press the strawberries close together into the whipped cream. Decorate the dish with strawberries for an extra special touch.

Sugar Cake

Makes about 8 portions

5 oz/140 grams flour
6 oz/170 grams sugar
½ teaspoon vanilla essence
1 teaspoon baking powder
2 eggs
2½ fl oz/75 ml water
5 oz/75 grams margarine or butter
Butter and breadcrumbs or flour for preparing
   the tin

Fasten the metal knife attachment onto your food processor.

Measure all cake ingredients into the food processor. Divide the margarine into 6 to 8 pieces before adding. Mix for 20 to 30 seconds. Pour into a 9-cm/22-cm round cake tin that has been greased and sprinkled with breadcrumbs. Bake in the lower half of a preheated 350°F/180°C/gas mark 4 oven for about 40 minutes. Let the cake cool before taking it out of the tin.

Orange Cake

Strawberry Meringue Gâteau

Makes 6 to 8 portions

3 egg whites
6 oz/170 grams sugar
Butter and breadcrumbs or flour for preparing
  the tin

filling and topping

14 fl oz/400 ml whipping cream, whipped
1–1½ lb/450–700 grams strawberries
Roasted sliced almonds

Beat the egg whites into firm, stiff peaks. Carefully fold in the sugar. Spread out onto lightly buttered greaseproof paper that has been sprinkled with flour. Spread it in 2 7-inch round layers. Bake in a 300°F/150°C/gas mark 1 oven for 20 minutes. Reduce the oven temperature to the lowest heat possible. Continue cooking until the meringue feels dry and light, about 40 to 50 minutes. Fill the meringue with whipped cream and sliced strawberries. Spread the whipped cream over the cake. Press large strawberries close together into the whipped cream. Sprinkle almonds on top.

The meringue layers can be made in advance, but do not put the cake together until just before it is to be served.

Temptation Cake

Makes 10 portions

nut cake rounds

4 oz/115 grams chopped hazel nuts
4 oz/115 grams sugar
3½ oz/100 grams butter
½ oz/15 grams flour
2 tablespoons cream

filling

About 2 pints/1¼ l vanilla ice cream

decoration

8 fl oz/220 ml double cream, whipped into peaks
1 lb/450 grams fresh berries, preferably
  redcurrants or raspberries

Mix all the cake round ingredients together in a saucepan. Let the mixture melt, stirring constantly and vigorously. It must not boil. Make 2 rounds by spreading out the nut mixture on greaseproof paper on 2 baking sheets. Use a third of the mixture for each round. Spoon out the last third of the mixture in small dabs on a third sheet, also covered with greaseproof paper. Bake in a preheated 350°F/180°C/

Orange and Chocolate Mousse Cake

gas mark 4 oven for 15 to 20 minutes. The baking sheets can all be in the oven at the same time, with the small ones on the bottom. Change positions several times during baking. Let the rounds cool. Remove them carefully from the sheets, using a spatula. Keep them in a dry place until just before serving.

Place one large round on a cake dish. Place ice cream balls close together, or lay ½-inch/1-cm ice cream slices on top. Place the second round on top of the ice cream.

Garnish with the piped whipped cream and plenty of fresh redcurrants, raspberries or strawberries, depending on the season. The little rounds can be used as extra decoration.

Tutti-Frutti Cake

Makes about 8 portions

shortcrust pastry
8 oz/225 grams self-raising flour
4 oz/115 grams sugar
4 oz/115 grams butter or margarine
½ egg

lemon filling
3½ oz/100 grams butter or margarine
2½ oz/75 grams sugar

1½ eggs
½ oz/15 grams flour
1 tablespoon grated lemon peel

topping
About 8 fl oz/220 ml whipped cream
Mixed berries and fruits; for example, raspberries, bananas and redcurrants

Smoothly work together the flour, sugar, butter and ½ egg, using your fingertips.* Refrigerate for 20–30 minutes. Roll out the dough. Line a lightly greased 9-inch/22-cm pie dish with the dough. Mix all the filling ingredients together in a saucepan. Heat carefully, stirring constantly, until the butter has melted. Pour the filling into the pastry lined pie tin. Bake in a 350°F/180°C/gas mark 4 oven for 15 to 20 minutes. Cool completely.

Dab the whipped cream onto the cold cake or press it through a forcing bag in an attractive design. Garnish generously with berries.

The cake can be made in advance and stored in the freezer. Do not add the whipped cream and berries until time to serve the cake.

*To measure ½ egg, blend the yolk and white of a whole egg, measure and divide in half.

Brandy Sponge, Old Fashioned Gingerbread Cake & Cinnamon Cake

Twelfth Day of Christmas Cake

Makes about 10 portions

3½ oz/100 grams butter or margarine
4 oz/115 grams sugar
4–6 oz/115–170 grams coarsely chopped
   almonds

icing

3½ oz/100 grams butter
1½ oz/45 grams icing sugar
1 tablespoon instant coffee
1 egg yolk
3 oz/85 grams cooking chocolate
12 fl oz/350 ml double cream for whipping
Cocoa

Beat the butter and sugar together until light. Add the almonds. Spoon half of the mixture into a lightly greased shallow tin. Bake in a 350°F/180°C/gas mark 4 oven for about 15 to 20 minutes. Let the cake cool before removing it from the tin. Place it on a flat surface. Bake the other layer.

To make the icing, beat the butter with the icing sugar until smooth. Add the instant coffee and the egg yolk.

Melt the cooking chocolate over a double boiler. Let it cool before beating it into the butter mixture. Spread the icing over one cake layer.

Whip the cream. Spread about half of the cream over this layer. Place the second layer on top. Decorate with the rest of the cream. Sprinkle the cocoa on top, using a sieve. Refrigerate the cake until serving time.

Celebration Cake

Makes about 15 portions

4 cake layers
8 egg whites, cold
14 oz/400 grams sugar
6 oz/170 grams marzipan, cold

chocolate mousse filling

1 lb/450 grams plain chocolate, or half plain and
   half milk chocolate, melted
1 pint/½ l whipping cream, whipped
4 oz/115 grams caster sugar
4 egg yolks

decoration
Small thin chocolate pieces in different shapes

Lightly Frozen Cake

Cherry and Marzipan Cake

Cake layers: draw 4 9-inch/22-cm circles on 4 sheets of greaseproof paper. Grease the insides of the circles.

Pour the egg whites into a large bowl. Beat the whites vigorously for 10 minutes, using an electric beater. They should be whipped into very stiff peaks. Add sugar a little at a time. Beat vigorously until the sugar has been added and the mixture has become stiff and satiny, glossy smooth.

Grate the marzipan. Mix slightly less than half the meringue with the marzipan and stir. Mix in the rest of the meringue. Divide among the 4 circles on the buttered greaseproof paper. Spread into even layers. Bake one layer at a time on the lowest rack in a preheated 300°F/150°C/gas mark 1 oven for 25 to 30 minutes. Each layer is done when it feels dry and has become slightly browned. Let cool on a rack. Carefully remove the paper when the layers have cooled.

It is easiest to make the chocolate mousse in 2 large bowls. Break the chocolate into pieces. Melt it slowly in a large pan over a double boiler, carefully stirring occasionally. Let the chocolate cool.

Whip 12 fl oz/350 ml whipping cream in each bowl.

Whip half the chocolate into one bowl and half the chocolate into the other, using an electric beater. Add 2 oz/60 grams sugar and 2 egg yolks to each bowl. Beat vigorously into a fluffy mousse. Refrigerate the mousse for about half an hour.

Spread the mousse on the layers. Spread slightly more mousse on the top layer. Put the layers together. Chill the cake for a couple of hours.

Decorate to taste. Keep the cake chilled until serving time.

Basic Layer Cake

Makes 12 portions

6 oz/170 grams butter or margarine, softened
6 oz/170 grams sugar
2 eggs
Few drops vanilla essence
12 oz/345 grams self-raising flour, sifted
½ teaspoon salt
About ¼ pint/140 ml milk

Beat the butter, sugar and eggs in a large bowl. Sift the dry ingredient together; add alternately with milk to the butter mixture. Beat until smooth after each addition. Pour into 2 greased and floured, 9-inch/22-cm layer cake tins.

Bake in a preheated 350°F/180°C/gas mark 4 oven 30 minutes, or until the cake is done. Cool in tins on wire racks 10 minutes. Turn out onto racks; cool completely. Fill and ice as desired.

Strawberry Meringue Gâteau

Combine the sugar, water, salt and white vinegar in a heavy saucepan. Cook over medium heat, stirring constantly until clear. Without stirring, cook until the mixture forms a thin thread when dropped from a spoon (242°F/114°C on a confectioner's thermometer).

Beat the egg whites until stiff. Add the hot syrup, beating constantly. Continue beating until the icing holds its shape. Add the vanilla and blend well.

Advent Stars

Makes about 40 biscuits

6–8 oz/170–225 grams butter or margarine
8 oz/225 grams sugar
Grated peel of 1 lemon
2 eggs
11 oz/315 grams self-raising flour
1 egg, beaten
Chopped almonds

Beat the butter and sugar together until light and fluffy. Add the lemon peel; the eggs, one at a time; and, finally, the flour. Thinly roll out the dough. Cut

Cherry and Marzipan Cake

Carrot Cake Icing

Makes icing for 1 cake

8 oz/225 grams cream cheese
4 oz/115 grams butter, softened
2 teaspoons vanilla essence
12 oz/345 grams icing sugar
6 oz/170 grams pecan nuts, finely chopped
12 oz/345 grams coconut

Cream the cheese and butter, then slowly add icing sugar, beating until light. Add the vanilla and beat until absorbed. Add the pecans and coconut. Mix until well distributed.

Tropical Icing

Makes icing for 1 cake

1 lb/450 grams sugar
½ pint/¼ l water
Pinch salt
1 teaspoon white vinegar
3 egg whites
½ teaspoon vanilla essence

Celebration Cake

out, using a large, star-shaped cutter. Brush with beaten egg. Dip in almonds. Place the biscuits on a greased baking sheet. Bake in a 400°F/200°C/gas mark 6 oven until pale light-yellow in colour.

Apple Squares

Makes about 50 squares

4–8 oz/115–225 grams self-raising flour
6 oz/170 grams sugar
3½ oz/100 grams butter or margarine
8 fl oz/220 ml milk
1 egg
4 or 5 apples
A little sugar
Several knobs of butter

Mix the flour and sugar.

Finely chop the butter into the mixture until it resembles breadcrumbs.

Beat the milk and egg together. Add to the flour mixture. Quickly make into a batter. Pour into a baking tin, 10 × 14 inches/25 × 35 cm, that has been covered with buttered greaseproof paper. Press wedges of apple close together into the batter. Sprinkle with

sugar. Place knobs of butter on top. Bake in a 425°F/220°C/gas mark 7 oven for 15 to 20 minutes. Cut the cake into pieces when it has cooled.

Variation: Add 1 teaspoon cinnamon and 1 teaspoon ginger to the flour mixture.

Almond Butter Cream Squares

Makes about 30 squares

6–8 oz/170–225 grams almonds
8 oz/225 grams sugar
6 egg whites
8 oz/225 grams sliced almonds

butter cream

3 egg yolks
4 fl oz/110 ml milk
3 oz/85 grams sugar
3 oz/85 grams butter, soft

Grind the almonds. Mix them with the sugar.

Beat the egg whites until stiff peaks form. Carefully fold them into the almond and sugar mixture. Spread onto well buttered greaseproof paper that has been sprinkled with flour. Spread into a rectangle of about 9 × 14 inches/22 × 35 cm. Sprinkle with the sliced almonds. Bake in a 350°F/180°C/gas mark 4 oven for about 20 minutes. Immediately remove the cake from the paper. Let it cool on a rack.

To make the butter cream, mix the egg yolks, milk and sugar in a saucepan. Simmer, beating vigorously, until the cream thickens. Add the butter. Let it melt in the warm cream mixture. Stir well. Let the mixture

Sugar Cake

Swedish Coffee Cake Ring

become cold and thick.

Divide the almond cake into 2 parts. Put the 2 parts together with the cream mixture between the layers. Refrigerate. Cut into small squares.

The squares are excellent to freeze. They taste best when served cold.

Variation: Bake the almond mixture as a round cake and ice the top with the butter cream.

Oatmeal Nut Biscuits

Makes about 40 biscuits

4½ oz/130 grams butter or margarine
2–3 oz/60–85 grams ground hazelnuts
8 oz/225 grams oatmeal
6 oz/170 grams sugar
Almost 1 teaspoon baking powder
3 oz/85 grams plain flour

decoration

Hazelnuts

Work all the biscuit ingredients together into a smooth dough. Rub the oatmeal grains between your hands if they are large. Roll the dough into small balls. Place them on a greased biscuit sheet. Press a nut into the centre of each one. Bake in a 350 to 400°F/

180 to 200°C/gas mark 4 to 6 oven for 10 to 12 minutes.

Butternuts

Makes 125 biscuits

8 oz/225 grams hazelnuts
6–8 oz/170–225 grams butter
5½ oz/155 grams sugar
About 6 oz/170 grams flour
¼ teaspoon baking powder
Pinch salt

Roast the nuts in the oven. Rub them between the palms of your hands to remove the skins. Chop the nuts into large pieces or divide them in half.

Work the ingredients together on a baking board. Refrigerate the mixture, if desired. Roll out into a cake, about ½ inch/1 cm thick. Place onto a lightly floured cutting board. Put it into the refrigerator.

Cut the chilled mixture into small cubes 1 × 1 inch/ 2½ × 2½ cm or slightly smaller. Place the cubes onto a greased baking sheet. They can be placed fairly close together. Bake in a 400°F/200°C/gas mark 6 oven for 10–12 minutes.

Vanilla Sticks

Makes 60 to 70 biscuits

2 oz/60 grams marzipan
6–8 oz/170–225 grams butter or margarine
2 oz/60 grams sugar
1 egg
1 teaspoon vanilla essence
¼ teaspoon baking powder
About 8 oz/225 grams plain flour

for brushing and decorating
1 egg white
Chopped almonds
Crystallised sugar

Finely grate the marzipan. Mix all ingredients together. Roll out into finger-thick lengths. Cut these into ½-inch/1-cm long pieces.

Brush with egg white. Dip in chopped almonds and sugar.

Bake the biscuits on a greased baking sheet in a 350°F/180°C/gas mark 4 oven for about 10 minutes.

Tutti-Frutti Cake

Chocolate Meringue Squares

Makes 20 to 25 squares

chocolate mixture

3½ oz/100 grams margarine or butter
2½ oz/75 grams sugar
3 egg yolks
3 oz/85 grams self-raising flour
3 tablespoons cocoa
2½ fl oz/75 ml milk

meringue mixture

3 egg whites
6 oz/170 grams sugar
4 oz/115 grams chopped hazelnuts

Cover a baking tin with greaseproof paper. Grease it with margarine.

Beat the margarine and sugar together until airy. Add the egg yolks, one at a time.

Mix together the flour and cocoa. Alternate adding this mixture and the milk to the egg and yolk mixture. Spread into the baking tin, using a rubber spatula.

Whip the egg whites into dry peaks. Whip in the sugar. Spread the meringue over the chocolate mixture. Sprinkle with the nuts. Bake in the centre of a preheated 350°F/180°C/gas mark 4 oven for 20–25 minutes. Let the cake cool. Cut it into squares with a sharp knife.

Brandy Wreaths

Makes 50 to 60 biscuits

6–8 oz/170–225 grams soft butter or margarine
3 oz/85 grams icing sugar, sifted
8 oz/225 grams flour
1½ tablespoons brandy

Mix all the ingredients together into a workable dough. Refrigerate. Roll the dough out into very thin rolls that are slightly smaller than the diameter of a pencil. Twist the rolls around each other, 2 by 2. Cut the twisted roll into pieces about 4½ inches/11 cms long. Shape the pieces into wreaths on a greased baking sheet. Bake in a 350°F/180°C/gas mark 4 oven for about 10 minutes.

Ginger Biscuits

Makes about 40 biscuits

6 oz/170 grams butter or margarine
12 oz/345 grams oatmeal
2½ oz/75 grams sugar
4 oz/115 grams golden syrup
2 teaspoons ginger
Pinch salt

Melt the butter. Stir in the remaining ingredients. Mix well. Spread onto a piece of buttered greaseproof paper on a 9×13-inch/22×33-cm baking

Temptation Cake

sheet. Smooth the surface with a spatula. Bake in a 350°F/180°C/gas mark 4 oven for 8 to 10 minutes. Cut the cake into pieces when it has cooled. Loosen from the baking sheet.

Cinnamon Squares

Makes 49 squares

8 oz/225 grams butter
8 oz/225 grams sugar
1 egg, separated
8 oz/225 grams self-raising flour
1½ tablespoons cinnamon
1 teaspoon salt
12 oz/345 grams nuts, chopped

Cream the butter and sugar and add the egg yolk. Add flour, cinnamon and salt. Press into a generously greased 8 × 14-inch/20 × 35-cm tin or 2 8-inch/20-cm square tins.

Beat the egg white until foamy. Spread on top of the mixture. Press the chopped nuts on top of this. Bake at 325°F/163°C/gas mark 3 for 30 minutes. Allow to cool slightly and cut into squares.

Coconut Squares

Makes about 50 squares

5 eggs
14 oz/400 grams sugar
7 oz/200 grams self-raising flour
2 tablespoons cocoa
8 fl oz/220 ml water
12 oz-1 lb/345–450 grams butter or margarine

coconut icing
3½ oz/100 grams butter or margarine
14 oz/400 grams coconut
6 oz/170 grams sugar
2 tablespoons strong coffee
2 eggs

Beat the eggs and sugar mixture together until very light.

Blend the flour with cocoa. Sift it into the mixture. Boil the water and butter until the butter melts. Add to the mixture. Pour into a large baking tin, about 12 × 16 inches/30 × 40 cms, which has been covered with buttered greaseproof paper. Bake in a 400°F/200°C/gas mark 6 oven until the cake is almost done, about 20 minutes.

Twelfth Day of Christmas Cake

Make the icing while the cake is baking. Beat together all the icing ingredients in a saucepan. Bring to the boil, stirring constantly. Spread the icing over the partially baked cake. Bake it for another 10 minutes in a 425°F/220°C/gas mark 7 oven until the icing is a nice colour.

Chocolate Flavour Biscuits

Makes about 100 biscuits

6–8 oz/170–225 grams butter or margarine
6 oz/170 grams sugar
8 oz/225 grams self-raising flour
1 egg
4 teaspoons cocoa
½ teaspoon vanilla essence

for brushing and decorating
1 egg
Crystallised sugar
Chopped almonds

Mix all the ingredients together into a workable dough. Refrigerate. Roll out into a thin dough. Cut out with a biscuit cutter.

Brush with a beaten egg. Dip in sugar and chopped almonds.

Place on a greased baking sheet. Bake in a 400°F/200°C/gas mark 6 oven for about 8 minutes.

Almond Butter Cream Squares

Christmas Biscuits

Makes about 50 biscuits

6 oz/170 grams brown or white sugar
12 oz/345 grams treacle or golden syrup
2 oz/60 grams boiled and finely chopped bitter
  orange peel
1½ teaspoons cinnamon
1 teaspoon cloves
1 teaspoon ginger
2½ oz/75 grams butter or margarine
2 eggs, beaten
4 fl oz/110 ml soured cream
1 level tablespoon bicarbonate of soda
12–14 oz/345–400 grams plain flour

decoration
Almonds, chopped into pieces.

Bring the sugar, treacle or syrup and spices to the boil in a saucepan. Add the butter. Stir until butter melts. Let cool. Add the eggs, cream, bicarbonate of soda and flour. Dab onto a greased biscuit sheet. Dab about 1 tablespoon of mixture with plenty of space between the dabs. Stick a piece of almond down into the middle of each. Bake in a 350°F/180°C/gas mark

4 to 400°F/200°C/gas mark 6 oven for about 8 to 10 minutes. Carefully remove from the biscuit sheet while they are still warm. Leave to cool on a rack under a cloth.

Christmas Ginger Biscuits

Makes about 200 biscuits

5 oz/140 grams butter or margarine
8 oz/225 grams sugar
4 oz/115 grams treacle or golden syrup
4 fl oz/110 ml water
½ tablespoon ginger
1 tablespoon cinnamon
½ tablespoon cloves
1 teaspoon finely ground cardamom
½ tablespoon bicarbonate of soda
12 oz/345 grams flour

Stir the butter, sugar and treacle or syrup until smooth. Add the water, spices and bicarbonate of soda. Work in the flour. Make into a workable mixture on a baking board. Let stand overnight.

Roll out into a thin dough. Cut out biscuits with a biscuit cutter. Bake in the middle of a 425°F/220°C/gas mark 7 oven for about 5 minutes. Leave to cool on the biscuit sheet.

Orange Snaps

Makes 14 biscuits

5 oz/140 grams margarine
2 eggs
2½ oz/75 grams sugar
A little vanilla essence
5 oz/140 grams flour

decoration
1½ oz/45 grams icing sugar
3 to 4 teaspoons orange juice
Chopped candied orange peel

Melt the margarine. Let it cool. Beat in the eggs, sugar, vanilla and flour. Spoon onto a greased, round, shallow tin. Bake for about 10 minutes in a 400°F/200°C/gas mark 6 oven. Let cool. Curl them around a greased, paper covered, thin, cylindrical shaped object.

Mix the icing sugar with the orange juice. Brush over the biscuits when they have stiffened. Sprinkle with the orange peel.

Orange Soup

Granny Bows

Makes about 100 biscuits

5 oz/140 grams butter or margarine
4 oz/115 grams sugar
1 egg
5 oz/140 grams self-raising flour

for brushing and decorating
1 egg white
Crystallised sugar
Chopped almonds

Stir the butter until soft. Mix in the sugar and egg. Add the flour. Save a small amount of flour for rolling out the dough. Make into a workable dough and refrigerate.

Roll out the dough thinly (half the dough at a time). Cut out biscuit bows with a biscuit cutter.

Brush with the egg white. Dip in sugar and almonds. Bake on a greased baking sheet in a 350°F/180°C/gas mark 4 oven for about 10 minutes.

From left: Ginger Biscuits, Granny Bows, Oatmeal Nut Biscuits, Vanilla Sticks, Chocolate Flavour Biscuits, Brandy Wreaths and Brown Biscuits

Butter Biscuits

Makes 60 biscuits

5 oz/140 grams butter
10 oz/285 grams sugar
2 eggs
12 oz/345 grams self-raising flour
1½ teaspoons salt
1 teaspoon vanilla essence

Cream the butter, sugar and eggs together until light and foamy. Sift the flour and salt together and add to the first mixture. Add vanilla. Mix until smooth. Chill.

Roll to a ¼-inch/½-cm thickness on a slightly floured board. Cut out with a biscuit cutter. Sprinkle with sugar and bake in a 350°F/180°C/gas mark 4 oven 12 to 15 minutes.

Brown Biscuits

Makes about 45 biscuits

½ beaten egg (see starred note in Tutti-Frutti Cake recipe)
½ teaspoon cinnamon
½ teaspoon ground cardamom

Chocolate Meringue Squares

5 oz/75 grams melted butter or margarine, cooled
2½ oz/75 grams chopped almonds
3 ground bitter almonds
2 oz/60 grams brown sugar
5 oz/140 grams self-raising flour
1 teaspoon baking powder
Crystallised sugar in which to dip the biscuits

Mix the egg with the spices. Stir in the butter, almonds and brown sugar. Add the flour, which has been blended with the baking powder. Roll into small round balls. Lightly press sugar into the balls. Place on a greased biscuit sheet. Bake in a 350°F to 400°F/180°C to 200°C/ gas marks 4 to 6 oven for 10 to 12 minutes.

Christmas Gingerbread

Makes 175 to 200 biscuits

10 oz/285 grams sugar
10 oz/285 grams treacle or golden syrup
6–8 oz/170–225 grams butter or margarine
8 fl oz/220 ml double cream
2 tablespoons ginger
1 tablespoon bicarbonate of soda
7 oz/200 grams flour

Heat the sugar, treacle or syrup and butter. Stir so that the butter melts. Let the mixture cool. Stir in the cream, ginger, bicarbonate of soda and most of the flour. Let stand overnight.

Thinly roll out the dough. Cut out biscuits with a biscuit cutter. Bake them on a greased biscuit sheet in a 400°F to 425°F/200°C to 220°C/ gas marks 6 to 7 oven for 5 to 7 minutes.

Cinnamon and Clove Biscuits

Makes about 100 biscuits

14 oz-1 lb/400–450 grams butter or margarine
8 oz/225 grams golden syrup
2 teaspoons cinnamon
2 teaspoons ground cloves
1 oz/30 grams bitter orange peel
2 teaspoons bicarbonate of soda
4 oz/115 grams almonds, chopped
11 oz/315 grams plain flour

Heat the butter, syrup and sugar in a saucepan. Let cool. Add the spices, bicarbonate of soda, almonds and flour. Work together into a dough. Shape the dough into rolls 1½ inch in diameter. Refrigerate them until firm.

Cut the rolls into thin slices. Bake on a greased biscuit sheet in a 400°F/200°C/gas mark 6 oven for about 7 minutes.

Chocolate Walnut Biscuits

Makes 12 biscuits

8 oz/225 grams sugar
2 eggs, well beaten
2 squares cooking chocolate
4 oz/115 grams butter or margarine
4 oz/115 grams self-raising flour
¼ teaspoon salt
8 oz/225 grams black walnuts, finely chopped
1 teaspoon vanilla essence
Sifted icing sugar

Gradually add the sugar to the eggs. Melt the chocolate with butter, then stir into the eggs. Sift the flour and salt together. Add the flour mixture to the chocolate mixture and add nuts and vanilla.

Bake in a greased 15 × 10 × 1-inch/38 × 25 × 3-cm Swiss roll tin in a 350°F/180°C/gas mark 4 oven 12 to 15 minutes. Cool slightly in the tin; dust with icing sugar. Cool completely in the tin on a rack. Cut into 2-inch/5-cm bars.

Gingerbread Christmas Cookies

Gingerbread Heart Village

Large Gingerbread Shapes

Quantity varies

5 oz/140 grams butter or margarine
12 oz/345 grams treacle or golden syrup
8 fl oz/220 ml water
1 tablespoon cinnamon
1 tablespoon ginger
1 tablespoon cloves
About 1½ lb/700 grams self-raising flour

lemon icing
1 egg white
14 oz/400 grams icing sugar
1 teaspoon lemon juice

Stir the butter, sugar and treacle or syrup together until smooth. Add the water, spices and flour. Use a larger amount of flour when making a gingerbread house. Make into a workable dough on a baking board. Refrigerate well covered overnight.

Work the dough. It should be rather firm if it is to be rolled out into different shapes. Large figures and large parts of the house should be cut out on the baking sheet. They easily lose their shape when moved. Bake in a 350-400°F/180–200°C/gas marks 4–6 oven. Let the shapes cool on the sheet.

To make the icing, mix the egg white, icing sugar and lemon juice together. Stir until the icing becomes thick and is firm enough to keep its shape. The consistency can be varied, using more egg white or icing sugar. Decorate large figures with icing.

Gingerbread-Hearts Village: to make this village, place 3 hearts together with their tips up. The size of the huts can be varied from tiny to extra large, depending on the size of the hearts used.

The recipe given for larger figures is ideal if the huts are to be of the larger variety. But if you are only going to make small huts, use the recipe for Christmas Ginger Biscuits (see above) as this dough is also easy to roll out.

After baking, decorate the hearts with icing, making doors and windows.

Glue the sides of the hearts together by dipping the biscuit edges into sugar that has been melted in a frying pan. The sugar becomes hard very quickly, so put the hearts together as soon as you have dipped them in the sugar. The points of the hearts meet at the top of the huts. Marzipan is suitable for the chimneys. Press the icing through a forcing bag and go over all the edges. Place the huts on a bed of cotton wool. Add some Santas and some greenery. Sprinkle icing sugar over the huts.

Butternuts

American Brownies

Makes about 35 brownies

4 eggs
14 oz/400 grams sugar
7 oz/200 grams cooking chocolate
1 lb/450 grams butter or margarine, melted
10–12 oz/285–345 grams chopped nuts (walnuts or almonds)
7 oz/200 grams plain flour
2 teaspoons baking powder

icing
About 7 oz/200 grams cooking chocolate

Beat the eggs and sugar together until light.
Break up the chocolate. Melt it over low heat. Stir occasionally.
Stir the butter into the egg mixture. Add the chocolate and nuts. Add the flour, which has been well mixed with the baking powder. Bake in a small baking tin in a 400°F/200°C/gas mark 6 oven for about 20 minutes. Cut into 1½ to 2-inch/4 to 5-cm squares. Let cool.
Ice with melted, cooled cooking chocolate.

Drinks and Preserves

Home Made Apple Juice

Quantity varies

Apples
¼ to ½ teaspoon ascorbic acid

Rinse the apples and remove the stalks. Cut them into large wedges. The core and peel should not be removed. Put the apples through a blender or food processor. The result should be a thick, somewhat cloudy juice. Strain through a fine tammy sieve. Add ascorbic acid as this will help the juice keep longer.

Pour the finished raw juice into suitable freezing containers. Freeze. Remember that it will take some time to thaw when you want to use it.

Brown, Red and White

Makes 2 large glasses

brown
4 oz/115 grams plain chocolate
½ pint/¼ l boiling milk, preferably skimmed
2 oz/60 grams sugar
Few drops vanilla essence
4 to 5 leaves fresh peppermint or
    ¼ teaspoon peppermint oil
8 fl oz/220 ml crushed ice

red
2½ fl oz/75 ml light rum (optional)
2 egg whites
1 lb/450 grams fresh red berries or redcurrants
7 fl oz/200 ml water
8 fl oz/220 ml crushed ice
6 oz/170 grams sugar

white
14 fl oz/400 ml milk
7 fl oz/200 ml crushed ice

1 tablespoon whisky or brandy
¼ teaspoon nutmeg

A long drink, with or without alcohol, really hits the spot on a mild summer's evening. Choose between a brown, a red or a white.

To make the brown: break the chocolate into pieces and beat it, with the hot milk, in the mixer. Add the rest of the ingredients and beat until everything is well blended and the ice had disappeared. Serve immediately.

To make the red: mix all ingredients in a mixer and beat until the ice has melted and the berries have blended evenly. Pour immediately into cold glasses. Substitute water for rum if preferred.

To make the white: pour the milk, ice and whisky or brandy into a mixer. Beat until the ice has melted and the milk becomes foamy. Pour into cold glasses. Sprinkle with nutmeg. Serve immediately.

Egg Nog

8 servings

6 eggs, separated
8 oz/225 grams sugar
1 pint/½ l double cream
1 pint/½ l milk
½ pint/¼ l Irish whiskey
¼ pint/140 ml rum
Nutmeg

Beat the egg yolks until pale yellow, then gradually beat in half the sugar. Beat the egg whites until stiff, not dry, and add the remaining sugar. Combine both mixtures. Stir in the cream, milk, whiskey and rum. Mix well and serve with a sprinkling of nutmeg.

Fruity Wine Punch

Homemade Apple Juice

stirred into a small amount of juice, and then fill warm, clean bottles up to the brim. Seal immediately.

Dilute the concentrate with water when serving. Use more water than with other juices when making juice from currants. Allow 1½ pints/850 ml water per 5 lbs/2¼ kilos well ripened blackcurrants and 14 fl oz/400 ml water for a similar quantity redcurrants. Dilute with water when serving.

Fruity Wine Punch

8 servings

2 oranges
1 well ripened mango
2 kiwi fruits
1 bottle cold dry white wine
14 fl oz/400 ml dry white vermouth
2 bottles tonic water, chilled
8 fl oz/220 ml orange juice (preferably frozen)
Ice cubes

Peel one of the oranges, removing as much of the pith as possible. Wash the other orange and the kiwi

Homemade Fruit Juice

Home Made Fruit Juice

About 8 servings

5 lbs/2¼ kilos berries, well ripened, picked over
15 fl oz/425 ml water
4 oz/115 grams sugar per pint/½ l drained juice
¼ teaspoon sodium benzoate per 2 pints/1¼
   juice

Boil the water and the cleaned berries (currants do not need to be cleaned, just rinsed, and the stone need not be removed from cherries) until they become runny, about 10 minutes. Crush the berries against the side of the pot while boiling. Strain the mixture through a fine tammy sieve. Do not let it drain for more than 30 minutes.

Measure the juice and pour it back into the pan. Bring to the boil, add the sugar and bring to the boil again. Skim the surface as necessary.

Add the sodium benzoate, which has first been

fruits and cut into thin slices. Peel the mango and cut into small pieces. Other fruits may also be used, such as well ripened pears or cut grapes from which the seeds have been removed.

Place all the fruit, with the exception of the un-peeled orange, in a bowl or jug that holds at least 4½ pints/2½ litres. Pour in the wine and the ver-mouth, cover and refrigerate for several hours so that the fruit absorbs the wine flavour.

Just before serving pour in the chilled tonic water and orange juice and add the sliced, unpeeled orange and ice. Serve with a punch spoon in each glass so that the wine soaked pieces of fruit can be tasted.

Hot Buttered Rum

1 serving

2½ fl oz/75 ml light rum
Juice of 1 small lemon
1 small strip lemon peel
1½ teaspoons brown sugar
1 oz/30 grams butter

Place a long spoon in a tall glass. Pour the rum into the glass. Add the lemon juice and peel. Pour in enough boiling water, over the handle of the spoon, to fill the glass. Stir in the brown sugar. Add the butter and stir until melted.

Garnish with a slice of lemon and additional lemon peel.

Mulled Wine

6 servings

4 oz/115 grams sugar
2½ fl oz/75 ml water
2 slices of orange
6 cloves
2 cinnamon sticks
¼ pint/140 ml orange juice
1 bottle red wine

Boil the sugar, water, slices of orange, cloves and cinnamon for 5 minutes. Remove from the heat. Add the juice and wine. Keep hot but do not boil. Serve with cinnamon sticks or slices of orange.

Cider can be substituted for the wine. Sweeten to taste.

Summer Freshness

1 serving

1 to 2 slices kiwi fruit
1 to 2 sliced strawberries
Dab orange sherbet
About ½ pint/¼ l chilled sparkling cider or
  champagne

Cover the bottom of a glass with kiwi slices and strawberries. Add a dab of sherbet and fill the glass with cider or champagne.

Green Tomato Preserve

Makes about 2 1 lb/450-gram jars

2¼ lbs/1 kilo small green tomatoes
Water

juice
8 fl oz/220 ml distilled white vinegar
14 fl oz/400 ml water
11 oz/315 grams sugar
1 piece cinnamon
8 cloves

Cherry Jam

Prick the skins of the tomatoes and boil them in water until almost soft. Drain off the water. Bring the juice to the boil with the spices, which should be placed in a small muslin bag. Skim well. Add the tomatoes to the juice and simmer over a low heat until soft.

Place the tomatoes in earthenware or glass jars with a draining spoon. Let the juice boil until slightly syrupy. Remove the spices (save them), and pour the juice over the tomatoes. Seal the jars.

Pour off the juice after a couple of days and cook it together with the spices. Skim the surface of the juice and pour once more over the tomatoes. The tomatoes should be completely covered by the juice. Seal the jars tightly and store in a cool place.

Summer Freshness

Green Tomato Preserve

Green Tomato Marmalade

Makes 3–4 8 oz/225 gram jars

2¼ lbs/1 kilo green tomatoes
Water
Grated peel of 2 washed lemons
4 to 5 pieces whole ginger
22 oz/620 grams sugar

Rinse the tomatoes, cut into pieces and put through a mincer. Place them in a stewing pan. Add a small amount of water, lemon peel and ginger. Boil the tomatoes until soft in a covered pan. They should be well mashed. Stir occasionally.

Add the sugar and boil, uncovered, until the mixture becomes the consistency of marmalade—25 to 30 minutes. Shake the pan several times while boiling. Remove the pieces of ginger and skim well.

Pour into warm, clean jars. Seal tightly. Store in a cool place.

Mixed Berry Jam

Red and Green Tomato Marmalades

Cherry Jam

Makes about 3 lbs/1350 grams

2¼ lb/1 kilo bitter cherries
1½ lb/700 grams sugar

Clean, rinse and stone the cherries. Place them in a jam pan and slowly bring to the boil over a low heat. Boil for 5 minutes. Add the sugar. Boil the jam slowly, without stirring, for 15 minutes. Shake the pan occasionally. Skim the surface as necessary.

Pour the jam into warm, clean jars. Seal well. Store in a dark, cool place.

Cherry jam will have a special taste if almonds are added. It will also taste delicious if several tablespoons of brandy are stirred into it when it is made.

Red Tomato Marmalade

Makes 3–4 8 oz/ 225 gram jars

2¼ lb/1 kilo ripe tomatoes
2 lemons
22 oz/620 grams sugar

Dip the tomatoes into boiling water and peel them. Cut them into pieces. Brush the lemons well, peel them and shred the peel thinly. Squeeze the lemons.

Mix the tomatoes, lemon peel and juice together and place in a stewing pan. Boil, uncovered, for about 30 minutes. Stir in the sugar and boil for another 25–30 minutes, uncovered, until the mixture begins to have the consistency of marmalade. Shake the pan several times while cooking. Skim well.

Pour into warm, clean jars. Seal tightly. Store in a cool place.

Blackcurrant Jelly

Carrhub

Plum Jam

Makes about 2 1 lb/450 gram jars

2¼ lbs/1 kilo plums
2½ fl oz/75 ml water
Just over 1 lb/450 grams sugar

Rinse the plums and stone them. Place them in a pan and cover with the water. Simmer the plums over a low heat until they start to break up into pieces. Remove any peel that floats to the top with a draining spoon.

Add the sugar and simmer for 15 to 20 minutes. Shake the pan occasionally while it is simmering.

Skim the jam well and pour it into warm, clean jars. Seal tightly. Store in a cool place.

Note: the plums can also be boiled without having first stoned them. When the plums start breaking up the stones will rise to the surface and can be removed with a draining spoon. Then add the sugar.

Carrhub

Makes about 6 lb/About 3 kilos

2¼ lb/1 kilo carrots
2¼ lb/1 kilo rhubarb
2¼ lb/1 kilo sugar

Peel the carrots and cut into small pieces. Using the metal knife attachment on the food processor, purée the carrot pieces. Do not fill the processor more than half full each time. Pour the carrot mixture into a 10-pint/5½-litre pan.

Peel and chop the rhubarb and purée as for the carrots.

Boil the carrot and rhubarb purées together with the sugar until the mixture reaches the desired consistency, about 1 hour. Stir occasionally.

Pour the mixture into clean, warm jars and leave to cool. Store in a cool place and eat promptly, or else freeze it. If it is to be stored in the freezer, cool first. Pour the jam into freezer containers and seal tightly.

Plum Jam

Mixed Berry Jam

Makes about 4 lb/About 2 kilos

5 lbs/2¼ kilos berries
1 to 2 lbs/450 to 900 grams sugar
½ teaspoon citric acid

Boiled jam may be made using one kind of berry or several kinds. A favourite jam is one made from both raspberries and bilberries. Other tasty mixed jams include: strawberry and gooseberry, strawberry and rhubarb, red and blackcurrants with raspberry, blackcurrant and bilberry, currants and bitter cherry.

Clean the berries well (only rinse if that is all that is needed). Alternate berries and sugar in a stewing pan and allow the mixture to stand and draw for several hours.

Place the pan over a low heat and warm up the mixture. Shake the pan occasionally, but avoid stirring the jam. Bring to the boil and simmer, uncovered, for 15- 20 minutes or until the berries start to sink. Skim as necessary.

Remove the pan from the heat and stir in the citric acid, which has been mixed with a little of the jam. Pour into warm, clean jars. When cooled seal tightly and store in a cool, dark place.

Blackcurrant Jelly

Makes 4–5 lb/2–2¼ kilos

2¼ lb/1 kilo blackcurrants
14 fl oz/400 ml water
2 lb/900 grams sugar per 2 pints/1¼ l drained juice

Bring berries and water to the boil over a low heat (do not add the sugar). Shake the pan occasionally, but avoid stirring. Bring to the boil and simmer, uncovered, for 15 to 20 minutes or until the berries sink to the bottom of the pan. Skim as necessary.

Pour the juice into a saucepan and allow it to boil for 5 minutes. Stir in the sugar, a little at a time, and then boil the juice without stirring until it passes the jelly test. (Jelly Test: pour a little jelly on a plate and pull a spoon right through it—if the jelly does not flow back together it is ready).

Let the jelly stand for a few minutes before skimming it well. Pour it into small, clean, warm jars and leave to cool. Seal tightly and cool in a cool, dark place.

For Redcurrant Jelly: use 8 fl oz/220 ml water for each 2¼ lb/ 1 kilo of currants. Boil as for blackcurrant jelly.

Note: if the jelly does not become firm, you can add pure pectine. Use 1 teaspoon pure pectine per 2 pints/1¼ litres juice (jelly), 1 teaspoon citric acid and 2 teaspoons sugar. Stir this mixture into a small amount of the hot juice. Mix this into the rest of the jelly and allow to boil for 1 minute.

Marrow or Pumpkin jam

Makes about 12 lb/5½ kilos

About 9 lb/4 kilos marrow or pumpkin
Water
Salt (1 tablespoon per 2 pints/1¼ l water)

juice
11 fl oz/ 325 ml distilled white vinegar
15 fl oz/425 ml water
1½ lb/700 grams sugar

3 to 4 pieces mace
3 pieces ginger
1 teaspoon white peppercorns
2 teaspoons yellow mustard seed

Peel and halve the marrow or pumpkin lengthways. Remove the seeds and cut the halves into pieces. Boil them in lightly salted water until just soft.

Bring the juice ingredients to the boil. Put the spices in a muslin bag. Boil several pieces at a time until they are soft and clear. When done, remove with a draining spoon and put into clean jars.

Bring the juice back to the boil and boil gently for a short time. Skim as necessary. Leave to cool. Remove the spice bag and pour the juice over the pieces of marrow or pumpkin. They should be completely covered by the juice. Place a tightly fitting lid on each jar and store in a cool place.

Marrow or Pumpkin Jam

Index